Race, Ethnicity, and the Cold War

A GLOBAL PERSPECTIVE

EDITED BY

Philip E. Muehlenbeck

Vanderbilt University Press
Nashville

© 2012 by Vanderbilt University Press
Nashville, Tennessee 37235
All rights reserved
First printing 2012

This book is printed on acid-free paper.
Manufactured in the United States of America

Library of Congress Cataloging-in-Publication Data on file
LC control number 2011034147
LC classification number D842.R28 2012
Dewey class number 305.8009'45—dc23
ISBN 978-0-8265-1843-9 (cloth)
ISBN 978-0-8265-1844-6 (paperback)
ISBN 978-0-8265-1845-3 (e-book)

Race,
Ethnicity,
and the
Cold War

Contents

PREFACE

In the past decade scholarship examining the ways in which race and ethnicity influenced US foreign policy during the Cold War has flourished to the point of establishing its own subgenre.[1] Yet what is striking is the dearth of scholarship in the English language that focuses on the ways in which race and ethnicity influenced the domestic and foreign policies of states *other* than the United States during this time period. This volume is an initial step toward rectifying this problem. It attempts to show that race and racism were not the original sin of the United States, but rather had an impact on the Cold War policies of countries all over the world.

The introduction and first two chapters of this book attempt to provide some context for the study of race, ethnicity, and the Cold War by providing a brief overview of the ways in which these variables affected US foreign policy and how the decolonization of Asia and Africa changed the international discourse on race and influenced the global Cold War. The second section uses case studies across time and geography to demonstrate the impact that race and ethnicity had on decolonization. The third and fourth sections examine how the variables of race and ethnicity interconnected the Cold War domestic and foreign policies of numerous states across the globe.

This volume is not comprehensive, of course, nor could such a collection of essays ever hope to be so. Unfortunately, several important topics—such as how diplomats from India and Communist China used their darker skin and colonial past in an attempt to gain Third World allies in the developing world or how the "White Australia Policy" (which restricted nonwhite immigration to Australia) affected that country's relations with its Asian neighbors—go unexamined here. However, by broadening the study of race, ethnicity, and the Cold War away from America's shores and toward the rest of the world, this volume—with its multidisciplinary approach and emphasis on multiarchival and multinational research (primary source research for this project being conducted in thirteen different countries)—aspires to serve as inspiration for further research on how race and ethnicity affected the Cold War policies of states other than the United States.

I would like to thank the following individuals for offering peer review comments on one or more chapters of this volume: Jan Asmussen, Tim Borstelmann, Daniel Byrne, Michael Conniff, Darren Dochuk, Cary Fraser, Julie Gilmour, Piero Gleijeses, Will Gray, Julie Hesler, Anna Jaroszyńska, Michael Krenn, David Lewis-Coleman, Argyris Mamarelis, Dominique Marshall, Filipe de Menses, Jim Meriwether, James E. Miller, Eric Morgan, Lise Namikas, Meredith Roman, Tim Scarnecchia, Tom Schwartz, Nico Slate, Kirk Tyvela, and the anonymous readers for Vanderbilt University Press.

I would also like to extend a special thanks to Ismail Ginwala, Elizabeth Kostendt, and Katherine Meier-Davis, students at George Washington University who assisted me in editing these chapters with an eye toward comprehension by an advanced undergraduate student. Finally, Eli Bortz, my acquisitions editor at Vanderbilt University Press, was an integral part of this project from conception to completion. This volume is a much better final product because of his involvement.

Note

1. Influential works on how race and ethnicity influenced US foreign policy during the Cold War include: Carol Anderson, *Eyes off the Prize: The United Nations and the African American Struggle for Human Rights, 1944–1955* (Cambridge: Cambridge University Press, 2003); Thomas Borstelmann, *The Cold War and the Color Line: American Race Relations in the Global Arena* (Cambridge, MA: Harvard University Press, 2003); Alexander DeConde, *Ethnicity, Race, and American Foreign Policy* (Boston: Northeastern University Press, 1992); Mary Dudziak, *Cold War Civil Rights: Race and the Image of American Democracy* (Princeton, NJ: Princeton University Press, 2000); James Meriwether, *Proudly We Can Be Africans* (Chapel Hill: University of North Carolina Press, 2002); Brenda Gayle Plummer, *Rising Wind: Black Americans and U.S. Foreign Affairs, 1935–1960* (Chapel Hill: University of North Carolina Press, 1996), and as editor, *Window on Freedom: Race, Civil Rights, and Foreign Affairs, 1945–1988* (Chapel Hill: University of North Carolina Press, 2003); and Penny M. Von Eschen, *Race against Empire: Black Americans and Anticolonialism, 1937–1957* (Ithaca, NY: Cornell University Press, 2001).

INTRODUCTION

The Borders of Race and Nation

Nico Slate

In January 1947, seven months before becoming prime minister of independent India, Jawaharlal Nehru sent a secret note to the first Indian ambassadors to the United States and China. "In the U.S.A. there is the Negro problem," he wrote. "Our sympathies are entirely with the Negroes." Nehru explained, however, that representatives of India should "avoid any public expression of opinion which might prove embarrassing or distasteful to the Government or people of the country where they serve." In particular, Nehru stressed that India "must be friendly" with both the United States and the Soviet Union without alienating either superpower.[1] Maintaining "sympathies" for African Americans while remaining on good terms with the American government would prove challenging for Nehru—complicating his efforts to remain nonaligned in the Cold War. His note highlights the many dilemmas that faced anticolonial freedom fighters as they became the leaders of postcolonial nation-states in the midst of an increasingly polarized world. The Cold War heightened the difficulty of reconciling the demands of international diplomacy with older commitments to a transnational politics of racial emancipation.

Nehru's challenge is but one of many routes by which race and ethnicity entered into Cold War dynamics. Conversely, the Cold War itself influenced the social, cultural, and political meanings of race and ethnicity throughout much of the world. Reading this volume demonstrates the diversity of the reciprocal linkages between race, ethnicity, and the Cold War. Building on conceptions of the Cold War that go well beyond US-Soviet relations, this volume offers insight into a range of distinct but often intersecting transnational histories.[2]

Much of the historical literature on race, ethnicity, and the Cold War focuses on the American dimensions of what this volume makes clear was a global story. Scholars of American foreign relations and of transnational African American history have offered two distinct but not contradictory narratives linking the Cold War and the struggle for racial justice in the United States. Some scholars have argued that the Cold War provided a useful context in which civil rights activists could pressure American politicians to combat American racism. During the Second World War, advocates of "double victory" had aimed to link victory at home against racism with victory abroad against fascism. One facet of the double victory campaign involved publicizing the opposition to American racism that had developed in regions vital to the war effort, such as China and India. The racial status quo, advocates of double victory warned, risked giving credence to the Japanese claim to defend the nonwhite world. The argument that American racism damaged American foreign relations became even more compelling as decolonization accelerated and as the Soviet Union positioned itself as a bulwark for those oppressed by imperialism and white supremacy worldwide. Segregation, lynching, and other brutal facets of American racism offered a propaganda windfall for the Soviets. At stake, advocates of racial justice warned, was the support of the recently decolonized countries of Asia and Africa. American politicians became increasingly concerned about the link between racism and anti-Americanism, especially at times of crisis, such as the violence that accompanied the attempted integration of the public schools of Little Rock, Arkansas, in 1957. To the degree that such concerns motivated American politicians to act, it has been argued, the Cold War contributed to the achievements of the American civil rights movement.[3]

The impact of the Cold War on the struggle for racial justice was, however, far from uniformly positive. While the foreign policy implications of American racism troubled some American politicians and provided opportunities for advocates of racial equality, anti-Communist hysteria hampered many civil rights organizations. Prominent left-leaning African Americans, such as W. E. B. Du Bois and Paul Robeson, found themselves harassed at home and denied the right to travel abroad. As left-leaning advocates and organizations were marginalized, the national offices of mainstream civil rights organizations such as the NAACP hewed ever closer to the political center. Once vibrant coalitions between civil rights and labor activists weakened as unions came under attack and themselves purged more militant members.[4]

Like the domestic consequences of the Cold War for the civil rights movement, the impact of the Cold War on the significance of race in American foreign relations was decidedly mixed. While American presidents and diplomats strove to woo newly emerging Asian and African nations, American policy toward the global South remained infused with racial bias and paternalism. As Michael L. Krenn's essay argues, Cold War considerations did little to inspire American politicians to rid American foreign policy of its historic racialized underpinnings. Krenn's chapter in this volume helps to foreground the global implications of the many linkages between race, American foreign policy, and the Cold War.

Transnationalizing the history of race, ethnicity, and the Cold War reveals contradictions similar to those that marked the American experience. More than just echoing the scholarship on race and the Cold War in the United States, however, the chapters in this volume provide unique insight into the complex ways in which the Cold War both aided and limited struggles against white supremacy throughout much of the world. As Henley Adams makes clear in his chapter on race and the Cold War in Cuba, it was not only the American government that attempted to shield its domestic racial inequalities from the outside world. The Cuban government attacked racism in the United States, both to frustrate its inveterate enemy and to secure support at home among black Cubans. At the same time, however, Cuban leaders resisted fully challenging the legacy of racial inequality in Cuba and the ongoing racial prejudice of many white Cubans. In keeping with Marxist theory, Cuban authorities worked to prevent racial consciousness from developing among black Cubans, preferring to explain racial discrimination as a result of class inequality. As Maxim Matusevich demonstrates in his chapter on black students in the Soviet Union, a Marxist opposition to black racial consciousness also influenced the experiences of African students in the Soviet Union. Like the Cuban government (and the American government, for that matter), the Soviets had a difficult time reconciling the image they projected to the world with the realities confronting some black students in the Soviet Union. While detailing the positive experiences of a range of black visitors in the USSR, Matusevich's chapter highlights the difficulties confronting black students, especially those who embraced the growing transnational interest in black power, the black arts movement, and black studies.

Adams and Matusevich offer a transnational complement to the literature on the difficulties facing American politicians when foreign visitors experienced prejudice in the United States. In August 1955, newspapers in India and the United States offered headlines detailing an incident in which Indian ambassador G. L. Mehta faced racial discrimination at the Houston airport. Mehta's encounter with Jim Crow was far from unusual for Indian visitors, despite the fact that Indians continued to occupy a gray zone in a system theoretically based on distinctions between black and white. With India independent and nonaligned, incidents such as that faced by Ambassador Mehta created pressure on the American government. In 1961, the Kennedy administration launched a concerted effort to end racial discrimination—not against all nonwhites, however, but specifically against foreign diplomats.[5] The question remained: could the public relations disasters that resulted when diplomats confronted Jim Crow force systematic changes that would affect more than just powerful visitors? In the case of diplomats from India or other non-African countries it was especially unclear whether Jim Crow would be directly challenged or whether it would simply be modified to favor nonwhites who could (some of the time) be distinguished from black Americans. Would Indians object as strongly if the ambassador of Ghana had been denied service at the Houston airport? What about the daily discrimination faced by the black residents of Houston? For decades, a colored cosmopolitanism, built on antiracist and anti-imperial conceptions of the colored world, had inspired many Indians to voice solidarity with African Americans. After Indian independence, however, the history of Afro-Indian solidarity offers few examples of colored cosmopolitanism trumping more narrow nation-based forms of identity.[6]

By examining questions of both race and ethnicity, this volume probes the relative strength of race-based versus more narrowly ethnicity-based forms of transnational solidarity. Historian Frederick Cooper has urged scholars to examine "why some affinities in some contexts give rise to groups with a hard sense of uniqueness and antagonism to other groups, while in other instances people operate via degrees of affinity and connection, live with shades of grey rather than black and white, and form flexible networks rather than bounded groups."[7] The sociologist André Béteille puts the point well: "It is not enough to know that boundaries exist between groups, one must also examine the situations under which some boundaries are ignored and others become significant."[8] In their examination of "the Cyprus issue" in Greece and among Greek Americans, Zinovia Lialiouti and Philip E. Muehlenbeck demonstrate how ethnic affiliation, based on ties of language, culture, and nation, could mobilize a particular community to protest foreign policy decisions. Similarly, Eric L. Payseur, in discussing the political activism of Polish Canadians, reveals how the bonds of ethnicity could forge connections between diasporic communities and their country of origin. In both cases, the Cold War provided a platform on which political coalitions could be built both at home and abroad. The Cold War helped strengthen the boundaries that connected Greeks in the United States with Greeks elsewhere and Poles in Canada with Poles elsewhere. Both chapters also highlight the importance of multiculturalism (in the United States and Canada) in contributing to the sense of ethnic solidarity that underpinned ties with the country of origin. It is tempting to differentiate race and ethnicity by noting how often racial affiliations crossed multiple national borders, while ethnicity tended toward a more demarcated affiliation based in a particular nation-based community. In the case of

Cyprus, however, the bonds of ethnicity were able to link Greek Americans not just to Greece but also to Greeks in Cyprus. As scholarship on Indian or Chinese migrants has shown, diasporic linkages based on ethnicity could and did extend across much of the globe.[9]

The work of Lialiouti, Muehlenbeck, and Payseur suggests that the political activism of Greek Americans and Polish Canadians had less of an impact on the Cold War than, vice versa, the Cold War had on the political mobilization of those particular communities. This is not to say, however, that race and ethnicity played no role in the high politics of the Cold War. Mark R. Beissinger makes a strong case for the role that "ethnic nationalism" played in the collapse of the Soviet Union. Reading his study along with the work of Payseur on Polish Canadians highlights the importance of studying how transnational ethnic linkages contributed to the end of the Cold War. The reverse relationship, in which the end of the Cold War affected race and ethnicity, is evident in the discussion that Henley Adams offers of the "special period" in which economic troubles disproportionately disadvantaged blacks in Cuba following the collapse of the Soviet Union.

The intersections between race, ethnicity, and the Cold War took on special importance in Africa. Several chapters demonstrate the centrality of Africa and African history, not just to the former imperial powers and Africans themselves, but also to many other parts of the world. Ryan M. Irwin's chapter indicates the vital role that apartheid played in the reconceptualization of international politics in the early 1960s. Henley Adams traces how Cuba's military involvement in Angola influenced the manner in which racial issues were broached by the Cuban government at home. Luís Nuno Rodrigues highlights the role of race in the decolonization of Portuguese Guinea. His discussion of the efforts of the Portuguese military to "win hearts and minds" strongly echoes Michael Krenn's analysis of the racialized nature of American involvement in Vietnam. While probing the ways in which race influenced how American policy makers viewed Papuan claims to independence, David Webster notes that Papuans themselves turned to a racial conception of the "Negroid race" to establish links with African nations. In his words, "they tried to turn 'race' into a diplomatic asset, transforming marginalization and powerlessness into a tool they could wield internationally."

While the following chapters focus on issues of race and ethnicity, Michael Donoghue's piece reveals how race has historically been interconnected with questions of gender and of sex. His close analysis of a rape case in the Panama Canal Zone demonstrates the transnational consequences of the historic interconnections between American racism and sexual control. It was not just within the territorial boundaries of the United States that white men encouraged each other to violence by conjuring images of black assaults on "white womanhood." Just as in the United States, Donoghue demonstrates, security concerns based in anti-Communism crippled efforts to achieve economic justice in the postwar Canal Zone. Complementing Donoghue's chapter, Maxim Matusevich reveals that it was not just Americans who linked race and sex. Sexual relationships with Russian women often created tensions between black students and Soviet citizens. Recognizing the global prevalence of interconnected efforts to control women and racial others underscores the importance of feminists such as Kamaladevi Chattopadhyaya who confronted the intersections of racism, imperialism, and sexism.[10] Transnational linkages between race, sex, and class make evident Barbara Fields's classic statement: "Only when set next to contemporary ideas having nothing to do with race can ideas about race be placed in the context of the ideological ensemble of which they form a part."[11]

While demonstrating the impact of the Cold War on "resurgent Nazi masculinity," Katrina M. Hagen's probing analysis of German perceptions of the conflict in Congo reveals a lesson relevant to all the contributions in this volume—the role of history in linking race, ethnicity, and the Cold War. Hagen focuses, in particular, on the legacies of National Socialism for the debate regarding German involvement in Congo. Scholarship on race and ethnicity in the twentieth century has long recognized the Second World War as a key turning point. While giving birth to the Cold War, the Second World War also fundamentally restructured race relations on a global scale. The war directly fed antiracist struggles throughout the world. In addition, the war helped delegitimize racism through its association with Nazi Germany and to a lesser extent imperial Japan. Hagen's analysis demonstrates how contested memories over the Nazi past became enmeshed in debates over decolonization and the Cold War. More broadly, her chapter illuminates the role that history and memory played in linking race, ethnicity, and the Cold War.

Today, it is memories of the Cold War that influence linkages between race and a new set of international relations. In the preface to the second edition of his autobiography, *Dreams from My Father*, Barack Obama linked the struggle against religious fundamentalism in the wake of September 11, 2001, to the struggle against racism. He began by referencing Francis Fukuyama's oft-cited conception of the end of history that accompanied the fall of the Berlin Wall. Turning from 1989 to 2001, Obama focused on the global consequences of the events of September 11. "History returned that day with a vengeance," he wrote, before adding, "as Faulkner reminds us, the past is never dead and buried—it isn't even past." Obama's reference to Faulkner implicitly linked the ongoing legacies of the Cold War to the ongoing legacies of the racial injustice that Faulkner immortalized in his writings. Obama personalized this linkage by locating his own story in relation to the struggle "between those who embrace our teeming, colliding, irksome diversity, while still insisting on a set of values that binds us together, and those who would seek, under whatever flag or slogan or sacred text, a certainty and simplification that justifies cruelty toward those not like us."[12] Obama connected his own efforts to transgress racial boundaries to his desire to forge links of understanding and interconnectedness across national, religious, and ethnic boundaries. His election raised hopes in many parts of the world that what was obviously a key moment (if not necessarily a turning point) in the history of race in the United States would usher in a new era in the history of American foreign relations and of global interconnectedness more generally. It remains to be seen to what degree such hopes will prove justified. By uncovering the transnational history of linkages between race, ethnicity, and global conflict, this volume makes clear that the challenge of grappling with, in Obama's words, our "teeming, colliding, irksome diversity" marked not just the United States, but many parts of the world. Perhaps recognizing the global nature of this challenge can serve as one step toward confronting the many boundaries that continue to divide human beings from each other and from our shared history.

Notes

1. Jawaharlal Nehru, "Note for Asaf Ali and K. P. S. Menon," January 22, 1947, K. P. S. Menon Papers, Nehru Memorial Museum and Library, New Delhi.
2. For one global approach to the Cold War, see Odd Arne Westad, *The Global Cold War: Third World Interventions and the Making of Our Times* (Cambridge: Cambridge University Press, 2005).
3. See Jonathan Rosenberg, *How Far the Promised Land? World Affairs and the American Civil Rights Movement from the First World War to Vietnam* (Princeton, NJ: Princeton University Press, 2006); Thomas Borstelmann, *The Cold War and the Color Line: American Race Relations in the Global Arena* (Cambridge, MA: Harvard University Press, 2001); Mary Dudziak, *Cold War Civil Rights: Race and the Image of American Democracy* (Princeton, NJ: Princeton University Press, 2000); and Brenda Gayle Plummer, *Rising Wind: Black Americans and U.S. Foreign Affairs, 1935–1960* (Chapel Hill: University of North Carolina Press, 1996).
4. See Nikhil Pal Singh, *Black Is a Country: Race and the Unfinished Struggle for Democracy* (Cambridge, MA: Harvard University Press, 2004); Carol Anderson, *Eyes off the Prize: The United Nations and the African American Struggle for Human Rights, 1944–1955* (Cambridge: Cambridge University Press, 2003); and Penny M. Von Eschen, *Race against Empire: Black Americans and Anticolonialism, 1937–1957* (Ithaca, NY: Cornell University Press, 1997).
5. Calvin B. Holder, "Racism toward Black African Diplomats during the Kennedy Administration," *Journal of Black Studies* 14, no. 1 (September 1983): 31–48.

6. Nico Slate, "A Coloured Cosmopolitanism: Cedric Dover's Reading of the Afro-Asian World," in *Cosmopolitan Thought Zones: South Asia and the Global Circulation of Ideas*, ed. Sugata Bose and Kris Manjapra (New York: Palgrave Macmillan, 2010).

7. Frederick Cooper, *Colonialism in Question: Theory, Knowledge, History* (Berkeley: University of California Press, 2005), 9.

8. André Béteille, *Society and Politics in India: Essays in a Comparative Perspective* (London: Athlone Press, 1991), 56.

9. Claude Markovitz, *The Global World of Indian Merchants: Traders of Sind from Bukara to Panama* (Cambridge: Cambridge University Press, 2000), and Wang Gungwu, *The Chinese Overseas: From Earthbound China to the Quest for Autonomy* (Cambridge, MA: Harvard University Press, 2000).

10. Nico Slate, "'I Am a Coloured Woman': Kamaladevi Chattopadhyaya in the United States, 1939–41," *Contemporary South Asia* 17, no. 1 (March 2009): 7–19.

11. Barbara Fields, "Ideology and Race in American History," in *Region, Race, and Reconstruction: Essays in Honor of C. Vann Woodward*, ed. J. Morgan Kousser and James M. McPherson (New York: Oxford University Press, 1982), 152

12. Barack Obama, *Dreams from My Father: A Story of Race and Inheritance*, rev. ed. (New York: Three Rivers Press, 2004), x.

References

ARCHIVES
K. P. S. Menon Papers, Nehru Memorial Museum and Library, New Delhi, India

SELECTED PUBLISHED WORKS
Anderson, Carol. *Eyes off the Prize: The United Nations and the African American Struggle for Human Rights, 1944–1955*. Cambridge: Cambridge University Press, 2003.

Béteille, André. *Society and Politics in India: Essays in a Comparative Perspective*. London: Athlone Press, 1991.

Borstelmann, Thomas. *The Cold War and the Color Line: American Race Relations in the Global Arena*. Cambridge, MA: Harvard University Press, 2001.

Cooper, Frederick. *Colonialism in Question: Theory, Knowledge, History*. Berkeley: University of California Press, 2005.

Dudziak, Mary. *Cold War Civil Rights: Race and the Image of American Democracy*. Princeton, NJ: Princeton University Press, 2000.

Ellison, W. James. "Paul Robeson and the State Department." *Crisis* 84 (May 1977): 184–89.

Fields, Barbara. "Ideology and Race in American History." In *Region, Race, and Reconstruction: Essays in Honor of C. Vann Woodward*, edited by J. Morgan Kousser and James M. McPherson, 143–77. New York: Oxford University Press, 1982.

Gungwu, Wang. *The Chinese Overseas: From Earthbound China to the Quest for Autonomy*. Cambridge, MA: Harvard University Press, 2000.

Holder, Calvin B. "Racism toward Black African Diplomats during the Kennedy Administration." *Journal of Black Studies* 14, no. 1 (September 1983): 31–48.

Layton, Azza Salama. *International Politics and Civil Rights Policies in the United States, 1941–1960.* New York: Cambridge University Press, 2000.

Markovitz, Claude. *The Global World of Indian Merchants: Traders of Sind from Bukara to Panama.* Cambridge: Cambridge University Press, 2000.

Obama, Barack. *Dreams from My Father: A Story of Race and Inheritance.* Rev. ed. New York: Three Rivers Press, 2004.

Plummer, Brenda Gayle. *Rising Wind: Black Americans and U.S. Foreign Affairs, 1935–1960.* Chapel Hill: University of North Carolina Press, 1996.

Rosenberg, Jonathan. *How Far the Promised Land? World Affairs and the American Civil Rights Movement from the First World War to Vietnam.* Princeton, NJ: Princeton University Press, 2006.

Singh, Nikhil Pal. *Black Is a Country: Race and the Unfinished Struggle for Democracy.* Cambridge, MA: Harvard University Press, 2004.

Slate, Nico. "A Coloured Cosmopolitanism: Cedric Dover's Reading of the Afro-Asian World." In *Cosmopolitan Thought Zones: South Asia and the Global Circulation of Ideas,* edited by Sugata Bose and Kris Manjapra, 213–35. New York: Palgrave Macmillan, 2010.

———. "'I Am a Coloured Woman': Kamaladevi Chattopadhyaya in the United States, 1939–41." *Contemporary South Asia* 17, no. 1 (March 2009): 7–19.

Von Eschen, Penny. *Race against Empire: Black Americans and Anticolonialism, 1937–1957.* Ithaca, NY: Cornell University Press, 1997.

Westad, Odd Arne. *The Global Cold War: Third World Interventions and the Making of Our Times.* Cambridge: Cambridge University Press, 2005.

PART I

Race and the International System

CHAPTER 1

Token Diplomacy

The United States, Race, and the Cold War

Michael L. Krenn

The problem of the twentieth century," declared the African American intellectual W. E. B. Du Bois in 1903, "is the problem of the color line." By the time the Cold War began to take shape following World War II, US foreign policy makers might well have argued that one of the great problems facing their own nation was the slow but steady erosion of the color line that for over a century quite literally divided the races and helped white Americans understand not only other peoples but themselves and their respective places in the world. At home, the walls of Jim Crow segregation were being steadily chipped away as African Americans spearheaded a movement for civil rights. Abroad, nations in Africa, Asia, and elsewhere that had suffered under the yoke of Western colonialism demanded an end to imperialism, white supremacy, and oppression. Even worse, they often pointed their fingers at the United States as a nation wracked with racial problems and wondered out loud whether such a society could truly carry the banner as "leader of the free world."

For US policy makers, the Cold War period was one of dealing—not always terribly successfully—with these numerous assaults on the old racial order, both at home and abroad. African American demands for equality and a greater role in US society; African and Asian nations clamoring for recognition of their status as sovereign states and decrying any notions of racial superiority and inferiority; Soviet propaganda on America's racial problems casting doubt on US claims to its status as leader of the free world—all these issues swirled, exploded, and intertwined in such complex ways that American officials were initially left dumbfounded in terms of a comprehensive response. In reaction to the increasing attacks on the color line, the United States adopted a policy that might reasonably be referred to as "token diplomacy."

The Historical Context of Race and US Foreign Policy

Before leaping directly into those tumultuous years following World War II and attempting to understand how American views on race adapted to a rapidly changing international environment, it would be useful to understand the history of the role played by race in US foreign policy prior to the beginnings of the Cold War. Two things are immediately, and painfully, obvious: first, that ideas about race were ingrained in America's dealings with the rest of the world from the very start of the American nation; second, that once part of the US view of the world and its people race (and racism) proved to be remarkably adaptable to the changing needs of America's foreign policy throughout the decades. Somewhat like a powerful virus, racism—even when the very fundamentals of the racist outlook were challenged or attacked—was able to mutate and reformulate itself to suit the demands of US diplomacy.

Ideas of race and racism certainly did not begin with the English colonists who, quite literally, carved new lives out of the New World in the sixteenth, seventeenth, and eighteenth centuries.[1] Since at least the 1500s, the English people had become more and more fascinated with stories of their own "race": the mythical Anglo-Saxons.[2] The English colonists who braved the wilds of the New World carried with them the notion that in some ways they were continuing the march of Anglo-Saxon expansion and progress. It was not long, however, before those general concepts of the Anglo-Saxon race were honed to a new sharpness through increased contact with "inferior" peoples. Interactions with the Native Americans, and the later importation of African slaves, provided the English settlers with living proof of their own superiority.

By the first decades of the nineteenth century, the United States was a nation that defined itself not only in terms of its political, social, and economic institutions, but also in very distinct and—so it was believed at the time—immutable racial terms. The Anglo-Saxon mythology transferred almost seamlessly into the American experience and with the break from England a new and more vigorous racial offshoot—the Anglo-American—had taken root in the national psyche. As the new nation's power grew, and as the vision of the United States as not merely a continental, but a world power took on greater clarity, race and racism would take their place as components of the young empire's foreign policy.

In the first half of the nineteenth century, for example, race played an important role in shaping and guiding the belligerent aggression that characterized the idea of Manifest Destiny. The United States now turned its attention to the lands farther west—Texas, California, and the other massive chunks of territory controlled by Mexico. Here, again, race played a vital role in supporting the aggressive American attitude toward the acquisition of Mexican lands. Just as Americans defined their own racial characteristics during the late 1700s and early 1800s, so, too, did they define the salient features of other races. Always acting under the assumption that Anglo-Americans occupied the top rung of what historian Michael Hunt has called the "hierarchy of race," it naturally followed that all other races took their place in descending order beneath the superior whites. Latin Americans, it was generally agreed, occupied a somewhat medium position—lower than the Caucasian, no doubt, but higher than the Native American or African.[3]

When in the 1820s the Mexican government allowed American colonists to settle in its northern province of Texas, what ensued was more than a clash of cultures; it was a clash of races. One notable Texan, Stephen Austin, espoused a popular view of the Mexican people: "To be candid the majority of the whole nation as far as I have seen them want nothing but tails to be more brutes than the apes." The Mexicans, it was quickly decided, were unworthy to hold such valuable land as Texas and California. In 1846, ten years after the American settlers in Texas successfully rebelled against Mexican rule, the United States and Mexico were at war. For many Americans, the conflict was inevitable.[4] By 1848, the war was over and the United States had stripped Mexico of two-thirds of its territory. Anglo-American destiny had been served.

Just fifty years later, the United States again embarked on a period of aggressive expansionism. This time, however, the goal was not the displacement of "inferior" races so that the white race might have the land it needed to progress and prosper. Instead, markets in which to sell American goods and secure needed raw materials were the aims of US policy. This period of overseas expansion coincided with a new phase in the development of racist thinking. The publication of Charles Darwin's theories on evolution in the 1850s, 1860s, and 1870s created a great deal of controversy, but they also served to sharpen and somewhat modify the dominant racial thinking. What emerged from the discussion and debate over Darwin's theories, specifically as they applied to the human race, was the idea of "social Darwinism." The idea, largely attributed to Englishman Herbert Spencer, posited that just as in the jungle, competition for survival also took place in human society. A number of influential Americans, including sociologist William Graham Sumner and amateur historian and popular writer John Fiske, were immediately taken by the precepts of social Darwinism. Phrases such as the "struggle for survival" and the "survival of the fittest" entered into common usage. Even the best-known man of the cloth of the late nineteenth century in the United States, Reverend Josiah Strong, could see the process of social Darwinism as God's will, put into action by the expansion of the Anglo-Saxon race to all corners of the earth. As Strong dramatically concluded, "And can any one doubt that the results of this competition of races will be the 'survival of the fittest?'"[5]

In some ways, of course, this trumpeted the old message of Manifest Destiny. However, the new American expansionism was quite different in its aims. The ultimate goals of what Walter LaFeber refers to as the "new empire"—consumers for American goods, workers to unearth and grow the raw materials demanded by the American marketplace—decreed a different fate for the people in the lands that came under American control. Such people as the Filipinos—"liberated" from their colonial masters in the Spanish-American War of 1898—could obviously not be left to their own devices. As Senator Albert Beveridge asked in his usual florid style: "Shall we leave them to themselves? Shall tribal wars scourge them, disease waste them, savagery brutalize them more and more? Shall their fields lie fallow, their forests rot, their mines remain sealed, and all the purposes and possibilities of nature be nullified?" President William McKinley, shortly after the American conquest of the Philippines, appealed to the highest counsel—God—who answered his worried prayer, telling the president that "there was nothing left for us to do but to take them all, and to educate the Filipinos, and uplift and civilize and Christianize them."[6]

Of course, racism had a more brutal side, which was fully on display during the Filipino Insurrection and the battle against Japan in World War II. The Filipinos, it turned out, were mostly Christian when the Americans arrived in 1898 and seemed intent on resisting President McKinley's (via God's) will to "civilize" them. The result was a three-year war between Filipino revolutionaries and US forces (1899–1902) in which tens of thousands of the former died from battle or starvation and exposure to the elements as American troops engaged in wholesale destruction of crops and villages. As congressional hearings later revealed, torture was a common practice for the US soldiers as was a strong and persistent racism. As one US enlisted man wrote to his parents about the "nigger fighting business": "I am in my glory when I can sight my gun on some dark skin and pull the trigger." During World War II, racism against the Japanese quickly crossed the line of simply reducing the humanity of the enemy (the easier to kill them). The famous US aviator Charles Lindbergh toured the Pacific battlefields in 1944 and came away visibly shaken by the racism and cruelty of the US servicemen he saw in action: the wholesale collecting of gold teeth from Japanese corpses; ears and noses cut from dead Japanese; and even the occasional Japanese skull taken as a war prize. When coming back through Hawaii Lindbergh was surprised to be asked whether he had any human bones in his luggage. Apparently, the customs official had "found a large number of men taking Japanese bones back home for souvenirs. He said he had found one man with two 'green' Jap skulls in his baggage." Little wonder that historian John Dower labels the conflict in the Pacific a "war without mercy." From the extermination of the Native American, the displacement of the Mexicans, and the "uplift" of the Filipinos to the war against the Japanese, racism not only served as a motivating factor but also served to heighten and intensify the levels of violence.[7]

Yet, when World War II came to a close it seemed that also coming to a close was the role of racism in US foreign policy. Even the Japanese, once defeated, were taken back into the fold and lavished with American aid. The discovery of the concentration camps spread throughout Nazi-occupied Europe brought home in the starkest ways possible the ultimate conclusion of the racially inspired lunacy of theories of a "master race." In addition, the war seemed to open the way for the development of a powerful movement in the United States that within two decades would help inspire the most far-reaching civil rights legislation in the nation's history.

Token Diplomats

Particularly in the years since the tragedy of 9/11, much of the publicity coming out of the US Department of State accentuated the "face" of America's diplomacy. The message of this new theme, illustrated by accompanying photographs, included men and women of all races—white, Hispanic, Asian American, and African American—was clear: America's diplomacy was representative of (and represented by) all the nation's people. An underlying theme, of course, was that in a world seemingly torn asunder by ethnic, religious, and racial conflicts the United States remained a beacon of hope as a nation where different people from so many different backgrounds lived in peace and progress.

Prior to the Cold War, however, the Department of State presented a very different face to the world: white, male, and mostly Protestant. In the years following the Civil War a handful of African Americans were appointed to a small number of overseas posts, usually by Republican administrations seeking to reward the loyalty of black voters. By and large, however, blacks (as well as women and Jewish Americans) were rarely present in America's foreign policy–making bureaucracy. Even the passage of the Rogers Act in 1924, which established guidelines for admission to the prestigious Foreign Service based entirely on merit, did little to crack open what some African American newspapers already referred to as the "lily-white club." The act did nothing to dissipate the elitist attitudes of the white males who dominated the Department of State. Their solutions for getting around the Rogers Act included "failing" African American candidates who made it to the oral examination part of the process for one reason or another and requesting an "unofficial" policy of telling women and blacks who applied that there simply were not enough openings available. These machinations were effective: a mere five African Americans managed to enter the Foreign Service in the quarter century after the Rogers Act came into effect. For these hardy few, however, career opportunities were extraordinarily limited. All of them were inserted into what came to be known as the "Negro circuit"—an endless round of assignments to undesirable postings in Liberia, the Azores, the Canary Islands, or Madagascar.[8]

For African Americans, however, the Cold War brought new—if still extremely limited—opportunities. Black men (and a handful of black women) found themselves holding new positions in their nation's official diplomatic efforts. Edward R. Dudley was named the first African American ambassador in American history in 1949 when the US mission in Liberia was raised to embassy status. Ten years later, Professor John Morrow was selected by the Dwight Eisenhower administration to serve as ambassador to Guinea, becoming the first black ambassador to a nation outside of Liberia. In 1961, Clifton Wharton Sr. broke another important color barrier when he became the first African American ambassador to a non-African nation, taking over as head of the US mission in Norway. In 1965, Patricia Roberts Harris was named the first African American woman ambassador when she accepted an assignment to Luxembourg. A number of other black Americans served in various foreign policy roles during the 1950s and 1960s, including membership on the US delegation to the United Nations.[9]

While civil rights groups and African American newspapers celebrated these high-profile appointments, and while each of the recipients was well deserving of the honor, much more than a desire to redress past discrimination or simple matters of merit went into the decisions to name black ambassadors, State Department officials, and UN representatives. Race, in one form or another, was a constant ingredient in the selection of each African American diplomat and US officials who made the appointments usually did so with very distinct propaganda goals in mind. The African American men and women who were selected were undoubtedly highly qualified, but the demands of what might reasonably be called "token diplomacy" usually outweighed considerations of merit.

A 1949 Department of State memorandum was one of the first official analyses concerning the use of African Americans as US diplomats. The crux of the matter was summed up in the memo's title—"Countries to which an

Outstanding Negro might Appropriately be sent as Ambassador." The racial angle quickly came into play as the report cited Romania or Bulgaria as first choices. As the memo noted, sending an "outstanding Negro as Ambassador to one of the iron curtain countries should serve to counteract the Communist propaganda that Americans are guilty of race discrimination." After that, it was slim pickings: Latin American countries would exhibit "initial hostility" to a black US diplomat; Arab nations would see such as appointment as an "affront"; and only Switzerland, Norway, and Denmark in Europe were satisfactorily "highly civilized and enlightened and generally without the race prejudice found in other places." (Apparently, the irony of the United States— one of the most racially segregated nations on the planet—commenting on the "racial enlightenment" of other countries was entirely lost on the writer of the memo.) Equally troubling was that the report could identify just one "outstanding Negro" to serve abroad: future Nobel Prize winner Ralph Bunche. In fact, Bunche was approached by the Department of State both for assistant secretary positions in Washington and for ambassadorial appointments abroad. Bunche adamantly refused service in the segregated environment of Washington and disparaged the notion of having to serve overseas in one of the "Negro circuit" nations. Instead, he went on to a brilliant career working with the United Nations. Little wonder, then, that only two African Americans were named to the prestigious Foreign Service Officer level during the Truman years and the majority of African Americans serving as diplomats overseas continued to see their opportunities limited.[10]

Problems continued during the Eisenhower years, when the tokenism inherent in the appointment of African American diplomats became painfully obvious. In discussing appointments to the US delegation to the United Nations an Eisenhower adviser complained to Secretary of State John Foster Dulles that "what we really are stuck on is a negro." He made it clear that the problem was entirely "political," since the "boss" (Eisenhower) has been "critized [sic] for not having appointed a negro to high office." Dulles was unimpressed; only eminent individuals should be on the delegation. And in what was plainly a Freudian slip, the secretary noted that few if any African Americans could "come through an FBI check lily white, because all of their organizations had been infiltrated at one time or another [by the Communists]." When an African American finally ascended to rank of chief of mission to a nation other than Liberia in 1958, the nation chosen for the breakthrough was none other than Romania—one of the Iron Curtain nations named in the 1949 memorandum. Clifton Wharton Sr., who toiled in the Department of State for over thirty years prior to being named US minister to Romania, certainly deserved the honor. The real reason for the appointment, however, was made clear in a story in *U.S. News & World Report*: Romania, an Eastern bloc nation that had been "sharply critical of the U.S. for 'suppressing' Negroes,'" was "in for a surprise" since "Mr. Wharton is a Negro." Certainly the negative international publicity given to the 1957 incidents in Little Rock (which also spurred the development of the "Unfinished Business" exhibit at the 1958 world's fair—as we will see) was also part of the reasoning.[11]

Throughout the Cold War African Americans continued to be appointed to some high-profile positions within the US foreign policy–making bureaucracy. Yet, if we examine ambassadorial appointments from the year 1949, when the first African American ambassador was appointed, through the late 1980s, when the Cold War came to an end, the "tokenism" inherent in the use of African Americans as diplomats becomes strikingly apparent. During that period nearly 1,400 ambassadorial appointments were made by US presidents. A mere sixty went to African Americans, which translates to just over 4.3 percent of all appointments. Where such appointments were made is equally telling. Sixty-seven percent of all African American ambassadors served in Africa, compared to 28 percent of all US ambassadors named to Africa. When one includes appointments to Caribbean nations then nearly 80 percent of African American ambassadors during the Cold War served in countries that were predominantly or entirely black.[12]

As the appointment of African American diplomats demonstrates, the ongoing Cold War with the Soviet Union was as much a battle of words and ideas as it was of bullets and economic aid packages. And in that battle, the United States suffered from what one observer referred to as an "Achilles' heel"—the racial problems arising from the treatment of African Americans. The initial American response was simply to dismiss the Soviet propaganda as "lies" and "exaggerations." But the constant stream of lynchings, beatings, bombings, and other vicious racial incidents in the postwar years belied these attempts. In desperation, the United States government turned to counter-propaganda, issuing pamphlets, books, and movies describing the fabulous progress of African Americans. The government also sponsored trips by notable African Americans such as Louis Armstrong, Dizzy Gillespie, Marian Anderson, and even the Harlem Globetrotters, all designed to show the world that black Americans were just as free and successful as any white American.[13]

When plans began for America's participation at the 1958 World's Fair to be held in Brussels, a striking idea emerged from some intellectuals and officials. Since the racial "cat," so to speak, was most certainly out of the bag, why not confront the problem head-on? Why not admit to the problem that the whole world could see anyway, and then try to explain what the United States was doing to deal with the issue. The end result of these discussions was the "segregation" section of what was known as the Unfinished Business exhibit at the fair. The United States put three of its problems on display: soil erosion; urban housing; and segregation. In three connected rooms, visitors to the exhibit were shown the problem of segregation; the progress being made to alleviate the problem (more education for African Americans, better jobs, etc.); and, in the final room, the hope for the future, portrayed by a picture of white and black children playing ring-around-the-rosy. The segregation section came in for scathing criticisms—mostly from Southern US congressmen. Their withering assault forced an almost immediate closure of the exhibit, but defenders quickly pointed out that the Europeans who visited Unfinished Business by and large left favorably impressed by America's honesty and seeming commitment to racial equality. After a brief reopening of a modified exhibit (the picture of the children playing was shrunk in size, and a picture of an African American man dancing with a white woman was removed), the attacks began anew. Eisenhower, never a strong supporter of civil rights to begin with, buckled and the segregation exhibit was closed for good.

The importance of the closing was clear. In a battle between Cold War policies (supposedly the driving force for the American government during the post–World War II period) and American racism, race trumped national security. Despite the fact that the "Unfinished Business" exhibit was an effective counterpropaganda tool in the war of words with the Soviets, the power of American racism simply overrode any and all other concerns. It was a telling moment in the history of race and US foreign relations.

The Modernization of Racism

During the nineteenth century, when the United States embarked on the creation of an overseas empire and increased its economic entanglements with not only Europe but Asia, Latin America, and even Africa, a small group of anti-imperialists in America asked why their nation needed to become involved with these faraway lands and peoples. The imperialists were quick to answer that nothing less than the progress of civilization was at stake. With the United States needing more and more markets for its gushing industrial production and more and more natural resources to feed those industries (and the American people), it was more necessary than ever before to have those dubbed by Rudyard Kipling "the white man's burden" perform their roles as consumers and producers in the world economy. And when the anti-imperialists (whose racism equaled or exceeded that of the imperialists) asked what American colonialism in places like the Philippines could accomplish given the low level of their human inhabitants, the answer was provided at the Louisiana Exposition of 1904. One of the most popular exhibits at this World's Fair, held in St. Louis, was the so-called Philippine Reservation. Here, visitors got a firsthand view of American progress in action. Hundreds of Filipinos had been rounded up and delivered to the fair. In one part of the reservation, American tourists were able to see the "natural" state of the Filipinos—half-naked savages who lived in grass huts (one male became famous as the "missing link" of evolution between the apes and man). In the other part of the reservation, visitors witnessed the amazing transformation that had taken place since the arrival of the Americans in 1898: Filipinos in Western garb, trained in orderly schools, working at industrial tasks, and singing the national anthem.[14] The paternalistic side of American racism was on display for all the world to see.

By the 1950s, however, the idea of a Philippine Reservation would have been unimaginable. At the Asian-African Conference held in Bandung, Indonesia, in April 1955 representatives from twenty-nine nations that had endured colonialism, bigotry, and exploitation made it clear that Western imperialism was on its last legs. Perhaps not surprisingly, one of the most damning speeches came from one of the delegates from the Philippines. He railed against European and American colonialism, in which the peoples of Africa and Asia were "systematically relegated to subject status not only politically and economically, and militarily—but racially as well." He warned his listeners in the West that the conference was a "sober and yet jolting reminder to them that the day of Western racism is passing along with the day of Western power over non-Western peoples."[15]

The eventual passing of Western colonialism, however, did not mean the disappearance of two questions that still lingered among American policy makers and intellectuals: How did one explain the underdevelopment of nations in Africa, Asia, and Latin America? And what role should the United States play in ameliorating that underdevelopment? Derogatory references to "gooks," "niggers," "chinks," and "darkies" as the reasons for those nations' lack of economic progress hardly seemed designed to win friends and influence people in these newly freed countries. Regardless, answers to those questions were needed quickly, because looming over the imminent demise of Western control over those nations was the threat of Communism's moving to fill the power vacuum with promises of economic development and equality for all workers. Out of this complex and troubling picture emerged a new, and seemingly more benign, theory of underdevelopment in the so-called Third World.

Modernization, as the theory came to be known, gradually gathered steam among US officials, political scientists, and economists during the period after World War II. MIT political economist Walt Whitman Rostow issued the best-known and most influential description of modernization theory with the 1960 publication of his book *The Stages of Economic Growth: A Non-Communist Manifesto*. (Rostow would use the fame generated by the book to go on to serve as a foreign policy adviser to John F. Kennedy and Lyndon

Johnson.) The essence of the theory was that all societies and nations moved along the same well-defined paths toward progress and economic development. Evolving from so-called traditional societies characterized by a more or less tribal structure and primitive subsistence agriculture and hunting, each culture progressed through what Rostow referred to as the "stages" of economic growth, eventually becoming the modern, urban, industrial societies evident in the United States and Western Europe. Modernization proponents admitted that many nations—particularly those in Asia, Africa, and Latin America—seemed to have more trouble passing through the various stages of development. These road bumps were ascribed to what Rostow called "bottlenecks"—poor political institutions, inadequate schooling and health care, and corrupt economic systems—that kept such nations from achieving the "take-off" point toward progress and prosperity. In this way, the problem of underdevelopment was ascribed not to racial factors, but to cultural and institutional issues.[16]

Thus, modernization had the patina of being a nonracial explanation for the different rates of economic development between the Western and non-Western nations. The word "patina" is apt, for lying beneath the scholarly jargon of modernization theory were some very old ideas about superiority and inferiority. As geographer James Blaut notes, whether the underdevelopment of nations inhabited by people of color was described in cultural or genetic terms the end result was the same: a need for "European [or American] guidance and 'tutelage.'" Ascribing the progress of the Western nations to their better "culture" was merely another—and better—way of explaining Western superiority. After all, if hundreds of years of Western involvement in the non-Western world failed to break the "bottlenecks" impeding development, then a natural conclusion soon arose: "a cultural, not genetic, superiority appeared in the European cultural pool very long ago and, just like genetic superiority, it has led ever since to a great rate of development for Europe and to a level of development which, at each moment in history, is higher than that of non-European cultures." Replacing the older, now disreputable theories of genetic racism came a newer, perhaps more palatable "cultural racism."[17]

The impact on American foreign policy became apparent almost immediately. Let us examine US policy toward Latin America in the postwar years as one example. References to Latin America's lack of economic and political development were now framed in the new, preferred cultural terms. As one State Department report noted, democracy was "alien" to Latin America, and the former colonial masters—Spain and Portugal—"deliberately suppressed" any movement in that direction. Another official noted the obstacles to progress: illiteracy, "feudal" societies, lack of a middle class. With these views in mind, US policy toward the region took shape, a policy that relied largely on the concept of American "guidance" of the "dependent, inarticulate, and politically impotent" peoples of Latin America. When Latin American nations, feeling they had done their fair share during World War II, called for a "Marshall Plan" for their region, the US answer was clear. As one American official explained, the Marshall Plan had been designed to "help a highly industrialized intricate economy." To try and replicate this in Latin America was futile, for "one could no more impose a Marshall plan on Central America than you could pick up Detroit and put it down in the middle of a Brazilian jungle. The basis for it wasn't there."[18]

Despite the high-sounding rhetoric of "modernization theory," race was never very far from these discussions. One State Department study made note of eight major differences between the United States and Latin America. Prominently featured was a comparison of "% white population." Not surprisingly, the Latin American nations praised most highly for their "development" were those that just coincidentally had the highest percentage of white population: Argentina, Uruguay, and Costa Rica. As another report suggested, the United States faced difficult problems in Latin America, such as the "efforts to assimilate millions of Indians who are heirs of a different type of civilization," and a "great variety of breeds of people reacting in their own way to our public and diplomatic behavior (origins, including European, and African, Moorish and indigenous, and complex crisscrossing)." Other reports noted that some Latin Americans were "not a logical people and have short memories"; others were noted for their "mental deviousness and difficulty of thinking in a straight line." Negotiating with such people about even insignificant issues was "rather like consulting with babies as to whether or not we should take candy away from them." When it came to complicated issues of economic development, the racial divide grew even wider. Latin American views on the matter were described as "plain cockeyed" or "the stuff of fantasy." When asked what the Latin Americans really wanted in terms of economic aid from the United States, one American official declared: "I think frequently they didn't know for sure. . . . What they wanted and what they needed were very frequently entirely different. . . . They thought one just pressed a button and out spewed steel or whatever." In even more patronizing language, a former US ambassador to four Latin American nations dismissed the notion that even massive amounts of American aid would really help most underdeveloped nations. You could not, he argued, compare US aid to nations like Greece or Israel, whose people were not "tribal," with nations whose citizens were "just out of the palm trees." In these situations, "the closer to the palm tree the object of American aid is, the less likely it is to utilize American assistance to his or our advantage."[19]

Under the new guise of "modernization theory," racism continued to influence American foreign policy. When the idea of race began to lose its biological foothold in the post–World War II years, it simply rebounded by attaching itself quite easily and seamlessly to cultural explanations of the unique prog-ress of the Anglo-Saxon world and the continuing backwardness and lack of civilization in the nonwhite world. The amazing resiliency of racism, how-ever, allowed it to stave off challenges during the Cold War, emerging rela-tively unscathed and continuing to play an important role in America's foreign relations.

The Dark Continent

In dealing with the demands for independence that began to pulse through Africa in the post–World War II period, US officials found themselves in an extremely uncomfortable situation. On the one hand, it was obvious to most observers that the old colonial British, French, Belgian, Portuguese, and Span-ish regimes were weakening almost daily. On the other hand, US statesmen did not believe that black Africans were capable of sustaining stable, anti-Communist self-government. The US policy toward Africa, therefore, care-fully (and, in many ways, disingenuously) trod a diplomatic tightrope. While publicly declaring their support for freedom and anticolonialism, in private US officials remained committed to a policy of incremental independence for the black population of Africa. The policy came into sharpest focus in South Africa, where the United States continued its support of an odious apartheid regime even in the face of rising violence and black demands for equality in that nation.

For most US officials prior to the Cold War, Africa was indeed the "dark continent"—in more ways than one.[20] There was a temporary increase in US interest in Africa during World War II. American troops were stationed at bases on the continent and even engaged in combat with Axis forces in North Africa. With the end of the war, however, Africa again virtually disappeared from the US diplomatic radar. Two forces combined to push American inter-est to its highest levels during the Cold War. The first was the development of strong nationalist movements in colonized Africa. Struggling against Brit-ish, French, Belgian, Portuguese, and Spanish imperialism, these movements often looked to the United States for encouragement and assistance. They were sorely disappointed in America's tepid official response. Public rhetoric about the American commitment to anticolonialism continued through the 1950s and early 1960s, but officially US diplomats expressed deep concern over the ability of Africans to rule themselves. As a National Security Council report from the late 1950s explained, the African people were far too "immature and unsophisticated" to weather the rigors incumbent upon independence.[21]

The second challenge that increased the US interest in Africa was the fear of Communist encroachment. Here, too, race played a factor. One of the biggest problems facing the United States in Africa was what one report called the "anti-white and anti-Western sentiment" on that continent. Of course, much of that had to do with the oppressive colonial regimes under which much of the population of Africa struggled for existence. After a visit to Africa in 1957, Vice President Richard Nixon concluded that another component of that sentiment was the "skillful propaganda primarily inspired by the enemies of freedom" that portrayed a "consistently distorted picture of the treatment of minority races in the United States." As he further explained, the Communist threat in Africa had been underestimated and Communist agents were effective because they could "clothe themselves in Islamic, racist, anti-racist, or nationalist clothing." Nixon's answer was simple: use more effective counterpropaganda telling the "true story" of racial progress in the United States.[22]

With America's focus on Europe and the Far East during the early Cold War, the United States—despite the challenges mentioned earlier—seemed content to leave the African continent to its white, European colonial allies. For at least one group in the United States, however, this rather passive indifference to Africa sparked outrage. At the same time African Americans were pushing for civil rights at home they also became more involved with and outspoken about America's foreign relations. African American journalists, civil rights leaders, and politicians were unrelenting in their attacks on European colonialism and the racism that was one of its foundations. As the executive editor of the influential black newspaper the *Pittsburgh Courier* declared, it was time for the United States to stop focusing so much on the rebuilding of the colonial nations of Europe and turn its attention to the "1600 million human beings, mostly colored," who made up "two-thirds of the world's population, but enjoy only one-sixth of the world's income." The National Association for the Advancement of Colored People regularly denounced colonialism as "unjust and a threat to world peace" and ran numerous columns and editorials calling on the European nations to end their imperialist rule in Africa. As the European hold on Africa began to crack, African Americans called on the United States to accept the new reality and adopt proactive policies toward the new black nations on that continent. Congressman Charles Diggs, following a visit to Africa in 1961, pleaded with US policy makers to "learn to consider the problem of the new African nations from the African's concept not those of the European colonists." Independence was "coming to Africa and the Africans are going to run the show."[23]

In particular, African Americans were frustrated and angry over the passive US response to the repugnant apartheid regime of South Africa. Neither the Truman nor the Eisenhower administration showed any inclination to engage in condemnations of the government of South Africa or in diplomatic activities geared toward influencing changes in the racially divided African nation. One of the reasons was explained by Eisenhower himself, who in response to suggestions that the United States support a strong anti-apartheid resolution in the United Nations argued that he "could not escape the feeling that we are not entirely in a different position ourselves. . . . If we vote for a tough resolution, we may find ourselves red-faced—in other words concerning our own Negro problem." Other reasons included the fact that South Africa was a consistent anti-Communist ally of the United States, providing generous amounts of valuable minerals including diamonds, gold, and uranium to the Cold War struggle. Even the Kennedy and Johnson administrations, despite their rhetoric of freedom and actions taken in regard to civil rights for African Americans, were reluctant to directly challenge the white regime in South Africa in any meaningful fashion.[24]

Throughout the Cold War years African Americans, in particular, remained vociferous critics of the apartheid regime in South Africa and of the United States government that supported it.[25] Roy Wilkins, executive secretary of the NAACP, lashed out at the South African government following the Sharpeville Massacre in 1960, in which security forces fired into a crowd of black protestors, killing sixty-nine people and injuring nearly two hundred others. This act, Wilkins declared, put South Africa "outside the pale of Western democratic society." However, Wilkins noted that the United States also bore much of the blame since the weapons used on the protesters might well have been purchased using aid provided by the American government. In the mid-1960s, as the civil rights movement gathered steam in the United States, black criticism of apartheid intensified. *The Crisis*, the official publication of the NAACP, argued that "racism, whether in Alabama, New York, or South Africa, is an abomination in the eyes of God and men." The situation in South Africa was particularly odious, since it was the "only country in the world officially dedicated to a policy of racism . . . reminiscent of Hitlerism."[26]

In the late 1960s and early 1970s, the anti-apartheid movement in the United States continued to gather strength and once again African Americans were in the forefront. Charles Diggs, a vocal and influential congressional opponent of the South African regime, became chair of the House Subcommittee on Africa and began a number of hearings into American corporate and political involvement with the apartheid government. The Congressional Black Caucus was formed in 1971, and US relations with South Africa became one of its issues of interest. Yet African Americans and other anti-apartheid foes found themselves confronted with the unreceptive, unsympathetic, and often painfully racist attitudes of the administration of Richard Nixon and his national security adviser, Henry Kissinger.[27]

Nixon, as tapes of his White House conversations reveal, often used derogatory terms to describe African Americans and Africans. In an infamous conversation with Kissinger, the president declared, "Henry, let's leave the niggers to Bill [Secretary of State William Rogers] and we'll take care of the rest of the world." Kissinger's assistant, Alexander Haig, was famous for creating peals of laughter by pretending to play tom-tom drums whenever matters related to Africa arose at meetings. Not surprisingly, such thinking influenced the Nixon administration's attitude toward South Africa. Faced with growing criticism of the apartheid regime in the United States, Kissinger—in his famous National Security Study Memorandum 39—asked the National Security Council to come up with an analysis of the problems faced in southern Africa. The resulting study laid out what would later be labeled by critics as the "tar baby solution," since they believed that its policy recommendations would ensnare the United States in a hopeless and inescapable position. In essence, the document suggested that the United States establish even closer relations with the white government of South Africa because "the whites are here to stay and the only way that constructive change can come about is through them." There was "no hope for the blacks to gain the political rights they seek through violence, which will only lead to chaos and increased opportunities for the communists." It was necessary, therefore, to adopt a "selective relaxation of our stance against the white regime." In addition, the US government should "take diplomatic steps to convince the black states of the area that their current liberation and majority rule aspirations in the south are not attainable by violence and that their only hope for a peaceful and prosperous future lies in closer relations with white-dominated states."[28]

In many ways, the situation reminded one of the civil rights struggles that had taken place in the United States since the late 1800s. Again and again, African Americans were told that the path to equal civil rights was one paved with patience and accommodation. Token gestures were made toward "equality": in 1896 the Supreme Court, in the *Plessy v. Ferguson* case, ruled that "separate" schools, seats on public transportation, and so forth for African Americans were entirely acceptable as long as they were "equal." It was not until nearly sixty years later, in the *Brown v. Topeka Board of Education* (1954) Supreme Court ruling, that segregated schools were declared unconstitutional and Southern states were directed to begin desegregation with "all deliberate speed." Violence erupted in places like Little Rock, Arkansas, as whites protested the decision. By the mid-1960s only a tiny fraction of African American students were attending previously all-white schools. Only the rising tide of the civil rights movement, led by charismatic people such as Martin Luther King Jr., finally pushed the US government to pass far-reaching civil rights legislation. Old habits—and old prejudices—whether at home or abroad did not die easily.

Indian Country

In many ways, all the intersections between race and US foreign policy during the Cold War ended up in the jungles of Vietnam. The Vietnam War served as a sort of societal mirror into which a horrified American public would look during the years 1965–1973 and see reflected all the racial schisms and theories that helped define their nation's Cold War diplomacy. In that war against North Vietnam (a nation roughly the size of New Mexico) and the National Liberation Front forces in South Vietnam, many of the racial aspects of American foreign relations were played out: the hubris and patronizing ideas behind modernization theory; the conflicted roles played by African Americans; and, as had happened so many times in the nation's past when race entered into US relations with other peoples, violence that beggared the imagination.

For many American policy makers, Vietnam was the place where the theory of modernization found its practical application. Here was a country with a long and brutal history of colonial rule now, in the post–World War II period, threatened by Communism from within led by Ho Chi Minh. Following the defeat and eventual withdrawal of the French colonialists in 1954 the United States embarked on a nearly two-decade experiment in what American officials referred to as "nation building." Even the phrase itself captured the US hubris and racially tinged paternalism so apparent in the Cold War years. Ignoring the fact that Vietnam had been a nation nearly nine hundred years before the American war for independence, US officials blithely assumed that no nation worthy of the name had ever existed in Southeast Asia. Faced with a dangerous power vacuum following the French departure and the threat of Ho's Communist movement, America simply decided that it must build the nation of South Vietnam from the ground up. It would be no easy task, as the US ambassador to South Vietnam stated so clearly in 1963: "My general view is that the US is trying to bring this medieval country into the 20th Century."[29]

Not all Americans, however, were quite as sure about the US mission in Vietnam. In particular, African Americans expressed very grave concerns over what they perceived as double-edged racism inherent in the war. When casualty figures from 1965 indicated that African Americans made up nearly 25 percent of all US combat deaths in Vietnam (while making up less than 11 percent of the total US population), the black community saw a dangerous double standard at work. The most vocal and visible black critic was Martin Luther King Jr. Fresh from spearheading civil rights victories at home in 1964 and 1965, by 1967 King worried that the war in Vietnam was destroying everything to which he had devoted his life's work. In a sermon in April

1967, King vented his frustrations, calling the United States the "greatest purveyor of violence in the world today." He now watched in horror and sorrow as the war continued, "devastating the hopes of the poor at home. It was sending their sons and their brothers and their husbands to fight and die in extraordinarily high proportions to the rest of the population." Every day America was "faced with the cruel irony of watching Negro and white boys on TV screens as they kill and die together for a nation that has been unable to seat them together in the same schools. So we watch them in brutal solidarity burning the huts of a poor village, but we realize that they would never live on the same block in Detroit. I could not be silent in the face of such cruel manipulation of the poor."[30]

But it was in the jungles of Vietnam, where the "brutal solidarity" of US troops was on display every day, that the racial aspects of the war came into sharpest focus. A number of historians, including Richard Drinnon, have commented on the fact that the war in Vietnam called up references to past US conflicts with people of color. In particular, the conflict in Vietnam was often compared to the wars against Native Americans in the wild west of the late nineteenth century. As one news report put it, US soldiers considered "all areas outside their small circular fortresses . . . to be 'Indian Country.'" The difficulty, as a US officer put it, was that "it is very hard to plant the corn outside the stockade when the Indians are still around. We have to get the Indians farther away in many of the provinces to make good progress." And in a tip of the hat to the war against the Filipinos following the Spanish-American War, the derisive term "goo-goo" (applied to the Filipinos because of their small, "doll-like" physiques) was transformed into "gooks" to describe the newer Vietnamese enemy.[31]

Even US officials who had serious doubts about America's involvement in Vietnam could not avoid the racial issue. George Ball, one of the most vocal dissenters in the Johnson administration, expressed his misgivings in a famous 1965 memorandum to the president by arguing: "No one can assure you that we can beat the Viet Cong . . . no matter how many hundred thousand *white, foreign* troops we deploy. No one has demonstrated that a white ground force of whatever size can win a guerrilla war." Even Ball could not have foreseen, however, that his drawing of the racial lines between the United States and the enemy it faced in Vietnam would have such devastating and violent blowback. With the adoption of a strategy of attrition (in essence, killing more of the enemy than they kill of your forces until they are forced to submit), the only real measurement of "progress" in the conflict became the "body count": stacking up enemy bodies like cords of wood. As the pressure for even more and faster progress increased, US soldiers adopted the informal MGR—the "mere gook rule." It was simplicity itself: if it's dead, and it's Vietnamese, it's the enemy. Not surprisingly, distinctions between foes and civilians blurred to the point of no return—and that point occurred on March 16, 1968, when US troops massacred nearly four hundred women, children, and elderly Vietnamese in the village of My Lai. Just a few miles away, other American soldiers slaughtered nearly one hundred peasants in My Khe. Although initially claiming that a savage firefight at My Lai had resulted in a terrific American victory, the cover for the massacre finally blew in 1969 and one of the commanders of the US troops that day was charged with murder. Even here, however, American officials could not stop themselves from drawing the color line: the lieutenant was indicted on the charge of murdering "at least" 102 "Oriental human beings." As with "Indians" and "goo-goos" in the past, the Vietnamese were discovering the price of American progress.[32]

Conclusion

As World War II came to a close and the Cold War started heating up, the time seemed well suited to a reconsideration of Du Bois's famous declaration about the problem of the "color line." Much had changed. The racism that had been a bulwark of the old colonial systems of oppression was under attack and the question now seemed one of when, not if, the imperial framework would completely collapse. The racist jargon that had been a consistent element of US foreign policy appeared to be in full retreat. Few officials, after all, wished to be lumped in with the racist lunacy that engulfed Germany and led to the Holocaust. At home, too, African Americans were pushing for greater civil rights and equal participation in the American political, economic, and social systems. In some ways, the Cold War appeared to give even added urgency to a full and complete denunciation of racism by the United States, both at home and abroad. What else could be expected of the self-anointed "leader of the free world"?

However, a close examination of US foreign policy during the Cold War reveals that race and racism still played important roles. This is not to argue, of course, that racism was the single most important determinant of American Cold War diplomacy. What the evidence does suggest is that to ignore or dismiss the role of race is a serious omission. As it had in America's past, racism ably adapted itself to the new needs and challenges of US foreign policy. In response to African American demands for more participation in the foreign policy–making bureaucracy and foreign criticisms of America's racial practices, a policy of token appointments of black diplomats and the selective use of African Americans in the propaganda war with the Communists arose.

When the more direct (and now publicly discredited) aspects of racism could not be used to explain underdevelopment in areas of the globe populated by people of color and the continuing need for US guidance even as new, independent nations arose in those areas, the cultural racism of modernization theory nicely filled the gap. Africa, which had historically been consigned to the back of the diplomatic bus by American officials, found itself facing an official US attitude that combined disparagement of black Africans' ability to govern themselves with patronizing encouragement of evolutionary progress toward independence. Still more insulting was the continued US embrace of the apartheid regime of South Africa, even in the face of denunciations by African Americans and much of the international community.

Finally, all the racist hens had come home to roost in the Indian Country of Vietnam. Here, again, was a medieval society desperately in need of American know-how and resolve. It remained for the United States to literally pull the Vietnamese peasant out of the muck and mire of their rice paddies. When some of the Vietnamese seemed reluctant to embrace this promised land of modernization, America responded with force. Even here, however, race was front and center. As King noted, how could one ignore the obvious ironies inherent in a nation sending its poor and black young men halfway across the globe to kill (and be killed by) poor and yellow young men in Vietnam? And as the grisly war of attrition hit its stride, the racist "mere gook rule" meant that Vietnamese friends and foes alike would be added to the body count.

The Cold War certainly marked a different era of America's foreign relations. As the examples in this chapter have attempted to demonstrate, however, racism—as it had for the first 150 years of the nation's history—continued to play its virulent and destructive role in the construction and implementation of US diplomacy. Instead of taking the lead in the international and domestic assault on the color line, US officials fell back into old habits, biases, and theories with disturbing ease. Within the framework of its token diplomacy, America could give lip service to equality, freedom, and civil rights while at the same time maintaining a generally steadfast adherence to the old notions of white superiority.

Notes

1. For analysis of the development of racial thinking, see Ivan Hannaford, *Race: The History of an Idea in the West* (Baltimore: Johns Hopkins University Press, 1996); Michael P. Banton, *Race Relations* (New York: Basic Books, 1967) and *The Idea of Race* (Boulder, CO: Westview Press, 1978); Pat Shipman, *The Evolution of Racism:*

Human Differences and the Use and Abuse of Science (New York: Simon and Schuster, 1994); and George M. Fredrickson, *Racism: A Short History* (Princeton, NJ: Princeton University Press, 2002).

2. For studies of the development of the Anglo-Saxon mythology and how it took hold in early America, see Reginald Horsman, *Race and Manifest Destiny: The Origins of American Racial Anglo-Saxonism* (Cambridge, MA: Harvard University Press, 1981); Richard Drinnon, *Facing West: The Metaphysics of Indian-Hating and Empire-Building* (Norman: University of Oklahoma Press, 1997); Winthrop D. Jordan, *The White Man's Burden: Historical Origins of Racism in the United States* (London: Oxford University Press, 1974); and Thomas F. Gossett, *Race: The History of an Idea in America* (Dallas: Southern Methodist University Press, 1963).

3. Analyses of the developing US attitudes toward Latin Americans are found in James William Park, *Latin American Underdevelopment: A History of Perspectives in the United States, 1870–1965* (Baton Rouge: Louisiana State University Press, 1995); Albert K. Weinberg, *Manifest Destiny: A Study of Nationalist Expansionism in American History* (Baltimore: Johns Hopkins University Press, 1935); Arnoldo de León, *They Called Them Greasers: Anglo Attitudes toward Mexicans in Texas, 1821–1900* (Austin: University of Texas Press, 1983); Thomas R. Hietala, *Manifest Design: Anxious Aggrandizement in Late Jacksonian America* (Ithaca, NY: Cornell University Press, 1985); Fredrick B. Pike, *The United States and Latin America: Myths and Stereotypes of Civilization and Nature* (Austin: University of Texas Press, 1992); John J. Johnson, *A Hemisphere Apart: The Foundations of United States Policy toward Latin America* (Baltimore: Johns Hopkins University Press, 1990); and David J. Weber, "'Scarce More Than Apes': Historical Roots of Anglo American Stereotypes of Mexicans in the Border Region," in *New Spain's Far Northern Frontier: Essays on Spain in the New West, 1540–1821*, ed. David. J. Weber (Albuquerque: University of New Mexico Press, 1979), 295–307.

4. Austin quote found in Weber, "'Scarce More Than Apes,'" 89, 92.

5. For a good introduction to the impact of social Darwinism in America and England, see Robert C. Bannister, *Social Darwinism: Science and Myth in Anglo-American Social Thought* (Philadelphia: Temple University Press, 1979). For two interesting views on how social Darwinism influenced one of America's leading figures, consult Thomas G. Dyer, *Theodore Roosevelt and the Idea of Race* (Baton Rouge: Louisiana State University Press, 1980); and David Burton, "Theodore Roosevelt's Social Darwinism and Views on Imperialism," *Journal of the History of Ideas* 26 (1965): 103–18. Strong quote is found in "Josiah Strong on the Superiority of the 'Anglo-American Race,' 1891," in *Major Problems in American Foreign Relations, Volume I: To 1920*, 4th ed., ed. Thomas G. Paterson and Dennis Merrill (Lexington, MA: D. C. Heath, 1995), 350–53.

6. Studies examining the impact of race in the Spanish-American War and Filipino Insurrection that followed include Rubin Francis Weston, *Racism in U.S. Imperialism: The Influence of Racial Assumptions on American Foreign Policy, 1893–1946* (Columbia: University of South Carolina Press, 1972); Philip W. Kennedy, "Race and American Expansion in Cuba and Puerto Rico, 1895–1905," *Journal*

of Black Studies 1 (1971): 306–16; Christopher Lasch, "The Anti-Imperialists, the Philippines, and the Inequality of Man," *Journal of Southern History* 24 (1958): 319–31; and Eric T. Love, *Race over Empire: Racism and U.S. Imperialism, 1865–1900* (Chapel Hill: University of North Carolina Press, 2004). John J. Johnson, *Latin American in Caricature* (Austin: University of Texas Press, 1980), is an interesting look at how racial stereotypes were reflected in the editorial cartoons of the time. Beveridge quote is found in Gossett, *Race*, 329; McKinley quote is found in "William McKinley's Imperial Gospel, 1899," in *Major Problems in American Foreign Relations, Volume I: To 1920*, 4th ed., ed. Thomas G. Paterson and Dennis Merrill (Lexington, MA: D. C. Heath, 1995), 424.

7. For the "nigger fighting business" quote, see James Bradley, *Flyboys: A True Story of Courage* (Boston: Little, Brown, 2003), 70; John W. Dower, *War without Mercy: Race and Power in the Pacific War* (New York: Pantheon Books, 1986); and Charles A. Lindbergh, *The Wartime Journals of Charles A. Lindbergh* (New York: Harcourt Brace Jovanovich, 1970), 879–80, 882–83, 903, 919, 923.

8. The best studies of the early Foreign Service and its exclusionary hiring policies can be found in Robert D. Schulzinger, *The Making of the Diplomatic Mind: The Training, Outlook, and Style of United States Foreign Service Officers, 1908–1931* (Middletown, CT: Wesleyan University Press, 1975), chs. 1–3, and Martin Weil, *A Pretty Good Club: The Founding Fathers of the U.S. Foreign Service* (New York: Norton, 1978), chs. 1–3. Jake C. Miller, *The Black Presence in Foreign Affairs* (Washington, DC: University Press of America, 1978), ch. 1, provides a brief but useful examination of early African American diplomats. For a more detailed look at the period from 1924 through 1952, see Michael L. Krenn, *Black Diplomacy: African-Americans and the State Department, 1945–1969* (Armonk, NY: M. E. Sharpe, 1999), chs. 1, 3. The Department of State was well aware of the situation confronting these black diplomats. The steady policy of discriminatory hiring, assignment, and promotion practices was clearly laid out in a memorandum, "Policy of the Department of State with reference to the assignment and transfer of Negro personnel of the Foreign Service," prepared by Harold Sims, May 10, 1949, contained in George McGhee to John Peurifoy, January 19, 1950, Papers of Edward R. Dudley, Box 1, Folder 8, Amistad Research Center.

9. For a brief survey of African Americans appointed to positions in the Department of State, see Office of Equal Employment Opportunity, Department of State, "A Chronology of Key Negro Appointments in the Department of State and the Foreign Service, 1869–1969," May 1969, furnished to the author from the personal papers of Ronald D. Palmer. More detail on these various appointments can be found in Krenn, *Black Diplomacy*, chs. 3, 5, and 7.

10. Christian Ravndal to Mr. Peurifoy, May 23, 1949, State Department Correspondence, Box 35, Folder 1948–49, no. 16, Confidential Files, Papers of Harry S. Truman, Harry S. Truman Library; "Bunche Blasts D.C. Jim Crow," *Pittsburgh Courier*, June 11, 1949, 1, 4, 13. For more details on Bunche's career, see Brian Urquhart, *Ralph Bunche: An American Life* (New York: Norton, 1993); Benjamin Rivlin, ed., *Ralph Bunche: The Man and His Times* (New York: Holmes and Meier, 1990); and Peggy Mann, *Ralph Bunche: UN Peacemaker* (New York: Coward, McCann, and

Geoghegan, 1975). For the figures on African American diplomats during the Truman administration, see Krenn, *Black Diplomacy*, 63–64.

11. "Telephone Conversation with Gov. Adams," July 17, 1953, 1:56 P.M.; "Telephone Conversation with Gov. Adams," July 17, 1953, 5:25 P.M., Papers of John Foster Dulles, Telephone Calls Series, Box 10, White House Telephone Conversations-May to December 31, 1953 (2) File; and "Telephone Conversation with Leonard Hall," May 6, 1953, Dulles Papers, Telephone Calls Series, Box 1, Telephone Memoranda (May–June 1953) (2) File, Dwight D. Eisenhower Library (hereafter DDEL), Abilene, KS. For the Wharton appointment, see Krenn, *Black Diplomacy*, 108–9; and "Clifton R. Wharton Gets Ready for Rumania," *U.S. News and World Report*, February 21, 1958, 22.

12. Michael L. Krenn, "'Outstanding Negroes' and 'Appropriate Countries': Some Facts, Figures, and Thoughts on Black U.S. Ambassadors, 1949–1988," *Diplomatic History* 14 (Winter 1990): 131–41.

13. Naima Prevots, *Dance for Export: Cultural Diplomacy and the Cold War* (Hanover, NH: University Press of New England, 1998); Uta Poiger, *Jazz, Rock, and Rebels: Cold War Politics and American Culture in a Divided Germany* (Berkeley: University of California Press, 2000); and Penny M. Von Eschen, *Satchmo Blows Up the World: Jazz Ambassadors Play the Cold War* (Cambridge, MA: Harvard University Press, 2004). As Von Eschen notes, Armstrong was initially reluctant to play the role of unofficial American "ambassador" because of his anger over the treatment of African Americans in the United States. The intersections between America's race problem and the Cold War are examined in Mary L. Dudziak, *Cold War Civil Rights: Race and the Image of American Democracy* (Princeton, NJ: Princeton University Press, 2000); Thomas Borstelmann, *The Cold War and the Color Line: American Race Relations in the Global Arena* (Cambridge, MA: Harvard University Press, 2003); Brenda Gayle Plummer, *Rising Wind: Black Americans and U.S. Foreign Affairs, 1935–1960* (Chapel Hill: University of North Carolina Press, 1996); Penny M. Von Eschen, *Race against Empire: Black Americans and Anticolonialism, 1937–1957* (Ithaca, NY: Cornell University Press, 1996); Michael L. Krenn, *Black Diplomacy: African-Americans and the State Department, 1945–1969* (Armonk, NY: M. E. Sharpe, 1999); and Plummer, *Window on Freedom: Race, Civil Rights, and Foreign Affairs, 1945–1988* (Chapel Hill: University of North Carolina Press, 2003).

14. For the best analysis of the 1904 World's Fair and the Philippine Reservation in particular, see Robert W. Rydell, *All the World's a Fair: Visions of Empire at American International Expositions, 1876–1916* (Chicago: University of Chicago Press, 1984), 154–83.

15. "Statement of Carlos P. Romulo, Member of the Cabinet, Chairman of the Philippine Delegation to the Asian-African Conference, Bandung, Indonesia," reprinted in Carlos P. Romulo, *The Meaning of Bandung* (Chapel Hill: University of North Carolina Press, 1956), 68–69. An interesting analysis of the American response to the conference is found in Cary Fraser, "An American Dilemma: Race and Realpolitik in the American Response to the Bandung Conference, 1955," in *Window on Freedom*, 115–40.

16. Walt Whitman Rostow, *The Stages of Economic Growth: A Non-Communist Manifesto* (Cambridge: Cambridge University Press, 1960). Several excellent studies

of the development of modernization theory and its application to American foreign policy during the Cold War have appeared over the last fifteen years: Nils Gilman, *Mandarins of the Future: Modernization Theory in Cold War America* (Baltimore: Johns Hopkins University Press, 2003); David Engerman et al., eds., *Staging Growth: Modernization, Development, and the Global Cold War* (Amherst: University of Massachusetts Press, 2003); and Michael E. Latham, *Modernization as Ideology: American Social Science and "Nation Building" in the Kennedy Era* (Chapel Hill: University of North Carolina Press, 2000).

17. James M. Blaut, "The Theory of Cultural Racism," *Antipode: A Radical Journal of Geography* 23 (1992): 289–99.

18. Problem Paper, August 29, 1949, Record Group 59, Office Files of the Assistant Secretary of State for Inter-American Affairs (Edward G. Miller), 1949–1953, Box 10, National Archives and Records Administration (hereafter NARA), College Park, MD; John Cabot, "Summary of Remarks at conference on U.S. Foreign Policy, June 4 and 5, 1953," John Foster Dulles Papers, Box 75, Seeley G. Mudd Manuscript Library; Central Intelligence Agency, "Conditions and Trends in Latin America Affecting US Security," December 12, 1952, Papers of Harry S. Truman, President's Secretary's Files, Intelligence File, Box 254, Central Intelligence Reports, NIC 67-75, Harry S. Truman Library; and George Elsey, Oral History, July 17, 1969, 376–77, Harry S. Truman Library. For a good general overview of the application of modernization theory to Latin America, see Park, *Latin American Underdevelopment*, 167–203; see also Michael L. Krenn, *The Chains of Interdependence: U.S. Policy toward Central America, 1945–1954* (Armonk, NY: M. E. Sharpe, 1996), ch. 2.

19. Untitled problem paper, July 5, 1949, Record Group 59, Miller Files, Box 10, NARA; "The Caribbean Republics," August 24, 1954, *Foreign Relations of the United States, 1952–1954,* 4, 383; problem paper, August 29, 1949, RG 59, Miller Files, Box 10, NARA; Walter N. Walmsley to Paul Nitze, May 9, 1952, RG 59, Miller Files, Box 10, NARA; Hallet Johnson to Department of State, October 15, 1946, RG 59, Decimal File FW818.00/10-1546, NARA; Rudolf Schoenfeld to Miller, September 5, 1952, RG 59, Miller Files, Box 7, NARA; Miller to Paul Daniels, April 7, 1952, RG 59, Miller Files, Box 7, NARA; Francis Truslow to Miller, March 12, 1951, RG 59, Miller Files, Box 4, NARA; J. Robert Schaetzel, "Analysis of Latin American Proposals," March 1948, Record Group 353, Records of the Department of State: Interdepartmental and Intradepartmental Committees, Box 2, NARA; Dennis FitzGerald, Oral History, May 26, 1976, 8–9 (DDEL); and Ellis Briggs, Oral History, June 19, 1970, and October 15, 1972, 3 (DDEL).

20. See Dennis Hickey and Kenneth C. Wylie, *An Enchanting Darkness: The American Vision of Africa in the Twentieth Century* (East Lansing: Michigan State University Press, 1993), 8–13; and Peter Duignan and L. H. Gann, *The United States and Africa: A History* (Cambridge: Cambridge University Press, 1984), chs. 1–4, for good overviews of US attitudes and policies toward Africa prior to World War II.

21. National Security Council, "U.S. Policy toward South of Sahara Prior to Calendar Year 1960," July 31, 1957, Record Group 273, Records of the National Security Council, Box 5, Folder "NSC 5719," NARA. For more on US attitudes toward Africa

following World War II, see Duignan and Gann, *The United States and Africa*, ch. 5; Thomas J. Noer, *Cold War and Black Liberation: The United States and White Rule in Africa, 1948–1968* (Columbia: University of Missouri Press, 1985); and Thomas Borstelmann, *Apartheid's Reluctant Uncle: The United States and South Africa in the Early Cold War* (New York: Oxford University Press, 1993).

22. "Africa: Problems of United States Policy," c. 1956, enclosed in John Hoover to Various American Missions, February 17, 1956, RG 59, 611.70/2-1756, NARA; "The Vice President's Report to the President on Trip to Africa, February 28–March 21, 1957," White House Office, Office of Special Assistant for National Security Affairs, Special Assistant Series, Subject Subseries, Box 10, Vice President (1) January 1954–April 1957 file (DDEL); and Memorandum, "Discussion at the 335th Meeting of the National Security Council, Thursday, August 22, 1957," August 23, 1957, Eisenhower Papers, National Security Council Series, Box 9, 335th Meeting of NSC, August 22, 1957 file (DDEL).

23. "NAACP Stand on Colonialism and U.S. Foreign Policy," *Crisis* (January 1955): 23–26; William Worthy Jr., "Our Disgrace in Indo-China," *Crisis* (February 1954): 77–83; "Portuguese Colonialism," *Crisis* (February 1956): 102–4; "Unrest in Angola," *Crisis* (June–July 1960): 383–85; P. L. Prattis, "New Look at the World," *Crisis* (April 1953): 201–4, 255; and Krenn, *Black Diplomacy*, 115.

24. "Telephone Calls, March 30, 1960, 4:20," Eisenhower Papers, Ann Whitman File, DDE Diary Series, Box 48, Telephone Calls March 1960 file (DDEL). For analyses of the various administrations' policies toward Africa, see Thomas J. Noer, *Cold War and Black Liberation: The United States and White Rule in Africa, 1948–1968* (Columbia: University of Missouri Press, 1985); Borstelmann, *Apartheid's Reluctant Uncle*; Richard D. Mahoney, *JFK: Ordeal in Africa* (New York: Oxford University Press, 1983); Terrence Lyons, "Keeping Africa off the Agenda," in *Lyndon Johnson Confronts the World: American Foreign Policy, 1963–1968*, ed. Warren I. Cohen and Nancy Bernkopf Tucker (Cambridge: Cambridge University Press, 1994), 245–78; Thomas J. Noer, "New Frontiers and Old Priorities in Africa," in *Kennedy's Quest for Victory: American Foreign Policy, 1961–1963*, ed. Thomas J. Paterson (New York: Oxford University Press, 1989), 253–83; and Gerald E. Thomas, "The Black Revolt: The United States and Africa in the 1960s," in *The Diplomacy of the Crucial Decade: American Foreign Relations in the 1960s*, ed. Diane B. Kunz (New York: Columbia University Press, 1994), 363–78.

25. Studies of the anti-apartheid movement, and African Americans' role in the movement, include Abdul S. Minty, "The Antiapartheid Movement and Racism in Southern Africa," in *Pressure Groups in the Global System*, ed. Peter Willetts (New York: St. Martin's Press, 1982), 28–45; Milfred C. Fierce, "Selected Black American Leaders and Organizations and South Africa, 1900–1977," *Journal of Black Studies* 17 (March 1987): 305–26; Donald R. Culverson, *Contesting Apartheid: U.S. Activism, 1960–1987* (Boulder, CO: Westview Press, 1999); and Steven Metz, "The Anti-Apartheid Movement and the Populist Instinct in American Politics," *Political Science Quarterly* 101, no. 3 (1986): 379–95.

26. Roy Wilkins to Christian Herter, March 22, 1960, Papers of the NAACP, Group III, Box A35, Africa, South Africa, 1956–1965, and undated file, Library of

Congress; and "Action against Apartheid," *Crisis* (June–July 1965): 359–61, 396.

27. Donald R. Culverson, "From Cold War to Global Interdependence: The Political Economy of African-American Antiapartheid Activism, 1968–1988," in *Window on Freedom*, ed. Brenda Gayle Plummer, 227–28. See also Stephen Metz, "Congress, the Antiapartheid Movement, and Nixon," *Diplomatic History* 12 (1988): 165–85.

28. Seymour M. Hersh, *The Price of Power: Kissinger in the Nixon White House* (New York: Summit Books, 1983), 110–11; and National Security Council Interdepartmental Group for Africa, "Study in Response to National Security Study Memorandum 39: Southern Africa," December 9, 1969, *nsarchives.chadwyck.com/nsa/documents/SA/00379/all.pdf.*

29. *Pentagon Papers* (Boston: Beacon Press, 1971), 2:790; Loren Baritz, *Backfire: A History of How American Culture Led Us into Vietnam and Made Us Fight the Way We Did* (New York: William Morrow, 1985), 129–77; and John Mecklin, *Mission in Torment* (Garden City, NY: Doubleday, 1965), 74, 76.

30. Peter B. Levy, "Blacks and the Vietnam War," in *The Legacy: The Vietnam War in the American Imagination*, ed. D. Michael Shafer (Boston: Beacon Press, 1990), 211.

31. Drinnon, *Facing West*, 368, 369, 455.

32. *Pentagon Papers*, 4:615 (the words "white, foreign" are italicized in the original); for a discussion of the development of the mere gook rule, see Philip Caputo, *A Rumor of War* (New York: Holt, 1996). The best analysis of My Lai and the resulting cover-up is found in Seymour M. Hersh, *Cover-Up* (New York: Random House, 1972).

References

ARCHIVES

Amistad Research Center, Tulane University, New Orleans, LA

Dwight D. Eisenhower Library, Abilene, KS

Harry S. Truman Library, Independence, MO

Library of Congress, Washington, DC

National Archives and Records Administration, College Park, MD

National Security Archive (Online)

Personal papers of Ambassador Ronald D. Palmer, Washington, DC

Seeley G. Mudd Manuscript Library, Department of Rare Books and Special Collections, Princeton University, Princeton, NJ

PERIODICALS

The Crisis

Pittsburgh Courier

U.S. News and World Report

SELECTED PUBLISHED WORKS

Bannister, Robert C. *Social Darwinism: Science and Myth in Anglo-American Social Thought*. Philadelphia: Temple University Press, 1979.

Banton, Michael P. *The Idea of Race*. Boulder, CO: Westview Press, 1978.

———. *Race Relations*. New York: Basic Books, 1967.

Baritz, Loren. *Backfire: A History of How American Culture Led Us into Vietnam and Made Us Fight the Way We Did*. New York: Morrow, 1985.

Blaut, James M. "The Theory of Cultural Racism." *Antipode: A Radical Journal of Geography* 23 (1992): 289–99.

Borstelmann, Thomas. *Apartheid's Reluctant Uncle: The United States and South Africa in the Early Cold War*. New York: Oxford University Press, 1993.

———. *The Cold War and the Color Line: American Race Relations in the Global Arena*. Cambridge, MA: Harvard University Press, 2003.

Bradley, James. *Flyboys: A True Story of Courage*. Boston: Little, Brown, 2003.

Burton, David. "Theodore Roosevelt's Social Darwinism and Views on Imperialism." *Journal of the History of Ideas* 26 (1965): 103–18.

Caputo, Philip. *A Rumor of War*. New York: Holt, 1996.

Culverson, Donald R. *Contesting Apartheid: U.S. Activism, 1960–1987*. Boulder, CO: Westview Press, 1999.

———. "From Cold War to Global Interdependence: The Political Economy of African-American Antiapartheid Activism, 1968–1988." In *Window on Freedom*, edited by Brenda Gayle Plummer, 221–38. Chapel Hill: University of North Carolina Press, 2003.

de León, Arnoldo. *They Called Them Greasers: Anglo Attitudes toward Mexicans in Texas, 1821–1900*. Austin: University of Texas Press, 1983.

Dower, John D. *War without Mercy: Race and Power in the Pacific War*. New York: Pantheon Books, 1986.

Drinnon, Richard. *Facing West: The Metaphysics of Indian-Hating and Empire-Building*. Norman: University of Oklahoma Press, 1997.

———. "The Metaphysics of Empire-Building: American Imperialism in the Age of Jefferson and Monroe." *Massachusetts Review* 16 (1975): 666–88.

Dudziak, Mary L. *Cold War Civil Rights: Race and the Image of American Democracy*. Princeton, NJ: Princeton University Press, 2000.

———. "The Little Rock Crisis and Foreign Affairs: Race, Resistance, and the Image of American Democracy." *Southern California Law Review* 70 (September 1997): 1641–1716.

Duignan, Peter, and L. H. Gann. *The United States and Africa: A History*. Cambridge: Cambridge University Press, 1984.

Dyer, Thomas G. *Theodore Roosevelt and the Idea of Race*. Baton Rouge: Louisiana State University Press, 1980.

Engerman, David, Nils Gilman, Mark Haefele, and Michael E. Latham, eds. *Staging Growth: Modernization, Development, and the Global Cold War*. Amherst: University of Massachusetts Press, 2003.

Fierce, Milfred C. "Selected Black American Leaders and Organizations and South Africa, 1900–1977." *Journal of Black Studies* 17 (March 1987): 305–26.

Foreign Relations of the United States, 1952–1954. Washington, DC: US Government Printing Office, 1983.

Fraser, Cary. "An American Dilemma: Race and Realpolitik in the American Response to the Bandung Conference, 1955." In *Window on Freedom*, edited by Brenda Gayle Plummer, 115–40. Chapel Hill: University of North Carolina Press, 2003.

———. "Crossing the Color Line in Little Rock: The Eisenhower Administration and the Dilemma of Race for U.S. Foreign Policy." *Diplomatic History* 24, no. 2 (Spring 2000): 233–64.

Fredrickson, George M. *Racism: A Short History*. Princeton, NJ: Princeton University Press, 2002.

Gilman, Nils. *Mandarins of the Future: Modernization Theory in Cold War America*. Baltimore: Johns Hopkins University Press, 2003.

Gossett, Thomas F. *Race: The History of an Idea in America*. Dallas: Southern Methodist University Press, 1963.

Hannaford, Ivan. *Race: The History of an Idea in the West*. Baltimore: Johns Hopkins University Press, 1996.

Hersh, Seymour M. *Cover-Up*. New York: Random House, 1972.

———. *The Price of Power: Kissinger in the Nixon White House*. New York: Summit Books, 1983.

Hickey, Dennis, and Kenneth C. Wylie. *An Enchanting Darkness: The American Vision of Africa in the Twentieth Century*. East Lansing: Michigan State University Press, 1993.

Hietala, Thomas R. *Manifest Design: Anxious Aggrandizement in Late Jacksonian America*. Ithaca, NY: Cornell University Press, 1985.

Horsman, Reginald. *Race and Manifest Destiny: The Origins of American Racial Anglo-Saxonism*. Cambridge, MA: Harvard University Press, 1981.

Johnson, John J. *A Hemisphere Apart: The Foundations of United States Policy toward Latin America*. Baltimore: Johns Hopkins University Press, 1990.

———. *Latin America in Caricature*. Austin: University of Texas Press, 1980.

Jordan, Winthrop D. *The White Man's Burden: Historical Origins of Racism in the United States*. London: Oxford University Press, 1974.

Kennedy, Philip W. "Race and American Expansion in Cuba and Puerto Rico, 1895–1905." *Journal of Black Studies* 1 (1971): 306–16.

Krenn, Michael L. *Black Diplomacy: African-Americans and the State Department, 1945–1969*. Armonk, NY: M. E. Sharpe, 1999.

———. *The Chains of Interdependence: U.S. Policy toward Central America, 1945–1954*. Armonk, NY: M. E. Sharpe, 1996.

———. "'Outstanding Negroes' and 'Appropriate Countries': Some Facts, Figures, and Thoughts on Black U.S. Ambassadors, 1949–1988." *Diplomatic History* 14 (Winter 1990): 131–41.

———. "'Unfinished Business': Segregation and U.S. Diplomacy at the 1958 World's Fair." *Diplomatic History* 20 (1996): 591–612.

Lasch, Christopher. "The Anti-Imperialists, the Philippines, and the Inequality of Man." *Journal of Southern History* 24 (1958): 319–31.

Latham, Michael E. *Modernization as Ideology: American Social Science and "Nation Building" in the Kennedy Era*. Chapel Hill: University of North Carolina Press, 2000.

Levy, Peter B. "Blacks and the Vietnam War." In *The Legacy: The Vietnam War in the American Imagination*, edited by D. Michael Shafer, 209–32. Boston: Beacon Press, 1990.

Lindbergh, Charles A. *The Wartime Journals of Charles A. Lindbergh*. New York: Harcourt Brace Jovanovich, 1970.

Love, Eric T. *Race over Empire: Racism and U.S. Imperialism, 1865–1900*. Chapel Hill: University of North Carolina Press, 2004.

Lyons, Terrence. "Keeping Africa off the Agenda." In *Lyndon Johnson Confronts the World: American Foreign Policy, 1963–1968*, edited by Warren I. Cohen and Nancy Bernkopf Tucker, 245–78. Cambridge: Cambridge University Press, 1994.

Mahoney, Richard D. *JFK: Ordeal in Africa*. New York: Oxford University Press, 1983.

Mann, Peggy. *Ralph Bunche: UN Peacemaker*. New York: Coward, McCann, and Geoghegan, 1975.

Mecklin, John. *Mission in Torment*. Garden City, NY: Doubleday, 1965.

Metz, Steven. "The Anti-Apartheid Movement and the Populist Instinct in American Politics." *Political Science Quarterly* 101, no. 3 (1986): 379–95.

———. "Congress, the Antiapartheid Movement, and Nixon." *Diplomatic History* 12 (1988): 165–85.

Miller, Jake C. *The Black Presence in Foreign Affairs*. Washington, DC: University Press of America, 1978.

Minty, Abdul S. "The Antiapartheid Movement and Racism in Southern Africa." In *Pressure Groups in the Global System*, edited by Peter Willetts, 28–45. New York: St. Martin's Press, 1982.

Nash, Gary B. "Red, White, and Black: The Origins of Racism in Colonial America." In *The Great Fear: Race in the Mind of America*, edited by Gary B. Nash and Richard Weiss, 1–26. New York: Holt, Rinehart and Winston, 1970.

Noer, Thomas J. *Cold War and Black Liberation: The United States and White Rule in Africa, 1948–1968*. Columbia: University of Missouri Press, 1985.

———. "New Frontiers and Old Priorities in Africa." In *Kennedy's Quest for Victory: American Foreign Policy, 1961–1963*, edited by Thomas J. Paterson, 253–83. New York: Oxford University Press, 1989.

Park, James William. *Latin American Underdevelopment: A History of Perspectives in the United States, 1870–1965*. Baton Rouge: Louisiana State University Press, 1995.

Paterson, Thomas G., and Dennis Merrill, eds. *Major Problems in American Foreign Relations, Volume I: To 1920*. 4th ed. Lexington, MA: D. C. Heath, 1995.

Pentagon Papers. Boston: Beacon Press, 1971.

Pike, Fredrick B. *The United States and Latin America: Myths and Stereotypes of Civilization and Nature*. Austin: University of Texas Press, 1992.

Plummer, Brenda Gayle. *Rising Wind: Black Americans and U.S. Foreign Affairs, 1935–1960*. Chapel Hill: University of North Carolina Press, 1996.

———, ed. *Window on Freedom: Race, Civil Rights, and Foreign Affairs, 1945–1988*. Chapel Hill: University of North Carolina Press, 2003.

Poiger, Uta. *Jazz, Rock, and Rebels: Cold War Politics and American Culture in a Divided Germany*. Berkeley: University of California Press, 2000.

Prevots, Naima. *Dance for Export: Cultural Diplomacy and the Cold War*. Hanover, NH: University Press of New England, 1998.

Rivlin, Benjamin, ed. *Ralph Bunche: The Man and His Times*. New York: Holmes and Meier, 1990.

Romulo, Carlos P. *The Meaning of Bandung*. Chapel Hill: University of North Carolina Press, 1956.

Rostow, Walt Whitman. *The Stages of Economic Growth: A Non-Communist Manifesto*. Cambridge: Cambridge University Press, 1960.

Rydell, Robert W. *All the World's a Fair: Visions of Empire at American International Expositions, 1876–1916*. Chicago: University of Chicago Press, 1984.

Schulzinger, Robert D. *The Making of the Diplomatic Mind: The Training, Outlook, and Style of United States Foreign Service Officers, 1908–1931*. Middletown, CT: Wesleyan University Press, 1975.

Shipman, Pat. *The Evolution of Racism: Human Differences and the Use and Abuse of Science*. New York: Simon and Schuster, 1994.

Thomas, Gerald E. "The Black Revolt: The United States and Africa in the 1960s." In *The Diplomacy of the Crucial Decade: American Foreign Relations in the 1960s*, edited by Diane B. Kunz, 363–78. New York: Columbia University Press, 1994.

Urquhart, Brian. *Ralph Bunche: An American Life*. New York: Norton, 1993.

Von Eschen, Penny M. *Race against Empire: Black Americans and Anticolonialism, 1937–1957*. Ithaca, NY: Cornell University Press, 1996.

———. *Satchmo Blows Up the World: Jazz Ambassadors Play the Cold War*. Cambridge, MA: Harvard University Press, 2004.

Weber, David J. "'Scarce More Than Apes': Historical Roots of Anglo American Stereotypes of Mexicans in the Border Region." In *New Spain's Far Northern Frontier: Essays on Spain in the New West, 1540–1821*, edited by David J. Weber, 295–307. Albuquerque: University of New Mexico Press, 1979.

Weil, Martin. *A Pretty Good Club: The Founding Fathers of the U.S. Foreign Service*. New York: Norton, 1978.

Weinberg, Albert K. *Manifest Destiny: A Study of Nationalist Expansionism in American History*. Baltimore: Johns Hopkins University Press, 1935.

Weston, Rubin Frances. *Racism in U.S. Imperialism: The Influence of Racial Assumptions on American Foreign Policy, 1893–1946*. Columbia: University of South Carolina Press, 1972.

CHAPTER 2

A Wind of Change?

White Redoubt and the Postcolonial Moment in South Africa, 1960–1963

Ryan M. Irwin

In July 1963, US Secretary of State Dean Rusk held a private meeting with Dr. Willem Naude, the ambassador of South Africa.[1] "A rough time [is] ahead," Rusk explained as the representative sat down in his office. "We are under enormous pressure but do not intend to give in." Several members of the UN African group states at the United Nations had successfully protested the practice of apartheid—South Africa's system of institutionalized racial discrimination—in the Security Council that year and pressure was rapidly mounting in the General Assembly for mandatory economic sanctions against South Africa. The ambassador looked across Rusk's desk and noted that it was "ironical" that ten years earlier they had been allies in the Cold War and now his country was being isolated in its struggle against a "common enemy." He went on to assert: "The United States [is] to a large degree responsible for releasing these revolutionary forces in the world. The goal of a great power should be to play down tensions and try to get people to talk together, but the United States without even opening its mouth [has] released dangerous forces in the world." Rusk paused for a moment before responding: "[I wonder] if these forces [are] not deeply rooted in the nature of man. [I wonder] if this discourse has not been going on for 2,000 years. Did not man, like most animals, not like to be pushed around too much?"[2]

The secretary of state's comments were meant as a subtle jab at the ambassador, but they reflected the fact that new themes were reshaping how politicians approached international affairs. In many ways, the world was in the midst of a revolutionary transformation. Since the end of World War II, the Cold War between the United States and the Soviet Union had formed the parameters of world conflict and dominated global forums like the United Nations. For many American elites, the foremost accomplishments of the postwar era had been the solidification of US power in Western Europe and the Pacific Rim, while the greatest threats were the Soviet Union's dominance over Eastern Europe and the rise of Communist China. The concept of containment seemed unassailable and few questioned the overriding importance of the Cold War. Under the surface, however, advocates for the decolonization of Africa and Asia were articulating a systematic rebuttal of this paradigm. With the onset of first-wave decolonization in the late 1940s, these actors gained a voice at the United Nations and established the foundation for what would become the postcolonial critique. Rather than focusing on national security issues or great power politics, they placed precedence on the problems of white racism and economic exploitation. The Cold War, to their minds, was a diversion from the more important struggles being waged along the North-South axis.

This thesis came into focus as dozens of African and Asian states gained their independence in the late 1950s and early 1960s. Concepts of sovereignty, freedom, and development—long defined in reference to European history— reemerged as contested ideas in these years, with actors using discourses of human rights, racial equality, and nationalism to expand their authority at the United Nations. As Rusk surveyed these developments in the summer of 1963, he no doubt recognized that South Africa's internal policies were placing it at the epicenter of this new drama. The issue of apartheid not only monopolized debate at the General Assembly that year; it also shaped *how* the "2,000-year-old" struggle of humankind against its oppressor was being presented to the world community. The choice between order and justice that subtly permeated Rusk's conversation with the South African ambassador, in effect, was a choice between the Cold War narrative of postwar events and the emerging story of postcolonial emancipation.

This chapter examines the apartheid debate from an international perspective. Focusing on the brief moment between 1960 and 1963, it looks at how three influential actors—the African group at the UN, the US government, and the South African government—framed the stakes and meaning of apartheid in the immediate wake of second-wave or African decolonization. Sitting at the nexus of Cold War politics and decolonization, apartheid was the quintessential border of the postcolonial decade. For symbolic and political reasons, each side in this story tried to police, reconceptualize, and control legitimate forms of knowledge about South Africa. As this contest unfolded, the apartheid question became a microcosm of the postcolonial era, revealing the deep-seated differences between actors in the First and Third Worlds, as well as the paradoxical nature of change in the late twentieth century.

In explicating this story, this chapter forwards three interlocking arguments. First, resistance to apartheid subtly influenced how anticolonial sentiment was expressed in the years after decolonization. Couched in the language of Third World nationalism and Cold War neutrality, the actions of African nation-states vis-à-vis South Africa did not illustrate political immaturity, but rather a latent effort to reconstitute global politics in ways that embraced universal human rights and nonracialism. Black nationalists, quite literally, used their influence in the United Nations to broaden the definition of legitimate international behavior. Second, the United States reacted to these efforts with an agenda born from the Cold War. America's own national myth worked in conjunction with the UN Charter to buttress anti-apartheid efforts on a rhetorical level, but US officials were always more concerned with maintaining America's hegemony at the United Nations than with confronting racism in South Africa. Finally, as world opinion turned definitively against the Nationalist government in the early 1960s, Afrikaner elites tried retooling their country's image in ways that transcended debate at the UN and strengthened ties with Western nations. Their efforts were not entirely successful, but they did expose important connections between older forms of racial paternalism and the new discourse of modernization in the post–World War II years.

When taken together, these points offer insight on the complex relationship between the Cold War and decolonization. The African bloc's inability to elicit support for economic sanctions was tied most directly to the divergence between its political goals and the security and economic priorities of Western policy makers. Equally important, however, was the shifting nature of political space in the postcolonial moment. As African elites grew more adept at using their numbers to shape discourse at the United Nations, US leaders began to pull away subtly from the organization and the idea that it could be a bulwark of American global power. This shift—and the underlying attitudes that supported it—both eroded the tentative authority of new nation-states at the international level and opened the door for subsequent South African propaganda initiatives at the nonstate level. Although the language of empire changed undeniably in the postcolonial years, global politics continued to reflect and reinforce older forms of pan-European hegemony.

Internationalizing Apartheid

On January 27, 1960, the British prime minister, Harold Macmillan, arrived in the Union of South Africa to deliver a stern message. Having spent much of the late 1950s managing decolonization movements within the British Commonwealth, he sought to warn the white population of South Africa that a "wind of change" was blowing through their continent. Speaking before a special joint session of Parliament on February 3, he argued: "Whether we like it or not, [the] growth of [African] national consciousness is a political fact. We must all accept it as a fact. Our national policies must take account of it." Macmillan went on to explain that the world was being divided into three groups, with the Western powers and Communists now competing to garner loyalty from newly independent nonwhite peoples. In his words, "The great issue in this second half of the twentieth century is whether the uncommitted peoples of Asia and Africa will swing to the east or to the west." When placed against this backdrop, the situation in South Africa was becoming vitally important. "It is the basic principle for our modern Commonwealth that we respect each other's sovereignty in matters of internal policy," Macmillan declared. "[But] we must recognize that, in this shrinking world in which we live today, the internal policies of one nation may have effects outside it."[3] The British prime minister, in short, was asking the Union of South Africa to recognize that it was becoming a liability to the West in the postcolonial era of world politics.

Macmillan's words reverberated throughout South African society. Since gaining its independence in 1910, the Union had worked from the assumption that its position among the Western powers was unassailable. The basis of this partnership, in the minds of many South African elites, was the inherent superiority of white civilization and a common commitment to racial paternalism. As European countries like France and Great Britain relinquished control of their colonial holdings in Africa and Asia, however, these twin principles receded from global discourse. In their place emerged concepts of development, universal equality, and political self-determination.[4] Although India and other Asian states subjected the Nationalist government to criticism as early as 1946, its economic and strategic niche in the Cold War alliance system insulated it from concrete action through the 1950s.[5]

Macmillan's speech was interpreted widely as the harbinger of major change. "South Africa can only have one answer to this challenge," contended Cape Town's *Die Burger* the day after the British prime minister's speech. "We cannot hand over any part of Africa for which we are responsible. . . . The state of emergency we have been plunged into by Western panic can only be fought with united forces. It is a struggle for civilization."[6] As a colonial nation in an increasingly postcolonial world, South Africa had essentially reached a crossroads between nonracial reform and continued minority domination. Its response was made clear in mid-February, when South African prime minister Hendrik F. Verwoerd publicly declared: "The world is suffering from a psychosis which makes it think only of the brown and black man and disregard the role of the White man." Claiming that Western countries were "sacrificing their only real and stable friend . . . for something that will not succeed," Verwoerd emphatically concluded that there would be "no mixing of the races."[7]

South Africa's decision to embrace white domination was born from policies dating back to 1948. Capitalizing on a general climate of anxiety after World War II, the Afrikaner Nationalist party had achieved electoral supremacy that year by explicitly promising to reinforce laws that segregated the country's various ethnic groups.[8] While Macmillan conceptualized the dilemma of decolonization through the lens of the Cold War, most white South Africans were more concerned with the concrete task of holding on to political and economic power in the Union. On a basic level, apartheid institutionalized state control over the movement of black African laborers in white urban centers. After 1948, the government invested enormous state resources in robbing nonwhites of their remaining civil liberties, criminalizing various forms of labor activism, and forcing black Africans into overcrowded ghettos at the outskirts of cities. To support these programs, the Nationalist party not only expanded the government's military capabilities, but also forced blacks to carry identification cards whenever they left local townships to work in industrial centers.

Dissatisfaction among black South Africans exploded only a month after Macmillan departed the country in early 1960. On March 21, twenty thousand Africans surrounded a small police station in the township of Sharpeville and demanded to be arrested for not carrying their travel passes. Led by a political group called the Pan Africanist Congress (PAC) and inspired by the lessons of India's independence, they hoped to overflow South Africa's jails and provoke a crisis within the government. The police responded by opening fire on the crowd. Within a half hour, sixty-seven people were killed and nearly two hundred were injured.[9]

The Sharpeville Massacre triggered a sense of panic within the Nationalist party. Acknowledging that the protests were only one part of a nationwide upheaval involving hundreds of thousands of Africans, the minister of justice declared a state of emergency on March 22 and warned ominously that the country was on the brink of a race revolution. Mass arrests occurred in the following weeks as riots spread throughout the country.[10] Standing before the House of Assembly a week after the initial outburst, Prime Minister Verwoerd explained: "These disturbances we are experiencing must be seen against the background . . . of similar occurrences in this country, in the whole of Africa, and around the world."[11] The "wind of change" that Macmillan had described had arrived on the shores of South Africa. And the Union's response was dramatically clear.

Language of Dissent

The protests were indeed closely related to broader changes in African politics during the postwar era. For over five decades, the dominant nonwhite political organization in the Union of South Africa was the African National Congress (ANC). Subscribing to a nonracial social platform, the group worked steadily to unite the country's various blacks, Indians, and Coloreds under an inclusive political banner.[12] In 1959, Robert Sobukwe, an activist from Johannesburg, created the Pan Africanist Congress to challenge directly the ANC's leadership position in South Africa. His goal was straightforward—to incorporate more confrontational methods into the struggle against the Nationalist party and accelerate the assault on apartheid. But the language he used to frame these efforts broke radically with ANC dogma. Arguing that "government must be of the African, by the African, and for the African," the PAC explicitly rejected the utility of cooperation between racial groups and declared that black Africans would have "complete political independence by 1963."[13]

The assertiveness and race consciousness of this platform was tied closely to developments occurring in the rest of Africa. Sobukwe was keenly in tune with the ideas of political leaders like Ghana's President Kwame Nkrumah. The independence of Ghana in 1957, in many ways, legitimized the political demands of other African territories and spread Nkrumah's unique version of African nationalism through intellectual circles in the late 1950s. Linked with pan-African ideas of an older generation of diaspora intellectuals like W. E. B. Du Bois and Marcus Garvey, African nationalism provided a language to address the challenges of postcolonialism in ways that were uniquely African.[14] For Sobukwe and his supporters, it provided "the only liberatory creed" that could "weld the illiterate and semi-literate masses . . . into a solid, disciplined and united fighting force; provide them with a loyalty higher than that of the tribe; and give formal expression to their desire to be a nation."[15]

As an ideological framework, African nationalism had two parts. Domestically, its advocates embraced the fair distribution of wealth through society and government investment in local infrastructures. "What other countries have taken three hundred years or more to achieve, a once dependent territory must try to accomplish in a generation if it is to survive," Nkrumah explained in the mid-1950s. "Capitalism is a difficult system for a newly independent nation, hence the need for a more socialistic society."[16] The goal was not to reject the tenets of modern industrialism, but to remedy the problems of underdevelopment in ways that strengthened communities and rejected economic exploitation. African nationalists hoped to promote development by balancing the needs of urban industrialism with their own mythic, precolonial African past. As Sobukwe explained at the PAC's Inaugural Conference, African nationalists would borrow the "best from the East" and "the best from the West" while "retain[ing] and maintain[ing]" the continent's "distinctive personality."[17]

At the international level, anticolonialism was the conceptual linchpin of African nationalism. According to Nkrumah, "[Africa's] safety [could] not be assured until the last vestiges of colonialism [were] swept from Africa." Political independence was the gateway to economic and social progress. Ghana's foreign minister, Alex Quiason-Sackey, tied this theme directly to the superpower struggle: "Colonialism is the source of all the troubles which afflict mankind in our age. It is the root cause of the desire to possess arms. Therefore, it is the root cause of the arms race and the problem of disarmament."[18] Rather than locating global turmoil in the subversive nature of Communism or the political economy of capitalism, African nationalists focused on the dangers of white colonialism. This racialized explanation of power was ubiquitous in the years surrounding decolonization. By flattening visions of the pan-European world (in ways that ironically mirrored the intellectual processes discussed in Edward Said's *Orientalism*), it buttressed the larger political project known as the Third World.[19]

The year 1960 was a moment of confluence. The Sharpeville Massacre occurred just as thirteen new African states emerged onto the global stage. While countries like India had criticized the Union's treatment of Indians and other nonwhites through much of the 1950s, decolonization opened space for a more forceful confrontation with the South African government.[20] For many of these African states, the system of apartheid represented a direct affront to the very notion of black liberation. Not only did it blatantly exploit Africans for economic advancement, but also it embraced the logic and methods of colonial domination. By modernizing the methods of white domination, the Union essentially positioned itself as the chief antagonist of the burgeoning African nationalist movement.

Young South African activists in the PAC and ANC rallied to the idea that their struggle was at the forefront of a worldwide revolution. "The beginning of the end of an era has begun," claimed the ANC's *Congress Voice* in 1960. "The day for which the oppressed and exploited people throughout the world have yearned and struggled so long, has at long last arrived. . . . [W]ith the recent accession of thirteen new independent African states . . . the [United Nations], which up to [now] has been a stronghold of the big imperialists and colonial powers, has now become the stronghold of the anticolonial forces."[21]

Believing that they could garner support for international sanctions by exposing the brutality of the Nationalist regime, the ANC and PAC put aside many
of their differences in the months after Sharpeville and sent foreign representatives abroad. As they established offices in Cairo, Accra, Dar es Saalam,
London, and New York, both organizations exhibited newfound confidence in
the potential for change in South Africa.[22]

This energy was also captured in a speech by Kwame Nkrumah before the
UN General Assembly in September. Introduced by W. E. B. Du Bois as "the
undisputed voice of Africa," Nkrumah claimed that "the United Nations [was]
the only organization that [held] out any hope for the future of mankind."
Although "the flowing tide of African nationalism" had the potential to "sweep
away" everything in its path, new African nations wanted only to eliminate
colonialism on their continent. Referring specifically to South Africa, the Ghanaian president argued, "The interest of humanity compels every nation to
take steps against such inhuman policy and barbarity and to act in concert to
eliminate it from the world."[23] The events at Sharpeville were tragic, but they
provided evidence that the "wall of intense hate" that protected South Africa
was beginning to crumble.

The time for change had arrived.

The American Pivot

As the most powerful member of the Western bloc and the dominant state at
the United Nations, the United States played an important role in determining
whether African nationalist demands would actually affect the government of
South Africa. In late 1958, the Union's foreign minister, Eric Louw, acknowledged to the American ambassador: "I wish to be frank. A specific and strong
resolution against South Africa voted for by a majority of nations in [the] U.N.
does not matter so much as one might expect. What matters more than . . . all
other votes put together is [the position] of [the] U.S. in view of its predominant position of leadership in [the] Western world."[24] As new African states
gained their independence in 1960 and railed at the United Nations against the
system of apartheid, Louw's statement grew increasingly relevant. Functioning
as the pivot between the old colonial order that South Africa supposedly epitomized and the new visions of world order that African nationalists embraced,
the approach of American policy makers became tremendously important in
the early 1960s. Although the United States viewed the African continent as
peripheral to its Cold War interests, its policies nonetheless shaped the boundaries of the debate on apartheid.

The American approach was both conflicted and complex. On the one hand, the United States had important political and financial investments in the Union. A report from the early 1960s explained the economic importance of South Africa: "The international standing of the U.S. dollar and, by extension, the stability of the integrated Western monetary system, is to a degree dependent on the orderly marketing of gold." South Africa accounted for about 65 percent of the Western bloc's gold production, the loss of which could put considerable strains on the US gold supply and the integrated Western monetary system.[25] When placed against the backdrop of the establishment of a NASA tracking station in 1960 and nearly $600 million worth of private American investment in the Union, these ties represented tangible and substantial links between the United States and South Africa.[26]

On the other hand, US leaders were cognizant that these ties might affect America's containment strategy in Africa. In discussing the issue at the first tripartite talks on Africa between the United States, Great Britain, and France in 1959, one participant stated: "In the world-wide political and strategic context, Africa is both a prize and a battlefield. If the Communists occupy or infiltrate too many countries we will lose the Battle for the Atlantic, Europe will be in danger, our communications in the Far East will be cut, and we will lose a tremendous source of raw materials."[27] While not all American policy makers agreed with such vaguely threatening assessments, they recognized that South Africa was "one of the West's greatest propaganda liabilities" in the new era of decolonization because it embodied "the most flagrant kind of 'colonialism.'"[28] Stated plainly, the United States viewed the debate over South Africa through the lens of the Cold War. South Africa's racial policies were not so much morally reprehensible as they were strategically inconvenient.

This underlying apathy over the morality of apartheid was buttressed by the general view that African nationalism was more an emotional outburst than a cogent alternative to the East-West global narrative. As historian Matthew Connelly and others have demonstrated, American policies during the period of decolonization often relied on older assumptions to support views on containment. In Connelly's words, "Even at the height of the Cold War, discourses about development and civilizational conflict helped delineate the shifting borders between North and South, the 'West' and 'the rest.'"[29] Against the backdrop of African independence and the debate over apartheid, traditional white American assumptions about blacks as being backward and uncivilized often permeated discussions among policy makers.[30]

During a National Security Council meeting in mid-1958, for example, one official commented: "The Spirit of 1776 is running wild throughout [Africa]. The various states and colonies want independence now, whether they are ready for it or not." Specifically referencing Ghana's President Nkrumah, he called such trends "terrifying."[31] During another NSC meeting in 1960, Vice President Nixon commented that "some of the peoples of Africa have been out of the trees for only about fifty years" and suggested that "politically sophisticated diplomats" could easily subvert black nationalism and reorient "the African people toward the Free World." President Dwight Eisenhower argued similarly that South Africa was the only country in the entire continent that could actually govern itself. Relying on a binary that subtly undercut the logic of African nationalism, he said that African leaders were "putting the cart before the horse" by placing more precedence on political independence than economic development.[32] These views— grounded in the vocabulary of prewar race relations—helped structure American assumptions about South Africa. The situation was noteworthy because it triggered the ire of new African countries, but beyond its symbolic importance many policy makers actually shared the racialist attitudes that buttressed the Union's policy of apartheid.

When President Eisenhower first heard that the US Department of State had issued a statement expressing "regret" about the Sharpeville Massacre, he called a meeting with Secretary of State Christian Herter. Learning that the statement was made by a bureau chief working on his own accord, Eisenhower said that if it were his decision, he would "find another post for the bureau chief" and recommended that the State Department apologize immediately to the Union government. Concurring with the president's comments, Secretary Herter framed the statement as a "breach of courtesy between two nations."[33] When pressure built for the UN Security Council to address the violence in South Africa during the following week, Eisenhower and Macmillan held a private meeting at Camp David to formulate a response. To the president's mind: "One could not sit in judgment on a difficult social and political problem six thousand miles away." Noting that the United States had its "own problem" with race and indicating his sympathy with his "friends in Atlanta on some of their difficulties," the president promised that the Security Council resolution would "express regret about the disturbances" without committing the Western bloc to a serious confrontation with South Africa.[34]

The president's comments revealed a deeper dimension of the US approach toward apartheid. At the end of the Eisenhower administration, American society was effectively standing on the brink of its own revolution in race relations. As Mary Dudziak and Thomas Borstelmann have noted, many nonwhites viewed the ascension of John Kennedy in 1961 as the harbinger of new policies toward black political demands.[35] During the presidential campaign he not only referred to Africa as "the most important area in the world" but also indicated his belief that "the lands of the rising peoples" would play a critical role in "the defense and expansion of freedom."[36] For many African nationalists, the central question of 1961 became whether the new president would back up his rhetoric with decisive action.

The Battleground

Indications that the debate over South Africa was entering a new stage became increasingly apparent as 1961 proceeded. Frustrated by Macmillan's earlier overtures and eager to garner more political autonomy, the Union withdrew from the British Commonwealth that March in order to create an independent republic. When it applied for reentry a few days later, several African member states established preconditions that made its readmission contingent on domestic political reform. "South Africa is one of the senior members of the Commonwealth," Verwoerd said during a Commonwealth meeting in London on March 23. "No self-respecting member of any voluntary organization could . . . be expected to retain membership in what is now becoming a pressure group."[37] South Africa withdrew permanently the following day and began fostering closer relations with Southern Rhodesia and the Portuguese territories.

Pressures mounted again when African and Asian countries joined together on July 18 to force the issue of apartheid onto the agenda of the UN General Assembly.[38] Diplomatic warfare carried over into a resolution that was submitted by thirty-two African and Middle Eastern nations in October. Rejecting the passive language that had characterized previous resolutions against South Africa, the resolution proposed that all UN member states break their diplomatic ties with the republic, close their ports to South African ships, boycott South African goods, deny passage to South African aircraft, and recognize apartheid as a direct threat to "international peace and security." The resolution was withdrawn in November because an Indian resolution against South Africa garnered more support, but the events that autumn revealed that African nations were beginning to use their numbers to place new pressure on South Africa.[39] The United Nations and the British Commonwealth were becoming the diplomatic battlegrounds where African nationalists confronted the forces of colonialism and racism.

The debate over whether the United Nations could take action against South Africa pivoted largely on an interpretation of the Charter of the United Nations. While Article 2(7) forbade the United Nations from "interven[ing] in matters which are essentially within the domestic jurisdiction of any state," Article 14 gave the General Assembly the ability to "recommend measures for the peaceful adjustment of any situation . . . it deems likely to impair the general welfare or friendly relations between nations." African nationalists came to believe that if they could demonstrate that South Africa represented a danger to "the maintenance of international peace and security," the Security Council would be obligated to take action under the provisions of Chapter VII, which outlined the Council's role in dealing with member-state aggression.[40]

In pursuing this goal, they offered a revealing twofold rationale that framed apartheid as both transnationally violent and innately expansionistic. In arguing the first point, African nationalists consistently referred to notions of pan-Africanism and asserted that brutality against South African blacks was a provocation against all Africans. Ali Mazrui, a young East African scholar who went on to help establish the field of African studies, framed the point well in a 1962 article to the *Times* of London. To his mind, the tendency to define black South Africans as "Bantu" was an epistemological byproduct of colonialism. "The term 'Bantu' is not territorially restrictive. And in any case the word 'African' has now assumed greater dignity, and is therefore preferred by many of the leaders of Africa." Pointing toward specific speeches by African leaders such as Robert Sobukwe and Kwame Nkrumah, he explained that most blacks now viewed their efforts "as part of a continental struggle in a more real sense than ever Nehru or Sukarno saw themselves as part of an Asian struggle." Apartheid was not just an assault against blacks in South Africa; it was an attack on Africa as a whole. Using a line of logic that laid a foundation for what would become postmodern theory, he approached the fluidity of African identity as "an excellent example" of how "semantics" could "create myths and symbols" that "changed the map of realities" at the international level.[41]

In supporting the case that apartheid was expansionistic, African nationalists were more concrete, drawing attention to the colonial relationship between South Africa and the neighboring region of South-West Africa (Namibia). South Africa had been granted a League of Nations mandate over the region after World War I, but such ties were widely seen as illegitimate in the postcolonial era. In early 1960, Ethiopia and Liberia—the only African nations with historical connections to the League of Nations—formally challenged the basis of this mandate with litigation at the International Court of Justice.[42] Paul Proehl, a professor of law at UCLA in the 1960s, suggested at the time that the case was "symbolic" of the broader "confrontation between black and white."[43] However, its meaning was more concrete. The South-West Africa case was a contest over the terms of legitimacy in the decolonized world. And although the final decision was not reached until 1966, the African bloc's ability to win the first phase of the trial in 1962 was interpreted widely as a step toward changing the traditional balance between universal human rights and national sovereignty at the international level.[44]

These initiatives did not go unnoticed by the United States. In June 1962, the State Department—in a policy paper entitled "The White Redoubt"—cast these breakthroughs in dire terms. Connecting events in South Africa directly to the revolution in Algeria, officials noted that blacks now faced whites "across a sea of developing hate." The language used was telling: "[South Africa] is, in effect, a last white stronghold against black invasion from the north and racialist-inspired upheavals from within."[45] Like the Eisenhower administration, the Kennedy administration subtly cast Africans as barbarians at the gates of whiteness, treating the tensions in southern Africa as an outgrowth of black extremism rather than a byproduct of South Africa's system of racial injustice. During a briefing just before the General Assembly in 1962, Undersecretary of State George Ball relayed this message to the president, saying that the United States was facing "a series of dilemmas with mounting pressures from the Africans and Asians for rapid solutions to the most complicated 'hard core' colonial problems." Although he predicted that support for sanctions and action in South-West Africa would expand in the next General Assembly, he argued that the president needed to "vigorously oppose" such "irresponsible" action.[46]

When Ghana and other African countries indeed submitted an expanded version of their 1961 resolution during the seventeenth General Assembly, American representatives accused them of "casting doubt on the efficacy of the sanction process," causing "dissension among Member States," and "seriously weakening the authority of the United Nations."[47] A circular telegram from the State Department explained that while the "United States continues to favor the achievement of self-determination by dependent peoples throughout the world," the actions of anticolonial nations at the United Nations reflected an "unjustified doctrinaire extremism and impracticality" that was making the United States look "soft on colonialism."[48] For Americans, it was a forum for establishing consensus on Cold War issues; for new anticolonial states it was a mechanism for transforming the existing world order. As new African nations grew more adept at using their numbers to shape the United Nations' political agenda, American officials became increasingly frustrated by their inability to control the terms of global politics.

This underlying divergence expanded into a direct confrontation in 1963. In late May, various African governments assembled at Addis Ababa, Ethiopia, to establish the Organization of African Unity and formulate a unified front against apartheid. In their opening resolution, they not only reaffirmed their commitment to the UN resolution they had passed the previous year, but also expressed "deep concern" with the racial discrimination against African Americans in the United States. Indeed, as the American civil rights movement garnered more media attention and the US government took concrete steps toward civil rights legislation, African nationalists retooled their strategy toward the United States. In a meeting at the State Department over the status of South-West Africa, one African diplomat went so far as to assert that the US government had "an obligation" to address the situation in the Republic of South Africa because it was willing to support civil rights activists in the American South.[49]

African nationalists understood that meaningful success was contingent on US willingness to support the resolutions they were passing at the UN General Assembly. When the issue of apartheid went before the Security Council in August 1963, it appeared that a breakthrough might be at hand. In a statement before the Council that dramatically departed from previous US admonitions, representative Adlai Stevenson declared:

> We all suffer from the disease of discrimination in various forms, but at least most of us recognize the disease for what it is: a disfiguring blight. In many countries, governmental policies are dedicated to rooting out this dread syndrome of prejudice and discrimination, while in South Africa we see the anachronistic spectacle of the Government of a great people which persists in seeing the disease as the remedy, prescribing for the malady of racism the bitter toxic of apartheid.

He went on to assert that "just as the United States was determined to wipe out discrimination" on its domestic front, it would "support efforts to bring about a change in South Africa." Acknowledging that apartheid was preventing the full independence of Africa, Stevenson's declaration was accompanied with a US pledge that the Security Council would help "end the sale of all military equipment" to the republic by the end of the calendar year.[50] The statesman's words represented the strongest condemnation against South Africa that any Western government had ever made.

However, the new US position ignored the broader political platform of African nationalists and said nothing about the issue of economic sanctions. The true sentiment of American policy makers was captured well in private conversations between the summer and fall of 1963. In a meeting with the South African ambassador, Dr. Willem Naude, on the eve of the UN sanctions debate, Secretary of State Rusk spoke frankly about attitudes within the Kennedy administration. Keeping his comments strictly off the record, Rusk admitted that the United States was willing to embrace a nonintegrationist solution to South Africa's problems. "A breath-taking step has a better chance of success than something small and pedestrian," the secretary of state explained with candor. By shifting South Africa to a "federal or confederal" political system, whites would be able to eliminate local discrimination against blacks while maintaining exclusive control over "external affairs and defence." The South African ambassador—who interpreted this plan as a sign of "fresh thinking and an abandonment of the hackneyed clichés of the New Frontier" —responded with enthusiasm. Writing to Pretoria the following evening, Naude noted that if South Africa could "present [its] situation in terms of [Mr. Rusk's] own terminology [it] might be able to make a great deal of 'progress' in getting the U.S. to understand [its] situation, without moving an inch from [its] declared policies." From South Africa's perspective, the overture was a sign that the Americans were "willing to agree—albeit reluctantly—to explore, if not yet to follow, [the] road of separate development" in South Africa.[51]

Such a sentiment was echoed by President Kennedy himself during an October meeting with British officials about African demands for economic sanctions against the Nationalist government. In his words, the United States had "gone along on the arms embargo" but "would not go beyond that and would not support sanctions." The question, to his mind, was now "how best to stop them."[52] A memo from the National Security Council staff later that month cast the situation in policy terms: "In the past several years . . . we have sailed an improvised, often erratic course between the antagonists, with a series of minor concessions to the Africans as the pressures mounted, while avoiding an irreparable break with the . . . South Africans. While this has been the most sensible—indeed the only sensible—course open to us, we are beginning to run out of sailing room. I think we can gain some space for maneuver, and continue to defer the dilemma, if we raise our present tactic to a deliberate, systematic policy."[53]

Shifting the Debate

The South African government watched the global apartheid debate with a mixture of anxiety and resentment. "[This] goes deeper than a 'publicity problem with political overtones,'" explained one high-ranking official in January 1961. "[These attacks] have become a full scale international political problem affecting the *survival* of South Africa itself."[54] To the minds of many Afrikaner elites, criticism from abroad was pushing South Africa toward economic collapse. Indeed, the foreign capital that had propelled the country's manufacturing growth during the postwar years evaporated rapidly in the wake of the Sharpeville Massacre, as global investors grew wary that unrest was a sign of a coming racial war. In the months that followed the riots, more than seven hundred million pounds disappeared from South Africa's economy.[55] At the end of 1960, banking officials lamented openly that "the net outflow of capital" was having "an appreciably adverse effect on the country's monetary reserves and financial markets." To address these problems, they encouraged the government to "exert itself in every possible way to revive the confidence of foreign investors."[56]

Toward this end, the government vastly expanded its propaganda machine and implemented an ambitious "programme of action" in the years after Sharpeville. Hoping to transcend their difficulties at the United Nations, South African officials focused their attention on nongovernment actors and global capitalists. "This total war against South Africa is being waged on the publicity front," explained the director of intelligence, P. J. Nel, in late 1960. Stepping back from the situation, he noted resentfully that "when we put forward our case, our words and good intentions are doubted. . . . Our country is stable, our economy healthy and our people are better off than in other parts of the continent. We are a Christian country, democratic, and free from corruption. Why are we being attacked about things which are glossed over in . . . embryonic dictatorships such as Ghana?" For Nel, the answer was tied to the insights of social psychology: "It is clear that the resistance against our message, at least in the U.S.A., can be ascribed to hidden, subconscious factors."[57] With the "survival" of South Africa contingent on economic integration with the West, the task before the South African Information Service was clear—to attack these "subconscious factors" in tangible and incremental ways.

Government officials advanced a plan that was layered and subtle. In South Africa, the government would begin a systematic effort of "planned internal press canvassing." In Nel's words: "The press should become priority number one. It was the press that conditioned the adverse popular opinion against South Africa; the press is the major means to be used to remedy the situation." Conceiving this work as the "top commitment of the Information Service of South Africa," he recommended the development of intimate relationships with "important internal correspondents" and "manageable foreign correspondents." Members of the press were to be treated literally as guests of the Nationalist party. To reinforce the authority of the state, cabinet members and other officials were instructed to release information to the public through press conferences rather than "impersonal" news releases. For the director, these initiatives would not simply dampen the influence of South Africa's critics—they guaranteed better understanding of South Africa's race problems. Demanding in "the strongest terms" that this program be kept secret from "the press, the Parliament and the public," the director confidently asserted that it provided an "answer to press control."[58]

Conceived as "the first bulwark of counter-attack," this program was coupled with an aggressive public relations campaign in Washington, DC, and New York City. On one level, South Africa's goal was political. As the director of intelligence explained: "Everything indicates that the Kennedy regime is going to be strongly influenced by liberal and progressive elements. An influential P.R. man can assist us in mustering a strong group of sympathetic people around Vice President Johnson and Senators Fulbright and Mansfield." On a deeper level, however, the South African government hoped to fundamentally change US perceptions of apartheid. Claiming that Americans were conditioned to "accept the simplistic solution of an eventual explosion as the only possible outcome" in South Africa, officials turned to private organizations like the Institute for Motivational Research for guidance in their approach to propaganda. Using newly developed social science concepts and research methods, the Institute and its "team of Ph.D.'s" analyzed the "latent" and "emotional" reasons for anti-apartheid sentiment in the United States. South African officials embraced the organization's findings. First, many Americans viewed the Nationalist government as a "colonial power" in South Africa. Second, everyday Americans tended to juxtapose the rigidity of apartheid with America's "progressive" approach toward race. And third, few Americans understood the "economic realities" of South African society. "Armed with these data," the director of intelligence declared, "we can now apply a strengthened information service with a new prospect of success and new techniques to swing public opinion within the foreseeable time into our favour."[59]

By 1965, the annual budget of South Africa's Information Service exceeded a million pounds and it was distributing periodicals, educational pamphlets, and propaganda movies in a variety of languages around the world, in addition to coordinating regular speaking tours by various government officials. On one level, the Information Agency worked to disconnect the country's domestic race policies from the narrative of anticolonialism. Keywords like "stability," "coexistence," and "self-government" permeated South African information pamphlets. To strengthen their case, propagandists juxtaposed the situation in South Africa with the supposed immaturity and volatility of other African nations. This effort was premised on South African exceptionalism: "Neither in Algeria nor in [Kenya] can the white communities be regarded as constituting a unique, separate and self-contained nation."[60] The *South Africa Digest* editorialized: "It is essential to remember that the forces and influences that have arisen in Algeria, West Africa, the Congo, and East Africa are not coordinated. To believe this would be to misunderstand the confused, shifting and immature character of the African."[61] Similarly, in a speech before European capitalists, South Africa's foreign minister argued that economic pressures from African nations like Ghana were signs of "political immaturity—the sort expected from small boys or a certain modern type of irresponsible teenager." Unrest in places like the Congo, to his mind, would have a "healthy effect" on the Western world by reminding foreigners that "[South Africa] is the only country with the necessary knowledge to ensure positive trade relations."[62] Relying on highly paternalistic language, the government tried to convince Western authorities that the rest of

Africa was fundamentally different from South Africa. Black African states were inherently "unstable" and "unpredictable," while the Union remained a bastion of modern capitalism.

When addressing the unrest inside their own borders, government officials dwelled often on the specter of Communism. The African National Congress had long-standing ties with the South African Communist Party, but few African nationalists—especially within the PAC—counted themselves genuine Communists in the early 1960s.[63] As criticism of apartheid mounted, however, South African propagandists made the case that black activism and Communism were a singular phenomenon. "Nothing would satisfy the Communists except a successful revolution in South Africa, and nothing would satisfy the extremist Africans except the introduction of one-man-one-vote into the constitution," explained an official in 1963.[64] For many white South Africans these two dangers were interconnected. By positioning themselves between the Western bloc and imaginary Communist masses, government advocates conveyed the message that they were defenders of Western values in the African continent.

Most importantly, South African propagandists lauded the merits of their industrial society. Nearly every propaganda item from the early 1960s made some reference to the country's high standard of living and complex manufacturing sector. The goal, according to the Information Service, was to "present to the world the true picture of South Africa" by focusing on themes like "industrial and social progress; science and education; cultural development; opportunities for investment; tourist attractions; and the way of life of South Africans at work and play."[65] Recognizing that colonial themes of white civilization no longer resonated abroad, the South African government used concepts of industrialization and modernization to reestablish its place in the capitalist world. The goal was not to engage directly the African nationalists in a debate over apartheid, but to manipulate underlying Western assumptions about blacks and emphasize the pragmatic importance of social stability and economic vitality. Understanding that economic integration with countries like the United States and Great Britain was the key to South Africa's place in the postcolonial world, Afrikaner elites worked deliberately outside the parameters of the United Nations to influence the nature of the debate on their country. Their efforts revealed important aspects of *how* the gap between older modes of "civilizational" thinking and the newer discourse of "modernization" was bridged in the years after the Second World War. Explicit racial paternalism receded from global discourse in the wake of decolonization, but racialist thinking still offered subtle reference points that helped frame economic, political, and cultural relations in the Cold War.

Conclusion

By the mid-1960s, the economy of South Africa was vibrant and strong, but the country was politically isolated from the world community. Although it remains difficult to measure the exact impact of South Africa's information campaign, it seems telling that the country had little difficulty receiving a series of loans from the International Monetary Fund and World Bank in the early 1960s to deal with its economic downturn. According to Reserve Bank officials, the ability to secure such loans "indicate[d] the beginning of an increase in foreign confidence in the maintenance of order, stability and prosperity in South Africa."[66] By the end of 1963, despite the Security Council's arms embargo and near universal condemnation of apartheid at the UN General Assembly, South African officials reflected that events had turned out "better than expected."[67] The situation had demonstrated "the value of positive, non-political propaganda" in creating "an effect essentially political."[68] On October 18, a delegation from Pretoria privately notified the US secretary of state that South Africa was "seriously and urgently" considering withdrawal from the United Nations. Although the Nationalist government had made similar declarations in the mid-1950s, its latest overture was coupled with a revealing qualifier. Noting that the organization only embarrassed and harassed their country, representatives argued that withdrawal would "reduce the difficulties for certain countries with whom South Africa has had long and friendly ties."[69] The message was clear— positive relations were not contingent on developments at the United Nations.

For a unique but fleeting moment in the early 1960s, African leaders like Kwame Nkrumah genuinely believed they could change South Africa and destroy the remnants of colonialism by mobilizing support in the United Nations. Such confidence was inspired by the sense that a racial revolution was occurring around the world that placed African interests at the vanguard of human progress. Motivated by a set of priorities that centered on North-South issues of white racism and economic exploitation, nationalists throughout the Third World were similarly working from within the United Nations to transform world opinion and the world order. Their concerns, however, were not shared by dominant international actors like the United States. In the minds of many American leaders, the political demands of Africans and Asians were inconvenient outbursts that distracted from the more important concerns of the Cold War. The inability of African countries to garner support for economic sanctions against South Africa at the United Nations exposed important realities about the limited nature of political change in the postcolonial era.

Equally important, it revealed the paradoxes that emerged as the Cold War superpowers supplanted traditional European empires in the years after World War II. Political space emerged for the articulation of alternative visions of world order—visions rooted in themes of racial justice, national sovereignty, and human rights—but actual initiatives were compromised by the imperatives of national security ideology and world capitalism. These points were not lost on people living in the Third World. By the late 1960s, as it became increasingly obvious that the Afro-Asian coalition and its nationalist leaders could not deliver on promises of change, political momentum in southern Africa (as well as the Middle East and Southeast Asia) began shifting toward leaders outside the traditional nation-state system. By the late 1960s, with war raging in Vietnam, the optimism once associated with the "postcolonial moment" was supplanted widely by feelings of frustration and disillusionment. And the United States, in the minds of many, stood imaginatively as the world's cynical "New Empire."

Notes

1. This chapter was previously published as an article in *Diplomatic History* 33, no. 5 (November 2009): 897–925, and is reprinted with the permission of *Diplomatic History* and Wiley Periodicals Inc. The author thanks Robert McMahon, Peter Hahn, and Tim Borstelmann for early feedback on the essay, as well as the George C. Marshall Foundation, the Society for Historians of American Foreign Relations (SHAFR), the Mershon Center, and the Kirwin Institute for their generous financial support.

2. Telegram to Secretary for Foreign Affairs (Top Secret), July 17, 1963, Verhoudings met die Verenigde State var Amerika, Volume 1, Departement Van Buitelandse Sake (BTS) 1/33/3, Archives of the South African Ministry of Foreign Affairs (ASAMFA); and Memorandum of Conversation, July 17, 1963, US Department of State, *Foreign Relations of the United States: Foundations of Foreign Policy (FRUS) 1961–1963*, 2:639–43.

3. Full speech quoted in Nicholas Mansergh, *Documents and Speeches on Commonwealth Affairs, 1952–1962* (London: Oxford University Press, 1963), 347–51.

4. For the best overview of this process, see Frederick Cooper, *Decolonization and African Society: The Labor Question in French and British Africa* (New York: Cambridge University Press, 1996).

5. For an overview of South African–US relations in the 1940s and 1950s, see Thomas Borstelmann, *Apartheid's Reluctant Uncle: The United States and Southern Africa in the Early Cold War* (New York: Oxford University Press, 1993); and Thomas Noer, *Cold War and Black Liberation: The United States and White Rule in Africa, 1948–1968* (Columbia: University of Missouri Press, 1985).

6. *Die Burger*, February 8, 1960, Mr. H. Macmillan's Visit: Press Cuttings, BTS 22/2/20/9, South Africa National Archives and Record Service (hereafter NARS).

7. "P.M. Responds to Macmillan," *South Africa Digest* 7 (1960): 6, 10 (capitals in the original).

8. The term "Afrikaner" (or "Boer") refers to South Africans of Dutch heritage. They constituted the majority of the white population, but British settlers were also present in the country. The two groups clashed frequently during the first part of the twentieth century. In many ways, the 1948 election was crucial because it marked the moment when Afrikaners took control of the government. They maintained control until 1994. The divisions within the white South African community and the emergence of white nationalism in South Africa are important and relevant topics, but they will not be explored here. See Leonard Thompson, *A History of South Africa*, 3rd ed. (New Haven, CT: Yale University Press, 2000); and William Beinart, *Twentieth-Century South Africa*, 2nd ed. (New York: Oxford University Press, 2001).

9. For the government version of events, see *A Précis of the Reports of the Commissions Appointed to Enquire into the Events Occurring on March 21 1960 at Sharpeville and Langa: A Fact Paper* (Johannesburg: South African Institute of Race Relations, 1961); for a reporter's version, see Bernard Sachs, *The Road from Sharpeville* (New York: Dial, 1961).

10. "Drastic Steps Justified to Stop Reign of Terror," *South Africa Digest* 7 (1960): 8, 10.

11. "S.A. the West's Most Faithful Ally in Africa," *South Africa Digest* 7 (1960): 7.

12. "Coloreds" is a South African term used to describe individuals with mixed African and European heritage; for a brief overview of ethnic groups in South Africa, see Philip Curtin, ed., *African History* (Boston: Longman, 1978), 277–331, 487–94.

13. "The PAC Speaks," *Contact*, May 30, 1959, 12.

14. For the political thought of Kwame Nkrumah, see *The Autobiography of Kwame Nkrumah* (New York: International Publishers, 1957); Pierre Moukoko Mbonjo, *The Political Thought of Kwame Nkrumah* (Lagos, Nigeria: University of Lagos Press, 1998); and Ndabaningi Sithole, *African Nationalism* (London: Oxford University Press, 1968). For an examination of African nationalism's place in postcolonial thought, see Robert Young, *Postcolonialism: A Very Short Introduction* (Oxford: Blackwell, 2001).

15. The State of the Nation, August 2, 1959, Robert Sobukwe Collection, Liberation Archives, University of Fort Hare (UFH).

16. Nkrumah, *Autobiography*, 101.

17. Opening Address, April 4, 1959, Robert Sobukwe Collection, Liberation Archives, UFH.

18. Nkrumah, *Autobiography*, 34; and Quiason-Sackey, quoted in Francis Wilcox, *UN and the Nonaligned Nations* (New York: Foreign Policy Association, 1962), 13.

19. See Ania Loomba, Frederick Cooper, and Jed Esty, eds., *Postcolonial Studies and Beyond* (Durham, NC: Duke University Press, 2005).

20. For a documentary overview of Indian protest at the UN, see UN Office of Information, *The United Nations and Apartheid, 1948–1994* (New York: UN Office of Information, 1994), 221–42.

21. "U.N.O. and Colonialism," *Congress Voice*, November 1960, 5.

22. An important literature exists on these exile activities. For an introduction, see Scott Thomas, *The Diplomacy of Liberation: The Foreign Relations of the African National Congress since 1960* (London: I. B. Tauris, 1996); Morgan Noval, *Inside the ANC* (Washington, DC: Selous Foundation Press, 1990); and South African Democracy Education Trust, *The Road to Democracy in South Africa, Volume I (1960–1970)* (Paarl, South Africa: Zebra Press, 2004).

23. Osagyefo at the United Nations, September 23, 1960; full text available at *www.nkrumah.net* (accessed January 12, 2006).

24. Telegram from the Embassy in South Africa to the Department of State, November 7, 1958, *FRUS, 1958–1960*, 14:732.

25. Memorandum from the Acting Assistant Secretary of Defense (Bundy) to the Deputy Secretary of Defense (Gilpatric), June 7, 1961, *FRUS, 1961–1963*, 21:595–97.

26. Memorandum from the President's Special Assistant for National Security Affairs (Bundy) to President Kennedy, July 13, 1963, National Security Files, Countries Series: South Africa, John F. Kennedy Presidential Library (JFKL), Boston, MA.

27. Memorandum of Conversation, April 16, 1959, *FRUS, 1958–1960*, 14: document 14.

28. Letter from the Acting Director of the Office of Southern Africa Affairs (Hadsel) to the Ambassador in Egypt (Byroade), [Enclosure: US Policy toward South Africa], August 3, 1956, *FRUS, 1955–1957*, 18:789–90.

29. Matthew Connelly, "Taking Off the Cold War Lens," *American Historical Review* 105, no. 3 (June 2000): 742.

30. For an overview of work on American policy in Africa, see Gerald Horne, "Race to Insight," in *Explaining the History of Foreign Relations*, ed. Michael Hogan and Thomas Patterson (New York: Cambridge University Press, 2005), 323–35.

31. Memorandum of Discussion at the 365th Meeting of the National Security Council, May 8, 1958, *FRUS, 1958–1960*, 14:49.

32. Memorandum of Discussion of 432nd Meeting of the National Security Council, January 14, 1960, *FRUS, 1958–1960*, 14:5–76.

33. Editorial Note, *FRUS, 1958–1960*, 14:741–42.

34. Memorandum of Conversation, March 30, 1960, *FRUS, 1958–1960*, 14:745–46; the United States was in a position of influence over the resolution because Ambassador Henry Cabot Lodge was the chair of the Security Council in April 1960.

35. See Mary Dudziak, *Cold War Civil Rights: Race and the Image of American Democracy* (Princeton, NJ: Princeton University Press, 2000), 152–54; and Thomas Borstelmann, *The Cold War and the Color Line: American Race Relations in the Global Arena* (Cambridge, MA: Harvard University Press, 2001), 135–40.

36. Kennedy campaign speech, November 1, 1960, JFKL, *www.jfklink.com/speeches* (accessed December 13, 2006); and John Kennedy's Special Appeal to Congress, May 25, 1961, Office Files: Speeches, Box 34, JFKL.

37. Mansergh, *Documents and Speeches*, 387.

38. As mentioned earlier, it was on the agenda periodically throughout the 1950s but focused mostly on the rights of Indian laborers in South Africa. The relations between African nationalists and the broader Non-Aligned Movement warrant significant analysis but fall outside the parameters of this chapter. This tension is examined in my broader work. It seems enough to say that India was a key member

of the Non-Aligned Movement and its decision to support the more radical platform of African nationalists in 1962 was an important moment in the anti-apartheid initiative at the United Nations. For further information, consult documents in UN Office of Information, *The United Nations and Apartheid, 1948–1994*, 221–42.

39. Ibid.

40. Ibid.

41. Ali Mazrui, "Why Does an African Feel African?," February 12, 1962, *Times*; and Africa: Political Situation and Developments, Vol. 6, BTS 1/99/1, NARS.

42. The case is discussed at length in my larger work. For an introductory overview of the basic legal debate, see *Ethiopia and Liberia v. South Africa: The South West Africa Cases, Occasional Papers no. 5* (Los Angeles: South African Department of Information, 1968). For a pro–South African perspective, see John Wellington, *South West Africa and Its Human Issues* (Oxford: Clarendon, 1967). For a pro-African perspective, see Ronald Segal and Ruth First, eds., *South West Africa: Travesty of Trust* (London: Deutsch, 1967). For a more balanced perspective, see John Dugard, *The South West Africa/Namibia Dispute: Documents and Scholarly Writing on the Controversy between South Africa and the United Nations* (Berkeley: University of California Press, 1973); and Solomon Slonim, *South West Africa and the United Nations: An International Mandate in Dispute* (Baltimore: Johns Hopkins University Press, 1973).

43. *Ethiopia and Liberia v. South Africa: The South West Africa Cases, Occasional Papers no. 5*, 34.

44. The relationship between legitimacy and power is crucial to this argument. Although international historians are only beginning to approach this topic seriously, international relations theorists have made positive headway in recent years. See Ian Hurd, *After Anarchy: Legitimacy and Power in the United Nations Security Council* (Princeton, NJ: Princeton University Press, 2007). For further information on legal strategy, see Richard Falk, *Reviving the World Court* (Charlottesville: University of Virginia Press, 1986).

45. "The White Redoubt," June 28, 1962, National Security Files, Countries Series: Africa, JFKL.

46. Memorandum from Acting Secretary of State Ball to President Kennedy, August 16, 1962, National Security Files, Subjects Series: United Nations (General), 7/62–8/62, Box 311, JFKL.

47. *Yearbook of the United Nations* (New York: United Nations Office of Public Information, 1961), 97.

48. Memorandum from Secretary of State Rusk to President Kennedy, undated, National Security Files, Subjects Series: United Nations (General), 9/62–12/62, Box 311, JFKL; and Circular Airgram from the Department of State to Certain Posts, August 30, 1962, *FRUS, 1961–1963*, 25:483–84.

49. Memorandum of Conversation, November 23, 1962, *FRUS, 1961–1963*, 21:623.

50. UN Office of Information, *The United Nations and Apartheid, 1948–1994*, 254–57.

51. United States/South Africa Relations (Top Secret), July 24, 1963, Verhoudings met die Verenigde State var Amerika, Volume 1, BTS 1/33/3, Archives of the South African Ministry of Foreign Affairs (ASAMFA).

52. Memorandum of Conversation, October 4, 1963, *FRUS, 1961–1963*, 21:471.

53. Memorandum from William H. Brubeck of the National Security Council Staff to the President's Special Assistant for National Security Affairs, October 29, 1963, National Security Files, Countries Series: South Africa, JFKL.

54. Die Sekretaris Van Buitelandse Sake, January 5, 1961, South African Public Relations Activities in USA, Vol. 1, BTS 1/33/3/1, NARS (emphasis in original).

55. Report of the Fortieth Ordinary General Meeting, *South African Reserve Bank* (1960), 14–16.

56. Ibid., 13–15.

57. Program om Openbare Betrekkinge in die V.S.A. te verbeter, November 30, 1960, South African Public Relations Activities in USA, Vol. 1, BTS 1/33/3/1, NARS.

58. Ibid.

59. Ibid.

60. Persoonlik en Vertroulik, Maart 4, 1960, Mr. Harold MacMillan: Visit to the Republic as Guest of the Republic Government, BTS 22/2/20, Volume 2, ASAMFA.

61. "Many Do Not Come to U.N. with Clean Hands," *South Africa Digest* 7 (1960): 22, 15.

62. "S.A. Unjustly Attacked by Africa Countries," *South Africa Digest* 10 (1963): 5, 2.

63. For an explanation of the relationship between the Communist party and the ANC, see Nelson Mandela, *Long Walk to Freedom* (Boston: Back Bay Books, 1995), 73–75, 91, 115–17.

64. "Praemonitus, Praemonitus," September 21, 1962, Advertising Campaigns and Reactions, BKL, 318–25, NARS.

65. Memorandum to Secretary for Information, December 1, 1962, Advertising Campaigns and Reactions, BKL, 318–25, NARS.

66. South African Reserve Bank, *Annual Economic Report* (1962) (Pretoria: Hayne and Gibson, 1962–1972), 10–11.

67. Ibid. (1963), 10.

68. Quoted in "South Africa Sells Her Image Abroad: The Propaganda Machine of the South African Government," African National Congress, *Sechaba*, April 1967.

69. Memorandum of Conversation (Secret), October 18, 1963, National Security Files, Countries Series: South Africa, 9/30/63–10/29/63, JFKL.

References

ARCHIVES
Archives of the South African Ministry of Foreign Affairs, Pretoria, South Africa
John F. Kennedy Presidential Library, Boston, MA
National Archives, Kew (London), United Kingdom
National Archives and Records Administration (II), College Park, MD
Robert Sobukwe Collection, Liberation Archives, University of Fort Hare (UFH), Fort Hare, South Africa
South Africa National Archives and Record Service, Pretoria, South Africa
UN Archives and Records Management, New York, NY

PUBLISHED DOCUMENT COLLECTIONS

African National Congress. *African National Congress Collection, 1928–1962*. Microfilm.

———. *Sechaba, 1967–1972*. Microfilm.

———. *South Africa Freedom News, 1963–1966*. Microfilm, Reels 1–6, 17–39.

Karis, Thomas, and Gwendolen M. Carter. *From Protest to Challenge: A Documentary History of African Politics in South Africa, Volume 3, 1953–1964*. Stanford: Hoover Institution Press, 1977.

Karis, Thomas, and Gail Gerhart. *From Protest to Challenge: A Documentary History of African Politics in South Africa, Volume 5, 1964–1979*. Stanford: Hoover Institution Press, 1977.

Mansergh, Nicholas, ed. *Documents and Speeches on Commonwealth Affairs, 1952–1962*. London: Oxford University Press, 1963.

Pan Africanist Congress. Collections and Documents. Microfilm.

———. *Pan Africanist Congress of South Africa: Material from the Collection of Gail Gerhart*. Microfilm.

South African Reserve Bank. *Annual Economic Report*. Pretoria: Hayne and Gibson, 1962–1972.

———. *Report of Ordinary General Meeting of Stockholders*. Johannesburg: Cape Times, 1956–1970.

UN Office of Information. *General Assembly Official Records*. New York: UN Office of Information, 1946–2012.

———. *Security Council Official Records*. New York: UN Office of Information, 1946–2012.

———. *The United Nations and Apartheid, 1948–1994*. New York: UN Office of Information, 1994.

US Department of State. Confidential US State Department Central Files. *South Africa: Internal Affairs and Foreign Affairs*. Frederick, MD: University Publications of America, 1985. Microfilm, Reels 28–37.

———. Office of the Historian. *Foreign Relations of the United States: Foundations of Foreign Policy, 1958–1960, Volume 14: Africa*. Washington, DC: US Government Printing Office.

———. Office of the Historian. *Foreign Relations of the United States: Foundations of Foreign Policy, 1961–1963, Volume 21: Africa,* and *Volume 25: United Nations*. Washington, DC: US Government Printing Office.

———. Office of the Historian. *Foreign Relations of the United States: Foundations of Foreign Policy, 1964–1968, Volume 24: Africa,* and *Volume 33: United Nations*. Washington, DC: US Government Printing Office.

———. Office of the Historian. *Foreign Relations of the United States: Foundations of Foreign Policy, 1969–1972, Volume 1: Foundations, Volume 5: United Nations,* and *Volume E-5, Part 1: Sub-Saharan Africa*. Washington, DC: US Government Printing Office.

PERIODICALS
Die Burger (Johannesburg)
New York Times
South Africa Digest
The Star (Johannesburg)
Times (London)
Washington Post

SELECTED PUBLISHED WORKS
Borstelmann, Thomas. *Apartheid's Reluctant Uncle: The United States and Southern Africa in the Early Cold War.* New York: Oxford University Press, 1993.
———. *The Cold War and the Color Line: American Race Relations in the Global Arena.* Cambridge, MA: Harvard University Press, 2001.
Chakrabarty, Dipesh. *Provincializing Europe: Postcolonial Thought and Historical Difference.* Princeton, NJ: Princeton University Press, 2001.
Cooper, Frederick. *Africa Since 1940: The Past of the Present.* New York: Cambridge University Press, 2002.
———. *Decolonization and African Society: The Labor Question in French and British Africa.* New York: Cambridge University Press, 1996.
Cooper, Frederick, and Randall Packard, eds. *International Development and the Social Sciences: Essays on the History and Politics of Knowledge.* Berkeley: University of California Press, 1997.
Connelly, Matthew. *A Diplomatic Revolution: Algeria's Fight for Independence and the Origins of the Post–Cold War World.* New York: Oxford University Press, 2001.
Culverson, Donald. *Contesting Apartheid: U.S. Activism, 1960–1987.* Boulder, CO: Westview Press, 1999.
Davenport, Rodney, and Christopher Saunders. *South Africa: A Modern History.* 5th ed. New York: Macmillan Press, 2000.
Dudziak, Mary. *Cold War Civil Rights: Race and the Image of American Democracy.* Princeton, NJ: Princeton University Press, 2000.
Gaddis, John. *Strategies of Containment: A Critical Appraisal of Postwar American National Security.* 2nd ed. New York: Oxford University Press, 2005.
Gaines, Kevin. *American Africans in Ghana: Black Expatriates and the Civil Rights Era.* Chapel Hill: University of North Carolina Press, 2006.
Gandhi, Leela. *Postcolonial Theory: A Critical Introduction.* New York: Columbia University Press, 1998.
Grubbs, Larry. "Workshop of a Continent: American Representations of Whiteness and Modernity in 1960s South Africa." *Diplomatic History* 32, no. 3 (June 2008): 405–39.
Guelke, Adrian. *Rethinking the Rise and Fall of Apartheid: South Africa and World Politics.* New York: Palgrave Macmillan, 2005.
Horne, Gerald. *From the Barrel of a Gun: The United States and the War against Zimbabwe, 1965–1980.* Chapel Hill: University of North Carolina Press, 2001.
Lauren, Paul Gordon. *Power and Prejudice: The Politics and Diplomacy of Racial Discrimination.* New York: Westview Press, 1988.

Leffler, Melvyn. *A Preponderance of Power: National Security, the Truman Administration, and the Cold War.* Stanford, CA: Stanford University Press, 1991.

Louis, William Roger. *The Ends of British Imperialism: The Scramble for Empire, Suez, and Decolonization.* New York: I. B. Tauris, 2006.

———. *Imperialism at Bay: The United States and the Decolonization of the British Empire, 1941–1945.* New York: Oxford University Press, 1978.

Louw, Eric P. *The Rise, Fall, and Legacy of Apartheid.* New York: Praeger, 2004.

Love, Janice. *The U.S. Anti-Apartheid Movement: Local Activism in Global Politics.* New York: Praeger, 1985.

Maier, Charles. "Consigning the Twentieth Century to History: Alternative Narratives for the Modern Era." *American Historical Review* 105, no. 3 (2000): 807–31.

Nkrumah, Kwame. *Ghana: The Autobiography of Kwame Nkrumah.* New York: International Publishers, 1957.

Noer, Thomas J. *Soapy: A Biography of G. Mennen Williams.* Ann Arbor: University of Michigan Press, 2005.

———. *Cold War and Black Liberation: The United States and White Rule in Africa, 1948–1968.* Columbia: University of Missouri Press, 1985.

Onslow, Sue, ed. *Cold War in Southern Africa: White Power, Black Liberation.* London: Routledge, 2009.

South African Democracy Education Trust. *The Road to Democracy in South Africa, Volume I (1960–1970).* Paarl, South Africa: Zebra Press, 2004.

Thomas, Scott. *The Diplomacy of Liberation: The Foreign Relations of the African National Congress since 1960.* London: I. B. Tauris, 1996.

Thompson, Leonard. *A History of South Africa.* 3rd ed. New Haven, CT: Yale University Press, 2000.

Thörn, Håkan. *Anti-Apartheid and the Emergence of a Global Civil Society.* London: Palgrave, 2009.

Young, Robert. *Postcolonialism: An Historical Introduction.* London: Blackwell, 2001.

PART II

Race, Ethnicity, and Decolonization

CHAPTER 3

Race, Labor, and Security in the Panama Canal Zone

The 1946 Greaves Rape Case, Local 713,

and the Isthmian Cold War Crackdown

Michael Donoghue

Near midnight on February 24, 1946, a twenty-five-year-old North American woman walked home alone from the Balboa Railroad station to her parents' home in Ancon on the Pacific side of the Panama Canal Zone. Daughter of one of the canal's division chiefs, she had just returned from Cristobal after a railroad trip across the isthmus. As she walked toward her home in the darkness, a labor truck loaded with West Indian workers finishing up the second shift drove by her. One of the truck's riders, Lester Leon Greaves, who worked for the US engineer depot at Corozal, eyed the woman closely, then asked the driver to drop him off at the next corner.[1]

Greaves, a twenty-year-old black Panamanian of West Indian descent, waited in the nearby bushes for the American woman to pass. When she did, he seized her and threw her down in the tall grass near Roosevelt Avenue close to the Canal Administration Building. There, according to police documents, he put his hand over her mouth to stifle her cries, tore off her panties, and raped her. Before fleeing, Greaves robbed his victim of twenty-four dollars from her pocketbook. In a state of shock, the American woman staggered to nearby Gorgas Hospital, where she reported the rape to doctors and later to the Canal Zone police.[2]

In a critical error during his struggle with the American woman, Greaves dropped his wallet containing his worker ID and union card. Finding these documents, Canal Zone police notified authorities in Panama, who picked up Greaves the next night near his Rio Abajo home and extradited him to the Canal Zone. While the United States exercised virtual sovereignty and extra-territoriality in the Canal Zone as a result of the 1903 Hay-Bunau-Varilla Treaty and the state-within-a-state that Washington had long operated there (including US courts, police, and law code), Zone officials still had to rely on Panamanian cooperation to bring in suspects from "the other side of the line." On that first February night, however, all available Canal Zone police had scoured the Zone in search of a young black man who fit the victim's description, resulting in a frightening night for the Zone's West Indian labor force. While electric with tension, Greaves's April 2 trial in US District Court at Balboa proved anticlimactic. Having already given a full and remorseful confession, Greaves simply pleaded guilty before Judge Bunk Gardner and waived his right to a jury trial. "Don't fret for me," he told his tearful relatives and friends. Gardner's sentencing of Greaves, however, reverberated for decades throughout Panama's nationalist struggle and US-Panamanian race relations. The judge sentenced Greaves to fifty years' imprisonment at Gamboa Penitentiary, the maximum sentence allowable under the Canal Zone Code. Gardner, a native of Kentucky, stated forcefully from the bench that the court "was familiar with the vicious and brutal details of the crime committed by the defendant, all of which the defendant confessed and admitted. . . . However, we want to take this occasion to recommend that *no Executive authority, ever, at any time, for any reason, under any condition, commute or remit the punishment provided by the judgment and order of this court or to grant a pardon to the defendant*" [judge's emphasis].[3]

The Greaves rape case sent shock waves through the Zone and the nearby Panamanian community. The brutal violation of a young US white woman by a black Panamanian fed into the worst US citizen fears and exposed the stark racial and national divisions within the enclave and in neighboring Panama. In the postwar years, under increasing pressure from Panamanian nationalism, the global decolonization movement, and the US civil rights struggle, the apartheid system of the Zone gradually weakened despite the determination of US officials, military leaders, and ordinary Zonians (US civilian canal workers) to uphold it. But a less explored impact of Greaves's crime rested on the rape's influence in strengthening the local US desire to maintain segregation in the Canal Zone, especially regarding West Indian labor. In the eyes of American authorities, reformist calls for an integrated canal labor force threatened the security of the strategic waterway at the very moment that the Cold War erupted in Europe, Asia, and Latin America. The Greaves case contributed pointedly to a US mentality that sought to separate and isolate West Indian labor within the Zone, beyond any integrated union that challenged traditional wage arrangements there and disconnected from dangerous nationalist influences in the republic. This fear of a "radicalized" labor movement in the Canal Zone set the stage for the Cold War crackdown on the isthmus. The combined US-Panamanian crusade to crush a newly emergent local union, deport its leaders, and purge canal labor of any leftist taint marked the opening salvo of a thirty-year struggle that linked many reformist efforts in and along the Zone to "red subversion."

Origins of Racial/Ethnic Divides in the Panama Canal Zone

Long before the Greaves rape case, one of the central clashes of power within the Canal Zone pitted the black West Indian against the white Zonian or US civilian inhabitant of the enclave. The animosity of Latin Panamanians toward the Antillean community played a key role in this racial divide as well. Even in the mid-1940s, despite gross racial discrimination within the Zone, many West Indians expressed more loyalty to Washington, their economic benefactor, than to Panama, which West Indians still viewed as hostile toward their presence on the isthmus. Thus West Indian leaders quickly condemned the Greaves assault in letters to the editor and op-ed pieces careful to note that the crime should not reflect on the decency and loyalty of the majority of West Indian workers.[4]

Latin Panamanian leaders responded more tepidly to the attack, which could, after all, be blamed on the Antillean minority, long despised as pernicious outsiders. US officials consigned West Indian labor to the most dangerous and arduous work and to minimal housing and rations. Very quickly a system of Jim Crow segregation had evolved in the US-administered Zone. West Indians slept, drank, and ate in separate facilities. Segregated "gold" and "silver" towns, schools, clubhouses, train compartments, buses, toilets, and commissaries mushroomed throughout the "Yankee Strip." Eventually silver and gold labor unions reinforced the stark racial divisions in wages and working conditions. Such unions reified the unequal two-tier salary system and near total lack of advancement for West Indian workers. Meanwhile Latin Panamanians continued to resent the US preference for "alien" West Indian labor. The fact that the early generations of West Indians refused to assimilate enthusiastically to Hispanic cultural norms provoked a unique form of cultural racism. "*Chombo*," the Panamanian equivalent of "nigger," emerged as the ubiquitous insult hurled at West Indians by majority Latin Panamanians.[5]

For generations, the majority of Panamanians associated crime and licentious sexuality in the republic with West Indians, who lived on both sides of the Canal Zone border and provided convenient scapegoats for the nation's intransigent socioeconomic problems. This denigration of the black West Indian encompassed one of the key dynamics of Panamanian identity politics. It should be noted that the term "Latin Panamanian" proves problematic, as the non–West Indian population on the isthmus encompassed a broad expanse of racial/ethnic groupings. Suffice to say that those Panamanians who spoke Spanish as their principal language and practiced Catholicism as their official creed came to view their embrace of both as key signifiers of loyalty and conformity to the Panamanian state and majority culture.

The 1946 Panamanian Constitution restored citizenship to West Indians and their children that had been stripped from them in the 1941 Constitution, but the National Assembly ratified the document a month *after* Greaves's arrest in February 1946. To most Latin Panamanians, Greaves was simply a *chombo de diablo*, or "evil nigger." His crime, however, contradicted other Panamanian stereotypes of the West Indian—that of the fawning "*Tio* Tom." Greaves represented an example of paternalism gone awry: a West Indian who repaid the Zonians for his privileged job by raping a US white woman.[6]

To their credit, Zonian leaders cautioned calm in the initial days following the crime. While notorious for their segregation, Zonians rarely practiced any of the beatings and never the lynching of blacks that white Southerners routinely committed. The early capture and conviction of Greaves also helped assuage any tendencies toward racial vengeance. Still, Zonian women decried the lack of security in the enclave. The Greaves case heightened racial tensions in the Zone at a very sensitive juncture in the postwar era. Following the Second World War, Americans conducted their own internal debate over the validity of segregation in a society that proclaimed itself leader of the free world. Try as it might, the Zone could not remain long isolated from such change. But the push for racial progress also inspired a strong counterreaction. After the war Zonians were experiencing marked anxiety at the very moment that the Greaves rape case filled the headlines. Rumors of federally enforced race reforms troubled them, as did scuttlebutt about the imposition of the federal income tax (Zonians had been exempt from this levy since 1914) and even the termination of the 25 percent tropical differential they had long enjoyed for working in the enclave. Might decolonization come next to the Canal Zone?[7]

Generally supportive of civil rights changes at the conclusion of the war, President Truman appointed retired brigadier general Frank McSherry to conduct a study of segregated labor, schools, and housing in the Zone. Released on June 1, 1947, the McSherry Report called for the abolishment of Jim Crow and the long-derided two-tier wage system. While critical of Zone racism, the report contained racist assumptions of its own. McSherry described West Indians as backward and in need of considerable instruction before they could attain the skill levels of whites. Zone and US military officials, together with their conservative congressional supporters, stonewalled the report's key recommendation that a single-wage system be established. They argued that pay increases for West Indians and Panamanians would bankrupt the canal's operation. But such claims masked deeper fears of the consequences of race mixing in the Zone for dominant US white workers.[8]

Therefore in place of the unequal gold/silver payroll, administrators implemented an unequal US rate/local rate payroll that continued to pay West Indians and Panamanians about one-third of what white Zonians earned, often for the same work. Veteran West Indian workers complained about training recently hired whites who quickly became their supervisors and earned three times their pay. Lester Greaves had labored under this system and remembered its many humiliations. "I was called nigger and boy every day that I worked for de whyte mon," Greaves recalled of his own pre-arrest experience. The gold and silver signs gradually came down near Balboa and Cristobal, the entry ports of the Zone where visiting dignitaries might take offense. But blacks and whites continued to use separate facilities in many cases right up until the late 1970s.[9]

But perhaps the greatest threat to Zonian hegemony on the isthmus exploded soon after the Greaves case in December 1947, when massive Panamanian rioting against the republic's acceptance of a controversial US base accord, the Filós-Hines Treaty, marked the ramp-up for Panamanian nationalism in the postwar era. This treaty would have allowed Washington to maintain thirteen World War II bases outside the Zone. The ferocious riots continued for three days and led to an eventual cave-in by US officials and a reluctant relinquishment of all US bases outside the enclave. This populist-driven uprising marked the first serious defeat for US imperialism on the isthmus. It was amid this atmosphere of change, uncertainty, and racial fear that West Indian canal workers made their bid for a new union to challenge the injustice of Canal Zone segregation.[10]

Early West Indian Attempts at Labor Reform in the Zone

While wildcat strikes by silver laborers protesting their inferior status burst forth periodically during canal construction, the first major Antillean strike erupted in 1920. In February of that year, the United Brotherhood of Maintenance of Way Employees and Railroad Shop Laborers (UB), the principal West

Indian union, launched a widespread walkout over a proposed two-cents-an-hour raise and no substantial improvements in housing and working conditions. Pan-Africanist and black nationalist leader Marcus Garvey lent public and financial support to the West Indian strikers. But Garvey's championing of the walkout played into American officials' hands in characterizing the strike as a "radical and racialist outpouring of hate against all legal authority." The US canal administration used every resource at its disposal to weaken and destroy this first attempt at West Indian self-determination. Countermeasures included police surveillance, spies, false allegations in newspapers, dismissals, eviction from canal housing, loss of commissary privileges, and even persecution from cooperative Panamanian officials who despised the West Indian presence and especially any show of black militancy.[11]

In the aftermath of the bitter 1920 strike, which Canal Zone authorities crushed, US officials blocked the formation of another West Indian union for over twenty years. But with a telling hypocrisy, the Canal Zone government accepted the unionization of gold—that is, overwhelmingly white—US canal workers into the AFL's Metal Trades Council (MTC) and those in white-collar positions into the Central Labor Union (CLU). As the national union of these gold locals, the AFL reneged on its brief wartime experiment in organizing blacks within the UB and returned to its traditional policy of barring minorities from its whites-only craft unions. Thus AFL unionization of US canal workers merely reified white supremacy in the enclave and constituted no security threat to the Canal in American officials' eyes.[12]

World War II and Changing Perceptions

The Second World War helped provoke fundamental change in US-Panamanian relations on a number of fronts, and labor was certainly one of them, though the immediate war crisis acted as a brake on reform. Panama was awash in American dollars, US soldiers, and construction projects, which led to a tripling of the nation's GDP between 1939 and 1945. The FDR administration had narrowly avoided a 1941 march on Washington from African American organizations over racial discrimination in defense plants, which led to the passage of the Fair Employment Act.[13] Following the 1935 Wagner Act, which legitimized and expanded union rights, FDR moved toward a closer alliance with organized labor, especially with the new Congress of Industrial Organizations (CIO), which in 1938 broke away from the conservative AFL. While many conservative Americans held deep suspicions toward the CIO's leftist agenda, the FDR administration preferred to have the silver workers of the Canal Zone organized under the CIO umbrella than supervised by Mexican labor leader Vicente Lombardo Toledano and his Confederación de Trabajadores de América Latina. Both Canal Zone and Washington officials regarded the aggressive and outspoken Toledano as an outright Marxist. Though never an official member of the Mexican Communist Party, he had allied himself publicly with the Soviet Union during the 1930s while the Mexican labor movement pursued its Popular Front policy.[14]

Even more frightening for authorities in Washington and the CZ government was the possible organization of West Indian labor under Juan Vicente Spiazzano Urriola, a worker activist and close friend of the labor attaché to the Argentine embassy in Panama. Spiazzano Urriola later became an official of the Perónista hemispheric union, Asociación de Trabadores de Latinamérica Sur. For US officials, if unionization must come, the CIO seemed a sweeter pill to swallow than either a pro-Communist or a pro-Axis international.[15]

Edward Gaskin and Local 713

The first green sprouts of organized labor in the World War II era emerged from the Zone's West Indian teachers. These highly educated children of the original canal workers taught in the segregated silver schools of the enclave. Viewed as a moderate and bourgeois sector of the silver labor force, they formed the Canal Zone Colored Teachers Association (CZCTA) in 1942 without arousing much US suspicion. Yet from this humble group the intellectual nucleus for the more militant Local 713 would arise. La Boca Normal School instructor Edward Gaskin emerged as a leading light in the effort to transform race and labor relations in the Zone. Born in 1918 in the silver town of Red Tank, Gaskin represented the new generation of West Indians on the isthmus known as criollos. They were the first generation born in Panama, the children of the original Antillean canal builders. As such they had a foot in each culture. And they proved more militant in standing up for their rights than had their parents, who had desperately needed their jobs just to survive and who had come out of a paternalistic plantation culture in Barbados and Jamaica.[16]

By war's end, the CZCTA and other silver worker groups evolved into the Canal Zone Workers' Union. In July 1946 it registered as Local 713 of the United Public Workers of America (UPW) under the aegis of the CIO. The union came into existence during a unique period of postwar conjuncture when the Truman administration still adhered to the Good Neighbor policy and Washington generally supported democratic, pluralistic governance in Latin America. This stand, which embraced much of the New Deal and encouraged populist impulses, shifted rapidly in 1947–1948 toward a Cold War hard line. The turnaround caught even State Department officials by surprise with its speed, as Washington abandoned earlier commitments to democratic institution building and electoral politics. West Indian canal workers would be among the first victims of this sudden closure of the democratic opening that had appeared so ascendant at the war's close.[17]

From April through June 1946 the International Labor Organization, prodded by Vicente Toledano at its spring conference in Mexico City, conducted an investigation into the Canal Zone's labor practices that set off alarm bells for US officials in the enclave. Even previous to this, the United Nations had petitioned its member states to file reports on the social, economic, and educational conditions in all their colonies and protectorates. It was within this touchy atmosphere that Washington allowed the new CIO affiliate, the UPW, to operate in the Zone and commissioned the aforementioned McSherry Report. State Department resistance to UN interference in the Canal Zone ran high. But cooler heads in the White House realized that the issue of racial segregation in the Zone—and in the American South—gave the Soviets a potent weapon with which to bludgeon Washington's claim to free-world leadership. Giving at least the appearance of supporting reforms would strengthen the US global image and help stem Communist expansion, especially in the strategic and decolonizing Third World.[18]

Still, Local 713's goals on the isthmus profoundly upset the applecart. Its leaders wanted to organize *all* non-US citizen labor in the Canal Zone, both West Indian and Latin Panamanians, into a single union. Worse, the UPW's stateside leadership encompassed a radicalism and aggression that unnerved the paternalistic traditions of the Canal Zone. Ed Cheresh, Len Goldsmith, and Jack Strobel, three Jewish Americans from the UPW's New York office, flew to the Canal Zone to facilitate the organizing campaign. All three came out of a wholly different, contentious New York City labor scene where hardball tactics and rhetoric constituted the norm. Philip Murray, the new, ambitious president of the CIO, supported their approach, at least on paper.[19]

Canal Zone governor Joseph Mehaffey (1944–1948), an old hand on the Zone and a relative progressive on race relations, regarded the local with mixed feelings. He could not envision how Latin and Antillean Panamanians could ever function together given their generations-old hostility and divergent political aims. Mehaffey also knew that he possessed a powerful counterweapon against Local 713, the animosity of the all-white Zonian AFL unions, which viewed this new CIO affiliate as a mortal enemy in both economic and racial terms. A key obstructionist technique that Mehaffey and Zonian labor leader Rufus Lovelady would later use to block advancement for the local-rate workers was to classify numerous canal jobs as "security positions" that required US citizens to fill their slots to prevent "unreliable foreigners" from putting the canal at risk. Reluctantly the governor assented to the CIO affiliate's certification but warned that it should never associate with any Panamanian union in the republic. Local 713 must remain a strictly Canal Zone entity that would bargain only with the United States and the Canal and not politic in Panama or adopt the republic's nationalist ideology. To further restrain the union, Mehaffey insisted that all its officers and members be employees of the US government or its agencies—and residents of the Canal Zone. He even demanded that the union renounce its right to strike and dismiss any members who advocated strikes.[20]

Gaskin and fellow officers Aston Parchment, Cespedes Burke, and Teodoro Nolan refused to knuckle under to these constraints, as they realized that such restrictions would enable Canal officials to decapitate the union leadership overnight by evicting them from their Zone housing and expelling them to Panama. Gaskin then issued his own battle plan, laying out Local 713's goals: an end to the gold/silver roll; a single job classification schema; an increased minimum wage; exemption from work with salary for all union representatives; and a retirement and pension plan for all non-US workers similar to the one US workers had enjoyed for years. Popular among a new generation of young workers who liked its forthright style, the union signed on some eleven thousand silver workers in a year. They marched and protested in the streets of Colón in early 1947, waving emotionally worded and pointed placards that denounced the second-rate salaries and living conditions of silver workers, which they compared to starvation wages and chicken coops.[21]

The Empire Strikes Back

The furor and fears that the Greaves rape case evoked reinforced Mehaffey's belief that the Jim Crow structure of the Canal Zone must endure despite the political price Washington paid for it in international forums. Mehaffey had earlier refused to reduce the fifty-year sentence of Lester Greaves, and he now stood shoulder-to-shoulder with the white supremacist gold workforce, despite his claims to the contrary. The governor had an additional powerful ally in the US military. Army chiefs of staff Generals Dwight D. Eisenhower and Omar Bradley, as well as Defense Secretary Louis Johnson, opposed the implementation of the McSherry reforms as they would later resist Truman's 1948 desegregation order. Besides the Panama Canal Company and Railroad, the US military in the Zone maintained its own two-tier wage scale that closely mirrored civilian Zonian practices. In addition to hiring West Indians as laborers for its dirtiest manual jobs, the army employed Kuna Indians in its barracks as janitors and mess boys. The army preferred Kunas to Latin Panamanians, who might constitute a security risk in the eyes of the more paranoid Cold

Warriors in uniform. Officers further claimed that the gold/silver system was essential to morale for the segregated Panamanian garrison. The US military had operated for decades under a so-called gentlemen's agreement with the Panamanian government that promised that Washington would never deploy African American soldiers in the Canal Zone.

Mehaffey made powerful arguments in favor of the two-tier system along the same lines as his white civilian workers recently aroused by the Greaves case. While he claimed he was personally sympathetic toward integration, he insisted that white workers, their families, and their unions would never accept darker-skinned Panamanians, and especially West Indians, working, eating, learning, and living alongside them as equals. A common euphemism that both Mehaffey and the US brass employed was that the Canal Zone embodied a unique "tropical" or "Caribbean" labor system that had existed for centuries, one that distant Washington liberals failed to comprehend. To an extent, Local 713's officials agreed with the governor and the military: the Canal Zone did indeed function under a traditional tropical system—that of the slave plantation.[22]

When actor, singer, and activist Paul Robeson visited Panama for ten days at the end of May 1947, Local 713 helped finance his trip and his concerts. At his performances, Robeson spoke in favor of the union's aspirations and against racial injustice and imperialism in Panama. He met with Gaskin and other leaders of the Antillean and Panamanian communities. The singer even alluded to the racist inequities of the Lester Greaves rape case, provoking greater global interest in the plight of the West Indian in the Canal Zone. Robeson, along with activists Max Yergin, W. E. B. Du Bois, and Ewart Guinier, served on the UPW's Citizens Committee to End Silver-Gold Jim Crow in Panama. While Governor Mehaffey and other Canal Zone officials were conspicuous by their absence at Robeson's concerts, Panamanian president Enrique Jiménez and his entire cabinet attended, shaking Robeson's hand before one concert to the thunderous applause of the crowd. But while the union had made progress on its organizational, educational, and political fronts, it was about to encounter a buzz saw of repression from a variety of opponents, foreign and domestic. Eliciting Robeson's support proved a mixed blessing, as had Marcus Garvey's aid to the 1920 strikers. Reactionary forces in Panama and the United States condemned black liberationists such as Robeson as radical, unwanted outsiders determined to stir up trouble among the peaceful natives. In the case of Robeson, criticism focused on his support of the US Communist Party and his admiration of Joseph Stalin. On a more local level, to the white US inhabitants of the Canal Zone Robeson represented the ultimate "uppity nigger," the type they thought they had put in his place with the Greaves rape sentence one year before.[23]

Meanwhile, in 1946 in the upper forty-eight, the Federal Bureau of Investigation began an investigation of Communist infiltration of Local 713's parent, the UPW. This marked the start of a broad US purge of leftist and Communist elements within the American labor movement. The House Un-American Activities Committee joined in on the condemnation of the union as a Communist front. Simultaneously, the Truman administration initiated its loyalty oath program, ostensibly to ferret out Communists in all agencies of the federal government. The Cold War crackdown south of the Rio Grande kicked into gear as well. Communist party membership in Latin America approached 400,000 in 1945, but by 1950 it dropped to 150,000 because the US government and conservative Latin Americans were determined to crush all possible Soviet subversion in the hemisphere—and many legitimate labor and populist movements as well. Under pressure from the White House, one Latin American nation after another broke diplomatic and trade relations with the Soviets.[24]

In 1947, Washington helped forge the Rio Pact and in 1948 the Organization of American States to secure South and Central America from the perceived yet exaggerated prospect of a Communist takeover. Other key security measures included the 1949 Mutual Defense Assistance Program, which funneled US arms to Latin American armies and police forces, and the 1946 creation of the US Army Caribbean School at Fort Amador in the Canal Zone that later morphed into a larger institution at Fort Gulick known as the School of the Americas (the new nomenclature actually began in 1963). A less glamorous but important Cold War support emerged in the 1949 Point Four Program, which channeled economic aid to sympathetic, anti-Communist governments and unions under the dictates of the 1947 Truman Doctrine. Panama and the all-white AFL unions of the Canal Zone would become early recipients.[25]

Remón and the National Guard: US Sentinels on the Isthmus

Another key instrument of power that both Governor Mehaffey and Washington wielded in their struggle against so-called radical labor in Panama was the National Police (after 1953, the National Guard) and its pro-US commander, Colonel José Antonio Remón (1908–1955). In 1931 Remón graduated from the Mexican Military Academy, one of the few Panamanian policemen of his era to receive professional education outside the country. He worked foremost to build the National Guard into a professional and independent institution with growing political influence, a small, nearly private army eligible for US military aid and equipment. His men trained at the nearby Caribbean School under US instructors, and his officers socialized with the US military at the multitudinous officers' clubs of the Canal Zone, often inviting their counterparts to receptions at the Cuartel Central.[26]

On one level Remón resembled any number of local proconsuls who supported US hegemony against their own citizens during the Cold War, such as Anastasio Somoza of Nicaragua, Rafael Trujillo of the Dominican Republic, or Fulgencio Batista of Cuba. On other levels, he, like the aforementioned leaders, was a complex man impelled by a variety of motives. An anti-Communist and supporter of Panama's cosmopolitan oligarchy in his early years of power, he gradually shifted into the camp of Panamanian nationalism. In opposition to much of the oligarchy, Remón would later enact serious social reform as president (1952–1955), a tradition of the left-leaning Panamanian military that continued under General Omar Torrijos's rule (1968–1981). He was also widely reported to have investments in Panamanian rackets such as prostitution and gun and drug smuggling, another Guard tradition. While in the immediate crisis of the late 1940s, he backed US efforts to repress Communists in the republic and labor reformists in the Canal Zone, Remón reached out to the West Indian community for political support when he ran for the presidency in 1952. During a 1953 White House meeting with President Eisenhower, Remón even petitioned for equal justice for Panamanians charged with crimes in the Canal Zone, an indirect reference to the controversial Lester Greaves case.[27]

Remón also played a hand in the unique racial dynamics of the Panamanian National Guard that cast the political conflicts of his era into many complex dimensions. Like most militaries, the Panamanian constabulary recruited from marginalized sectors of the population. Darker-skinned mestizos, mulattoes, and blacks from the interior made up a large part of its ranks, though only a few English-speaking West Indians, still regarded as cultural outsiders. The National Guard proved one of the more progressive institutions in Panamanian life with its racial openness and promotion of people of color. These freshly minted recruits reciprocated with heartfelt loyalty toward their *comandante*, "Chichi" (Babyface) Remón. Such personnel policies put the National Guard in direct class and racial conflict with its initial Cold War enemy, the Panamanian students and middle class, which tended to encompass whiter and lighter-skinned mestizos from the urban crucible. During the December 1947 anti–US base riots when Panamanian students and activists railed against the National Assembly's apparent sellout to *yanqui* imperialism, this racial component of the chief actors added to the crisis's animosities. Middle-class students looked down on the darker, poorer, less educated police as ignorant country *cholos* (Indians) and mulattoes. The police in turn despised the spoiled—and in their eyes, overprivileged—brats of the Panamanian bourgeoisie, *los hijos de la cocinera*, in popular parlance. No doubt such attitudes added to the ferocity of Remón's men in their repression of the 1947 protest with police dogs, water cannons, batons, and cavalry. They sent sixty of the demonstrators to the hospital, killed one, and paralyzed another for life.[28]

Besides keeping the students in line, Remón also proved adept in monitoring the small but outspoken Panamanian Communist Party, the Partido del Pueblo de Panamá (PDP) and its president, Celso Selano, whom Remón blamed for inflaming the students at the 1947 riots and for infiltrating the republic's unions. The Canal Zone police also tightened their surveillance over Local 713's leaders and operations, to the point where many felt that authorities shadowed them all the time, a mark of their good intuition. While Remón appreciated the relative weakness of the PDP, denigrated by many Panamanians as the Partido del Pelo Pubico (the Party of the Pubic Hair), it served his interests in receiving US funding and equipment to exaggerate the party's capabilities. Eventually agencies on both sides of the border identified some forty PDP members within Local 713 out of a membership of nearly sixteen thousand. This intelligence cooperation between US and Panamanian clandestine agencies helped solidify their joint vigilance against any untoward political developments on the isthmus. While Remón's initial instinct was to stay out of the Local 713 affair, he helped put pressure on the union by harassing its potential allies in Panama and maintaining a labor-hostile environment in the republic. Simultaneously he damped down nationalist protest that might have aided Local 713 in its larger social justice campaign.[29]

Racial and Political Showdown on the Isthmus: The Destruction of Local 713

In late 1947, Ed Cheresh, the first American UPW representative sent to Panama, purportedly resigned under pressure from the international back home. Upon his dismissal, he complained about Communist influence within the union. Undeterred, the UPW had already sent two fresh delegates, Max Brodsky and Joseph Sachs, to replace Len Goldsmith and Robert Weinstein, who were "not getting the job done," according to headquarters in New York. Brodsky and Sachs denied all Cheresh's charges, as did Nolan, who called Cheresh "a traitor and a rabble-rouser."[30] The two abrasive newly arrived reps got off on the wrong foot by offending not only Canal Zone officials but also the Antillean leadership of their own local. Their Jewish background and bellicose tactics unnerved even Gaskin. He felt he had made progress in building the union from a strong local base and did not appreciate Sachs's and Brodsky's interference or lack of understanding of the complex racial politics in Panama.

Gaskin even told a reporter that if the union's US leaders urged hostile actions against the Canal—that is, sabotage—"we'd throw them out bodily."[31] A small but important Jewish minority exerted some political and economic influence in Panama, but the Sephardic community had little contact with Canal Zone silver workers. On their own side of the border, many Panamanian Arnulfistas expressed open anti-Semitism toward them. Incongruous stereotypes about Jews in this period—that they were both socialist revolutionaries and exploitative capitalists—abounded on both sides of the Zone border and unfortunately did not endear Brodsky and Sachs to either the local communities or to the mostly Protestant, all-white US authorities.[32]

Back in the United States, Abram Flaxer, the president of the UPW international, faced increasing accusations that he was a Soviet puppet. As far as the FBI was concerned, Flaxer had several strikes against him. He had been born in Lithuania, later a part of the Soviet Union; he had joined the Communist Party in his youth; he took a pro-Soviet line on foreign policy in the late 1940s; and as if this was not bad enough, he was Jewish. Well aware by now of the negative connotations attached to the UPW in the States, in early 1948 Gaskin and West Indian ally George Westerman began to form a moderate breakaway faction within Local 713. Czechoslovakia fell into the Soviet camp in a coup that February, accentuating the fear that democratic states and organizations could easily descend to "Red slavery" via internal subversion. When Gaskin and his more politically astute allies pushed for a resolution in the local condemning Communism and pledging loyalty to the United States, it failed to pass. Gaskin now saw the Red writing on the wall and moved toward exiting the union. When the Canal court charged the Sachs-allied Nolan with check fraud, Gaskin's disillusionment with Local 713's New York faction magnified. Probably in desperation, Sachs threatened the popular Gaskin and his associates physically, and this proved the final straw for the West Indian leadership, who held personal dignity and nonviolence as core values.[33]

The Zone's district attorney, Daniel McGrath, successfully prosecuted Sachs for libel in Judge Bunk Gardner's court—the same judge who had sentenced Lester Greaves—after Sachs made derogatory statements regarding McGrath's handling of the Nolan check fraud case that sent Nolan to prison for a year. The court sentenced Sachs to six months in jail. Five months later, US ambassador to Panama Monnet Davis expelled UPW's regional director, Max Brodsky, from the Republic of Panama "for his communist associations." The State Department blocked passports for any future representatives from the international to travel to Panama. Davis even put the PDP on the US attorney general's subversive organizations list, a somewhat odd move since the PDP was a Panamanian and not an American political party.[34]

In January 1949 the Inter-American Confederation of Workers, an AFL affiliate, sent representatives to the Canal Zone to try to pick up the pieces of the fragmenting Local 713. AFL leaders felt that their union might have better success organizing the local-rate employees, given that the AFL already had a strong presence there through the MTC/CLU unions that represented all white US-rate workers. Washington encouraged this organizational drive under George Meany as a safer conduit for worker aspirations than the suspicious CIO, then undergoing an ideological purge. George Westerman, a key West Indian leader in the severely fractured Local 713, refused to accept a $10,000 bribe from the US embassy's political officer, Ed Clark, in exchange for Westerman's abandonment of Local 713 and embrace of the AFL.[35]

Back in the United States by the fall of 1949, the CIO'S civil war came to a head. The moderates under Philip Murray won and expelled eleven unions suspected of Communist affiliations. Among them was Abram Flaxer's UPW, the parent of Local 713. These riveting developments at the metropole facilitated Gaskin's and Westerman's decision to cut the cord with Local 713. They quickly formed a new CIO affiliate, Local 900, to negotiate with the Canal administration over wages and benefits from a politically safer platform. The new Canal governor, Francis Newcomer, who had replaced Mehaffey in 1948, concurred in their efforts.[36] On many levels the collapse of Local 713's attempt to organize all non-US laborers into a single union resembled the CIO's larger failure of the period, Operation Dixie—an effort to organize Southern workers mostly in the textile but also in the mining, lumber, and steel industries. Like Local 713's, the CIO's efforts south of the Mason-Dixon Line fell victim to both the Cold War and racial retrenchment. Southern managers and authorities could draw on appeals to paternalism and tradition in Southern labor relations, just as Canal Zone governors and bosses did in their war against Local 713. Even such sharp advocates of the West Indian cause as Ed Gaskin and George Westerman were to a degree taken in by US promises that under a more moderate local, the silver workers would be "taken care of." In the Deep South of this same period, white workers were held in thrall by national headlines decrying Communist treason in unions, while local headlines covered the lynchings of black men accused of assaulting innocent white women. The effects of this double-barreled psychic assault proved telling: Operation Dixie collapsed by 1952. The Lester Greaves case, while not publicized as egregiously by the Panamanian or Canal Zone press, played a similar role in galvanizing white workers to stand together and defend the racial status quo. After all, found among the documents at the rape scene, as reported in the initial coverage, was Greaves's Local 713 membership card.[37]

Aftermath of Destruction:
The Cold War Death of a Dream?

In July 1950, the Canal Zone government officially recognized Local 900 as the legitimate representative of the local-rate workforce. The new local elected Ed Gaskin as its first president in a brief moment of triumph. Three months later Governor Newcomer decertified Local 713. But while Gaskin and Westerman had read the tea leaves correctly on the growing support for civil rights in the United States, they had badly underestimated the power of racial backlash and Red-baiting to reach them on the isthmus.[38] Larger structural changes within the US Canal Zone apparatus also hampered their efforts. In 1950 under executive and congressional directives, the US-run Canal Zone underwent a major reorganization. An entirely new, more streamlined operation emerged under which the Canal would have to pay for itself solely through tolls and earn a profit as a business. As a result, major manpower and benefit cutbacks ensued.

When in September 1950 Ed Gaskin met with Governor Newcomer for the first time as Local 900 president, these reorganization plans had not yet been fully implemented. But Newcomer knew the figures and the general scope of the cutbacks. Gaskin brought a list of what he considered sixteen reasonable objectives from a labor leader who had proven his loyalty to the United States and the free world by breaking ties with a Communist-branded union. Among the most prominent demands were: a single wage scale; automatic step increases in job grades to narrow the gap between US and local-rate pay; equal pay for equal work; seniority in reductions-in-force and rehiring; regular grievance procedures; better housing, disability pay, pensions, and health care; and an end to racial segregation and discrimination. The governor rejected all sixteen requests. He did so on two bases: (1) segregation on the Zone was "natural" and its main participants, the whites, preferred it; and (2) the restructuring of the Canal conveniently eliminated the funds necessary to carry out any local-rate labor reforms. Gaskin was stunned. When one of his lieutenants vehemently protested the governor's stony rejections, Newcomer demanded an apology. The image of the white governor of the Canal Zone in his white tropical suit demanding that a black subordinate grovel before him cast the entire confrontation in its proper colonial format.[39]

But worse news was to come for the West Indian community. Given the increasingly liberal US Supreme Court decisions chipping away at *Plessy v. Ferguson*, culminating in 1954's *Brown v. Board of Education*, Canal Zone authorities began to protect themselves from future charges of discrimination in housing and education. They commenced a policy of evicting all but essential West Indian workers from their subsidized Canal Zone quarters, in effect dumping surplus Antilleans into the republic. US officials also set up a so-called Latin American school system in cooperation with Panama that would instruct all West Indian children in a Spanish curriculum, replacing the former colored school system of the Zone. In this manner, the Canal Zone attempted to immunize itself from charges of discrimination on the basis of race rather than nationality. US authorities claimed they were only helping West Indians assimilate toward the local nationality. They neglected to mention that they had deliberately impeded such a transculturation process for two generations when it served US purposes to play the West Indians off against the Latin Panamanians and vice versa.[40]

Gaskin soon found himself the target of a number of foes: racist whites, nationalist Panamanians, and the Cold War–obsessed US military. He faced constant harassment and reprimands from the Canal Zone government for continuing to speak out against Jim Crow in the Zone and in both the United States and Panama against such injustices as Lester Greaves's fifty-year sentence. In desperation, he played his last card: Colonel José Antonio Remón. Gaskin threw his support behind Remón's 1952 presidential bid. When Remón won, Gaskin backed his call for negotiations with the United States to revise the hated 1903 Hay-Bunau-Varilla Treaty and bring fundamental reform to the Zone. But in the eventual treaty signed in January 1955, Gaskin and the West Indians faced a subtle yet onerous betrayal by both sides. Washington to a large degree sacrificed the West Indians for better relations with Panama. US diplomats agreed to make all the Canal's West Indian workers subject to the Panamanian income tax for the first time. In a concession to Panamanian grocers, US officials also denied duty-free commissary privileges to West Indian canal workers who lived outside the Zone, a rapidly growing group because of the new housing policies. These twin hammer blows had the effect of reducing West Indians' real wages by about 20 percent. As one retired silver worker remembered: "De whyte man, he kick you when you down and he kick you when you dead." Even the West Indian workforce could not forgive Gaskin for this. He lost his election for a third term as union president.[41]

Canal authorities further punished Gaskin for breaking a cardinal rule of Zone labor relations by aligning his workers' grievances with Panamanian nationalism. The personnel office of the Panama Canal Company encouraged a separate breakaway union for all West Indian defense workers on the Zone's military bases, thus further weakening the local-raters' bargaining position as a single union, to the administration's benefit. This breakaway faction became Local 907 of the American Federation of State, County, and Municipal Employees. It siphoned off about a third of Local 900's laborers. Gaskin left the Canal Zone in 1956 and moved to New York, where he died in obscurity in 2001, deeply disillusioned by a number of betrayals.[42]

Paul Robeson, who journeyed to the isthmus in 1947 in behalf of Local 713, the West Indian racial plight, and the injustice of the Lester Greaves sentence, also fell victim to the pernicious alchemy of race and the Cold War. The State Department stripped him of his passport in 1950, cutting him off from his lucrative overseas performance income. Both Hollywood and Broadway blacklisted him. He ended his days isolated and in poor health, a shadow of his once towering talent as a singer, performer, and activist.[43]

And finally what of the fate of Lester Leon Greaves, whose crime had so polarized a racially divided Canal Zone on the eve of the Local 713 fight? Greaves worked the infamous Gamboa road gang in striped overalls for sixteen years at the Zone's federal prison. Like convicts in the segregated US South, he could be seen in leg irons fettered to his fellow prisoners of color, wielding a shovel, grading the thoroughfares of the Zone while white guards with shotguns eyed him. During Greaves's initial years in prison, the guards and authorities seemed to target and harass him deliberately. By the early 1950s greater acceptance of West Indians as productive citizens of the republic, a process advanced by Ed Gaskin, heightened local interest in the Greaves case. Previously indifferent Latin Panamanians gradually rallied around the convict, elevating his plight to a *cause célèbre* and an effective wedge issue when confronting Washington. When in 1958, Canal Zone Governor William Potter pardoned Gustave Smith and Gerald Thomas, two white GIs serving twenty-five-year sentences for the murder of a West Indian watchman, Panamanian protests of injustice toward Greaves intensified.[44]

Radical Panamanian writers even suggested that Zone officials had framed Greaves. They claimed that the girl who Greaves "supposedly raped" was actually his girlfriend. The two were interracial lovers and the police had "railroaded" Greaves for violating the Zone's chief sexual taboo, that against intimate relations between black men and white women. While such accusations appeared outlandish given Greaves's abuse and robbing of his victim, many Panamanians and West Indians sincerely questioned the charges against him. In interviews decades later, Lester Greaves continued to maintain his innocence and hint at previous relations with his victim.[45]

In 1962 Canal Zone governor William Carter, at President John F. Kennedy's direction, pardoned and released Greaves after sixteen years' hard labor. Washington granted the pardon as a goodwill gesture and part of Kennedy's hopes for a new, more egalitarian relationship with Panama. Thirty-five years old on the day of his release, Greaves went on to marry, have children, and work a variety of odd jobs, including a two-year stint as a furniture repairman in the Canal Zone, where he joined Local 900. At the invitation of the Panamanian government, he attended the handover of all police responsibilities in the remnants of the old Zone from the CZ police to the Panamanian constabulary on April 1, 1982. Today Greaves lives in San Miguelito, a suburb of the capital, an energetic and voluble character, still resentful of his professed mistreatment by "de whyte mon."[46]

The Greaves case heightened racial fears at a key moment in the history of the West Indian struggle in the Zone. Conjoined with Cold War paranoia and the cynical strategies of both Panamanian and US officials, the case played an important contextual role in undoing sincere hopes for reform on the eve of the US-Soviet confrontation. Race mattered in the Cold War and certainly in the Panama Canal Zone, where the unjust system of apartheid became linked in the minds of otherwise rational leaders with the necessity for security and tradition. This obsession with safeguarding strategic territory from alleged Soviet threats helped reify injustice for millions of people of color around the globe.

Notes

1. "Negro Rapes Young American Woman in Midnight Assault," *Panama American*, February 23, 1946.
2. For more details of the assault, see "U.S. Woman Assaulted in Balboa," *Star and Herald*, February 23, 1946; "Engineer Employee Held as Suspect in Zone Rape Case," *Star and Herald*, February 26, 1946; and "Criminal Assault Suspect Arraigned," *Star and Herald*, February 27, 1946.
3. "Criminal Assault," *Panama Tribune*, March 3, 1946. For Greaves's comments to his family in the courtroom, see "Rapist Sentenced to Fifty Years in CZ Pen," *Panama American*, April 2, 1946. For Gardner's admonition, see *Government of the Canal Zone vs. Lester Leon Greaves*, Criminal Case no. 3861, April 2, 1946, from the Lester Leon Greaves File, Part I, 55-K-2620, Records Division, Autoridad del Canal de Panamá (ACP) Corozal, República de Panamá.
4. "Criminal Assault."
5. For a good description of the origins and impact of the gold/silver roll system of the Canal Zone, see Michael L. Conniff, *Black Labor on a White Canal: Panama, 1904–1981* (Pittsburgh: University of Pittsburgh Press, 1985), 5–15. Dr. Conniff is the foremost and pathbreaking historian of West Indian labor in the Canal Zone, and the author is immensely indebted to his work for much of the background and inspiration for this essay; see also Velma Newton, *The Silver Men: West Indian Labour Migration to Panama, 1850–1914* (Kingston, Jamaica: Ian Randle Publishers, 2004); Lancelot Lewis, *The West Indian in Panama: Black Labor in Panama, 1850–1914* (Washington, DC: University Press of America, 1980); Rhonda D. Frederick, *"Colón Man a Come": Mythographies of Panamá Canal Migration* (Lanham, MD: Lexington Books, 2005); George W. Westerman, "Historical Notes on West Indians on the Isthmus of Panama," from Panama Canal Collection (PCC) Centro de

Recursos Tecnícos, Biblioteca del Autoridad de Panama, Balboa, Panama (CRT); and John Biesanz, "Race Relations in the Canal Zone," *Phylon* 11 (1950): 23–30.

6. For an early analysis of Panamanian perceptions toward the West Indian community on the isthmus, see Olmedo Alfaro, *El peligro antillano en la América Central: La defensa de la raza* (Panama: Imprenta Nacional, 1926); for a more recent analysis, see Marixa Lasso, "Race and Ethnicity in the Formation of Panamanian National Identity: Panamanian Discrimination against Chinese and West Indians in the Thirties" (MA thesis, University of Pittsburgh, 1996). For the Panamanian stereotypical view of the West Indian as a US Uncle Tom in literature, see Rafael L. Pernett y Morales, *Loma Ardiente y Vestida de Sol* (Panama: Biblioteca de Nacionalidad ACP, 1999), 107–9; Dimas Lidio Pitty, *Estación de Navegantes* (Panama: INAC, 1975), 303–9; Mirna Pérez-Venero, "Raza, color, y prejucios en la novelística panameña contemporanea de tema canalero" (PhD diss., Louisiana State University, 1973); and Alan Philips, "Afro-Central Americans: Rediscovering Their African Heritage," *NACLA Report on the Americas: The Black Americas, 1492–1992*, 25 (1992): 20–23.

7. For changing attitudes toward race during the postwar era and their international implications, see Thomas Borstelmann, *The Cold War and the Color Line: American Race Relations in the Global Arena* (Cambridge, MA: Harvard University Press, 2001); Penny M. Von Eschen, *Race against Empire: Black Americans and Anticolonialism, 1937–1957* (Ithaca, NY: Cornell University Press, 1997); George Lewis, *The White South and the Red Menace: Segregationists, Anticommunism, and Massive Resistance, 1945–1965* (Gainesville: University Press of Florida, 2004); Mary L. Dudziak, *Cold War Civil Rights: Race and the Image of American Democracy* (Princeton, NJ: Princeton University Press, 2000); Brenda Gayle Plummer, ed., *Window on Freedom*: *Race, Civil Rights, and Foreign Affairs, 1945–1988* (Chapel Hill: University of North Carolina Press, 2003); and Linda F. Williams, *The Constraint of Race: Legacies of White Skin Privilege in America* (University Park: Pennsylvania State University Press, 2003).

8. *McSherry Report on Housing and Labor Conditions in the Panama Canal Zone*, June 1, 1947, PCC, CRT; for stark differences in gold vs. silver salaries for the same jobs in the Zone, see "Labor Conditions in the Canal Zone: Personnel Policy Board of Office of the Department of Defense," September 7, 1948, Decimal File 220.846/230-741, 1947–1948, Box 11, Record Group 338, National Archives and Records Administration, College Park, MD (NARA); see also "Memorandum: Subject: United States Government Labor Relations in the Panama Canal Zone," *Foreign Relations of the United States (FRUS) 1948* (Washington, DC: US Government Printing Office, 1972), 9:682–83.

9. Lester Leon Greaves, interview with the author, San Miguelito, Panama, January 5, 2004.

10. For the Filós-Hines debacle, see "Rejection by the Panamanian Assembly of the Defense Sites Agreement," January 17–December 23, 1947, *FRUS 1947* (Washington, DC: US Government Printing Office, 1972), 13:881–948; see also Thomas L. Pearcy, *We Answer Only to God: Politics and the Military in Panama, 1903–1947* (Albuquerque: University of New Mexico Press, 1998), 109–33.

11. Julie Greene, *The Canal Builders: Making America's Empire at the Panama Canal* (New York: Penguin Group, 2009), 141–42, 263–64, 97–98, 369–70; and Conniff, *Black Labor*, 52–54.

12. "Huelga de los alquilos de 1925," special issue, *Revista Lotería* 213 (October–November 1973); George W. Baker Jr., "The Wilson Administration and Panama, 1913–1921," *Journal of InterAmerican Studies and World Affairs* 8 (April 1969): 279–93; John Major, *Prize Possession: The United States and the Panama Canal, 1903–1979* (New York: Cambridge University Press, 1993), 203–5, 285–96; and Walter LaFeber, *The Panama Canal: The Crisis in Historical Perspective* (New York: Oxford University Press, 1989), 65–70.

13. Paula F. Pfeffer, *A. Philip Randolph: Pioneer of the Civil Rights Movement* (Baton Rouge: Louisiana State University Press, 1990), 47–50, 89–91, 153–54; and Greaves interview with author.

14. Luis Fernando Alvarez, *Vicente Lombardo Toledano y los sindicatos de Mexico y los Estados Unidos* [Vicente Lombardo Toledano and the unions of Mexico and the United States] (Madrid: Editorio Praxis, 1995), 59–71; Martín Tavira Urióstegui, *Vicente Lombardo Toledano: Vida y Pensamiento* [Life and thought] (Mexico City: Fondo de Cultura Ecomica, 1999), 131–35; and Enrique Krauze, *Mexico: A Biography of Power* (New York: Harper Perennial, 1998), 509.

15. Jules Dubois, *Danger over Panama* (Indianapolis: Bobbs-Merrill, 1964), 188–89.

16. "Profile in Courage: Edward A. Gaskin," *www.afro-panamavisions.com*; and William Sinclair and Anthony MacLean, "Homenajae a un luchador [Homage to a fighter]: Edward Ashton Gaskin Stuart," *www.diadelaetnia.homestead.com/Gaskin.html.*

17. Leslie Bethel and Ian Roxborough, "The Postwar Conjuncture in Latin America: Democracy, Labor, and the Left," in *Latin America between the Second World War and the Cold War*, ed. Leslie Bethel and Ian Roxborough (New York: Cambridge University Press, 1992), 1–32; and Kevin Boyle, "Labour, the Left, and the Long Civil Rights Movement," *Social History* 30 (August 2005): 366–72.

18. Murray M. Wise, "Memorandum of a Conversation," and affiliated correspondence, January 23–November 25, 1946, *FRUS 1946*, 9:1149–67; ibid., 42–49, 54–64, 948–67; and State Department File 711.19/1-2346 RG 59, NARA.

19. Conniff, *Black Labor*, 112; Judith Stepan-Norris and Maurice Zeitlin, "Union Democracy, Radical Leadership, and the Hegemony of Capital," *American Sociological Review* 60 (December 1995): 829–50; and Pat Angelo, *Philip Murray, Union Man: A Life Story* (Philadelphia: Xlibris, 2003), 163–67.

20. State Department Decimal File 811F.504/5-1646, Mehaffey to Hines, May 5, 1946; Mehaffey to Wood, October 25, 1946, Panama Canal Company Washington Office, Subject Files, Labor: June–Dec. 1946, Box 204, RG 185, NARA; for security position ruse, see Davis to Marshall, August 18, 1948, Decimal File 220.846/230-741, 1947–1948, Box 11, RG 338, NARA; see also Major, *Prize Possession*, 217–21.

21. *Men of Gold, Men of Silver* (Local 713 pamphlet), July 13, 1946; Conniff, *Black Labor*, 113; and Raymond Allan Davis, "West Indian Workers on the Panama Canal: A Split Labor Market Interpretation" (PhD diss., Stanford University, 1981), 161–73.

22. For the racism inherent in this tropical labor theory as it related to Panama in the canal construction period, see C. L. G. Anderson, "The White Man in the Tropics,"

Journal of American Medicine 24 (May 20, 1908): 1780; and R. S. Irwin, "Native Labor in the Tropics," *Journal of American Medicine* 25 (June 10, 1908): 2076. For historical roots of the system, see Sidney W. Mintz, *Caribbean Transformations* (New York: Columbia University Press, 1989), 59–129. For arguments in favor of maintaining the gold/silver system and defending white privilege, see W. Tapley Bennett, "Memorandum of a Conversation," March 28, 1947, *FRUS 1947*, 8:950–53; and Mehaffey to Wood, October 25, 1946, Panama Canal Company Washington Office, Subject Files, Labor: June–December 1946, Box 704, RG 185, NARA.

23. Paul Robeson Jr., *The Undiscovered Paul Robeson: Quest for Freedom, 1939–1976* (Hoboken, NJ: Wiley, 2010), 125–26; Martin B. Duberman, *Paul Robeson* (New York: Knopf, 1988), 320–21; "Paul Robeson Thrills Panamanians," *People's Voice*, June 28, 1947; "Canal Officials Boycott Robeson Recital," *Panama American*, May 28, 1947; and Katherine Zien, "Politics in Motion: Robeson's 1947 Concerts in Panama" (unpublished paper, 2009).

24. Frank Kofsky, *Harry S. Truman and the War Scare of 1948: A Successful Campaign to Deceive the Nation* (New York: Palgrave Macmillan, 1995); Leonard White, "The Loyalty Program of the United States Government," *Bulletin of the Atomic Scientists* 7 (1951): 361–82; and Louise S. Robbins, "After Brave Words, Silence: American Librarianship Responds to Loyalty Programs, 1947–1957," *Libraries and Culture* 30 (Fall 1999): 345–65.

25. David Green, "The Cold War Comes to Latin America," in *Politics and Policies of the Truman Administration*, ed. Barton J. Bernstein (New York: Quadrangle Books, 1970), 141–59; and Leslie Gil, *School of the Americas: Military Training and Police Violence in the Americas* (Durham, NC: Duke University Press, 2004). For the Point Four Program, see *FRUS 1949* (Washington DC: US Government Printing Office, 1975), 1:757–88.

26. Larry LaRae Pippin, *The Remón Era: An Analysis of a Decade of Events in Panama, 1947–1957* (Stanford, CA: Stanford University Institute of Hispanic American and Luso-Brazilian Studies, 1964), 1–8; and Robert C. Harding II, *Military Foundations of Panamanian Politics* (New Brunswick, NJ: Transaction Publishers, 2001), 33–36, 38–41. The National Police grew in manpower from 959 men to nearly 3,000 under Remón's tutelage.

27. Pippin, *The Remón Era*, 6–8; Harding, *Military Foundations*, 82–107; "Memorandum by the Secretary of State to the President: The Situation in Panama," January 17–21, 1952, *FRUS 1952–1954* (Washington, DC: US Government Printing Office, 1983), 4:1391–98; and Leddy to Cabot, May 20, 1953, ibid., 1409–14, 1418–23.

28. Pippin, *The Remón Era*, 3, 7; Pearcy, *We Answer Only to God*, 95; LaFeber, *Panama Canal*, 89–90. For more on the *mentalité* of the Panamanian middle class, see Daniel Goodrich, *Sons of the Establishment: Elite Youth in Panama and Costa Rica* (Chicago: Rand McNally, 1966), 54–55; Pearcy, *We Answer Only to God*, 124–31; and "Remón Regrets Disturbances: Lauds Police," *Panama Star and Herald*, December 13, 1947. For Remón's personal friendship with Caribbean Command's commander in chief, General Matthew B. Ridgway, see "Remón Visita a General Ridgway," *La Nación*, April 9, 1949. For Remón as political kingmaker on the isthmus, see Harding, *Military Foundations*, 38–41; LaFeber, *Panama Canal*, 84–89; and Thomas

Leonard, "U.S. Perceptions of Panamanian Politics, 1944–1949," *Journal of Third World Studies* 5 (1988): 131–38.

29. "Colon Students Hold Protest Rally in Park," *Star and Herald*, December 14, 1947. For Remón's assistance in surveillance and repression of the PPP, see Memorandum: Intelligence Briefing on Subversive Elements in the Republic of Panama, November 19, 1949, File: Intelligence: Panama July–Dec. 1949, Box 14, RG 349, NARA; and Pippin, 36–39. For an example of US and Panamanian surveillance of the PDP, see Oldfield to Eleta, 24 August 1965, Tomo VI Departamento de Relaciones entre la República de Panamá y La Zona del Canal, 1964, Archivos y Recuerdos del Ministerio de Relaciones Exteriores (ARMRE), Quarry Heights, Panama, in which a West Indian former agent of the US Army Counterintelligence in Panama relates his ten-year experience as a US-paid "plant" within the PDP from 1946 to 1956; virtually all US embassy reports on security from this period mention cooperation between the US military's G-2, the Panamanian National Police, and Canal Zone's Internal Security Division.

30. "Local 713 Denies Cheresh's Charges," *Panama American*, February 6, 1948.

31. "Panama: Double Standard," *Time*, June 23, 1947.

32. State Department Decimal File 819.5043/2-648, US Embassy Memorandum: "Sensational Charges Brought against UPWA/CIO," Hall to Davis, February 6, 1948; File 811.5043/3-2048, US Embassy Memorandum: "Developments Following Charges Brought by Ed Cheresh against UPWA/Local 713," March 20, 1948, Box 5228, RG 59, NARA; and Conniff, *Black Labor*, 113–14.

33. Judith Stepan-Norris and Maurice Zeitlin, *Left Out: Reds and America's Industrial Unions* (Cambridge: Cambridge University Press, 2003), 117–19. For Teodoro Nolan's check fraud case, see "Trial of Theodore M. Nolan and Further Action by the District Attorney," Dispatch no. 196, March 20, 1948, American Embassy, State Department Decimal File 811.5403/3-2048, Box 5228, RG 59, NARA. For physical threats against Gaskin and Westerman, see Ted Scott's column, *Panama American*, February 29, 1948; and George W. Westerman's "The Passing Review," *Panama Tribune*, February 28, 1948.

34. "Brodsky Expelled from CZ: Governor Cites Red Connections," *Panama American*, March 12, 1949; and Major, *Prize Possession*, 223–24.

35. State Department Decimal File 711.19, Clark to Davis, April 6, 1949, Box 5189, RG 59, NARA, cited in Conniff, *Black Labor*, 115; as further proof of Westerman's firm anti-Communism, he wrote a long missive, *Blocking Them at the Canal* (n.p., 1952), that referred to Communist designs on the waterway's unions, in *Los papeles de Jorge Westerman*, Archivo de Ricardo J. Alfaro, Panama City, Panama (ARA), and wrote a sharp condemnation of Communists in Local 713 published in his own "The Passing Review" column, *Panama Tribune*, March 12, 1948. For Westerman's hostility to the AFL, see also Conniff, *Black Labor*, 115.

36. "Newcomer Recognizes New Local 900," *Panama American*, July 16, 1950. For Newcomer's hostile attitude toward labor reform in the Canal Zone, see Newcomer to Royall, October 21, 1948, *FRUS 1948*, 9:684–87.

37. Barbara S. Griffith, *The Crisis of American Labor: Operation Dixie and the Defeat of the CIO* (Philadelphia: Temple University Press, 1988); for racist quotes and

newspaper headlines on lynchings, see Katherine F. Martin, ed., *Operation Dixie: The CIO Organizing Committee Papers, 1946–1953*, 36, 49, 53–55, Microfiche Roll Labor Archives, University of Washington Library, Special Collections. For paternalism and the family labor system in Southern textile mills, see Jacquelyn Dowd Hall, James Leloudis, Robert Korstad, Mary Murphy, Lu Ann Jones, and Christopher B. Daly, *Like a Family: The Making of the Southern Cotton Mill World* (Chapel Hill: University of North Carolina Press, 2000); and "Negro Rapes Young American Woman in Midnight Assault," *Panama American*, February 23, 1946.

38. State Department Decimal File 819.062, Newcomer to Davis, July 19, 1950; 811F.062-3/1850, Box 5341 RG 59, NARA; also cited in Conniff, *Black Labor*, 116; "Local 713 Decertified in the CZ," *Star and Herald*, October 9, 1950.

39. Conniff, *Black Labor*, 115–16.

40. John Dorscher, "The People Caught in No-Man's-Land," *Tropic Magazine* (*Miami Herald*), December 12, 1976; "Between Two Fires," *Workman*, March 29, 1930; Conniff, *Black Labor*, 121–27; Justo Arroyo, "Race Theory and Practice in Panama," in *African Presence in the Americas*, ed. Carlos Moore (Trenton, NJ: Africa World Press, 1995), 155–67; and R. S. Bryce-Laporte, "Crisis, Contraculture, and Religion among West Indians in the Panama Canal Zone," in *Blackness in Latin America and the Caribbean: Social Dynamics and Cultural Transformations*, ed. Norman E. Whitten Jr. and Arlene Torres (Bloomington: Indiana University Press 1998), 1:100–118.

41. Conniff, *Black Labor*, 118–19; Trevor O'Reggio, *Between Alienation and Citizenship: The Evolution of the Black West Indian in Panama, 1903–1964* (Lanham, MD: University Press of America, 2006), 140–52; and Vincente Williams, interview with the author, Cardenas, Panama, April 14, 2004.

42. Conniff, *Black Labor*, 117–19; "Profile in Courage: Edward A. Gaskin," *www.afro-panamavisions.com*; and William Sinclair and Anthony MacLean, "Homenajae a un luchador: Edward Ashton Gaskin Stuart," *www.diadelaetnia .homestead.com/Gaskin.html*.

43. Duberman, *Paul Robeson*, 336–47, 363–70, 381–403, 435–45, 498–521; Paul Robeson Jr., *Undiscovered Paul Robeson*, 126–27, 163–68, 207–36, 239–42, 248–54; and Internal Correspondence, June 10, 1947, Federal Bureau of Investigation, FBI File 100-12304 [Paul and Essie Robeson], Microfilm Reel 9, Frames 14–32, from Zien, "Politics in Motion."

44. Prisoner Disciplinary Infraction Reports: Lester Leon Greaves, 1946–1962, Gamboa Penitentiary, Leon Greaves File, Part II, 55-K-2620, Records Division, ACP, Corozal, Panama; and Greaves interview with author.

45. Roberto Peñaloza, interview with the author, Curundu, Panama, April 1, 2002. For West Indian opinions on Greaves's innocence, Angus Brown, interview with the author, Gatun, Panama, June 10, 2002; and Albert Brown, interview with the author, Corozal, Panama, January 14, 2004. For Zonian viewpoints, Robert Taht, interview with the author, Balboa, Panama, May 11, 2001. For the complex issues of rape, sexual assault, and date or acquaintance rape possibly involved in the Greaves case, see Ann J. Cahill, *Rethinking Rape* (Ithaca NY: Cornell University Press, 2001), 109–42; Sally K. Ward, Jennifer Dziuba-Leatherman, Jane Gerard Stapleton, and

Carrie L. Yodanis, eds., *Acquaintance and Date Rape: An Annotated Bibliography* (Westport, CT: Greenwood Press, 1994); Lee Ellis, *Theories of Rape: Inquiries into the Causes of Sexual Aggression* (New York: Hemisphere Publishing Corporation, 1989); Robin Warshaw, *I Never Called It Rape: The Ms. Report on Recognizing, Fighting, and Surviving Date and Acquaintance Rape* (New York: Harper, 1994); and Lester Leon Greaves, interviews with the author, San Miguelito, Panama, January 5, 2004, and August 4, 2005.

46. For Zonian reaction to Greaves's presence at the ceremony, see Herbert and Mary Knapp, *Red, White, and Blue Paradise: The American Canal Zone in Panama* (San Diego: Harcourt Brace Jovanovich, 1984), 269–71; "Greaves Released Quietly: Famous Convict Returns to Family," *Star and Herald*, May 6, 1962; "Lester Greaves Attends Police Handover: Most Famous Prisoner Returns to Gamboa," *Panama American*, April 2, 1982; Prisoner Disciplinary Infractions Reports: Lester Leon Greaves, 1946–1962, Gamboa Penitentiary, Leon Greaves File, Part II, 55-K-2620, Records Division, ACP, Corozal, Panama; and Greaves interview with author, January 5, 2004.

References

ARCHIVES

Archivo de Ricardo J. Alfaro, Panama City, Panama

Center for Technical Resources, Panama Canal Authority Library (Centro de Recursos Tecnícos, Biblioteca del Autoridad de Canal de Panama), Balboa, Panama

Foreign Ministry Archives (Archivo del Ministerio de Relaciones Exteriores), Quarry Heights, Panama City, Panama

Library of Congress, Manuscript Division, Washington, DC

Library of Statistics and the Census (Biblioteca de le Direccion de Estadística y Censo), Panama City, Panama

National Archive (Archivo Nacional), Panama City, Panama

National Archives and Records Administration, College Park, MD

National Institute of Culture (Instituto Nacional de Cultura), Panama City, Panama

National Library (Biblioteca Nacional), Panama City, Panama

Panama Canal Authority Archives and Records Divsion (Archivo de Recuerdos de la Autoridad del Canal de Panamá), Corozal, Panama

PERIODICALS

Critica

El Siglo

Estrella de Panama/Star and Herald

La Hora

La Nación

Matutino

Miami Herald
New York Times
North American Congress on Latin America: Report on the Americas
Panamá América/Panama American
Panama Canal Review
Panama Tribune
República
Revista Loteriá
Revista Tareas
Time
Washington Post
Workman

SELECTED PUBLISHED WORKS

Alfaro, Olmedo. *El peligro antillano en la América Central: La defensa de la raza* [The danger of Antilleans in Central America: The defense of the race]. Panama: Imprenta Nacional, 1926.

Alfaro, Ricardo J. *Los canales internacionales: Panamá* [International canals: Panama]. Panama: Imprenta Nacional, 1957.

———. *Medio siglo de relaciones entre Panama y los Estados Unidos* [Half a century of relations between Panama and the United Status]. Panama: Imprenta Nacional, 1959.

Biesanz, John. "Cultural and Economic Factors in Panamanian Race Relations." *American Sociological Review* 14 (1949): 772–79.

———. "Race Relations in the Canal Zone." *Phylon* 11 (1950): 23–30.

Borstelmann, Thomas. *The Cold War and the Color Line: American Race Relations in the Global Arena*. Cambridge, MA: Harvard University Press, 2001.

Boyle, Kevin. "Labour, the Left, and the Long Civil Rights Movement." *Social History* 30 (August 2005): 366–72.

Bryce-Laporte, R. S. "Crisis, Contraculture, and Religion among West Indians in the Panama Canal Zone." In *Blackness in Latin America and the Caribbean: Social Dynamics and Cultural Transformations, Volume 1*, edited by Norman E. Whitten Jr. and Arlene Torres. Bloomington: Indiana University Press, 1998.

Conniff, Michael L. *Black Labor on a White Canal: Panama, 1904–1981*. Pittsburgh: University of Pittsburgh Press, 1985.

———. *Panama and the United States: The Forced Alliance*. Athens: University of Georgia Press, 2001.

———. "Panama since 1903." In *The Cambridge History of Latin America, Volume 7*, edited by Leslie Bethel, 603–42. New York: Cambridge University Press, 1990.

Davis, Raymond. "West Indian Workers on the Panama Canal: A Split Labor Market Interpretation." PhD diss., Stanford University, 1981.

Duberman, Martin B. *Paul Robeson*. New York: Knopf, 1988.

Fernando Alvarez, Luis. *Vicente Lombardo Toledano y los sindicatos de Mexico y los*

Estados Unidos [Vicente Lombardo Toledano and the unions of Mexico and the United States]. Madrid: Editorio Praxis, 1995.

Greene, Julie. *The Canal Builders: Making America's Empire at the Panama Canal*. New York: Penguin Group, 2009.

Harding, Robert C., II. *Military Foundations of Panamanian Politics*. New Brunswick, NJ: Transaction Publishers, 2001.

James, Joy. "US Policy in Panama." *Race and Class* 32 (1990): 17–32.

Johnson, Suzanne P. *An American Legacy in Panama: A Brief History of the Department of Defense Installations and Properties in the Former Panama Canal Zone*. Corozal, Panama: Directorate of Engineering and Housing, US Army Garrison–Panama, 1995.

Knapp, Herbert, and Mary Knapp. *Red, White, and Blue Paradise: The American Canal Zone in Panama*. San Diego: Harcourt Brace Jovanovich, 1984.

LaFeber, Walter. *The Panama Canal: The Crisis in Historical Perspective*. New York: Oxford University Press, 1989.

Lasso, Marixa. "Race and Ethnicity in the Formation of Panamanian National Identity: Panamanian Discrimination against Chinese and West Indians in the Thirties." MA thesis, University of Pittsburgh, 1996.

Lewis, Lancelot. *The West Indian in Panama: Black Labor in Panama, 1850–1914*. Washington, DC: University Press of America, 1980.

Major, John. *Prize Possession: The United States and the Panama Canal, 1903–1970*. New York: Cambridge University Press, 1993.

McPherson, Alan. "Courts of Public Opinion: Trying the Panama Canal Flag Riots." *Diplomatic History* 28 (January 2004): 83–112.

———. *Yankee No! Anti-Americanism in U.S.-Latin American Relations*. Cambridge, MA: Harvard University Press, 2003.

Newton, Velma. *The Silver Men: West Indian Labour Migration to Panama, 1850–1914*. Kingston, Jamaica: Ian Randle, 1984.

O'Reggio, Trevor. *Between Alienation and Citizenship: The Evolution of the Black West Indian in Panama, 1903–1964*. Lanham, MD: University Press of America, 2006.

Pearcy, Thomas L. *We Answer Only to God: Politics and the Military in Panama, 1903–1947*. Albuquerque: University of New Mexico Press, 1998.

Pérez-Venero, Mirna. "Raza, color, y prejucios en la novelistica panameña contemporanea de tema canalero" [Race, color, and prejudice in the contemporary Panamanian novels of the canal]. PhD diss., Louisiana State University, 1973.

Pernett y Morales, Rafael L. *Loma Ardiente y Vestida de Sol* [Burning hill and dress of sun]. Panama: Biblioteca de Nacionalidad ACP, 1999.

Pippin, Larry LaRae. *The Remón Era: An Analysis of a Decade of Events in Panama, 1947–1957*. Stanford, CA: Stanford University Institute of Hispanic American and Luso-Brazilian Studies, 1964.

Plummer, Brenda Gayle, ed. *Window on Freedom: Race, Civil Rights, and Foreign Affairs, 1945–1988*. Chapel Hill: University of North Carolina Press, 2003.

Robinson, William Francis. "Panama for the Panamanians: The Populism of Arnulfo Arias Madrid." In *Populism in Latin America*, edited by Michael L. Conniff, 157–71. Tuscaloosa: University of Alabama Press, 1999.

Stepan-Norris, Judith, and Maurice Zeitlin. *Left Out: Reds and America's Industrial Unions*. Cambridge: Cambridge University Press, 2003.

Von Eschen, Penny M. *Race against Empire: Black Americans and Anticolonialism, 1937–1957*. Ithaca, NY: Cornell University Press, 1997.

Zien, Katherine. "Politics in Motion: Robeson's 1947 Concerts in Panama." Unpublished paper, 2009.

CHAPTER 4

Race, Identity, and Diplomacy in the Papua Decolonization Struggle, 1949–1962

David Webster

As they gained independence, African governments were courted from many corners.[1] One of the most unusual was a group of unofficial diplomats from Papua, which was then still the Dutch colony of West New Guinea.[2] There, in the seas where Asia faded into the Pacific islands, a Papuan nationalist movement sought to insert itself into an Indonesian-Dutch diplomatic and military struggle for control of their homeland. The Dutch spoke of tutelage, the Indonesians of regaining a part of their territory still under colonial rule. The issue threatened to erupt into war before the US government intervened in 1962 and forced a settlement that saw the territory transferred to Indonesian rule, where it remains, restively, to this day.

Papuan nationalists touring Africa in 1962, months before the American-mediated settlement, carried with them a pamphlet. "BROTHERS AND SISTERS NEGROIDS!" it exhorted. "It's about time you break away from your busy work to listen to what we Papuans have to say! Many, many times you have heard about us from the Dutch and Indonesians, without having known us. Now we will take the floor ourselves. We are living in the Pacific, our people are called Papuans, our ethnic origin is the Negroid race."[3] The pamphlet made an audacious claim that mobilized ideas of race to back a demand for independence. As they traveled through Africa, their hosts remarked with surprise on their appearance. These inhabitants of a Dutch colony, claimed by Indonesia, "looked African." Armed with that perception, they tried to turn "race" into a diplomatic asset, transforming marginalization and powerlessness into a tool they could wield internationally.

It would be difficult to make a case for ethnic ties between Africa and the Melanesian Pacific, but the emergent Papuan nationalist movement neverthe-less seized on the dark skins and curly hair of many people in both areas. They lacked the strength to win their case internationally. Yet in deciding to press the case for Papuan-African commonality, they forged the identity that is still asserted in today's Papuan independence movement.

The case for the Papuans was not just one of diplomacy: it was an effort to convince the world that there was such a thing as a Papuan people. The claim was grounded in an assertion of racial difference between Papuans and Indo-nesians—something made clear in the title of the Papuan nationalist pamphlet *The Voice of the Negroids of the Pacific to the Negroids throughout the World.* The pamphlet's opening article, signed by nationalist leader Nicolaas Jouwe, conceded that the case could not be grounded in historical records, since the Papuans' ancestors were illiterate. Still, he wrote, "we Papuans know that we are an independent people and this is the time we want to fight before the international forum to remain ourselves. We do not want to be slaves any-more." Papuans were a distinct people who "differ[ed] from the Indonesians ethnologically not in the way the Indian differs from the Pakistani but like the people of Ghana in West Africa differ from the Chinese. . . . WE ARE PAPUANS AND WANT TO REMAIN PAPUANS!" Lest there be any mistaking its intent, *Voice of the Negroids* was copiously illustrated with photographs of Papuans. One depicted a Papuan teacher alongside Frédéric Guirma, Upper Volta's ambas-sador to the United Nations. "What is the ethnical difference between them?" the caption asked.[4] Similarly, an appeal from the Papuan National Commit-tee, the main vessel of Papuan nationalism, called on "all negroid peoples in the world" as "fellow tribesmen" to lend help.[5] Papuan nationalists continu-ally stressed difference from Indonesia as foundational to their nation. "The Papuan people form a nation, which has the right to its territory and its national State, in the same way as the other peoples of the world," one public meeting resolved in a motion to UN Secretary-General U Thant. "The Papuans are not Indonesians."[6] Grounded in claims of difference and claims of inter-national justice, the Papuan nationalist case looked to the United Nations for support. As a host of new African states joined the United Nations, they found hope in identification with Africa's decolonization wave and with Africans.

The period leading up to the publication of *The Voice of the Negroids* saw Papuans form an identity within the context of Dutch-Indonesian struggle, defining themselves along lines of "race." The idea that Papuans were a race apart from Indonesians was very much a product of colonial administration and anthropology. Yet Papuan nationalists sought to reclaim and redeploy the idea that they were "black" for their own ends. This was partly to build a unifying sense of nation within Papua, but equally it had pragmatic diplomatic goals, as a strategy to build international support for Papuan independence. Diplomatic struggle drove identity formation. Papuan nonstate diplomats donned the hallowed pan-African mantle. This gave them a claim to the dignity of independence, and offered the prospect of overseas supporters able to lend weight to their claims for a separate future from the regional giant, Indonesia.

Yet it also left them victim to ideas of space and place implicit in Western minds. If they were black, that made them, to many in the West, primitive. A claim for independence was rendered into an argument against independence. Diplomatic thinking of the day "situate[d] black subjects and their geopolitical concerns as being elsewhere (on the margin, on the underside, outside the normal)," to quote Katherine McKittrick and Clyde Woods. Writing on the history of Papua's transfer from Dutch to Indonesian rule has similarly tended to exclude Papuan voices, even though "the situated knowledge of these communities and their contributions to real and imagined human geographies are significant political acts and expressions."[7] In other words, Papuans were subjects in their own history, even though most historical accounts have omitted them.

The new Papuan identity was constructed internationally, rather than by factors from within the territory. It is best understood as part of the Africa-centered global wave of decolonization in the early 1960s. Papuans, told they were "black," reclaimed and redeployed the imposed race category. Rejecting any notion that they were part of another country, or destined for years of "tutelage," they demanded equality with other peoples, framing this claim in internationally accepted terms as a demand for decolonization and self-determination. The decolonizing "wind of change" in Africa offered a window for parallel Papuan hopes for decolonization, but Cold War politics slammed that window shut. Although it failed in its bid for independence, the Papuan claim to be in a sense African became foundational to Papuan nationalism. Before it could make claims that linked Papua to Africa in the 1960s, however, Papuan nationalism had to form within more limited regional spaces.

Papua in Indonesian and Melanesian Contexts, 1945–1959

Papuan identity emerged in the short period between the Indonesian independence declaration of 1945 and the Indonesian takeover of the 1960s. It was historically contingent—which does not make it less real or deeply held. International factors were key in identity formation. In 1944, Allied forces pushed the Japanese military out of New Guinea. General Douglas MacArthur established his base at what is now the Papuan provincial capital, Jayapura—then called Kampong Harapan, the village of hope. The arrival of African American soldiers made a major impression. Jouwe recalled the impression of these dark-skinned troops on local Papuans: "They saw how the Negroes, who were as black as we, were building roads, driving large army trucks, and were able to do all sorts of things as well as the Whites. They saw Black pilots, Black sailors, Blacks in beautiful uniforms with bottles of Coca-Cola. Of course they had no idea about racial discrimination in the USA. But what they saw opened their eyes. They had always been despised and treated as savages."[8] Another nationalist leader, E. J. Bonay, took away a similar impression of African American soldiers: "They worked and fought shoulder to shoulder with their white comrades. The Negro men flew fighter planes, commanded warships, fired artillery, and drove vehicles and so forth. . . . Seeing this, Papuans asked themselves why can the Negroes do these things and the Papuans not? Is not our skin color and hair the same?"[9]

Papuan elites had to contend with the fact of Indonesia's independence declaration, issued two days after the Japanese surrender. Was *merdeka* (freedom) to be realized in partnership with the new Republic of Indonesia, or in opposition to it? For Indonesian nationalists, there was no question: Papua was part of the Dutch East Indies, therefore part of Indonesia, and the proclamation settled the issue of self-determination once and for all. Dutch officials proposed an eventual independent Papua in union with the Netherlands. The proposal split the Papuan elite into two factions. Silas Papare emerged as the leader of those who rejected it, while Markus Kaisiepo, Nicolaas Jouwe, and others accepted it.[10] The idea of separating Papua from Indonesia went back to the 1930s, with some Dutch groups seeing it as a new tropical Holland to be carved out of the wilderness. These groups included fascists who sought a "white New Guinea."[11] In this vision, Papuans were invisible, part of nature. Colonial race scholarship rendered them as Melanesian rather than Indonesian, the anthropological catchall term for the rest of the Indies (plus present-day Malaysia, the Philippines, and Madagascar). Anthropology mapped race on lines of difference. Where the Indonesians were for the most part brown skinned and straight haired, Papuans' black skin and curly hair prompted their depiction as "Oriental Negroes" by turn-of-the-century Dutch explorers.[12] Nineteenth-century writers had speculated that Melanesians might be originally from Africa—they were "all children of Ham." As Gerald Horne has noted, a "blackbirding" trade in "Papuan savages" went back to the nineteenth-century construction of a "white Pacific" in Australia, the United States, and elsewhere.[13]

Papuan nationalists renamed the territory Irian, a term coined by Markus

Kaisiepo meaning the hot land that rises out of the tropical haze. Silas Papare established the first nationalist group, the Partai Kemerdekaan Irian Indonesia (PKII), the Irian Indonesian Independence Party. After planning an anti-Dutch uprising, Papare was jailed for a time, then founded the PKII in 1946 to seek independence from the Netherlands as an autonomous component of the new decentralized Indonesian Republic. Papare stressed that "the PKII will only recognize a government of its own choice, that is, constituted by the people and for the people."[14] If Papare represented one current in Papuan nationalism, Markus Kaisiepo represented the other. Kaisiepo was foremost among the early Papuan nationalists who rejected the path to independence as part of Indonesia. By the 1960s he was, in the words of an Australian diplomat, "regarded by the Dutch as the doyen of the Papuan elite."[15]

In the sense of newness and discovery, Papuan reactions echoed global feelings. "A wind *is* rising," wrote Walter White, who went on to head the NAACP—"a wind of determination by the have-nots of the world to share the benefits of freedom and prosperity which the haves of the earth have tried to keep exclusively for themselves." White deplored the return of such European holdings as Papua to their former colonial ruler. "Colored peoples, particularly in the Pacific, believed, whether correctly or not, that in its later stages the war was being fought to restore empire to Great Britain, France, Holland, and Portugal," he wrote. US policy, influenced by racialized thinking, tended to preach self-determination but sympathize with European governments. Washington took a pro-Dutch stance in the early stages of the Indonesian revolution, which drew the condemnation of African American anticolonialists at home. It shifted only after the new Republic of Indonesia proved its anti-Communist bona fides by crushing a Communist uprising in 1948.[16]

American and UN diplomacy saw the Netherlands accept Indonesian independence in 1949. The Indonesian-Dutch negotiations leading to this deal deadlocked over control of Papua. Papuan leaders complained that Papua's fate was being settled with no Papuans present, as if it was "a piece of merchandise."[17] Papuan nationalism was forming, with Indonesia defined as the "other." This process gelled under Dutch rule in the 1950s.

The postwar international climate made it necessary for the Netherlands to justify its continued colonial presence in Papua. Dutch authorities insisted that there were two different races in the Netherlands East Indies: on this, "we can trust the simple evidence of our own eyes."[18] By making race the reason for their presence in Papua, they set the boundaries within which a new Papuan or Melanesian identity could emerge. As Danilyn Rutherford has written, "the Papuan was born in a process of naming in which those designated as such had little part."[19]

The result was a colonial government that gave an unusually large responsibility to anthropologists. Plans drawn up in 1949 for a colonywide parliament were shelved for a series of local councils. A gradualist approach stressed political training but avoided firm target dates for independence. In the words of Governor Jan van Baal, himself a distinguished anthropologist: "Real independence is dependent on economic development."[20] Dutch colonialists wanted to prove they could succeed next to an Indonesia that was failing. At the United Nations, the Dutch government argued for a "sacred mission" in West New Guinea that represented "the natural self-respect of a guardian who has begun the upbringing of an infant and does not want to relinquish the responsibility until the child can stand on its own legs."[21]

Not surprisingly, Indonesian leaders were unimpressed with Dutch efforts to follow policies in New Guinea that they remembered all too well themselves. They derided claims for a separate Papuan political unit as racial pseudoscience. One Indonesian pamphlet argued that "no one can draw a distinct dividing line between the so-called Papua and Malay areas!"[22] The struggle to gain control of Papua became increasingly central to Indonesian political unity. Patriotic songs, for instance, harnessed Indonesian nationalism to the campaign to "restore West Irian to the fold of the motherland."[23]

Papuan nationalists again found themselves squeezed between these two states in conflict. When in 1949 the Dutch government accepted Indonesian independence but held on to Papua, Silas Papare and his followers moved to Indonesia to carry on the anticolonial struggle. Papare was appointed as one of three Papuan representatives in exile sitting in the Indonesian parliament. He founded the Irian Struggle Body, which continued to assert his right to speak for the Papuan people in international forums. In 1953 he was named a member of the Indonesian government's Irian Bureau, set up as an embryo for a future provincial government. His key role, however, was to serve as a concrete representation of Papuan pro-Indonesian sentiment—his story made regular appearances in Indonesian pamphlets produced for international consumption. Papare declared an autonomous province from exile in 1956, but the Indonesian government ignored this, announcing its own "autonomous province" soon afterward under the leadership of the Sultan of Tidore—best known for his dynasty's history as slave-traders along the Papuan coasts.[24]

If Papare had been squeezed out in the "autonomous province" episode, Markus Kaisiepo also felt a sense of betrayal the same year as Dutch churches began to call for talks with Indonesia. Kaisiepo shifted away from Christianity as a result, stressing instead indigenous beliefs and unambiguous Papuan nationalism. With Jouwe, Bonay, and fourteen other leaders, he signed a 1956 Papuan resolution that it must be Papuans who maintained peace and stability in their country, given the call of the Dutch church for Indonesian-Dutch talks.[25]

Although Dutch categorizing of race was formative, Indonesian attitudes on race also became decisive. The rejection of European racial classification was central to the Indonesian nationalist project, which asserted a single nation embracing all indigenous peoples throughout the archipelago.

Indonesian political depictions of Papua drew on ideas of center and periphery, civilization and savagery. Territory mattered, and the lingering Dutch presence on part of Indonesia's "body" was painted as an "amputation" by Indonesian leaders. President Sukarno, for instance, declared: "Compared to our archipelago, West Irian is the size of a *kelor* (horseradish) leaf, yet West Irian is part of our body. Would anybody allow one of his limbs to be amputated without putting up a fight? Does not a man cry out in pain if even the tiniest finger of his hand is cut off?" The idea of all ethnicities in the archipelago being Indonesian together was deeply rooted in Indonesian nationalism.[26] Nevertheless, and unlike other regionally based ethnic minorities, Indonesian nationalist depictions of Papuans tended toward racial caricature. One activist wrote about the need to "free" Papuans from their "stone age civilization," while noting their skills in music and sports; Foreign Minister Subandrio spoke of the need to get Papuans "down out of the trees even if we have to pull them down"; and Sukarno's audience reportedly appeared in blackface at one rally.[27] Indonesian nationalism, even as it extolled the struggle to gain control of Papua, othered the Papuan people.

The Indonesian-Dutch struggle was over who would possess the land. In Jouwe's words: "Papua was like a virgin girl, being ready to be married by anyone strong enough to get her."[28] Gendered concepts had also been present from the beginnings of the Indonesian nationalist movement, a project of freeing the feminine body of the motherland (Ibu Pertiwi) from colonialism through dynamic action by nationalist men. These gendered themes became stronger as the nationalist movement won its freedom in a war of revolution that spawned heroic memories, and then inherited a state apparatus. Dutch colonial rhetoric often feminized Indonesian men, and US colonial-period images did the same.[29] That legacy remained postindependence: US images portrayed Sukarno as a vain, emotional, and irrational ruler. But Sukarno's popularity at home only benefited when he was criticized for womanizing on his foreign trips, and he was careful to bolster his masculine image through the conjuring of national grandeur and the construction of grand projects and symbols like the National Monument in Jakarta, a column locals dubbed "Sukarno's last erection."

Throughout the 1950s, Western assumptions about Indonesian backwardness and incapacity reinforced strategic calculations that privileged European concerns. One typical note from a Western diplomat underlines this point:

> Looked at objectively and realistically in the light of current conditions in Indonesia, of course, acquisition of another vast stretch of primitive territory would be like piling Ossia upon Pelion. . . . But emotion, pride and bitterness compounded have expanded the issue of control over a rugged and backward South Sea tract of land into a political problem of global impact, possibly fraught with menace to the world's peace and certainly to its peace of mind.[30]

Only when this attitude began to shift, and racialized attitudes toward "primitive" Papuans began to grow, did this change.

Papua as "New Africa," 1960–1962

Racial categories in the Papuan-Indonesian conflict were very recent constructions. In adopting "race" as a marker of difference, Papuan nationalists embraced a new mental map of sharp division, rather than gradual shading, between Indonesia and Melanesia (islands of dark-skinned people). A sharp racial divide was then painted as a sharp ideological divide. "I don't believe that in the future we will be friendly with Asiatic people," Jouwe wrote. "They will become more and more communistic. We are a Pacific people."[31]

Nationalism surged as the Dutch government announced a ten-year plan for self-government. In 1961, a semi-elected New Guinea Council with a Papuan majority took office. With this step, Papuan nationalists became diplomatic actors. The council swiftly staked a claim as the legitimate international voice of the Papuan people. It resolved, for instance, that the Netherlands was "no longer free" to dispose of the territory without council consent.[32]

A Papuan National Congress convened in October 1961 to choose and deploy images of nationhood—a new flag and anthem—in the global diplomatic arena. Within a year, 95 percent of Papuan students could identify the new symbols. The Congress, "knowing that we are united as a people and a nation," demanded "our own position, equal to that of the free nations and in the ranks of these nations." Despite this, Indonesians and Americans believed that the new flag, designed by Jouwe, was a Dutch creation, and that the Dutch rather than a nationalist gathering had insisted on a name change from Netherlands New Guinea to West Papua. This ascribed to colonial rulers what was in fact the result of Papuan agency.[33]

A group of young Papuans formed the National Party, Parna, which called for tripartite Indonesian-Dutch-Papuan talks on the territory's future. One Dutch official dismissed their call as "naïve and infantile," evoking images of a Dutch father toward his Papuan children that still pervaded the Netherlands government.[34] Still, Parna was a significant political force, founded in a rejection of "father-son dependency" and complaints that the white minority was engaging in "apartheid," and willing to criticize the Dutch government for not moving quickly enough toward self-determination. It seemed driven by typical anticolonial sentiments, noting that "even today there are Netherlanders, and among those religious leaders in Papua country, who still regard the people of New Guinea as a herd of animals, who cannot think, who can only eat."[35] The reference to apartheid, meanwhile, indicated a global awareness and a sense of connection to decolonization struggles in Africa.

The initial space for Papuan race perceptions was Melanesia. In attempting to move Papuan mental maps to a Pacific rather than Southeast Asian setting and to build regional security partnerships, Dutch officials had sought to create links between their colony and the decolonizing Pacific islands, especially the Australian-administered half of the island (now Papua New Guinea). Papuan leaders used this opening presented by Dutch strategic calculations for their own ends, pressing for a "Melanesian Federation" including the whole island. At an Australian-Dutch administrative cooperation conference in 1961, Jouwe hoped for "the distant day when all Papuans from Sorong in West New Guinea to Samarai in East New Guinea will share common political feelings."[36] Kaisiepo attended South Pacific Commission meetings as a Papuan representative, where he was able to convince "leading persons of the Polynesian, Micronesian, and Melanesian peoples" to call on the United Nations to support "the unity of the Melanesian people which cannot be destroyed and who cannot be compelled to unite with any other people than the Melanesian people, based upon the unity of the Island of New Guinea."[37]

Yet Melanesia was not enough to meet the need for international diplomatic support. The nationalist mental map based on Melanesian racial identity therefore expanded to include Africa.

Kwame Nkrumah's Ghana in particular seized the global pan-African imagination. It was "a virile black republic headed by a disciple" of pan-Africanism, "the African American Camelot." Nkrumah declared: "For too long in our history Africa has spoken through the voice of others. Now what I have called the African Personality in international affairs will have a chance of making its proper impact and will let the world know it through the voices of its sons."[38] Sixteen more African countries joined the United Nations in 1960, shifting the balance of voting power and making African support a valuable asset. In the fall of 1961, the Papua case came to the United Nations as part of the General Assembly's declaration on how to implement the Declaration on the Granting of Independence to Colonial Countries and Peoples, passed the year before. Unlike the other colonial powers, the Dutch government had supported that resolution and brought forward a plan to end colonialism in Papua the following year, hoping its vote for rapid decolonization had earned it some credibility. Foreign Minister Joseph Luns offered to transfer sovereignty to the Papuans and administration to the United Nations, while still paying the costs of administration. Indonesian foreign minister Subandrio called that "a declaration of war," while his ambassador in Washington declared that the Dutch meant "not to give self-determination but to create separatism and finally to amputate Irian Barat [Papua] from Indonesian territory." Indonesian diplomats instead backed a proposal from India for bilateral Indonesian-Dutch talks.[39]

Into this battle entered the newly formed Brazzaville group, an association of thirteen "moderate" African countries, most of them newly independent from France. In their first joint diplomatic effort, the Brazzaville states offered a resolution endorsing Papuan self-determination that married Indian and Dutch resolutions by calling for bilateral talks, but also authorized implementation of the Luns plan if talks did not reach a speedy agreement. This would include a UN mission to decide on the territory's future. The Brazzaville resolution was the product of the diplomacy and desires of its African sponsors, who saw their own experience mirrored among Papuan nationalists. American officials in Washington were seeking a resolution and willing to accept some of the Indonesian arguments, but the US delegation to the United Nations rallied behind the Brazzaville group's efforts. "Real heroes were French-Africans who took on arduous task out of belief in principle of self-determination," the delegation reported. They had shown the "courage of their convictions" and won a "moral victory due to their steadfastness in resisting powerful pressures and blandishments to eliminate self-determination from their resolution."[40] In voting that followed bloc lines, the Brazzaville resolution fell short of the two-thirds needed for adoption. Most significantly, the UN experience permitted the expression of Papuan diplomacy.

The effort to identify with Africa trapped the Papuan leadership between two African camps. With African politics polarized between Brazzaville group "moderates" and Casablanca group "radicals," appeals to pan-African sentiment from outside had less space than they would after the formation of the Organization of African Unity in 1963. The two camps were especially divided on attitudes toward the Congo civil war. Indonesia backed Patrice Lumumba's central government, and in doing so won the support of African governments that sided with Lumumba. Indonesian officials argued with some success that the Dutch were trying to split Indonesia through a separate Papuan state, in the same way many African leaders thought Belgium was trying to split the Congo by backing separatists. Here, Jakarta deployed a powerful argument grounded in African-Asian solidarity and anticolonialism, recalling the 1955 Bandung conference and appealing to the Casablanca group's sympathy toward the new Non-Aligned Movement formed in Belgrade in 1961. Sukarno's notion of solidarity among the "new emerging forces" of Africa and Asia appealed more to some governments than did Papuan appeals to a putative pan-Africanism.

Papuan nationalists were further handicapped by the need to disarm Western concerns that their country might become "another Congo," fears that were already motivating policy. The US State Department's first study of the Papua problem evoked images of "witchcraft, the cutting off of the finger-ends of widows, and headhunting," and determined that "premature independence" would be counter to American and Western interests. Dutch officials warned of "a Congo situation" if they left Papua too quickly. "Another Congo cannot happen here," one Parna leader said, acknowledging the comparison.[41] Policy makers already disposed to view such cases as Papua through racial preconceptions did so all the more as Papuan diplomats stressed their identification with Africa. For many in the West, Africa still evoked images of the primitive. It was "the place of the savage, the natural abode of evil, the banquet hall of the cannibal, and the pit of blackness itself."[42] Yet the effort to disarm Western fears of another Congo alienated key African governments. When a Dutch diplomat told officials at Ghana's foreign ministry that premature withdrawal risked "a vacuum which would permit a situation similar to Congo to develop," he evoked only anger at colonial meddling in the Congo conflict.[43]

Both Washington and Jakarta saw the Papuans as mired in the Stone Age, a factor that eased American policy makers' journey from neutrality to a more pro-Indonesian stance on the Papua issue. There was no effort to ascertain Papuan views: ideas of Papua as hopelessly primitive underpinned a strategic calculation. Ironically, this came even as Papuan views were becoming clearer and more vocal in support of self-determination. The New Guinea Council issued a note on self-determination in February 1962 that made its stance crystal clear: "The Papuan people as an ethnological unit has the right to decide its own fate in pursuance of item 2 of the decolonisation resolution 1514 (XV). . . . As set out in item 6 of the Decolonisation Resolution of the United Nations No. 1514 (XV), an insufficient economic or social development of the population should in itself not justify the prevention of the right to self-determination from being exercised."[44] This statement was followed up with a decision to send missions overseas to African and Asian countries, including Indonesia; a call for independence by 1970 at the latest; and an acceptance of trusteeship by the United Nations or by any country other than Indonesia.

Similarly, Papuan exiles in Indonesia were moving toward a call for self-determination. Silas Papare and his supporters had worked closely with

Indonesian authorities until their declaration of an autonomous provincial government-in-exile failed to win Indonesian government support. In 1960, Papare was pensioned off, at age forty-two, from his position as an ex officio member of the Indonesian parliament. After the election of the New Guinea Council and the inauguration of new nationalist symbols, Papare told the American ambassador that he faced arrest for being too critical of Sukarno. Three New Guinea councillors had asked him to return and assist in an independence declaration, he said. Papuan nationalists were simply "awaiting his return before announcing independence." He said he wanted to return to be part of a new Papuan state, and asked for American aid to "assist and protect new nation." This episode came just days after Indonesian foreign minister Subandrio described Papare as "by far the best" of the Papuans living in Indonesia, and the likely candidate for governor of a future Indonesian province.[45] Papare's back-channel negotiations with members of the New Guinea Council were a sign that the two streams of Papuan nationalism, which had diverged in 1945–1949, were converging. Those nationalists proved too weak, however, to assert themselves as an international force independent of their respective patrons.

In Washington, Papua appeared as a land too hopelessly primitive to dream of self-determination. "For those Americans who could find it on a map," Bradley Simpson points out, "West New Guinea was a blank slate upon which they could write their fantasies about primitive people and the benefits of encounter with the West."[46] Stone Age images began to reach a wider American audience beginning with the 1961 Harvard-Peabody anthropological expedition to the Dani people of the interior mountains, and the many photographs of scantily clad Dani men and topless Dani women transmitted home. From it came a series of books and films such as the anthropological classic *Dead Birds*, often previewed in photographic spreads in US magazines.[47] Also prominent in Western depictions were the Asmat, profiled in the 1960 film *Le Ciel et la Boue* (released in English in 1961 as *The Sky Above, the Earth Below*). Michael Rockefeller, a promising young anthropologist whose family name always conjured attention, added a fascination with Asmat art, shipping large amounts of it home to New York. Asmat art, like "Negro art," allowed collectors to praise its beauty while still looking down on its makers as primitive.[48] In early 1962, Rockefeller drowned on an expedition to the Asmat. The search for his body, never found, featured the personal participation of his father, New York governor Nelson Rockefeller. This made headlines, and underlined the image of Papua as hopelessly exotic, hostile, and primitive.

Rockefeller's romantic swim and the still more romantic search for signs of his body (or even his miraculous survival) stirred American imaginations far more than did his fascination with Asmat artistic "remnants of a marvelous past."[49] Press accounts stressed unchanging timelessness. A photograph used in 1940 coverage of an American aircrew that crashed in the interior lands of the Dani peoples was used, as if current, in 1961—with "native of Shangri-La" now captioned instead as "Typical Native—More Primitive Than Civilized." If anything, the imagery had become *less* sympathetic to Dani peoples over time. In the 1940s, comic-book stories like "WAC in Shangri-La" celebrated adventure, but by the 1960s, the land and people seemed hostile. Helpful natives who had been "good farmers" in the 1940s comic became "a savage tribe focused on war" in a 1961 *New York Times* report.[50]

The land merged with the people in explorers' stories. Explorer Heinrich Harrer's 1962 mission to the interior aimed at both conquering the last unclimbed mountain and unearthing the secrets of the Dani people. His account combined with reports from the Harvard anthropologists to make the Dani the predominant representatives of West New Guinea in the US popular imagination: Harrer portrayed them as wild children, unpredictable as puppies, capable of enormous and thoughtless cruelties as well as "richly comic" moments.[51] A war over control of this land seemed absurd, yet one nevertheless loomed as Indonesian troops began to infiltrate Papua in support of their government's claim. National Security Adviser McGeorge Bundy cited a book of photographs, *Les papous coupeurs de têtes* (Papuan headhunters), as evidence that Papuans were far from "ready" for self-determination.[52] As Indonesian-Dutch tensions flared into jungle skirmishes and naval clashes, Indonesia began to receive significant shipments of Soviet arms. US policy makers began to work to avoid a war in Southeast Asia. Kennedy said "he had a couple of wars in Southeast Asia; and West New Guinea was one he would like not to have to fight. . . . Laos and Vietnam were enough."[53]

Kennedy administration thinking on Papua was consciously racialized. A war "would have been white men against the Africans, the Asians, and the Communists," Robert Kennedy recalled.[54] The administration already faced a divisive internal battle over civil rights that raised issues of American identity and racial inclusion. Its foreign policy aimed at winning over the global South, inhabited mainly by peoples of color. Civil rights progress at home aimed, in Mary Dudziak's telling, to recount "a story of progress, a story of the triumph of good over evil, a story of US moral superiority." Racism was America's "Achilles' heel" in foreign policy.[55] That approach would have been undermined by any conflict pitting Europeans against Third World countries along racial lines. Papua policy was not a case of US government ignorance of the Papuan political situation. With conceptions of the primitive in the background, the administration acted on its own mental maps. Those privileged the global over the local and saw autonomous regional developments mostly through Cold War lenses.

Visiting Indonesia, Robert Kennedy made remarks hinting at Papuan primitivism that enraged Papuan leaders. Drawing parallels to American history, a group of New Guinea councillors called those words "advice to Indonesia to eradicate Papuan people just like in history other people have been almost eradicated because they were so backwards not to know shotguns and firewater." In a telegram to the White House, they added: "Independence and democracy can be understood and practiced by common people even if they have not seen Harvard." This was filed with a State Department note stating, "There is no advantage to be gained in replying to these persons." Papuan resentment of the Kennedy administration role continues to linger. One recent nationalist publication complains of Kennedy's "Anti-Papua" feelings, arguing that the president's "disregard for West Papua" combined "America's economic and political interests" with "JFK's revengeful attitude toward West Papua," a result of the death of Michael Rockefeller.[56]

With few prospects of Western support, Papuan appeals to Africa seemed the only hope of generating new international support for self-determination. They continued to foster the Brazzaville connection, hosting a visit by the heads of the Upper Volta and Dahomey UN delegations in April 1962. American officials tried at the last minute to have the Dutch prevent this visit, expressing "qualms over this project" and worrying it would encourage the New Guinea Council to declare independence. They sought and obtained Dutch assurances that there would be no Papuan independence declaration in April.[57]

Dahomey's delegate, Maxime-Léopold Zollner, returned to New York "profoundly struck by the racial differences between the inhabitants of New Guinea and those of Indonesia." Ambassador Guirma of Upper Volta was also "deeply impressed by the ethnical differences between Papuans and the inhabitants of Indonesia which led him to disregard Djakarta's contention that West Irians are Indonesians." Papuan nationalists toured Africa in the first half of 1962. Visits and appeals included the Brazzaville group, with trips to Upper Volta, Senegal, Côte d'Ivoire, and Dahomey. But they aimed especially at key states seen as having strong Third World nationalist credentials: Ethiopia, Liberia, Nigeria, Ghana, the Congo, Guinea, and Sierra Leone. Kaisiepo said Papuans "did not want to be handed over to Indonesia like cattle" but would not declare a premature independence. The key effort was to win support in Ghana. There, officials were reportedly "struck not so much by the strength of the West New Guinea [Papua] case as by the color and the physiognomy of the West New Guineans, who they thought would look like Indonesians. Their strong resemblance to Africans surprised the Ghanaians and made at least one of the officials think that perhaps Ghana was supporting the wrong side in the dispute." That did not lead to any policy change, however: Ghana's alignment with Indonesia mattered more. "We share your views completely and stand behind you," the Papuans were told, "but Nkrumah is a great friend of Sukarno's and therefore we have to vote against."[58] The imperatives of Afro-Asian solidarity trumped Papuan appeals to pan-Africanism.

Sympathy was higher in newly independent Tanganyika, where Prime Minister Julius Nyerere's government proposed a ceasefire, a temporary Indonesian trusteeship accountable to the United Nations, and a UN office in Papua empowered to hold free elections on the territory's future sponsored elections as soon as "the United Nations thinks the time is ripe to do so." Tanganyikan diplomats called for immediate talks and offered to mediate. Tanganyika's "first faltering step" into diplomacy should not be taken seriously for its own sake, but simply as an example of poor planning in new African foreign ministries, the US embassy's report sniffed.[59]

In the first half of 1962, Indonesian-Dutch talks mediated by American diplomat Ellsworth Bunker led to a plan for transfer from Dutch to UN administration, followed by a transfer to Indonesia soon afterward, then some form of self-determination to be carried out by Indonesian authorities later on. This in effect accepted Indonesian arguments. US government pressure finally managed to extract Dutch agreement as well, and a final deal along those lines was signed in August 1962. Papuan nationalist leaders experienced that as betrayal. One petition called the Bunker plan "a fire that will burn us citizens of West Papua to death." A group of leaders in the nationalist stronghold of Biak "reject[ed] Mr. Bunker's proposal, because it leads to the enslavement and destruction of the people of Papua Barat by the modern imperialisme [sic] of Indonesia." Citing the UN resolution on ending colonialism in an appeal sent to the United Nations, Dutch authorities, and the Brazzaville states, they declared that "the rights of small nations are the same as those of the big nations. Thus the rights of the Papuans are the same as those of the Americans and the rights of the Papuans are the same as those of the Burmese." Based on the promise of independence, Papuan nationalists had defined their nation in opposition to Indonesia, but now they faced the prospect of early Indonesian rule.[60] Yet the cry for independence persisted. Parna renewed its call for independence by 1970. The Papuan National Council agreed to the Dutch-Indonesian deal but demanded that the UN authority recognize their flag and anthem and that a plebiscite be held by the end of 1963. A new Papuan National Front asked to send a delegation to UN headquarters to renegotiate the Bunker plan, calling for a plebiscite on self-determination to be held before the UN administration left, and for UN administrators to serve as deputies to Papuan counterparts. Pro-independence rallies across the territory waved signs with such messages as "We are not merchandise" and "How many Yankee dollars for selling Papua?" Similar sentiments came from outlying regions. A group in Manokwari, at the opposite end of Papua from the capital, announced:

"We stick to the flag of West Papua which is the nationalist symbol of West Papua."[61] From the Dani lands, only five years after the arrival of Dutch colonial administrators, anthropologist Karl Heider reported that "the enthusiasm for Papua Barat [West Papua] is great and, I think, mostly genuine. They have a flag, a song, and a name, and now a growing sense of identification. If Sukarno does take the country, he will be stuck with an area which is not only economically useless, but politically resentful."[62] Elite nationalism, driven by diplomatic imperatives, was being widely embraced.

This did not alter the determination of UN officials to manage a smooth transition to Indonesian rule. There was little knowledge of the situation on the ground, with UN officials for instance exclaiming with surprise that Papua's lingua franca was a version of Malay, as was Indonesia's (and, though this was not stated, Malaysia's too).[63] Indonesian officials stressed taking possession, more than liberation. Subandrio declared that Indonesia would "introduce civilization" in the interior and made it "quite clear that they have no intention of keeping . . . their agreement with the Netherlands" to hold a plebiscite.[64]

Although Parna leader E. J. Bonay was appointed as the first governor of the Indonesian province of West Irian, he was soon removed as untrustworthy, then arrested. Silas Papare, passed over for governor, was arrested during the UN administration period in 1962. One by one, Papuan leaders found their way into jail or exile. Nationalist groups formed to lobby for independence from bases in the Netherlands, Senegal, Japan, and elsewhere. The language of racial difference from Indonesia remained central. A heavily documented appeal to U Thant and to the UN Commission on Human Rights in 1965, for instance, concluded: "it is becoming clear to us that the Indonesians seriously intend to wipe out the 750.000 Papuans, of the NEGROID RACE, of[f] the face of their native earth, West Papua/West New Guinea, by brute force" and replace them with Indonesian migrants. "Papuans belong to a *Negroid race, not* Indonesian," a Papuan youth group wrote the same year.[65]

A flurry of international diplomacy in 1969 tried to ensure that the "act of free choice" held by Indonesia in keeping with the terms of the 1962 agreement would be a real act of self-determination, not a piece of political theater. Jouwe's Freedom Committee of West Papua–West New Guinea called on the United Nations to provide an armed peacekeeping and protection force. It argued that the United Nations was "co-responsible for the fate and future of the Papuan people," given its role in handing the territory over to Indonesian rule. The same call went out to key Western governments but was met with silence or rejection. UN observers were said to have a stack of Papuan protest letters "a foot thick" handed over by such clandestine methods as being hidden inside seashells.[66] When the act saw the 1,023 electors chosen by Indonesian authorities opt unanimously for integration into Indonesia, the majority of African governments refused to endorse the UN report accepting this as valid. Lingering sympathy for Papuan independence saw most Brazzaville states withhold their consent for Indonesian formal annexation. Ghana, now more convinced of the logic of the Papuan case and less in sympathy with General Suharto's New Order regime in Indonesia, tried without success to amend the UN resolution, taking note of the act to require a further chance for free choice by 1975. Fifteen African states refused in the General Assembly voting to "take note" of the UN representative's report, a result of Papuan lobbying of African governments.[67]

Indonesian rule, among its other harshly repressive aspects, aimed at removing the racial basis of Papuan identity. The "transmigration" program, for instance, aimed to move large numbers of Indonesian peasants from densely populated Java into Papua. Claims of racial difference nevertheless have been central to continued Papuan independence campaigning. Testifying to the UN Commission on Human Rights, for instance, the Free Papua Movement sought an end to "the obliteration of the Papuan Negroid or Melanesian people in West Papua" and recalled Brazzaville group support of the "Negroid people of West Papua." This support network continues to linger, seen for instance in recent lobbying for Papuan human rights by the US Congressional Black Caucus.[68]

Conclusion

There is nothing inevitable about the course of identity formation in Papua. It was driven by the contingent needs of the various diplomatic actors, and by international rather than domestic factors. The demands of diplomacy in the period from 1949 to 1962, however, formed the basis for what is now a lasting and deeply held Papuan sense of nationalism.

Papuans were first equated with Africans in the nineteenth century, in the context of European defining and ordering of races. Colonial rule then codified and entrenched those perceived differences. Dutch rule over Papua continued after the rest of the Dutch East Indies became independent as Indonesia. Once the territory had been split from Indonesia, a justification was needed. Dutch rulers found it in a renewed mission of tutelage over a people newly defined as Papuan or Melanesian through the work of colonial anthropologists. What had been a political convenience to justify colonialism became the rallying cry for a people coming to think of themselves as Papuans. To gain international support, they sought allies who could be seen to share their new identity. This meant in the first case ethnic Melanesian peoples in the South

Pacific, and then the African continent. Yet the same factors that led to identification with Melanesia and Africa cost Papuan nationalists their prospects of new overseas support. The idea that violence in the Congo was the result of "premature independence" forced Papuan leaders to offer reassurances to the West that cost them the prospect of support from such key African states as Ghana. The identification with Africa also reinforced Western policy makers' ideas that Papuans were "primitives" living in "the Stone Age" and thus not ready for self-determination. Papuan nationalists were not able to overcome these obstacles. For all their efforts to speak for themselves, they did not manage to make themselves heard internationally. Nevertheless, the identity forged in a diplomatic contest that peaked in the early 1960s continues to define the indigenous inhabitants of Papua. The strength of this identity is, if anything, stronger after half a century of Indonesian rule.

Notes

1. Parts of this chapter were previously published as a journal article, "Regimes in Motion: The Kennedy Administration and Indonesia's New Frontier, 1960–1962," *Diplomatic History* 33, no. 1 (January 2009): 95–123, and are reprinted with the permission of *Diplomatic History* and Wiley Periodicals Inc.
2. The territory has a multitude of names. Papua is the oldest name for the island also known as New Guinea. Both names appear in the current designation of the eastern half of the island, Papua New Guinea. The western half became the colony of Netherlands New Guinea (or West New Guinea). Papuan nationalists created the name Irian in the 1940's, and the term was adopted in Indonesia as West Irian (Irian Barat) even as the Dutch continued to use the name West New Guinea. Papuan nationalists selected the new name West Papua in 1961. In 1963, the territory became the Indonesian province of West Irian, and was then renamed Irian Jaya (Great Irian) in 1969. The Indonesian government renamed the province as Papua in response to local demand in 2001. For convenience, the name Papua is used throughout this chapter.
3. This and following quotes taken from *Voice of the Negroids in the Pacific to the Negroids throughout the World* (Papuan nationalist pamphlet published in Hollandia, 1962).
4. *Voice of the Negroids.*
5. Papuan National Committee appeal to "all fellow-tribesmen of the Negroids throughout the world," March 19, 1962.
6. "Motion à Son Excellence le Secrétaire general des Nations Unies," passed at meeting of four thousand Papuans, Numfor Island, July 24, 1962, UN Archives, S-0884-23-1.
7. Katherine McKittrick and Clyde Woods, *Black Geographies and the Politics of Place* (Toronto: Between the Lines; Cambridge, MA: South End Press, 2007), 4.

8. C. L. M. Penders, *The West New Guinea Debacle: Dutch Decolonisation and Indonesia, 1945–1962* (Honolulu: University of Hawaii Press, 2002), 89–90.

9. E. J. Bonay, unpublished memoir, cited in Richard Chauvel, *Constructing Papuan Nationalism: History, Ethnicity and Adaptation* (Washington: East-West Center, 2005), 40.

10. Onnie Lumintang et al., *Biografi Pahlawan Nasional, Marthin Indey dan Silas Papare* [A biography of national heroes Marthin Indey and Silas Papare] (Jakarta: Proyek Inventarisasi dan Dokumentasi Sejarah Nasional, Direktorat Jenderal Kebudayaan, Departemen Pendidikian dan Kebudayaan, 1997); and Richard Chauvel, "Decolonising without the Colonised: The Liberation of West Irian," in *Las relaciones internacionales en el Pacífico* (Siglos XVIII–XX): *Colonización, descolonización, y encuentro cultural* [International relations in the Pacific (18th–20th centuries): Colonization, decolonization, and cultural encounter], ed. M. Dolores Elizade, 553–74 (Madrid: Consejo Superior de Investigaciones Cientificas, 1997).

11. Danilyn Fox Rutherford, "Trekking to New Guinea: Dutch Colonial Fantasies of a Virgin Land, 1900–1942," in *Domesticating the Empire*, ed. Julia Clancy-Smith and Frances Gouda (Charlottesville: University Press of Virginia, 1998), 255–71; Frances Gouda, *Dutch Culture Overseas: Colonial Practice in the Netherlands East Indies, 1900–1942* (Amsterdam: Amsterdam University Press, 1995); Arend Lijphart, *The Trauma of Decolonization: The Dutch and West New* Guinea (New Haven, CT: Yale University Press, 1966); and Justus van der Kroef, "The Eurasians of West New Guinea," *United Asia* 14 (1962): 123–28.

12. Chris Ballard, Steven Vink, and Anton Ploeg, *Race to the Snow: Photography and the Exploration of Dutch New Guinea, 1907–1936* (Amsterdam: Royal Tropical Institute, 2001), 7.

13. Gerald Horne, *The White Pacific: U.S. Imperialism and Black Slavery in the South Seas after the Civil War* (Honolulu: University of Hawaii Press, 2007), 2, 63, 133.

14. Silas Papare, "The 'Partai Kemerdekaan Indonesia Irian' [Irian party for Indonesian Independence]," in Ministry of Information, *The Truth about West Irian* (Jakarta: Ministry of Information, 1956), 18–21; Wolas Krenak, "Mengenang Irian Barat 36 Tahun Silam: Kisah 'Orang-orang Merah' dan 'Tuan-tuan Merdeka'" [Commemorating West Irian 36 years ago: "Reds" and "Freedom Champions"], *Suara Pemabaruan*, April 30, 1999; "Keadaan Politik" [The political situation], unpublished document attributed to Free Papua Movement; Ministry of Foreign Affairs, *The Question of West Irian* (Jakarta: Ministry of Foreign Affairs, 1955), 30–32; Nonie Sharp, *The Morning Star in Papua Barat* (North Carlton, Australia: Arena, 1994), 94; and PKII resolution, March 1949, in Lumintang et al., *Pahlawan Nasional*, 86–87.

15. H. W. Bullock, "Netherlands New Guinea—Markus Kasiepo [*sic*]," memorandum for Australian Department of External Affairs, November 4, 1960, copy on file at Library and Archives Canada (hereafter LAC), Record Group 25/6149/50409-40[6.1].

16. Walter Francis White, *A Rising Wind: A Report on the Negro Soldier in the European Theater of War* (Garden City, NJ: Doubleday Doran, 1945), 155, 147; W. E. B. Du Bois

memorandum to NAACP secretary and board, September 7, 1948, cited in David Levering Lewis, *W. E. B. Du Bois: The Fight for Equality and the American Century, 1919–1963* (New York: Henry Holt, 2000), 534; and Robert J. McMahon, *Colonialism and the Cold War: The United States and the Struggle for Indonesian Independence, 1945–1949* (Ithaca, NY: Cornell University Press, 1981).

17. Penders, *Debacle*, 155.
18. *Western New Guinea and the Netherlands* (The Hague: Netherlands Government State Printing Office, 1954), 11.
19. Danilyn Fox Rutherford, "Trekking to New Guinea: Dutch Colonial Fantasies of a Virgin Land, 1900–1942," in *Domesticating the Empire: Race, Gender, and Family Life in French and Dutch Colonialism*, ed. Julia Clancy-Smith and Frances Gouda (Charlottesville: University Press of Virginia, 1998), 268.
20. Penders, *Debacle*, 396.
21. *Handbook on Netherlands New Guinea* (Rotterdam: New Guinea Institute, 1958), 5.
22. Ministry of Information, *The Truth about West Irian*, 5–7; and "West Irian and Pseudo-Science," *Indonesian Spectator*, May 15, 1958, 15.
23. "Bebaskan Irian" [Free Irian], in *Irian Barat*, ed. M. Silaban (Medan: Pustaka Sri, n.d.), 56.
24. Lumintang et al., *Pahlawan Nasional*; Ministry of Information, *The Autonomous Province of West Irian* (Jakarta: Ministry of Information, 1956); *The Case of West Irian (West New Guinea)* (Cairo: Indonesian Embassy, n.d.), 37–38; Ministry of Information, *The Truth about West Irian*, 13–17; and Ministry of Foreign Affairs, *The Question of West Irian* (Jakarta: Ministry of Foreign Affairs, 1955), 18, 30–32.
25. Kaisiepo oral history and letter to the Dutch Reformed Church in Sharp, *The Morning Star*; and Papuan public meeting resolution, July 1956, in *Nieuw Guinea spruikt zich uit* [New Guinea speaks out] (Hollandia, New Guinea: Netherlands New Guinea administration, 1956), 15–18.
26. R. E. Elson, *The Idea of Indonesia: A History* (Cambridge: Cambridge University Press, 2008), 63, 223; and Arend Lijpart, "The Indonesian Idea of West Irian," *Asian Survey* 1, no. 5 (July 1961): 9–16. The idea of countries as "geo-bodies" is explored in Thongchai Winichakul, *Siam Mapped* (Honolulu: University of Hawaii Press, 1994).
27. Herlina, *The Golden Buckle* (Yogyakarta, Indonesia: Gadjah Mada University Press, 1990), 82, 85, 292–9; Subandrio quoted in Peter Hastings, "Double Dutch and Indons," in *Melanesia: Beyond Diversity*, ed. R. J. May and Hank Nelson (Canberra: Australian National University Research School of Pacific Studies, 1982), 159; and Justus van der Kroef, *The West New Guinea Dispute* (New York: Institute for Pacific Relations, 1958), 41n116.
28. "Papuan Politicians Yesterday, Today, and Tomorrow," Free Papua Movement summary document.
29. Frances Gouda, "Languages of Gender and Neurosis in the Indonesian Struggle for Independence," *Indonesia* 64 (October 1997): 45–76; and Tineke Hellwig, "A Double Murder in Batavia: Representations of Gender and Race in the Indies," *Review of Indonesian and Malaysian Affairs* 35, no. 2 (Summer 2001): 1–32.
30. Canadian Embassy in Jakarta to Canadian DEA, April 25, 1960, LAC, RG25/6148/50409-40[4.2].

31. Henry S. Albinski, "Australia and the Dutch New Guinea Dispute," *International Journal* 16 (1961): 379; and Nicolaas Jouwe, "Conflict at the Meeting Point of Melanesia and Asia," *Pacific Islands Monthly (PIM)*, April 1978, 12.

32. Justus van der Kroef, "Recent Developments in West New Guinea," *Pacific Affairs* 34 (1961/1962): 281.

33. Manifesto of the First Papuan Congress, October 19, 1961; P. W. van der Veur, "Questionnaire Survey among the Potential Papuan Elite in 1962 West New Guinea," *Bijdragen tot de Taal-, Land- en Volkenkunde* 120 (1964): 445; "Ten Questions on the West Irian Dispute between Indonesia and the Netherlands," *Report on Indonesia (ROI)*, January 1962, 7; and W. W. Rostow memorandum to John F. Kennedy, November 30, 1961, John F. Kennedy Library (JFKL), National Security Files (NSF), Box 205.

34. Canadian Embassy in The Hague to DEA, December 16, 1960, and November 18, 1960, LAC, RG25/6149/50409[6.1].

35. Justus van der Kroef, "Nationalism and Politics in West New Guinea," *Pacific Affairs* 31 (1961/1962): 42; Penders, *Debacle*, 401, 407–19; "Dutch New Guinea Has a Political Party," *PIM*, September 1960, 23; "They Want a Republic," *PIM*, April 1961, 20; and "Dutch Plan Thwarted," *ROI*, December 19, 1961.

36. June Verrier, "Australia, Papua New Guinea, and the West New Guinea Question, 1949–1969" (PhD diss., Monash University, 1976), 203; and Bilveer Singh, *Papua: Geopolitics and the Quest for Nationhood* (New Brunswick, NJ: Transaction Publishers, 2008), 63–64.

37. Declaration of South Pacific nationalist leaders, 1962, UN Archives, S-0229-25-2.

38. James Campbell, *Middle Passages: African American Journeys to Africa, 1787–2005* (New York: Penguin, 2006), 317; Lewis, *W. E. B. Du Bois*, 565; Von Eschen, *Race against Empire*, 139–40; and Maya Angelou, *All God's Children Need Traveling Shoes* (New York: Vintage, 1991), 77.

39. Subandrio, *An Opening Address to the UN Political Committee* (Jakarta: Ministry of Foreign Affairs [1957]), 8; Benedict Anderson, *Imagined Communities*, 2nd ed. (London: Verso, 1991), 170–78; Luns speech to UN General Assembly, September 26, 1961, UN Office of Information, *General Assembly Official Records*, A/PV.1016, 90-1; US delegation at UN to Rusk, October 11, 1961, JFKL, NSF Box 205; *Indonesian Observer*, October 12, 1961; and "Nugroho Warns U.S. of Potential Danger in West Irian Dispute," *ROI*, May 1962, 11.

40. Secretary of State Dean Rusk to UN Ambassador Adlai Stevenson, November 24, 1961; Stevenson to Rusk, November 29, 1961, JFKL, NSF Box 205; and Howard P. Jones, *Indonesia: The Possible Dream* (New York: Harcourt Brace Jovanovich, 1971), 45.

41. Policy Planning Staff study, "The Problem of West New Guinea (West Irian)," October 12, 1960, JFKL, NSF Box 205; Dutch Ambassador J. H. van Roijen to US Ambassador Ellsworth Bunker, April 14, 1962, UN Archives, S-0884-22-5; and Herman Wajoi, cited in "Nationalist Stir Felt by Papuans," *New York Times*, April 3, 1961.

42. Charles J. Patterson, "What Is Africa to Me?," *Transition* 15 (1964): 20.

43. Canadian High Commission in Accra to DEA, January 10, 1962, LAC, RG 25/6149/50409-40[9].

44. New Guinea Council advisory note concerning the use of the right to self-determination, February 16, 1962, Appendix to Viktor Kaisiepo, "The Case of West Papua Sovereignty," background paper for expert seminar on treaties, agreements and other constructive arrangements between states and indigenous peoples, Geneva, December 15–17, 2003, UN document HR/GENEVA/TSIP/SEM/2003/BP.16.

45. US Embassy in Jakarta to State Department, December 15, 1961, and January 8, 1962, JFKL, NSF Box 205; and Lumintang et al., *Pahlawan Nasional*.

46. Bradley R. Simpson, *Economists with Guns: Authoritarian Development and U.S.-Indonesian Relations, 1960–1968* (Stanford, CA: Stanford University Press, 2008), 45.

47. Robert F. Gardner and Karl G. Heider, *Gardens of War: Life and Death in the New Guinea Stone Age* (London: Andre Deutsch, 1969); "The Ancient World of a War-Torn Tribe," *Life*, September 28, 1962; Peter Matthiesson, *Under the Mountain Wall* (New York: Ballantine, 1962); and Robert Gardner, *Making Dead Birds: Chronicle of a Film* (Cambridge, MA: Peabody Museum Press, 2007).

48. George Schuyler wrote that "Negro Art" reassured whites that Negro meant savage: "Even when he appears to be civilized, it is only necessary to beat a tom tom or wave a rabbit's foot and he is ready to strip off his Hart Shaffner & Marx suit, grab a spear and ride off wild-eyed on the back of a crocodile." Quoted in Campbell, *Middle Passages*, 205.

49. Rockefeller letter, July 10, 1961, in *The Asmat: The Journal of Michael Clark Rockefeller* (New York: Museum of Primitive Art, 1967), 43; and Milt Machlin, *The Search for Michael Rockefeller* (New York: Putnam, 1972).

50. Undated press clipping from scrapbook and "WAC in Shangri La" (1945), reprinted in Susan Meiselas, *Encounters with the Dani* (New York: International Center of Photography, 2003), 21, 29–31; "Rocky Son Lost in N. Guinea," *Boston Record American*, November 20, 1961, reprinted in Gardner, *Making Dead Birds*, 108; and Homer Bigart, "Harvard Expedition Discovers a Warrior Tribe in New Guinea," *New York Times*, April 5, 1961.

51. Heinrich Harrer, *I Come from the Stone Age* (London: Rupert Hart-Davis, 1964), 255.

52. Robert P. Martin, "War over This—?," *U.S. News and World Report*, February 5, 1962, 44; and McGeorge Bundy to Robert Gardner, August 18, 1962, reprinted in Meiselas, *Encounters with the Dani*, 114. Transmittal slips on file at JFKL indicate that Komer passed this book to Bundy as evidence of the primitiveness of all Papuans, not just the Dani.

53. Walter W. Rostow (interviewee), recorded interview by Richard Neustadt (interviewer), April 11, 1964 (pp. 88–89), JFKL Oral History Program.

54. Edwin O. Guthman and Jeffrey Schulman, eds., *Robert Kennedy in His Own Words* (Toronto: Bantam, 1988), 315–16.

55. Mary L. Dudziak, Cold *War Civil Rights: Race and the Image of American Democracy* (Princeton, NJ: Princeton University Press, 2002), 13, 29.

56. New Guinea councillors group telegram to President Kennedy, March 6, 1962; State Department Executive Secretary L. D. Battle to McGeorge Bundy of National Security staff, March 8, 1962, JFKL, NSF Box 206; and West Papuan Community,

West Papua: The Case We Knew/Papua Barat: Yang Kami Tahu (West Papua Community, 2000).

57. US Embassy in Jakarta to State Dept., March 31, 1962, and March 23, 1961, JFKL, NSF Box 206; and Rusk to US Embassy in the Hague, March 23, 1961, March 31, 1962, and April 1, 1962, JFKL, NSF Box 206.

58. Canadian delegation to UN memorandum, June 7, 1962, LAC, RG25/6150/50409-40[12.2]; Canadian Embassy in Accra to DEA, June 13, 1962, LAC, RG25/6150/50409-40[12.2]; and Canadian Embassy in Accra to DEA, January 10, 1962, LAC, RG 25/6149/50409-40[9].

59. Tanganyikan delegation to UN proposals to U Thant, April 9, 1962, UN Archives, S-0884-22-5; and US Embassy in Dar es Salaam to State Dept., April 11, 1962, JFKL, NSF Box 206.

60. Resolution signed by twenty-six Papuan leaders, cited in Penders, *Debacle*, 429; and undated [1962] Biak-Numfor declarations on file at UN Archives, S-0884-23-1.

61. Robin Osborne, *Indonesia's Secret War: The Guerrilla Struggle in Irian Jaya* (Sydney: Allen and Unwin, 1985), 31–32; Peter Savage, "Irian Jaya: Reluctant Colony," in *Politics in Melanesia*, ed. R. G. Crocombe and Ahmed Ali (Suva: University of the South Pacific, 1982), 90; Papuan National Front proposals, August 31, 1962, UN Archives, S-0279-25-5; and "Mass Protests by Papuans," *Sydney Morning Herald* (*SMH*), August 10, 1962.

62. Heider to Robert Gardner, January 11, 1962, in Gardner, *Making Dead Birds*, 111.

63. Note on declaration of Sorong Doom leaders, UN Archives, S-0884-23-1.

64. British Embassy in Jakarta to Foreign Office, June 7, 1963, LAC, RG25/6150/50409-40[13].

65. Freedom Committee of West Papua/West New Guinea, memorandum handed to UN Secretary-General's chef de cabinet, C. V. Narasimhan, November 19, 1965, UN Archives, S-0279-31-2; and Papuan Independent Movement, "The Exclamation from Jungle," June 1965.

66. Freedom Committee of West Papua/West New Guinea to U Thant, May 21, 1969, UN Archives, S-0279-25-12; "Irians Seek UN 'Protection' Force," *SMH*, May 27, 1969; "Papuan Asks If Canada Will Help," *Auckland Star*, June 26, 1969; "'Free Choice'—as Long as You Vote 'Yes,'" editorial, *Auckland Star*, July 19, 1969; and "Strong Opposition to Irian Vote," *New Zealand Herald*, July 14, 1969. The 1969 "act of free choice" is covered in detail in John Saltford, *The United Nations and the Indonesian Takeover of West Papua, 1962–1969: The Anatomy of Betrayal* (London: RoutledgeCurzon, 2002).

67. UN Office of Information, *Official Records of the General Assembly*, A/PV.1127, A/PV.1150.

68. I have discussed later Papuan nationalism in David Webster, "'Already Sovereign as a People': A Foundational Moment in Papuan Nationalism," *Pacific Affairs* 74, no. 4 (Winter 2001–2002): 507–28.

References

ARCHIVES
John F. Kennedy Library, Boston, MA
Library and Archives Canada, Ottawa, Ontario, Canada
UN Archives and Records Management, New York, NY

PUBLISHED GOVERNMENT DOCUMENTS, REPORTS, AND SERIALS
Handbook on Netherlands New Guinea. Rotterdam: New Guinea Institute, 1958.
Kaisiepo, Viktor. "The Case of West Papua Sovereignty." Background paper for expert
    seminar on treaties, agreements, and other constructive arrangements between
    states and indigenous peoples, Geneva, December 15–17, 2003.
Manifesto of the First Papuan Congress, October 19, 1961. *wpik.org/Src/whosewho.html.*
Ministry of Foreign Affairs. *The Question of West Irian.* Jakarta: Ministry of Foreign
    Affairs, 1955.
Ministry of Information. *The Autonomous Province of West Irian.* Jakarta: Ministry of
    Information, 1956.
———. *The Truth about West Irian.* Jakarta: Ministry of Information, 1956.
Nieuw Guinea spruikt zich uit [New Guinea speaks out]. Hollandia, New Guinea:
    Netherlands New Guinea Administration, 1956.
Papuan Independent Movement. "The Exclamation from Jungle," June 1965.
"Papuan Politicians Yesterday, Today, and Tomorrow." Free Papua Movement summary
    document.
Subandrio. *Indonesia on the March.* Jakarta: Department of Foreign Affairs, [1963].
———. *An Opening Address to the UN Political Committee.* Jakarta: Ministry of Foreign
    Affairs, [1957].
UN Office of Information. *Official Records of the General Assembly.* New York: UN
    Office of Information, 1946–2012.
Voice of the Negroids in the Pacific to the Negroids throughout the World. Pamphlet.
    Hollandia, New Guinea, 1962.
Western New Guinea and the Netherlands. The Hague: Netherlands Government State
    Printing Office, 1954.
West Papuan Community. *West Papua: The Case We Knew/Papua Barat: Yang Kami
    Tahu.* West Papuan Community, 2000.
Yamin, Mohammad. *A Legal and Historical Review of Indonesia's Sovereignty over the
    Ages.* Manila: Indonesian Embassy [1959].

PERIODICALS
Auckland Star
Indonesian Observer
Indonesian Spectator
Life
National Geographic
New York Times

New Zealand Herald
Pacific Islands Monthly
Report on Indonesia
Suara Pembaruan
Sydney Morning Herald
U.S. News and World Report

SELECTED PUBLISHED WORKS

Albinski, Henry S. "Australia and the Dutch New Guinea Dispute." *International Journal* 16 (1961): 358–82.

Anderson, Benedict. *Imagined Communities*. 2nd ed. London: Verso, 1991.

Campbell, James. *Middle Passages: African American Journeys to Africa, 1787–2005*. New York: Penguin, 2006.

Chauvel, Richard. *Constructing Papuan Nationalism: History, Ethnicity, and Adaptation*. Washington, DC: East-West Center, 2005.

———. "Decolonising without the Colonised: The Liberation of West Irian." In *Las relaciones internacionales en el Pacífico (Siglos XVIII–XX): Colonización, descolonización, y encuentro cultural* [International relations in the Pacific (18th–20th centuries): Colonization, decolonization, and cultural encounter], edited by M. Dolores Elizade, 553–74. Madrid: Consejo Superior de Investigaciones Científicas, 1997.

Dudziak, Mary L. *Cold War Civil Rights: Race and the Image of American Democracy*. Princeton, NJ: Princeton University Press, 2002.

Elson, R. E. *The Idea of Indonesia: A History*. Cambridge: Cambridge University Press, 2008.

Gardner, Robert. *Making Dead Birds: Chronicle of a Film*. Cambridge, MA: Peabody Museum Press, 2007.

Gouda, Frances. *Dutch Culture Overseas: Colonial Practice in the Netherlands East Indies, 1900–1942*. Amsterdam: Amsterdam University Press, 1995.

———. "Languages of Gender and Neurosis in the Indonesian Struggle for Independence." *Indonesia* 64 (October 1997): 45–76.

Harrer, Heinrich. *I Come from the Stone Age*. London: Rupert Hart-Davis, 1964.

Hastings, Peter. "Double Dutch and Indons." In *Melanesia: Beyond Diversity*, edited by R .J. May and Hank Nelson, 157–62. Canberra: Australian National University, Research School of Pacific Studies, 1982.

Hellwig, Tineke. "A Double Murder in Batavia: Representations of Gender and Race in the Indies." *Review of Indonesian and Malaysian Affairs* 35, no. 2 (Summer 2001): 1–32.

Herlina. *The Golden Buckle*. Yogyakarta, Indonesia: Gadjah Mada University Press, 1990.

Horne, Gerald. *The White Pacific: U.S. Imperialism and Black Slavery in the South Seas after the Civil War*. Honolulu: University of Hawaii Press, 2007.

Kroef, Justus van der. "The Eurasians of West New Guinea." *United Asia* 14 (1962): 123–28.

116 | *Race, Ethnicity, and the Cold War: A Global Perspective*

———. "Nationalism and Politics in West New Guinea." *Pacific Affairs* 31 (1961/1962): 38–53.

———. "Recent Developments in West New Guinea." *Pacific Affairs* 34 (1961/1962): 279–91.

———. *The West New Guinea Dispute.* New York: Institute for Pacific Relations, 1958.

Lewis, David Levering. *W. E. B. Du Bois: The Fight for Equality and the American Century, 1919–1963.* New York: Henry Holt, 2000.

Lijphart, Arend. "The Indonesian Idea of West Irian." *Asian Survey* 1, no. 5 (July 1961): 9–16.

———. *The Trauma of Decolonization: The Dutch and West New Guinea.* New Haven, CT: Yale University Press, 1966.

Lumintang, Onnie, et al. *Biografi Pahlawan Nasional, Marthin Indey dan Silas Papare* [A biography of national heroes Marthin Indey and Silas Papare]. Jakarta: Proyek Inventarisasi dan Dokumentasi Sejarah Nasional, Direktorat Jenderal Kebudayaan, Departamen Pendidikian dan Kebudayaan, 1997.

Markin, Terrence. *The West Irian Dispute: How the Kennedy Administration Resolved That "Other" Southeast Asian Conflict.* PhD diss., Johns Hopkins University, 1996.

McKittrick, Katherine, and Clyde Woods. *Black Geographies and the Politics of Place.* Toronto: Between the Lines/Boston: South End Press, 2007.

McMahon, Robert J. *Colonialism and the Cold War: The United States and the Struggle for Indonesian Independence, 1945–1949.* Ithaca, NY: Cornell University Press, 1981.

Meiselas, Susan. *Encounters with the Dani.* New York: International Center of Photography, 2003.

Osborne, Robin. *Indonesia's Secret War: The Guerrilla Struggle in Irian Jaya.* Sydney: Allen and Unwin, 1985.

Patterson, Charles J. "What Is Africa to Me?" *Transition* 15 (1964): 20–22.

Penders, C. L. M. *The West New Guinea Debacle: Dutch Decolonisation and Indonesia, 1945–1962.* Honolulu: University of Hawaii Press, 2002.

Rutherford, Danilyn Fox. "Trekking to New Guinea: Dutch Colonial Fantasies of a Virgin Land, 1900–1942." In *Domesticating the Empire*, edited by Julia Clancy-Smith and Frances Gouda, 255–71. Charlottesville: University Press of Virginia, 1998.

Saltford, John. *The United Nations and the Indonesian Takeover of West Papua, 1962–1969: The Anatomy of Betrayal.* London: RoutledgeCurzon, 2002.

Savage, Peter. "Irian Jaya: Reluctant Colony." In *Politics in Melanesia,* edited by R. G. Crocombe and Ahmed Ali, 20–22. Suva: University of the South Pacific, 1982.

Sharp, Nonie. *The Morning Star in Papua Barat.* North Carlton, Australia: Arena, 1994.

Silaban, M., ed. *Irian Barat* [West Irian]. Medan: Pustaka Sri, n.d.

Simpson, Bradley R. *Economists with Guns: Authoritarian Development and U.S.-Indonesian Relations, 1960–1968.* Stanford, CA: Stanford University Press, 2008.

Singh, Bilveer. *Papua: Geopolitics and the Quest for Nationhood.* New Brunswick, NJ: Transaction Publishers, 2008.

Verrier, June. "Australia, Papua New Guinea, and the West New Guinea Question, 1949–1969." PhD diss., Monash University, 1976.

Veur, Paul W. van der. "Political Awakening in West New Guinea." *Pacific Affairs* 36, no. 1 (1963): 54–73.

———. "Questionnaire Survey among the Potential Papuan Elite in 1962 West New Guinea." *Bijdragen tot de Taal-, Land- en Volkenkunde* 120 (1964): 424–60.

Von Eschen, Penny. *Race against Empire: Black Americans and Anticolonialism, 1937–1957.* Ithaca, NY: Cornell University Press, 1997.

Webster, David. "'Already Sovereign as a People': A Foundational Moment in Papuan Nationalism." *Pacific Affairs* 74, no. 4 (Winter 2001–2002): 507–28.

———. "Regimes in Motion: The Kennedy Administration and Indonesia's New Frontier, 1960–1962." *Diplomatic History* 33, no. 1 (January 2009): 95–123.

White, Walter Francis. *A Rising Wind: A Report on the Negro Soldier in the European Theater of War.* Garden City, NJ: Doubleday Doran, 1945.

CHAPTER 5

"For a Better Guinea"

Winning Hearts and Minds in Portuguese Guinea

Luís Nuno Rodrigues

Between 1961 and 1974 Portugal fought three colonial wars in its African territories of Angola, Mozambique, and Guinea. The authoritarian regime in Lisbon, led since 1932 by Oliveira Salazar (succeeded in 1968 by Marcelo Caetano), believed it was essential that the country maintain its presence in Africa and was not prepared to decolonize or to find a political solution for the colonial conundrum. Several attempts toward a gradual process of decolonization had been made in the early years of the decade, either by internal forces or by international pressure, but Salazar and the Portuguese political and military elite adamantly refused.

One of the most serious problems was the situation in Portuguese Guinea. The poorest and least populated Portuguese colony in Africa, Portuguese Guinea was a small territory of thirty-six thousand square kilometers situated between Senegal and the Republic of Guinea, with a total population of around five hundred thousand, 1 percent of them white or mulatto.[1] In January 1963, the nationalist movement African Party for the Independence of Guinea and of Cape Verde (PAIGC), led by Amílcar Cabral, carried out its first successful military operation against colonial domination. The PAIGC military successes were rapid, and in the following months the nationalists conducted several military operations, including ambushes and the laying of mines. Faced with a deteriorating situation, in May 1964 the Portuguese government appointed Brigadier Arnaldo Schultz as commander-in-chief in Guinea. Schultz gambled on an essentially military strategy, in which he sought to "counter-attack" and regain control of the areas occupied by the PAIGC. The results, however, were clearly unsatisfactory from Lisbon's point of view. During the following years, the Portuguese military continued to lose territory as the nationalists extended their operations into the eastern part of Guinea.[2]

In 1968, Oliveira Salazar decided that it was time to make new changes in the military leadership of Portuguese Guinea. He called Brigadier António de Spínola, a cavalry officer who, at fifty-one years old, had offered himself as a volunteer when the first Portuguese colonial war started in Angola in 1961. Within the Portuguese Army, Spínola had emerged as a respected and charismatic commander; Salazar, with whom Spínola's father had worked in the early 1930s, soon heard of his exploits.[3] A few months after Spínola's nomination, however, Salazar suffered a cerebral-vascular accident and was replaced by Marcelo Caetano.

Almost the entire time Spínola commanded Portuguese forces in Guinea, Marcelo Caetano was the head of government—the true center of political power in Lisbon. Spínola viewed Caetano's arrival in power with optimism. His hopes lay in the belief that the new prime minister would be able to put a different colonial policy in place. Spínola openly identified with the ideas of the new head of government, believing that relations between the metropole and its overseas provinces—as the regime in Lisbon preferred to call the colonies—should develop into a broader "federation" of "commonwealth" states. As Spínola recalled, not only did he have "high hopes" about Caetano's arrival in power, he was a true "marcelista"—a keen supporter of the new prime minister.[4]

In April 1969, Caetano decided to visit Portugal's African colonies. This trip was an important moment for the prime minister, who returned convinced it would be an "ignoble betrayal to the people and to the work that has been done [in Africa] to establish pacts with small groups that, against the wishes of the majority, by mere adventurism and maintained only by international support, upset the general peace in one or another small part of our immense territories of Angola and Mozambique." Negotiations with the so-called terrorists were not an option, but Caetano recognized that the Portuguese colonial problem could not be resolved without some sort of change. The continuation of a Portuguese presence in Africa required the development of a "policy for the future" that outlined a "satisfactory solution." This solution did not mean "abandoning the *Ultramar*," nor did it mean the "premature" proclamation of independence under "white minority rule." It was important to find an "intermediate way," which Caetano was to label "progressive autonomy."[5]

During the following years, the development of this new policy moved slowly, accompanied by often contradictory public statements. Facing pressure and resistance from the Portuguese extreme right wing grouped around President Américo Tomás, reformist Caetano was not able to put in practice a new colonial policy and the wars continued in Guinea, Angola, and Mozambique, with growing desperation from junior officers in the Portuguese Army. It was not until December 1970 that the policy of "progressive autonomy" was incorporated into a proposed constitutional revision the government presented to the National Assembly in Lisbon, more than two years after Caetano had taken office as prime minister. This proposal then had to wait until August 1971 before it passed into law.[6] In June 1972, under the terms of the new constitutional regulations, the Organic Law for the Portuguese Ultramar (Lei Orgânica do Ultramar Português) was finally approved. In December, the new colonial statutes were published, which granted the title of "state" to Angola and Mozambique, but not to Guinea. The regulations never had any practical result. Most important, however, was the fact that four years had passed since Caetano had taken office—years during which the wars in Africa continued. The policy of progressive autonomy conceived by Marcelo Caetano meant the necessary continuation of the wars, the regime's real Gordian knot. Even as he looked to introduce reformist laws, Caetano maintained the "military commitment" that over time was to fatally undermine all his "reform programs," both domestically and in the colonies, and that led to the military coup of April 1974.[7]

"Short-Term Military Collapse"

On arriving in Guinea, Spínola quickly understood that Portugal could soon be facing a "short-term military collapse." In his first serious analysis of the war in Guinea, in October 1968, he argued that the military situation had deteriorated progressively since the beginning of the conflict, as the expanding area over which the PAIGC was able to carry out its "guerrilla activities" demonstrated. Portuguese forces were clearly in an "inferior position," and over time the troops felt a growing "sense of frustration." Spínola was aware that this was a "critical" situation that had to be dealt with immediately by the government in Lisbon; otherwise, Portugal would lose "effective control" of Guinea. It was not only Guinea that was at risk, but the whole of the colonial empire: the eventual "success of the insurgency" in Guinea would produce in the international community "an unstoppable wave of support for the liberation movements in Angola and Mozambique."[8]

Spínola's observations on the ground and the information he had collected allowed him to appreciate the contrasts between the two forces opposing one another. On the one hand, the PAIGC's military forces were better organized, wholly suited to the demands of an insurgency, and equipped with weapons whose technical characteristics were also suited to this type of conflict. On the other hand, after almost six years of war in Guinea, Portuguese troops continued to have to make "local contingent adjustments to the organization of their basic combat units." Moreover, they lacked the "support of light weaponry" that matched their "needs for durability, simplicity, ease of transport and the fire power essential for anti-guerrilla warfare," and that would allow them to replace their pre–Second World War weapons. The intelligence services, he believed, were "not aggressive and lacked imagination" and their operations were "poorly co-ordinated." In Spínola's opinion, the Portuguese military in Guinea was marked by a "psychological climate of frustration while facing a better equipped enemy that was able to take full advantage of the physical and psychological environment in which he had always lived."[9]

Therefore, Spínola called for several changes on the military field. He called for a pay review for troops serving in Guinea that would place them on an equal footing with their comrades serving in Mozambique. He demanded, for himself, the "right to choose his operational commanders . . . in a state of exception and during the period in which the strategic effort is in effect in this theatre of operations" and called for the reinforcement of his "operational resources" in order to allow the establishment of more "balanced forces" and to guarantee "the creation of a nucleus of intervention forces equipped to retake the initiative." He asked that forces under his command be provided with the "light support weapons" and radio equipment essential for their operational activities. He proposed to change the organization of "combat units" and of command and logistics services, to review the "training program," to increase the number of African recruits, and to establish civil "self-defense" systems. Finally, he asked that Portugal's anticolonial aircraft defense system be transferred to Guinea and called for the creation of a radio station that would broadcast Portuguese "propaganda" throughout Guinea and its neighboring countries.[10]

Spínola also advocated closer cooperation with the Portuguese political police, PIDE (State Defence and Intervention Police). In a report to the minister for the Ultramar in October 1968, Spínola complained that PIDE was "symbolically" represented in Guinea, where it had only thirty agents for a population of around five hundred thousand.[11] With the arrival of Inspector Fragoso Alas to the colony, a few months later, the relationship between Spínola and PIDE improved significantly and the police played a significant role in Spínola's strategy.

There was, however, an aspect of the "Guinea problem" even more significant. Spínola categorically stated that this was a war that could not be won by force of arms in his report of October 1968: "As no-one today will deny, the fundamental aspects of a general counter-insurgency program are not conducted in military missions, but through economic development and by promoting the social well-being of the civil population." The phrase "military victory" was of no relevance in a counterinsurgency war. Spínola's analysis and conclusions were not necessarily original. In fact, the Portuguese military elite had established, since the early 1960s, a real doctrine of counterinsurgency in Portuguese Africa.

In the case of Guinea, Spínola claimed, nothing had been done during the preceding years to encourage any "real socio-economic development within the province." He therefore called for plans to be drawn up for a number of activities designed to promote economic development, which would demonstrate to the Guineans that "the better life promised by the enemy is part of our plans, complete with examples that are real or feasible in the short-term." Nevertheless, he accepted that the military aspects could not be separated from the social and economic ones, "because for the socio-economic development of the province to advance in sufficient time to eliminate the root causes of the insurgency . . . it was essential that the armed forces reduced the enemy's threat with a clear show of strength that would be sufficient to increase our prestige among the people."

Finally, Spínola had insisted since the beginning that the solution to the "problem of Guinea" should also be found on the political field. The military advances and the social-economic developments might make it possible for Portugal to negotiate with the rebels from a position of superiority. These negotiations could be conducted both at a local level, with the leaders of the Guinean military units, either at a central level with the leadership of the PAIGC or with the mediation of "moderate" African leaders. At a local level, Spínola would try to explore the racial divide that existed between the leadership of the PAIGC—mostly of Cape Verdean origin—and the leaders of the nationalist combat groups that were native Guineans. Portuguese Guinea itself had a very complex social configuration, with at least eighteen different ethnolinguistic groups.

With this three-pronged approach, Spínola believed that it was still possible to turn the situation around in Guinea. With the spectre of Goa—a former Portuguese territory in the Indian subcontinent, conquered by India in December 1961—hanging over the colony, Spínola stated categorically that if Portugal lost the province, "responsibility" could not be placed on the shoulders of a military that had never been provided with the conditions necessary to complete their mission. At the end of the day, the problem was beyond his ability to "resolve" and the "crucial moment" at which central government must "address the situation in Guinea directly and take the decision to better defend the national interest" had finally arrived.

This document served as the basis of the account Spínola gave at a meeting of the National Defense Council (CSDN—Conselho Superior de Defesa Nacional) in Lisbon at the beginning of November 1968. Having expressed his view, he added that he believed it essential for the CSDN to reevaluate the situation by clearly defining the military's mission in Guinea. As a soldier, Spínola accepted the mission the government had given him, as long as it was clearly defined and he had been given the "minimum means" to complete it. However, "in order to lead men in battle and to ask them to make the supreme sacrifice," it was necessary "to feel they were dying for a reason or, more clearly, for a goal that was within reach."[12]

Spínola nevertheless had reasons for being satisfied. At that moment the government had committed itself to mobilize and send Spínola whatever he thought necessary to both resolve the most important military problems and to launch the program for the colony's socioeconomic development. There remained, however, a great distance between words and action, and during Marcelo Caetano's visit to Bissau in April 1969 Spínola complained to the prime minister about the delays in the arrival of the promised matériel and reinforcements. The following month, as he reflected on his first six months in office, he lamented that as the "dry season" was about to end, only "a minimum fraction of the absolutely essential provisions" had been allocated to Guinea.[13]

The Cold War in West Africa

The international dimension of the war in Guinea was also a matter of concern to Spínola, who gradually began to see it as the most important factor in play. On the one hand, Portugal was a founding member of NATO, a member of the Western community; therefore it could count on political, diplomatic, and economic support from its Western allies, who also sold Portugal the majority of the military equipment used in the wars, especially West Germany and France.[14] On the other hand, the nationalist movements in Portuguese Africa received support from other African countries, from Cuba, from China, and from the Soviet Union and the Warsaw Pact countries. This general picture had some nuances. The United States, for instance, during the presidency of John F. Kennedy, had distanced itself from Portuguese colonial policy and even supported nationalists in Angola. Gradually, however, American policy makers moderated this attitude. Richard Nixon's arrival at the White House marked a significant change in terms of US policy toward Africa, with Henry Kissinger defending close cooperation with the "white regimes" in southern Africa. In the case of the Guinean nationalists, the most important source of support for the PAIGC was Fidel Castro's government in Cuba, which, according to historian Piero Gleisejes, was following its own policy in Portuguese Guinea, with Che Guevara meeting Amílcar Cabral in Conakry in January 1965. The Guinean nationalists also received strong support from Sweden and other Scandinavian countries.[15]

Since the early 1960s the situation in Portuguese Africa had also become one of the most debated issues in the United Nations. Portugal was criticized for its colonial policy and racial discrimination, and the United Nations considered the wars in Angola, Mozambique, and Guinea a threat to international peace and security. Several resolutions had been approved condemning Portuguese policies and calling for self-determination and independence in the colonies.[16] The Portuguese regime defended itself using several arguments. One of them became known as "Luso-tropicalism," based on a theory put forward by Brazilian sociologist Gilberto Freyre, according to which Portuguese colonialism had always been—and still was—different from those of other European colonial powers. Luso-tropicalism maintained that Portuguese colonizers historically had a special ability to deal with the "inferior races" and to promote them to a "superior level of civilization." According to this theory, Portugal was not even an empire; the territories in Africa were not colonies but merely "overseas provinces." These had the same rights and lived under the same laws as the "continental provinces" in "metropolitan" Portugal. Portuguese administration of these territories was a domestic matter, and therefore the United Nations had no jurisdiction over them.[17]

Besides this public rhetoric, Portuguese diplomacy paid special attention to the context of the Cold War and used other arguments in the corridors of international diplomacy. When President John F. Kennedy tried to implement a new African policy favoring self-determination and independence for Portuguese colonies, Salazar used the American military base in the Azores as a trump card. He was able by late 1962 to moderate the discourse of the Americans regarding Portuguese colonialism and even to reverse the votes of the US mission at the United Nations, which had been voting favorably on General Assembly and Security Council resolutions criticizing Portuguese colonial policy since March 1961.[18]

Another argument frequently used in Portuguese diplomacy was the strategic importance of the Portuguese colonies in West Africa for the control of the South Atlantic in the general context of the Cold War. Throughout the 1950s, Portugal tried to convince its partners in the Atlantic alliance that NATO should pay attention to the southern flank of the Atlantic Ocean, namely, to the Portuguese territories of São Tomé, Guinea, Cape Verde, and Angola. Some NATO military commanders even considered the possibility of establishing bases and facilities in those territories. The following decade, as the support from Cuba and the Soviet bloc to the nationalist movements in Portuguese Africa became evident, Portugal used the reverse argument: the triumph of the liberation movements would mean the implementation of Communist and pro-Soviet regimes in the former Portuguese colonies and, consequently, a military presence of the Soviets in the area.

Spínola himself used every occasion to put the situation in Portuguese Guinea in a larger international perspective. In December 1968, he received in Bissau an officer from the American embassy in Dakar, George Andrews. The commander-in-chief stated categorically that Guinea was "strategically important not only for Portugal, but also for the West." Spínola quoted Prime Minister Caetano as stressing to the Portuguese cabinet that it was important for NATO that Guinea and the Cape Verde islands "do not fall into unfriendly hands," and Portuguese authorities hoped for "greater understanding and support not only from NATO, but from Europe and the United States." Spínola added that Portugal had "the military and economic means to handle the situation alone without assistance, but that any help would, of course, be welcome." He personally hoped that, with the new Nixon administration, the United States "would come to appreciate the validity of the Prime Minister's assessment and would act accordingly." The major problem was that the Soviets and Chinese were aiding the PAIGC "in the hope that they would later be able to establish themselves in Portuguese Guinea and obtain a base on the South Atlantic." Strategically, Portuguese Guinea and Cape Verde were "inextricably intertwined" and "if Guinea were lost, so eventually would be the Cape Verde Islands." The leader of the PAIGC was, after all, a Cape Verdean and the rebellion would quickly spread to the islands if Portuguese Guinea were lost.[19]

"For a Better Guinea"

The Cold War context in which the war in Guinea was being fought was one more reason that Spínola was convinced that the conflict could not be ended by military means alone and that it was necessary to pay attention to native Guineans and to their social and economic condition. This would, Spínola believed, deprive the PAIGC and its Cape Verdean leadership of the arguments used to motivate the combatant troops. Spínola's main strategic weapon was his plan for the colony's economic and social development, a program he called For a Better Guinea. "Our plan," he wrote in December 1968, "is to ensure the swift attainment of this level of well-being, which can be represented by the slogan: a Better Guinea." If Portugal were to prove capable of achieving this goal, it would deprive the enemy of "the force of their reason and, with this, the people—which is the end goal of the counter-insurgency plan."[20]

Speaking to Guinea's legislative council at the beginning of December 1968, Spínola outlined the steps he had taken to implement this program during the first months of his mandate. Immediately upon his arrival in Bissau, he had asked the provincial services to conduct detailed studies that would allow him to assess the colony's major problems. Furthermore, he himself had established direct contacts with the Guineans and with the armed forces in every corner of the colony and listened to their "concerns and frustrations." After "five months of observation and many hours of meditation," he finally understood the "true situation" in Guinea. He then left for Lisbon, where he presented his findings to the government with the intention of formulating an "action plan." As a result of the meetings in Lisbon, the government of Guinea was granted "significant financial assistance" for the creation of a "better Guinea." This would provide him with the "minimum conditions necessary for the re-establishment of peace and order in the province and for the commencement of its socio-economic development." At this meeting with the legislative council in Bissau, Spínola announced some of the initiatives he intended to implement: "expansion of the infrastructural works currently being carried out in the province—in particular completion of the road and communications network; reconstruction of the ports in the interior and speeding up the province's economic integration through the immediate establishment of social improvement programs that will increase standards of living, of education and of sanitation."[21]

In March 1969, Spínola announced the birth of the "new Guinea" in a statement to the Guinean people. He spoke directly "to the good people of all Guinea," to those who lived "in the city, in the towns, in the villages (*tabancas*) and in the bush—even those in Senegal and the Republic of Guinea." In a paternalistic tone, Spínola declared to all the "children of this land" that, because Guinea lacked resources, the Portuguese government had decided to channel "large sums" to the colony and enable him to construct "a better Guinea," one with "paved roads, river ports, more primary and secondary schools and technical institutes, thus enabling the selection of the best and facilitating their access to senior positions within the administration." The "better Guinea," Spínola promised, would have an "extensive network of hospitals, maternity clinics and first aid posts" and "more urbanized settlements as a result of progress." Guinea would have "a better future than it had a past and present and would be able to fully realize its people's legitimate desire for progress." Progress and development, however, depended on the continuation of Guinea as a part of Portugal. The "new Guinea" was only possible because the territory was an "integral part of the Portuguese nation, which was obliged by its own constitution to encourage the development of its entire territory." The independence of Guinea, warned Spínola, would not be in the interests of the Guinean people—only of a minority of Cape Verdeans—and would "inevitably lead to its division or, more precisely, to its disappearance."[22]

Even on this matter, however, the public announcements contrasted with private utterances. On the eve of Caetano's visit to Guinea, Spínola wrote to the minister for the Ultramar complaining that the promised financial assistance was taking too long to arrive. Spínola reminded Silva Cunha that the promise to create a "better Guinea" had caused certain expectations among the Guinean people that could lead them to "adhere decisively to the national cause"; however, to make this happen it was important to put the words into action through the "fulfilment of the promises upon which we have based our propaganda" with the people. "Otherwise," he concluded, "we will miss this final opportunity to regain their support."[23]

Resettlement Plan and Public Works

In this struggle for the hearts and minds of the Guinean people, Spínola decided to go ahead first with his "resettlement and self-defense" plan, through which he would relocate the native population into settlements or villages controlled by Portuguese troops charged with keeping them "separate from the guerrillas and their demands for information, food and shelter." One of the "most effective procedures for denying the enemy the moral and material support they receive from the people" was, according to Spínola, "to resettle them under our control." However, it was also necessary to be aware that in Guinea the people have a "deep bond with their land, . . . strong links of an ethno-socio-economic nature," living in a "world of superstitions and beliefs" that would have to be violated if the people were to be resettled. The Portuguese military should accordingly develop "unrelenting and ongoing psychological activities that would encourage the people to want resettlement or accept its necessity." The soldiers should explain to Guineans how their geographical dispersion makes it difficult to protect them, meaning they are more likely to find themselves controlled by the enemy, while simultaneously explaining to them—"clearly and simply for their primitive minds"—the advantages that they will reap should they "collaborate with our authorities" and agree to live in the new villages. The idea could be summarized as this: "With us Heaven: with the enemy Hell."[24]

The basic idea behind this policy had to be transmitted to the people through the tribal "big men" and village "chiefs" assembled according to "traditional customs." For the Muslims living in Guinea it was appropriate to include the chiefs and the "Islamic clerics," using "trustworthy interpreters" with whom a dialogue could be attempted. It was important to convince the

Muslim clergy of their own interest in this subject and to assure its support for the Portuguese initiatives. It was also important to dispatch "duly prepared native agents" to listen to opinions and to "hammer out some of the themes around the hearth." More importantly, Portugal had to demonstrate "the truth of its words through the prompt realization of positive achievements in the first resettlements" by channeling the government's efforts to improve sanitation, education, and the economies of the new villages. In the settlements Portuguese troops should demonstrate their respect of "traditional religions" and allow Guineans "to practice their rituals." Radio and cinema should also be used to show the Guinean people "the positive results of resettlement and self-defense in such a way as the deeds will speak louder than the words."[25]

The new settlements established by Spínola and the Portuguese armed forces in Guinea represented much more than a military strategy. The settlements were normally an expansion of an existing village and consisted of simple houses constructed of locally available materials—namely, wood and clay—with zinc roofs.

Another important component of Spínola's program was a series of public improvement works. In large part, these resulted from the resettlement and self-defense program. Spínola sought to take advantage of the "resettlement phase" to "modernize native housing—from the rural and suburban areas into the urban centers—increasing the construction of settlements with houses wholly integrated into an urban setting, conveniently adjusted to the actual level of social life sought."[26] Accordingly, Spínola instructed the government public works service to come up with a series of urbanization plans for all population centers, from the "present or future council, district or administrative centers" to the "rural villages."[27] While in 1968 there were only 60 kilometers of paved road in Guinea, five years later there were 550 kilometers.

In schooling, the impact of direct intervention by the armed forces was even more significant. In January 1969, the Portuguese press reported Spínola "being acclaimed by natives" as he opened an army-built school in Mansoa. The reporting of these events was essential not only for their local impact, but also for the image of Spínola's government they projected at home and abroad. The *Diário da Manhã* reported "large crowds" that "enthusiastically applauded" Spínola and praised the "fine work within society the military are carrying out in this province as they also continue with their difficult task of defending the motherland's integrity."[28]

In June 1969, the new head of the education services division (RPSE—Repartição Provincial dos Serviços de Educação) took office. Spínola recalled at the time that for a long while the idea that access to education had been a "prerogative of the privileged classes, without reflection on the economic development of nations," had become generalized. Now it was thought that education was "the most profitable investment that a government can make." The Guinean people must quickly achieve "the minimum level corresponding to the cultural demands of today's world." In real terms, this meant the "universalization of primary education, placing a greater emphasis on intermediate technical education courses that reflect the province's economic needs and offering those with the best qualifications an opportunity to achieve their legitimate goals for upward mobility."[29]

The following month Spínola issued an order dealing with education in which he noted the "very small percentage of pupils presented for the fourth-grade exam." He contrasted this with the very considerable investment the PAIGC was making in primary education among the people under its control, as it "seeks to take maximum possible advantage from this fact in the propaganda war." On the Portuguese side, the picture was truly "dire," and, given the "lack of teachers and accredited monitors able to take control of the many village schools that need to come into service," there was no sign that this position would change any time soon. Given these circumstances it was necessary "to compromise on some more formal demands and take exceptional measures" that would permit the "full use of all the means available in the province: both civil and military." On the one hand, Spínola decided to push for the "maximum increase in the construction and provisioning of primary schools," while on the other he stipulated that in those areas in which there were military units, a military teacher must be assigned to provide primary education under the "academic supervision" of the education services.[30]

The Portuguese military assumed an increasingly important role in the delivery of primary school education in Guinea. According to data published by Cann, during the academic year 1970–1971, Portuguese military personnel administered 127 (43 percent) of the country's 298 primary schools—which tended to be schools it had constructed in sparsely populated areas—compared to the 31 percent of schools run by the educational services and the 27 percent run by missionaries. When Spínola returned to Portugal in 1973, around 30 percent of school-age children were attending classes.[31]

At the end of his four years in Guinea, Spínola was speaking of a true "social revolution" that had taken place since his arrival. This revolution had resulted in the implementation of "the tasks necessary for development—the real battlefield between the key ideas in the conflict." It had been possible to transform into "real achievements the promises the enemy had used to mobilize Guineans, . . . which meet the real and legitimate aspirations of the province's African population." According to Spínola, the PAIGC could be considered to have been truly "disarmed" as a result of the "program of social development that swept away the main reasons for the insurgency."[32]

Dealing with Race Issues

Winning over the Guinean people involved another matter Spínola believed fundamental: changing the Portuguese military's attitude toward the native population. In an order issued in December 1968, Spínola said it was necessary "to forget poor past behavior—to which we admit we have also contributed—and re-establish the atmosphere of reciprocal trust between European Portuguese and (native) Guinean Portuguese that is an absolutely necessary condition for the restoration of normal and peaceful life in the province." Portugal needs to "forgive" and to be "generous towards those who, responding to our call for a better Guinea, wish to exchange the path of insurgency for that of peace and of order."[33]

Some months later Spínola issued new instructions to his officers. Portuguese soldiers were told to change their behavior toward Guineans and particularly to avoid "any unjustified act of violence against the native population." Spínola again reminded his subordinates that "the struggle taking place in this province is essentially psychological, the ultimate goal of which is to win hearts and minds." Therefore, "fully aware of past mistakes and of the responsibility we all have to build the future," commanders at every level must "direct their activities among the people in such a way as will create a new psychological atmosphere in which there is no place for resentment or guilt." Spínola warned his men he would be "meticulous in punishing any unjustified act of violence against the native population, regardless of whether the victims of the violence were loyal or not."[34]

This new relationship Spínola hoped to establish with the Guineans also involved the release of political prisoners, particularly the publicity given to these releases. Without doubt, the most spectacular result of this policy came with the freeing of Rafael Barbosa, former president of the PAIGC's central committee, and a group of other political prisoners. Spínola ranked these liberations in August 1969 as "a psychological shock of unquestionable value in the struggle in which we are engaged."[35] In a speech he made upon his release, Rafael Barbosa recalled that five years earlier, "disillusioned by the promises of the winds of history he had stepped off the path and stopped behaving like a good Portuguese." He added that nothing now remained of this other than "repentance, . . . bitterness, and disillusion." Praising Spínola for both his "clemency" and his "dignity," Barbosa promised to be "as good a Portuguese" as the governor-general was.[36]

Another effort to overcome the racial divide and to win the hearts and minds of the Guineans were the so-called people's congresses (Congressos do Povo). These congresses gathered the various ethnic groups in Guinea and at the regional level included all the inhabitants of the particular council or administrative district in which the sessions were held. The various ethnic groups, represented mainly by members of the "upper layers of traditional society," including native monarchs, village chiefs, religious leaders, and tribal "big men," attended the annual meetings. The congresses had only "consultative power," however, and never passed any normative resolution in plenary session.[37]

According to Spínola, the first annual congress in 1970 defined the "basic principles" on which the "process of social renewal" in Guinea would be constructed. At the second congress, delegates debated economic matters, while the third congress, in July 1972, enabled the creation of "a broad regionalization of provincial structures," which for Spínola represented a "new and decisive step in the direction of Guinea's true integration into the national body."[38] At the opening of one of the congresses, Spínola was careful to stress the "principles" underlying these initiatives. The congresses allowed "the people to affirm and participate in collective life" without becoming a "pulpit from which they would voice eulogies or express undeserved gratitude and make requests for favors for minorities." Spínola asked that participants be allowed to "speak their minds, express their criticisms, present their complaints, say what is wrong and propose solutions without any fear of repercussion."[39]

Even critics of Spínola, such as Otelo Saraiva de Carvalho, did not hesitate to consider the people's congresses one of the "most important political events" in Guinea, and "an emotional and valid example of the possibilities of dialogue with people through their legitimate representatives." However, Otelo also noted that the members of the congresses represented only the Guinean population who lived in areas under Portuguese control, which meant people the authorities could trust. Moreover, the congresses—in which tribal divisions were as a rule maintained—had no "deliberative functions": they were strictly consultative. As a result it was possible to see the congresses as a "populist" initiative designed particularly to appeal to the native population.[40]

Spínola, however, claimed it was not possible for "terrorists" or their "supporters hiding in the bush" to be represented in these initiatives. Moreover, Guineans remained divided by the "tribal barrier" and continued to identify themselves with their people and for this reason "demanding" the "ethnic division of the congresses." According to this view, the congresses were less an exercise in "populism" than they were "a genuine attempt to listen to the problems of the popular masses, debated freely and without hindrance by their legitimate representatives in accordance with the stimulus injected by Spínola during his speeches." The governor-general frequently repeated the idea that "Congress is not here to applaud the governor, nor is it here to rubber-stamp the governor's policies; it is a place in which each person can say what they sincerely believe and openly make the criticisms they believe must be made."[41]

Africanization

Finally, one should mention the importance of the Africanization of Portuguese troops fighting in Guinea. Spínola provided a significant push to the drive to recruit Africans into the military in Guinea, in a move that was to become one of the most important aspects of Portugal's counterinsurgency in Africa. The involvement of African troops in the Portuguese military during the thirteen years of conflict in Africa began in an almost "marginal" and limited fashion; they occupied secondary roles, such as controlling the civilian population, gathering information, and scouting terrain.[42] However, as the wars progressed, their roles became increasingly important. When Caetano led the government, he sought to place greater emphasis on the recruitment of Africans, arguing this was justified "by the need to prevent the conflict from taking on the racial character of whites against blacks, because of their better adaptation to the environment, and because of the impossibility of meeting by any other means the commanders' constant requests for more men."[43]

The number of African recruits in Guinea increased significantly during Spínola's time as senior commander, from 14.4 percent in 1967 to 20.1 percent in 1974.[44] Spínola saw three advantages in this rise in the number of Africans under his command. First, it solved the chronic troop shortage mentioned earlier, with one-fifth of the Portuguese armed forces in Guinea being of African origin. Second, it was clear that African soldiers had better natural ability to adapt to the terrain, to assess the "civilian population's mood," and to gather information.[45] Spínola believed that African units were much "more efficient in certain missions" because of their "natural adaptation to the environment" and their "perfect understanding of the techniques of moving through and surviving in the jungle."[46]

Third, the process of Africanizing Portugal's military was a reflection of Spínola's ideological views on the need to increase the participation of Guineans in the creation of a "better Guinea." Spínola often publicly stated that the integration of many Guineans into Portuguese "militias" would be the best example of the success of his ethnic policies. Some of the Africans now integrated into the Portuguese military had previously been "on the side of the enemy, fighting against their brothers," but had recognized "the error of their ways" by deciding to fight for the "people's true cause." What mattered now was that this "enemy" understood that Guinea was "being defended by its people" and that in the near future, this task would be "completely given over to Africans."[47]

On the ground, these new African forces carried out some important missions. For example, the militias were stationed in as many villages and settlements as possible, where they were made responsible for their defense. Trained by the Portuguese army, they were commanded by the village chief and supplied with radios with which they could call for help in the event of a PAIGC attack. During the time Spínola was responsible for Guinea, the distinction between "normal" and "special" militias grew. While the former had the defensive task of protecting the civilian population from PAIGC attacks, the latter were employed in special counterinsurgency operations.[48] According to historian Borges Coelho, the creation and development of "special" militias in Guinea was a real "turning point" in terms of Portugal's employment of the African population in its military.[49]

Spínola did not hesitate to establish entirely African combat units that operated in a "more or less irregular and independent" manner with "increased levels of operational efficiency."[50] One example was the "black militia," a body of approximately forty combat units made up of more than eight thousand men.[51] The importance of the locally recruited "African Commandos" is also worthy of note. These units were, according to specialists, "highly effective in combat" and were wholly integrated into the logic of the "Africanization of the war." However, their most important feature was that they constituted a "policy tool for the progressive autonomy General Spínola was calling for." The African Commandos could become the "African military elite" Spínola hoped to establish as the "embryo of the armed forces of an independent Guinea integrated in the Portuguese sphere."[52]

The "special detachments of African riflemen," with their training and preparation center in Bolama, also carried out important duties, particularly through their participation in special operations. Spínola appointed Rebordão de Brito, a Cape Verdean, to command this unit. In January 1972, Spínola wrote a long letter to his friend the minister of the navy, Pereira Crespo, which clearly explains what he had in mind with the Africanization of Portuguese armed forces in Guinea:

> As you know I am pushing on with the increased Africanization of
> cadres of African units. . . . The companies of the army's African
> Commandos are now entirely commanded by Africans, although
> there remains a small administrative unit of Europeans and a
> European supervisor. I wish to similarly Africanize the last-raised
> detachment of riflemen, which has the advantage of—for the
> command of this detachment—having a First Lieutenant who, by

his color and exceptional fighting qualities, has all the attributes necessary to command. He is Lt Rebordão de Brito (Cape Verdean) and he is to receive a medal, the Torre e Espada [Tower and Sword]— which is well deserved—on 10 June. . . . Here, my dear friend, you have my proposal, which is part of a plan for the progressive replacement of the Portuguese rifle detachment with African rifle detachments with minimal European involvement. This—as you know as well as I—is the route by which the problems in the overseas provinces will be solved.[53]

Conclusion: The Failure of Spínola's Strategy

The success of the For a Better Guinea program, gradually implemented by Spínola since his arrival in Guinea, was limited. By the standards of the Portuguese administration in Africa, the achievements regarding the lives of the Guineans were impressive in areas such as housing, health, and education. The major problem, however, was that a policy of winning hearts and minds required much more time and should have been conceived as a long-term program, not as a short-term remedy for military decline. In 1968, after five years of war and with the Portuguese military on the verge of collapse, this was a clear case of too little, too late.

Yet it should be noted that Spínola's efforts to improve the image of colonial Portugal in Guinea and internationally was overshadowed by the launching of very aggressive military operations. These operations made Guineans doubt Spínola's true objectives and brought Portugal condemnation from the international community. In late 1969, for instance, Spínola gave direct orders to his troops to attack PAIGC military camps in Senegal, right across the Guinean-Senegalese border, from which the nationalists attacked Portuguese garrisons.[54] These "retaliations" were successful and caused a significant reduction in PAIGC military activities near the border. Spínola rejoiced, and in a meeting of his military commanders he said that this was indeed "the only language that the blacks consider and respect."[55]

The best-known example of these "special operations," however, was the invasion of Conakry by Portuguese troops in late 1970. Operation Green Sea, approved by the Portuguese government, had as its major goals the overthrow of Sékou Touré, the capture of Amílcar Cabral, the release of Portuguese prisoners, and the destruction of PAIGC military equipment that was stored in Conakry.[56] The invasion of Republic of Guinea was a failure from the Portuguese point of view. Although Portuguese prisoners were able to escape and some military equipment was destroyed, neither Sékou Touré nor Amílcar Cabral was in Conakry. In the aftermath, following a complaint from the Guineans, the

UN Security Council approved a resolution on December 8, 1970, condemning the invasion of Republic of Guinea by Portugal and considering Portuguese colonialism in Africa a "serious threat to the peace and security of independent African states."[57]

On a political level, however, Spínola was certainly more successful. In October 1970 he wrote an extensive document to Prime Minister Caetano urging that Portugal should evolve "urgently" toward a "federation," adopting a "political system" that assured the "autonomy of the several parts" of Portugal "under the authority of the central government."[58] He was also very active in Bissau, trying to find allies for a political solution to the Portuguese colonial conundrum. In 1972, Spínola was able to create a window of opportunity: with his declarations of intentions, with the practical results of his policies, and with his charisma and personal involvement, he caught the attention of the president of Senegal, Leopold Senghor. This prestigious African leader, interested in a peaceful solution for Portuguese Guinea and concerned about the growing influence of Sékou Touré over the PAIGC, offered to mediate between Portugal and the nationalist movement. In May 1972 Spínola went to Cap Skiring, in Senegal, to meet with the Senegalese leader. Senghor told him he had obtained the agreement of PAIGC and its leader, Amílcar Cabral, for a cease-fire and a period of "gradual transition" that could last a decade, with the gradual assumption of political and administrative functions by the native population. After this transition period, the people of Guinea would exercise an act of self-determination, defining then the future of its relationship with Portugal.[59]

The major problem for Spínola was that when he reported this breakthrough to Prime Minister Caetano, the answer was negative. Caetano would not allow Spínola or any Portuguese official to negotiate and to sit at the same table as Amílcar Cabral, the leader of what the Portuguese called a "terrorist movement" supported by the Soviet Union. This would be a humiliation, Caetano argued and, more than that, the first domino to fall in a game that would certainly extend to Angola and Mozambique, where the situation was considerably different. "For the general defense of our overseas territories," Caetano argued, "it is better to leave Guinea with an honorable military defeat than with a deal negotiated with the terrorists, opening the way for other negotiations."[60] Spínola realized then, in his own words, that Portugal had just lost "the last opportunity to solve with honor and dignity the problem of Guinea."[61]

A few months later, after receiving critical military equipment from the Soviet camp (Strela surface-to-air missiles), the PAIGC was able to inflict a series of military defeats to Portuguese troops in Guinea, and in September 1973 the nationalists unilaterally proclaimed the independence of the Republic of Guinea-Bissau. Meanwhile, in August of that year, Spínola had resigned and had come back to Portugal to write the book that detonated the democratic transition in 1974.

Notes

1. Aniceto Afonso and Carlos de Matos Gomes, *Guerra Colonial* [Colonial war] (Lisbon: Editorial Notícias, 2000), 91. In Angola in the early 1960s there were approximately 170,500 white Portuguese (3.5 percent of the total population) and in Mozambique 97,250 (approximately 1.5 percent). Data from Afonso and Gomes, *Guerra Colonial*, 60, 121.

2. A. E. Duarte Silva, *A Independência da Guiné-Bissau e a Descolonização Portuguesa* [The independence of Guinea-Bissau and Portuguese decolonization] (Porto: Afrontamento, 1997), 58.

3. Spínola's period in Angola is analyzed in Luís Nuno Rodrigues, *Spínola* (Lisbon: Esfera dos Livros, 2010), 51–84.

4. Interview with António de Spínola in 1992, in Manuel A. Bernardo, *Marcello e Spínola: A Ruptura. As Forças Armadas e a Imprensa na Queda do Estado Novo, 1973–1974* [Marcello and Spínola: The break; armed forces and press in the fall of the new state] (Lisbon: Editorial Estampa, 1996), 235.

5. Marcello Caetano, *Depoimento*, Rio de Janeiro/São Paulo: Distribuidora Record, 1974, 32.

6. Amélia Neves Souto, *Caetano e o ocaso do Império. Administração e Guerra Colonial em Moçambique durante o Marcelismo (1968–1974)* [Caetano and the decline of empire: Administration of the colonial war in Mozambique during Marcelismo] (Porto: Edições Afrontamento, 2007), 62.

7. Fernando Rosas, "O Marcelismo ou a Falência da Política de Transição no Estado Novo" [The Marcelismo or the failure of transition policy in the new state], in *Do Marcelismo ao Fim do Império* [Marcelismo and the end of empire], ed. J. M. Brandão de Brito (Lisbon: Editorial Notícias, 1999), 49.

8. António Spínola's Archive (hereinafter ASA), "Comando-Chefe das Forças Armadas da Guiné: O Problema Militar da Guiné. Seu Estudo e Proposta de Solução" [Chief command of the armed forces in Guinea: The military problem of Guinea; its study and proposal of a solution], October 1968.

9. Ibid.

10. Ibid.

11. ASA, "Província da Guiné. Análise da Situação dos Serviços da Guiné. Seus objectivos mínimos e necessidades" [Province of Guinea: Analysis of the services situation in Guinea; its minimum objectives and requirements], October 1968.

12. "Província da Guiné: Exposição do Governador e Comandante Chefe das Forças Armadas da Guiné ao Conselho Superior da Defesa Nacional" [Province of Guinea: Statement by the governor and commander in chief of the armed forces of Guinea to the Superior Council of National Defense], November 8, 1968, ASA.

13. "Proposta de reforço de meios e medidas necessárias para a concretização de um plano de contra-subversão no teatro de operações da Guiné apresentado ao Chefe do Estado-Maior General das Forças Armadas" [Proposal to strengthen the means and measures necessary for the realization of a plan of countersubversion in the operations theater of Guinea presented to the general chief of staff of armed forces], May 1, 1969, ASA.

14. For an overview of the international context of Portuguese colonialism in the period of the colonial wars, see António Costa Pinto, *O Fim do Império Português. A Cena Internacional, a Guerra Colonial, e a Descolonização, 1961–1975* [The end of the Portuguese empire: The international scene, the colonial war, and decolonization, 1961–1975] (Lisbon: Livros Horizonte, 2001). On West German and French support, see Ana Mónica Fonseca, *A Força das Armas: O apoio da República Federal da Alemanha ao Estado Novo (1958–1968)* [Force of arms: The support of the Federal Republic of Germany to the new state (1958–1968)] (Lisbon: Instituto Diplomático, 2007); and Daniel Marcos, *Salazar e De Gaulle. A França e a Questão Colonial Portuguesa (1958–1968)* [Salazar and De Gaulle: France and the Portuguese colonial question (1958–1968)] (Lisbon: Instituto Diplomático, 2007).

15. See Piero Gleijeses, *Conflicting Mission: Havana, Washington, and Africa, 1959–1976* (Chapel Hill: University of North Carolina Press, 2002), particularly chapter 9; and Tor Sellström, *A Suécia e as lutas de libertação nacional em Angola, Moçambique e Guiné-Bissau* [Sweden and national liberation struggles in Angola, Mozambique, and Guinea-Bissau] (Halmstad, Sweden: Nordiska Afrikainstitutet, 2008).

16. A. E. Duarte Silva, "O litígio entre Portugal e a ONU (1960–1974)" [The dispute between Portugal and the UN (1960–1974)], *Análise Social* 30, no. 130 (1995): 5–50.

17. See Cláudio Castelo, *O Modo Português de Estar no Mundo. O Luso-Tropicalismo e a Ideologia Colonial Portuguesa (1933–1961)* [The Portuguese way of being in the world: Lusotropicalism and the Portuguese colonial ideology (1933–1961)] (Porto: Afrontamento, 1999).

18. See Luís Nuno Rodrigues, *Kennedy-Salazar: A Crise de Uma Aliança. As relações Luso-Americanas entre 1961 e 1963* [Salazar-Kennedy: A Crisis of the Alliance; Luso-American relations between 1961 and 1963] (Lisbon: Editorial Notícias, 2002); and "Today's Terrorist Is Tomorrow's Statesman: The United States and Angolan Nationalism in the Early1960s," *Portuguese Journal of Social Science* 3, no. 2 (2004): 115–40.

19. "Portuguese Guinea: Discussion with Governor," from the US Embassy in Dakar to the State Department, December 26, 1968, National Archives and Records Administration, Central Foreign Policy Files, 1967–1969, Box 2440.

20. "Directiva no. 360/68. Campanha Psicológica de Recuperação" [Directive no. 360/68: Psychological recovery campaign], December 17, 1968, Historical Military Archive (HMA), 2nd Division, 4th Section, Box 226, no. 1.

21. António de Spínola, *Por uma Guiné Melhor* [For a better Guinea] (Lisbon: Agência Geral do Ultramar, 1970), 41–44.

22. *Diário de Notícias*, March 11, 1969, 5.

23. ASA, letter from António de Spínola to the minister for the overseas provinces, March 25, 1969.

24. "Comando Chefe da Guiné. Directiva de Propaganda no. 1" [Chief command of Guinea: Propaganda directive no. 1], September 30, 1968, HMA, 2nd Division, 4th Section, Box 226, no. 1.

25. Ibid.

26. "Directiva no. 57/69. Reordenamentos. Urbanização de Aglomerados Populacionais"

[Directive no. 57/69: Resettlements urbanization of population clusters], July 14, 1969, HMA, 2nd Division, 4th Section, Box 226, no. 1.

27. Ibid.

28. *Diário da Manhã*, January 22, 1969, 2.

29. Spínola, *Por uma Guiné Melhor*, 101–3.

30. "Directiva no. 60/69. Incremento da Instrução Primária" [Directive no. 60/69: Increase in primary education], from the commander in chief in Guiné, July 23, 1969, HMA, 2nd Division, 4th Section, Box 226, no. 2.

31. John Cann, *Contra-Insurreição em África. O modo português de fazer a guerra* [Counterinsurgency in Africa: The Portuguese way of war] (Lisbon: Edições Atena, 1998), 197–98.

32. António de Spínola, *Por uma Portugalidade Renovada* [For a renewed Portugality] (Lisbon: Agência Geral do Ultramar, 1973), 113–14.

33. "Directiva no. 360/68. Campanha Psicológica de Recuperação" [Directive no. 360/68: Psychological recovery campaign], December 17, 1968, HMA, 2nd Division, 4th Section, Box 226, no. 1.

34. "Comando Chefe das Forças Armadas da Guiné. Directiva no. 44/69" [Chief Command of the Armed Forces of Guinea: Directive no. 44/69], June 8, 1969, HMA, 2nd Division, 4th Section, Box 226, no. 2.

35. ASA, letter from António de Spínola to Venâncio Deslandes, July 31, 1969.

36. *Diário de Notícias*, August 5, 1969, 5.

37. Silva, *A Independência da Guiné-Bissau e a Descolonização Portuguesa*, 124.

38. Spínola, *Por uma Portugalidade Renovada*, 132–33.

39. Ibid., 88–92.

40. Otelo Saraiva de Carvalho, *Alvorada em Abril (I)* [Dawn in April (I)] (Lisbon: Edições Alfa, 1991), 86–88.

41. Ibid.

42. João Paulo Borges Coelho, "African Troops in the Portuguese Colonial Army, 1961–1974: Angola, Guinea-Bissau and Mozambique," *Portuguese Studies Review* 10, no. 1 (2002): 130.

43. Caetano, *Depoimento*, 169.

44. Figures cited by Coelho, "African Troops in the Portuguese Colonial Army," 136.

45. João Paulo Borges Coelho, "Da violência colonial ordenada à ordem pós-colonial violenta. Sobre um legado das guerras coloniais nas ex-colónias portuguesas" [From ordered colonial violence to the violent postcolonial order: About a legacy of colonial wars in the former Portuguese colonies], *Lusotopie* (2003): 182, 184. *www.lusotopie.sciencespobordeaux.fr/*.

46. Spínola, *Por uma Portugalidade Renovada*, 118.

47. Ibid., 76–78.

48. Cann, *Contra-Insurreição em África*, 137, 217.

49. Coelho, "African Troops in the Portuguese Colonial Army," 139–40.

50. Ibid.

51. Cann, *Contra-Insurreição em África*, 137.

52. Afonso and Gomes, *Guerra Colonial*, 204–5.

53. ASA, letter from António de Spínola to the minister of the navy, January 14, 1972.

54. ASA, "Directiva no. 78/69. Ideia de manobra para o Desenvolvimento Operacional na Época Seca de 1969/70" [Directive no. 78/69: Idea of maneuver for the operational development in the dry season of 1969/70], November 19, 1969.

55. "Reunião Mensal de Comandos. Acta no. 11" [Monthly meeting of commands: Transcript no. 11], HMA, 2nd Division, 4th Section, Box 226, no. 2.

56. ASA, "Acta da Reunião Extraordinária de Comandos realizada em 19 de Novembro de 1970" [Transcript of the extraordinary meeting of commands, November 19, 1970].

57. Silva, "O litígio entre Portugal e a ONU," 37.

58. ASA, "Algumas Ideias Sobre a Estruturação Política da Nação, Outubro de 1970" [Some ideas about the political structure of the nation, October 1970].

59. ASA, "Acta da reunião com o Presidente Senghor, em Cap Skiring, em 18 de Maio de 1972" [Transcript of the meeting with President Senghor, in Cap Skiring, May 18, 1972].

60. Caetano, *Depoimento*, 191.

61. António de Spínola, *País Sem Rumo. Contributo para a História de uma Revolução* [A country with no route: Contribution to the history of a revolution] (Lisbon: Scire, 1978), 42.

References

ARCHIVES

António Spínola's Archive, Lisbon, Portugal
Historical Military Archive, Lisbon, Portugal

PERIODICALS

Diário da Manhã
Diário de Notícias

SELECTED PUBLISHED SOURCES

Afonso, Aniceto, and Carlos de Matos Gomes. *Guerra Colonial* [Colonial war]. Lisbon: Editorial Notícias, 2000.

Bernardo, Manuel A. *Marcello e Spínola: a Ruptura. As Forças Armadas e a Imprensa na Queda do Estado Novo, 1973–1974* [Marcello and Spínola: the break—armed forces and press in the fall of the new state]. Lisbon: Editorial Estampa, 1996.

Caetano, Marcello. *Depoimento* [Testimony]. Rio de Janeiro/São Paulo: Distribuidora Record, 1974.

Cann, John. *Contra-Insurreição em África. O modo português de fazer a guerra* [Counterinsurgency in Africa: The Portuguese way of war]. Lisbon: Edições Atena, 1998.

Carvalho, Otelo Saraiva de. *Alvorada em Abril (I)* [Dawn in April (I)]. Lisbon: Edições Alfa, 1991.

————. *Cinco Meses Mudaram Portugal* [Five months that changed Portugal]. Lisbon: Portugália, 1975.

Castelo, Cláudio. *O Modo Português de Estar no Mundo. O Luso-Tropicalismo e a Ideologia Colonial Portuguesa (1933–1961)* [The Portuguese way of being in the world: Lusotropicalism and the Portuguese colonial ideology (1933–1961)]. Porto: Afrontamento, 1999.

Coelho, João Paulo Borges. "African Troops in the Portuguese Colonial Army, 1961–1974: Angola, Guinea-Bissau, and Mozambique." *Portuguese Studies Review* 10, no. 1 (2002): 129–50.

————. "Da violência colonial ordenada à ordem pós-colonial violenta. Sobre um legado das guerras coloniais nas ex-colónias portuguesas" [From ordered colonial violence to the violent postcolonial order: About a legacy of colonial wars in the former Portuguese colonies]. *Lusotopie* (2003): 175–93. *www.lusotopie.sciencespobordeaux .fr/*.

Fonseca, Ana Mónica. *A Força das Armas: o apoio da República Federal da Alemanha ao Estado Novo (1958–1968)* [Force of arms: The support of the Federal Republic of Germany for the new state (1958–1968)]. Lisbon: Instituto Diplomático, 2007.

Gleijeses, Piero. *Conflicting Missions: Havana, Washington, and Africa, 1959–1976.* Chapel Hill: University of North Carolina Press, 2002.

Marcos, Daniel. *Salazar e De Gaulle. A França e a Questão Colonial Portuguesa (1958–1968)* [Salazar and De Gaulle: France and the Portuguese colonial question (1958–1968)]. Lisbon: Instituto Diplomático, 2007.

Pinto, António Costa. *O Fim do Império Português. A Cena Internacional, a Guerra Colonial, e a Descolonização, 1961–1975* [The end of the Portuguese empire: The international scene, the colonial war, and decolonization, 1961–1975]. Lisbon: Livros Horizonte, 2001.

Rodrigues, Luís Nuno. *Kennedy-Salazar: a Crise de Uma Aliança. As relações Luso-Americanas entre 1961 e 1963.* [Salazar-Kennedy: A crisis of the alliance: Luso-American relations between 1961 and 1963]. Lisbon: Editorial Notícias, 2002.

————. *Spínola.* Lisbon: Esfera dos Livros, 2010.

————. "Today's Terrorist Is Tomorrow's Statesman: The United States and Angolan Nationalism in the Early 1960s." *Portuguese Journal of Social Science* 3, no. 2 (2004): 115–40.

Rosas, Fernando. "O Marcelismo ou a Falência da Política de Transição no Estado Novo" [The Marcelismo or the failure of transition policy in the new state]. In *Do Marcelismo ao Fim do Império* [From Marcelismo to the end of empire], edited by J. M. Brandão de Brito, 15–59. Lisbon: Editorial Notícias, 1999.

Sellström, Tor. *A Suécia e as lutas de libertação nacional em Angola, Moçambique e Guiné-Bissau* [Sweden and national liberation struggles in Angola, Mozambique, and Guinea-Bissau]. Halmstad, Sweden: Nordiska Afrikainstitutet, 2008.

Silva, A. E. Duarte. *A Independência da Guiné-Bissau e a Descolonização Portuguesa* [The independence of Guinea-Bissau and Portuguese decolonization]. Porto: Afrontamento, 1997.

————. "O litígio entre Portugal e a ONU (1960–1974)" [The dispute between Portugal and the UN (1960–1974)]. *Análise Social* 30, no. 130 (1995): 5–50.

Souto, Amélia Neves. *Caetano e o ocaso do Império. Administração e Guerra Colonial em Moçambique durante o Marcelismo (1968–1974)* [Caetano and the decline of the empire: Administration and colonial war in Mozambique during the Marcelismo (1968–1974)]. Porto: Edições Afrontamento, 2007.

Spínola, António de. *País Sem Rumo. Contributo para a História de uma Revolução* [A country with no route: Contribution to the history of a revolution]. Lisbon: Scire, 1978.

———. *Por uma Guiné Melhor* [For a better Guinea]. Lisbon: Agência Geral do Ultramar, 1970.

———. *Por uma Portugalidade Renovada* [For a renewed "Portugality"]. Lisbon: Agência Geral do Ultramar, 1973.

PART III

Race and the Interplay of Domestic and International Politics

CHAPTER 6

Testing the Limits of Soviet Internationalism

African Students in the Soviet Union

Maxim Matusevich

I n 2009, a BBC investigation focused on the lives of Africans in Moscow. A staggering 60 percent of the respondents reported having been physically assaulted in racially motivated attacks at some point during their residence in Russia.[1] The report, widely discussed in the blogosphere and international press, made little news in Russia. In fact, it hardly registered with the Russian public and was largely dismissed as yet another example of the West's insistent attempts to malign their proud and resourceful nation. In post-Soviet Russia, it seems, the plight of Africans and other ethnic minorities, routinely abused, beaten up, and even murdered, concerns very few. Indeed one can hardly expect much in the way of racial harmony in a country where the spokesman for the Federal Migration Service bemoaned in a recent interview the alleged disappearance of the "white race."[2] Fewer than three hundred people, many of them foreign students, showed up for the March against Hatred organized in St. Petersburg in October 2009 under the auspices of Russia's African Union and a small number of domestic human rights groups. In all-too-familiar fashion, the grisly murder of a young Ghanaian man in St. Petersburg on Christmas Day 2009, allegedly filmed by its neo-Nazi perpetrators, hardly made so much as a ripple in the complacent national media.[3] How tragically ironic that the country that had previously staked its reputation on waging global struggles against racism and colonialism would emerge in its post-Soviet reincarnation as a danger zone for people of color.

In part, the dramatic surge of racism and xenophobia in Russia after the Cold War can be attributed to the general breakdown of Soviet society that accompanied the dissolution of the Soviet Union. Soviet ideological pronouncements, as stale and obtuse as they had grown over the years, still provided the modicum of a moral code for the populace as well as a strict criminal code to regulate public behaviors of Soviet citizens. Still, in itself the Soviet collapse cannot account for the scope of the racist backlash against Africans and other minorities in Russia. Post-Soviet racism has deep roots in the Soviet past, paradoxically at the very time when the Soviet Union was widely recognized and even celebrated among Africans on the continent and in the diaspora as the laboratory of racial egalitarianism, the one great source of hope for oppressed racial minorities.[4] For example, the great pan-Africanist W. E. B. Du Bois visited the Soviet Union on several occasions before and after World War II, each time coming away amazed at the degree of racial acceptance he experienced there. As early as 1926 Du Bois eulogized Soviet Russia for its great strides toward colorblind egalitarianism: "I stand in astonishment and wonder at the revelation of Russia that has come to me. I may be partially deceived and half-informed. But if what I have seen with my eyes and heard with my ears in Russia is Bolshevism, I am a Bolshevik."[5]

There was nothing uniquely Du Boisian about these sentiments. During the 1920s and 1930s, dozens, probably hundreds, of African Americans, Afro-Caribbeans, and Africans trekked to the Soviet Union in search of a racial utopia. They apparently found what they were looking for. These black sojourners left numerous testimonials and memoir literature reflecting on their experience of equality and general acceptance in the "land of the Bolsheviks." Not just black celebrities like Du Bois or Claude McKay, Paul Robeson or Langston Hughes, but also other travelers—African American radicals, engineers and technicians, journalists, artists, even adventurists—partook of Soviet hospitality and, by many accounts, enjoyed the kind of equality denied them at home.[6] Even though the initial infatuation with the Soviet experiment would largely dissipate by the late 1930s (especially in view of the Nazi-Soviet pact of 1939), the memories of those early friendly encounters would continue to inform attitudes toward the Soviet Union in significant segments of the African American community and among many educated African elites in the colonies well into the postwar period.[7]

Africa Reconsidered: The 1957 Youth Festival

World War II changed the Soviet Union; it solidified its credentials as a nation-state and eventually its role as a superpower. The Soviet Union performed during the war as a highly centralized nation-state. Multiethnic, yes, but nevertheless increasingly seen at home and abroad as simply "Russia." Over the course of the war, Joseph Stalin had encouraged the resurgence of Russian nationalism, rightly recognizing its huge emotional potential in rallying the country around his leadership and against the Nazis. As is often the case with resurgent nationalism and those who exploit it for political ends, the nasty side effects were not long in coming. Toward the end of the war, Stalin, now himself a staunch Russian nationalist (despite his Georgian background), launched a series of devastating campaigns of ethnic cleansing. His ire fell on several minority groups suspected of disloyalty and collaboration with the Nazis. The Crimean Tartars, ethnic Germans, the Baltic peoples, the Chechens, the Ingush—all paid dearly for their imagined crimes of treason and were subjected to massive deportations.[8] The Jews were to follow. Stalin's last years in power were marked by the rise of state-sponsored anti-Semitism and thinly veiled attacks on Jewish intelligentsia, culminating in the infamous "Doctors' Plot" of 1953.[9] The intensification of the Cold War did little to alleviate Stalin's growing paranoia and the chauvinistic anxieties of his regime.

By the time of the tyrant's death in 1953, the Soviet Union had abandoned most of its early internationalist aspirations, its heady Comintern (Communist International) days now but a distant memory. Many of the Comintern's founders were either imprisoned or long dead. Stalin's profound xenophobia also stifled most ethnographic research. The field of African studies was not spared Stalin's wrath, with several of its founding fathers swept up in purges on account of their alleged "bourgeois leanings."[10] Soviet ideologues, despite vociferous (and by now routine) antiracist and anticolonial propaganda campaigns, nevertheless saw little revolutionary promise in the African continent.

The rise of Nikita Khrushchev and his subsequent denunciation of Stalinism at the Twentieth Party Congress in 1956 dramatically changed official Soviet attitudes toward African emancipation, which was now recognized for what it actually was, that is, a geopolitical reality. In the aftermath of Khrushchev's revelations, the country entered a relatively short period of so-called thaw, which, in contrast with the years of Stalinism, was a time of cultural and political awakening and comparative openness.[11] Africa was quickly coming into vogue with the Soviet political class, who, taking a cue from their bombastic leader, began to entertain hopes of a Marxist-Leninist future for postcolonial Africa. It was under these transformed circumstances that Soviet citizens were treated to a remarkable spectacle—amid Moscow's drabness, the appearance of a colorful cast of exotic characters: some thirty thousand international delegates of the 1957 Youth Festival.

By many accounts, African delegates enjoyed wide (and wild) popularity during the festival. The hotel reserved for African delegations quickly turned into a vibrant social spot, "the liveliest place" in town, with Soviet youth crowding its entrance in hopes of getting acquainted with the foreign new-comers.[12] Urban folklore circulated the wild tales of Russian girls throwing themselves at the striking-looking visitors. The rumors, undoubtedly greatly exaggerated, cast the festival as a veritable extravaganza of interracial love. Yet the gathering did excite Soviet citizens, unaccustomed to such close—not to mention intimate—contact with foreigners, pushing the most adventurous toward behaviors both risky and risqué. One of festival's unintended conse-quences was the appearance of a generation of biracial "festival kids," whose presence amid the Soviet populace would serve as a continuous reminder of that 1957 summer of love in Moscow.[13] Indeed, love was very much in the air. "Africa is shaped like a heart," gushed poet Evgenii Dolmatovsky, yet another contemporary observer smitten by the festival.[14]

The party and state authorities had planned the festival to showcase Soviet values, but the event overwhelmed them and produced some unanticipated and long-lasting ramifications. In August of 1957, millions of Soviet citizens received their first exposure to the lifestyles, mannerisms, aesthetics, cultural expressions, and political debates that contrasted most sharply with the Soviet norm.[15] The effects of the festival would linger on for decades; it provided an opening through which Western ideas and art forms began to seep into Soviet society.[16] Africans, so visible during the festival, would soon begin to arrive in the country in large numbers. They came to study, but in an ironic role rever-sal, they ended up educating the Soviets; they introduced a population steeped in parochialism to modern aesthetics, new art forms, and the liberation politi-cal discourse.

Institutional Initiatives and the Arrival of African Students

The 1957 Youth Festival contributed to rejuvenating the study of Africa in the Soviet Union. During his 1958 conversation with Nikita Khrushchev, Du Bois argued for the creation within the Soviet Academy of Sciences of "an institute for the study of Pan-African history, sociology, ethnography, anthro-pology and all cognate studies."[17] Du Bois's argument must have resonated with Khrushchev; in July 1959, the Communist Party's Central Committee adopted a special resolution providing for the creation of a research institute of African studies (later to be known as the Africa Institute).[18] Less than a year later another party resolution, in February 1960, stipulated the founding of a new university to train "the national cadres for the countries of Asia, Africa, and Latin America." Friendship University, later renamed Lumumba Univer-sity after assassinated Congolese prime minister Patrice Lumumba, would emerge as a flagship institution of higher learning, catering to the needs of Third World students and thus to the needs of Soviet foreign policy.[19]

As these institutional initiatives were being finalized, African students began to trickle into the Soviet Union. As of January 1, 1959, there were only seven students from sub-Saharan Africa officially enrolled in Soviet institutions of higher learning.[20] However, between 1960 and 1961 the number of African students in the USSR increased sevenfold, from seventy-two to over five hundred, eventually reaching some five thousand by the end of the decade.[21] By 1990, on the eve of Soviet collapse, the number of Africans in the country would rise to thirty thousand, or about 24 percent of the total body of foreign students.[22] Few of these students were committed Marxists. In fact, there is some evidence that even those who arrived with the backing of foreign Communist parties or their front organizations often lacked appropriate ideological credentials or at least failed to put them to good use once in the Soviet Union.[23] As a result, and in stark contrast to the black travelers of the prewar decades, African students of the 1960s and 1970s were less inclined to give the Soviets the benefit of the doubt. It is not that the prewar black sojourners never encountered racism or were not frustrated by instances of crude racial stereotyping while in the Soviet Union. The vast majority of black American travelers of the 1920s–1930s, on a tour away from Jim Crow America, put much faith in Soviet rhetoric and rationalized the many Soviet deficiencies as a necessary corollary to the newness of the socialist experiment.[24] Some three decades later the new black arrivals proved far less sanguine. Many of them also hailed from places steeped in political activism, charged with the energy released by the process of decolonization. They brought into the midst of Soviet society the very revolutionary fervor and liberation ethos that had marked Soviet Russia's entry into the world some forty years earlier.

African Students' Challenge to the Soviet Ritual

Accounts by African students in the late Soviet Union are replete with complaints about drab lifestyles, everyday regimentation, substandard dorm accommodation, and alleged *stukachestvo* (spying and reporting to authorities) by their Soviet fellow students.[25] Upon his arrival in Moscow in 1959, an East African student named Everest Mulekezi was quick to discover that he had to share his fourteen-by-sixteen dorm room with three other students, two of whom were "hand-picked" Russians. His hopes for a hot bath after a long and arduous journey were also dashed—hot water was available only once a week, on Wednesdays from five to eleven o'clock in the evening.[26]

Despite the prevailing climate of complacency and the relative timidity of their Soviet peers, Africans protested vociferously against poor living conditions, racist incidents, restrictions on travel within the Soviet Union, restrictions on dating Russian girls, and restrictions on forming national and ethnic student associations. As early as March 1960, African students in Moscow petitioned the Soviet government to curb the expressions of crude racism by Soviet citizens.[27] At about the same time, four African students (Theophilus Okonkwo of Nigeria, Andrew Richard Amar and Stanley Omar Okullo of Uganda, and Michel Ayieh of Togo) were expelled from Moscow State University for defying an administrative ban on the Black African Students' Union. Their expulsion and subsequent departure from the country received wide coverage in the Western press. The students publicly accused university officials of suppressing the union as well as of imposing severe restrictions on the circulation of "books and jazz records." Okonkwo, Amar, and Ayieh challenged the Soviet authorities in a biting open letter: "For the Soviet leaders to pose before the world as champions of oppressed Africa while they oppress millions in their own country and their satellites is hypocrisy at its worst."[28]

The death of a Ghanaian student in Moscow in December 1963, which his friends suspected to have been a homicide, occasioned an exceptionally angry reaction among African students in the Soviet Union.[29] They staged a protest march on the Kremlin demanding a "Bill of Rights" for African students in the country (the first unauthorized demonstration in the Soviet Union since the expulsion of Leon Trotsky in 1927).[30] The press was also raging back on the continent: "Why did our students . . . protest in Moscow recently?" exclaimed a particularly incensed African observer. "Was it not because . . . our boys had been insulted and attacked on trams, on the streets, in restaurants, in most public places? Could it be that our students have grown tired of the hypocrisy of Communism and the Soviet system?"[31] More trouble brewed in 1964 and 1965, with African students in the USSR frequently reporting racist attacks, fights with Soviet youngsters, and even feeling compelled to "carry knives for protection."[32] Komsomol officials at Moscow State University (MGU) grudgingly acknowledged several instances of scandalous behavior exhibited by Soviet students, but also argued that Africans and other foreigners at MGU had a limited understanding of the selfless and romantic nature of Soviet young men, many of whom preferred the hardship of toil in remote Siberia to the pleasures of Moscow highlife.

In May 1965, the Soviet authorities tacitly linked the African student community in the country with the idea of political subversion when they expelled a black American diplomat, Norris D. Garnett, for "conducting anti-Soviet work among students from African countries."[33] Garnett's departure from the scene hardly garnered the desired long-term effect, as the community of African students in the Soviet Union continued to be the source of multiple headaches for Soviet authorities. For example, in 1975, eight hundred African students went on a weeklong strike, this time in Kiev, in protest of the expulsion of a twenty-three-year-old Czechoslovakian girl for daring to marry a Nigerian fellow student. That same year, a Nigerian student sleeping in his dorm room in the city of Lvov was attacked by "a drunken Russian with a chisel." The attacker was reportedly incensed by the Nigerian's success with Russian and Ukrainian girls. The incident quickly turned into a major fight involving other Nigerian students who had come to the rescue of their compatriot, and as a result three of them were expelled "for attacking and beating up a Soviet citizen."[34]

Discrimination or alleged discrimination aside, the students' resentment, it was noted, stemmed from "the sole fact of their living in a communist country." Once in the Soviet Union, Africans, "even self-proclaimed leftists," had to reconcile "the obvious discrepancies between what is said and what actually exists." And what "actually existed" in the Moscow of 1960s and 1970s were "the crowded living conditions, lack of privacy, monotonous diet, inadequate sanitary facilities, and the overall drabness of life."[35]

By expressing their displeasure with the Soviet status quo (something that few of their Soviet peers dared do) and by challenging it through their "foreign" lifestyles and cosmopolitan aesthetics, some African students became the de facto conduits of dissent. They had more freedom of expression and travel (and quite often more money) than their hosts, and many of them arrived from postcolonial settings reverberating with spirited political debates.[36] Everest Mulekezi remembered intense political discussions he used to hold in his dorm room with some of his Russian friends, who were reportedly stunned by the openness and nonchalance with which Everest and his fellow Africans discussed politically sensitive matters. From a Soviet perspective, Everest, by encouraging his Russian friends to question authority and read the Western press, clearly acted as an agent of political subversion. By introducing them to jazz, he effectively subverted Soviet cultural values. It was in the course of one such "sedition session" that a Russian friend of Mulekezi's "buried his face in his hands" and conceded the truth of the African's argument: "It is true we're not free. . . . I am not free to read what Westerners read. I am not free to visit the West or even travel in my own country without a permit."[37] African students in Moscow articulated ideas manifestly out of sync with Soviet sensibilities in the pages of *Russian Journal*, Andrea Lee's perceptive memoir of her time in Russia. Lee records, for example, a memorable conversation she had in a smoke-filled Moscow kitchen with a stern-looking Eritrean student: "In my five years in Russia, I've come to hate everything about the Soviet system. Life here is a misery of repression—you yourselves know it. . . . The Soviet Union has educated me, though not in a way it intended."[38]

What Africa Actually Meant for the Soviets

Of course, not every single African student in the USSR set out on a collision course with the Soviet system. For many, the romantic aura surrounding their arrival in this strange new land never entirely wore off. Yet being an African in the Soviet Union also meant that one performed "foreignness" on a day-to-day basis. Blackness implied an almost automatic association with a number of political and cultural modern phenomena that taxed Soviet sensibilities. Antiracist and anticolonial movements carried a powerful liberation (and often implicitly religious) message, while the sorts of cultural production usually associated with black roots tended to be anti-authoritarian, both in form and content. The liberal wing of the Soviet intelligentsia sometimes embraced officially sanctioned liberation "causes" not out of any deep respect for Soviet foreign policy but rather because Africa's struggle for emancipation and freedom resonated with those whose own freedoms were significantly restricted. For example, having visited West Africa in the late 1950s, the bard of the Soviet "thaw," Yevgenii Yevtushenko, penned a series of emotionally charged and ideologically ambiguous poems. Following a long-established Western poetic canon, the poet exoticized Africa but also mused on a supposed commonality of fate between the savannah (Africa) and the taiga (Russia):

> Savannah, I'm the taiga
> I'm endless like you
> I'm a mystery for you
> And you're a mystery for me . . .
>
> Your sons desire for you
> Freedom eternal
> And toward them I'm filled with love
> Enormous like the pine trees of my land.[39]

On its surface the poem reads as yet another celebration of decolonization. Indeed, over the years the Soviets labored assiduously to domesticate and appropriate African anticolonial movements or to claim a kind of ideological kinship with the civil rights movement in the United States (the movement epitomized by a charismatic Baptist minister—by no means a natural ally of the Soviet Union).[40] Yet considering Moscow's own less than stellar record in that department, any discussion of human and civil rights, even by a poet generally loyal to the regime, was potentially subversive. Yevtushenko's ode to African emancipation, composed when hopes were running high for a long-lasting post-Stalin liberalization of Soviet society, can also be read as a hymn to freedom—African *and* Russian.

Even celebrating such bona fide black Communists as Angela Davis was far from an ideologically risk-free proposition. In 1972, the Soviet public followed closely the dramatic twists and turns of Davis's trial in the United States. Formidable propaganda resources were marshaled to wage a massive solidarity campaign in support of the imprisoned Californian professor. Indeed, in the early 1970s Angela Davis was a household name in the Soviet Union, the pages of Soviet newspapers filled with impassioned pleas for her freedom. According to Valentina Tereshkova, the first woman cosmonaut and chair of the Soviet Women's Committee, these powerful sentiments were shared by "millions of Soviet women," whose hearts apparently were "beating in unison" with Angela's heart.[41] Following her acquittal on a murder conspiracy charge, Davis triumphantly toured the Soviet Union, ushered around in black limousines and presented with honorary degrees and mountainous floral arrangements.[42] But strangely enough, the real impact of the trial and the subsequent visit lay outside Cold War politics. Angela Davis's name, and especially her world-famous hairdo (like Che Guevara's iconic image in the West), would become fixtures of Soviet popular culture. Handmade "Angela Davis canvas shopping bags" fetched top rubles on the black market and hairdressers skillful enough to replicate the legendary Afro established a devoted urban clientele. As often was the case with Western radicals transplanted on Soviet soil, Davis's political message mattered little to the seasoned (and increasingly cynical) populace. Of far greater import was the romantic aura of youthful anti-establishment rebellion surrounding the young Californian. There was little new or exciting for a Soviet citizen circa 1970 in Davis's Marxist pronouncements; her appeal lay elsewhere—in the stories of her daring escapes and concealed weapons; her transcontinental travels; and perhaps, in the fact that she had dared to appear braless at a public ceremony in her honor.[43]

Probably the most visible aspect of Africa's subversive challenge to Soviet values could be observed in the countercultural prominence of the types of artistic expression usually associated with African/black cultural tradition. Living in Moscow in the early 1960s, Andrew Amar noted the Russian students' fascination with jazz, as well as their awareness of its historical roots: "One of the things which often brought us together with the Russian students was listening to modern jazz music. Large numbers of them appreciated the better kind of jazz and also realized and acknowledged that it had developed from the folk music of the African people."[44] Early Soviet commentators saw in jazz the worst manifestations of Western decadence. They also fumed over the "jungle" and "uncivilized" roots of the music. When it came to criticizing jazz (and later rock), the gloves came off; Soviet cultural critics and commentators did not hesitate to tap into the basest racial stereotypes borrowed from the West. The great proletarian author Maxim Gorky explicitly linked jazz to the alleged savagery and unbridled sexuality of its performers.[45]

Africa and Africans thus occupied a highly ambiguous place in the Soviet's everyday life. While over the years the Soviet state and its ideologues exerted considerable effort to bring "Africa into the fold," the reality of the African presence in the USSR was far more multilayered and complex. As a propaganda weapon, Africa often jammed and even backfired, and as Soviet collapse loomed closer, the idea of Africa was playing at least a partially subversive role to the Soviet status quo. It is noteworthy then that African themes came to feature prominently in Soviet countercultural production, especially in the late Soviet period. In 1988, millions of Soviet citizens flocked to movie theaters to see what would become a classic "perestroika" film: *ASSA*.[46] By employing a grotesque but poignant pop-cultural symbolism, the film exposed to national scrutiny the debility of late-Soviet society. The movie's main character, an artsy and nonconformist "boy Bananan" (played by countercultural icon Sergey Bugaev, also commonly known by the nickname "Afrika"), turns himself into a protagonist of change.[47] Bananan's youth and lightness of being, his alternative lifestyle, his penchant for hippiesque outfits, and his eventual tragic end in the hands of mature and businesslike men (men of the establishment, no doubt) combined to put forward a quixotic vision of life in stark contrast to the moribund Soviet status quo. The stage name of the actor himself, "Afrika," makes the alien quality of the main character even more pronounced, as does the appearance of Bananan's best friend—a black-skinned Russian. Apparently, for the makers of this popular movie, Africa presented a point of reference so out of tune with daily Soviet experience, so remote and strange, as to endow the bearer of such a moniker with a distinctively dissident aura.

The idea of Africa and Africa's foreignness finds use in another celebrated and paradigm-changing perestroika film—Vassily Pichul's *Little Vera* (1989). One scene in particular never failed to elicit puzzled chuckles from the Soviet audience: a typical shabby Soviet flat and a little black boy glued to a television screen watching a popular Russian cartoon. The cartoon characters, three vicious-looking but highly likable pirates, break into a lighthearted song about Africa:

> Little kids,
> No matter what you do,
> Don't even think of
> Going to Africa for walks.
> Africa is dangerous,
> Africa is horrible.[48]

The irony of the scene that shows a black Russian child consuming a cultural production that treats Africa as an exotic, dangerous, and slightly ridiculous unknown could not fail to register with the viewers. The black boy's outward appearance made his absorption in the cartoon highly humorous. Yet the significance of this brief cinematic encounter with Africa went beyond a passing movie moment. *Little Vera* gives us a glimpse of popular Soviet imagery of Africa and alerts the viewer to Africa's presence in late-Soviet public and cultural domains. Yes, Africa is a somewhat unknown quantity, but not entirely so. The little boy in the movie did not just materialize out of thin air amid the clutter of Soviet domestic life (even if some of the viewers conclude that to have been the case)—his mother is white, hence his father had to be of African descent. His precise identity is left to our imagination—a foreign sailor, an African student, a romantic guerilla type training in the USSR, or maybe even a visiting black American musician (partisans of Soviet counterculture worshipped Louis Armstrong, Jimi Hendrix, Bob Marley, and others).

How telling it was that a cult classic like *ASSA* drew on the idea of Africa and "Africanness" in its treatment of the contemporary Soviet condition! Such contrasting imagery fleshed out the essentials of Soviet experience— its profound isolationism, the drabness of the mundane, the lack of color, and even the notoriously forbidding Russian climate. African students in the Soviet Union personified the contrast between Soviet insularity and the outside world, and in this capacity they routinely collided with the state and challenged by word and deed its values. They had fashioned for themselves a separate cultural and ideological space within the Soviet domain, an impressive achievement of free will beyond the wildest dreams of ordinary Soviet citizens. Any encounter with an African or a cinematic or literary African theme evoked for many the world outside Soviet ritual, differing from it in almost every respect. And it was in part for this very reason that Africa and Africans became early targets for the xenophobic propaganda campaigns of the late-Soviet period.

Popular Images of Blackness and the Racist Backlash during Perestroika

By the time Mikhail Gorbachev rose to power in 1985, the Soviets had long since solidified their credentials as supporters of African decolonization and liberation struggle. The Soviet Union participated (with varying degrees of success) in a number of African development and industrial projects. African students had become a common sight on most large Soviet campuses, where they stood out but also often enjoyed a degree of popularity among the student body. And the African presence was being felt in yet another, not entirely unexpected way: by the early 1980s a new generation of Soviet children of partial African ancestry began to enter Soviet public life.[49]

The post-1985 reforms ushered in a period of thorough reassessment of Soviet values and commitments, which also affected both the official and popular attitudes toward Africa and Africans. By exposing the structural deficiencies of the Soviet system, perestroika also invited an increasingly open and progressively critical discussion of the special place the USSR had come to occupy within the international community.[50] With the Cold War on the wane, many of the country's economic shortcomings were now blamed on its external liabilities. For too long, argued the avatars of perestroika, the Soviet Union had undermined its own economic base by channeling aid to Third World nations. The implication of such an argument was all too apparent: the Third World had been sponging off the USSR and thus degrading the quality of life for its citizens.[51] Even before the onset of reforms, people in the streets had been grumbling about "too much aid to Africans"—lamenting the privileges bestowed on African and other visitors, presumably at Soviet expense. For example, foreign students received much higher stipends—ninety rubles per month versus an average of thirty rubles allotted to Soviet students.[52] As early as 1963, professors from Moscow and Leningrad reported Soviet students complaining bitterly about the preferential treatment allegedly allotted to Africans at their colleges: "they are studying at our expense and eating our bread, of course it's unfair."[53]

Popularly accepted images of Africa and African lifestyles long present in the Soviet cultural tradition fed the growing paranoia. It was exactly the frequent representation of Africa as a place of carefree existence, where people (and cute cartoonish animals) cared little to nothing about "tomorrow," that turned Africa into a ready scapegoat for widespread discontent. Several generations of Soviet children, for example, grew up listening to the lovely tune "Chunga-Changa" as they watched a famous cartoon. In the cartoon, a racially diverse group of adorable and playful youngsters enjoy a problem-free life on a tropical (read: African) island, far from the drudgery and cold of the north. In a lighthearted song they celebrate the obvious benefits of this easy way of life:

> Chunga-Changa, the sky is blue
> Chunga-Changa, the summer's all year round
> Chunga-Changa, we live so merry
> Chunga-Changa, we sing little songs

Oh, what a miracle island, miracle island
It's so easy to live here
It's so easy to live here, Chunga-Changa
We are happy munching on coconuts and bananas
Munching on coconuts and bananas, Chunga-Changa.[54]

A very similar theme can be found in another popular cartoon, *The Lion Cub and the Turtle*, where several charming characters, unmistakably African animals, celebrate life in the sun without work. Sings the lion cub:

All I do is lie in the sun
And move my ears
I just lie and lie
And move my ears.[55]

Such "orientalist" representations of Africa and life in the tropics in general were not necessarily intentionally demeaning. More likely they reflected the generally benign views of "southern countries" widely held by Soviet citizens, a perspective only slightly marked by a certain condescension and paternalism. However, adverse economic circumstances expedited a not-so-illogical transition from paternalism, to distaste, to outright hostility toward the "Third World leeches."

A surge in anti–Third World sentiment accompanied new revelations about the alleged sources of Soviet underdevelopment. The Soviet Union, the public was led to believe, could not afford to support dependents in faraway exotic locations. Africans, the most visible representatives of the developing world in Soviet public spaces, now had to bear the brunt of what became a spontaneous campaign of denunciation of Soviet assistance abroad. Africans residing in the Soviet Union at the time reported a rise in the number of racist incidents as well as mounting difficulties in maintaining government scholarships to continue their education in the country.[56] In a series of letters to *West Africa*, Charles Quist-Adade, a Ghanaian residing in Leningrad, depicted a rather gloomy fate for the African in Gorbachev's Russia. According to Quist-Adade, a sense of desperation and insecurity permeated the lives of African students in the country of dying socialism. Prior to perestroika, he suggested, African students had been in a privileged class of their own, but, alas, not anymore.[57]

The neat arrangement was ended by a combination of skyrocketing inflation and new regulations imposing heavy financial burdens on foreign students in the Soviet Union, but not before it had produced widespread envy, resentment, and racial hatred among the general population. Glasnost lifted the flood gates to prejudice and crude racism and let loose antiblack senti-ments bordering on hysteria. Many Africans blamed Gorbachev's "revolu-tion" for not feeling safe in the streets and public places of Soviet cities. A Nigerian journalism student at Kazan University wrote to a Moscow news-paper: "One day I decided to have my lunch in a nearby café. As soon as I opened the door, I was met with jeers and cat-calls by young girls sitting around a table, laughing and cracking unfriendly jokes about me."[58] The enterprising Nigerians soon learned to play curious mind games to save their skin during their growing number of unfriendly encounters. One student, for example, when approached by a group of hoodlums, pretended to be an American black. The trick worked; the thugs, having abandoned their origi-nal belligerent intentions, "immediately simulated keen interest and began to ask questions about Stevie Wonder, Michael Jackson, etc."[59] Alas, other assault victims were either not as quick or simply less lucky. Between May and August of 1990, at least four Nigerian students were severely beaten up and one allegedly killed in Moscow on grounds ranging from "being a mon-key" to dating Russian girls.[60]

Considering the growing public paranoia about HIV/AIDS, for any African to approach a Russian girl was becoming an increasingly risky proposition. By the late 1980s the Soviet public had grown panicky about the alleged AIDS pandemic in the country. Ignorant in their understand-ing of the dreadful disease, Soviet citizens found themselves exposed to a media barrage of materials on AIDS, many of scientifically dubious content. Publications dealing with AIDS routinely portrayed Africans as primary transmitters of the virus (the first victim to have died was reported by *Len-ingradskaya Pravda* as having had her "first sexual contact with Africans ten years ago"). Another newspaper ran a feature story about an infected Ukrai-nian baby whose mother "had an affair with an African."[61] Soviet street folk-lore, with its characteristic sexual undertone, tied the much-professed (and mocked) love of Soviet officialdom for the developing world to the appear-ance of AIDS in Russia. A popular joke provided alternative transliterations for the original Russian *SPID* (AIDS) in which the term was variously inter-preted either as *Sotsialnoe Posledstvie Internatsionalnoj Druzhby* (Social Consequence of International Friendship) or *Spetsialny Podarok Inostrannyh Druzej* (Special Gift from Foreign Friends). Although Africans residing in the Soviet Union were far from amused, the joke encapsulated the growing popular dissatisfaction with the regime, which "wasted precious resources" on people who (in the words of one populist politician) "have just descended from the palm tree." Africans were rapidly becoming visible scapegoats for Soviet medical, economic, and political disasters.[62]

As Soviet-style paternalism gave way to outright and widespread hostility, the traditional Soviet concern for African liberation also withered away. The release of Nelson Mandela from a South African prison in February 1990, by any measure an event of historic proportions and one eagerly anticipated by the Soviets for decades, occasioned rather unenthusiastic coverage in the Soviet press. In fact, some of the "old Africa hands" at the Central Committee of the CPSU noted the measured tone of Gorbachev's congratulatory telegram to Mandela.[63] Africans residing in Russia on the eve of the Soviet collapse worried that the coverage of Africa was being reduced to simplistic stereotypes of its banes and woes. In the media, the very word "Africa" was often supplanted by *cherny kontinent* (black continent), the Conradian place of danger and wasted opportunities, and a proverbial black hole devouring scant Soviet resources.[64] In its later years the Soviet government, facing mounting economic troubles, proceeded to cut educational scholarships for Africans and other Third World students. After decades of governmental sponsorship, African students now were left to provide for themselves amid an increasingly unsympathetic and disintegrating society; many of them opted to leave the country altogether—in the words of the Mauritanian film director Abderrahmane Sissako, himself formerly a student in Moscow, their "relationship with Russia was over."[65] The stage was set for the debilitating wave of racism and xenophobia soon to sweep across post-Soviet spaces.

Notes

1. "Africans 'under Siege' in Moscow," BBC broadcast, August 31, 2009, *news.bbc .co.uk/2/hi/europe/8230158.stm* (accessed October 5, 2009).
2. "Predstavitel' FMS Rossii: Na Konu Vyzhivanie Beloi Rasy" [Representative of Russia's Federal Migration Service: At stake is the survival of the white race], BBC broadcast, April 20, 2011, *www.bbc.co.uk/russian/russia/2011/04/110420_fms_white_ race.shtml* (accessed May 10, 2011).
3. "Natsisty Zasnyalis' v Ubijstve" [Nazis filmed the murder], *Fontanka.ru*, January 15, 2010, *www.fontanka.ru/2010/01/15/072/* (accessed January 18, 2010).
4. See Paul Robeson, *The Negro People and the Soviet Union* (New York: New Century, 1950), 8.
5. W. E. B. Du Bois, editorial, *Crisis* 33, no. 1 (November 1926), 8.
6. See, for example, a recent study of black sojourners in the Soviet Union by Joy Gleason Carew: *Blacks, Reds, and Russians: Sojourners in Search of the Soviet Promise* (New Brunswick, NJ: Rutgers University Press, 2008).
7. For this argument, see Maxim Matusevich, "An Exotic Subversive: Africa, Africans, and the Soviet Everyday," *Race and Class* 49, no. 4 (2008): 57–81; see also

Matusevich, "Journeys of Hope: African Diaspora and the Soviet Society," *African Diaspora* 1, nos. 1–2 (2008): 53–85.

8. See Yitzhak M. Brudny, *Reinventing Russia: Russian Nationalism and the Soviet State, 1953–1991* (Cambridge, MA: Harvard University Press, 2000).

9. See Jonathan Brent and Vladimir Naumov, *Stalin's Last Crime: The Plot against the Jewish Doctors, 1948–1953* (New York: Norton, 2004).

10. Apollon Davidson and Irina Filatova, "African History: A View from behind the Kremlin Wall," in *Africa in Russia, Russia in Africa: Three Centuries of Encounters,* ed. Maxim Matusevich (Trenton, NJ: Africa World Press, 2007), 111–32.

11. For an exhaustive study of Khrushchev's role in this transition, see William Taubman, *Khrushchev: The Man and His Era* (New York: Norton, 2003).

12. Ibid., 9–10. See also "2-Week Revelry in Moscow Ends," *New York Times*, August 12, 1957.

13. Kristin Roth-Ey, "'Loose Girls' on the Loose? Sex, Propaganda, and the 1957 Youth Festival," in *Women in the Khrushchev Era*, ed. Melanie Ilič, Susan E. Reid, and Lynne Attwood (New York: Palgrave Macmillan, 2004), 75–95.

14. Russian State Archive of New History (RGANI), Department of Culture at CC CPSU, f. 5, op. 55, ex. 103 (January 1964–July 1965).

15. For a comprehensive overview of the festival's impact on Soviet society, see the recently published Pia Koivunen, "The 1957 Moscow Youth Festival: Propagating a New, Peaceful Image of the Soviet Union," in *Soviet State and Society under Nikita Khrushchev*, ed. Melanie Ilič and Jeremy Smith (London: Routledge, 2009), 46–65.

16. This argument has been recently made in Yale Richmond, *Cultural Exchange and the Cold War* (University Park: Pennsylvania State University Press, 2003).

17. See W. E. B. Du Bois, *The Autobiography of W. E. B. Du Bois: A Soliloquy on Viewing My Life from the Last Decade of Its First Century* (London: Oxford University Press, 2007), 18–19.

18. S. V. Mazov, "Sozdanie Instituta Afriki" [The creation of Africa Institute], *Vostok* 1 (January–March 1998): 80–88. See also Yu. M. Ilyin, *Institut Afriki, 1960–2004* [Africa Institute, 1960–2004] (Moscow: RAN, 2005).

19. Tsentr Khranenia Sovremennoj Dokumentatsii (TsKhSD), f. 4, op. 16, d. 783, l. 13 and d. 806, l. 19, 21. For more archival references, see Mazov, "Sozdanie Instituta Afriki."

20. Russian State Archive of Social and Political History (hereafter RGASPI), "Spravka o kolichestve studentov-inostrantsev iz kap i kolstran, obuchayushikhsya v vuzah SSSR na 1 yanvarya 1959" [A note on the number of foreign students from capitalist and colonial countries studying in the USSR as of 1 January 1959], f. 1M, op. 46, d. 248, list 12.

21. These numbers come from O. M. Gorbatov and L. Ia. Cherkasski, *Sotrudnichestvo SSSR so stranami Arabskogo Vostoka i Afriki* [Cooperation between the USSR and the countries of Arab East and Africa] (Moscow: Nauka, 1973). Also quoted in Julie Hessler, "Death of an African Student in Moscow," *Cahiers du Monde Russe* 47, nos. 1–2 (January–June 2006): 35.

22. V. V. Gribanova and N. A. Zherlitsyna, "Podgotovka studentov iz Afrikanskikh stran v vuzah Rossii" [Training of African students at Russian universities],

Publications of Africa Institute, www.inafran.ru/ru/content/view/77/51/ (accessed June 17, 2008).

23. A typical example was that of a young Somali student, Abdulhamid Mohammed Hussein, who having arrived in Moscow with references from Italian Communists proceeded to wreak havoc with Soviet and university authorities by engaging in a series of domestic disturbances and public scandals. His story was only one of many. See S. V. Mazov, "Afrikanskie Studenty v Moskve v God Afriki" [African students in Moscow in the year of Africa], *Vostok* 3 (May–June 1999): 91–93.

24. This argument is further developed in Maxim Matusevich, "Harlem Globe-Trotters: Black Sojourners in Stalin's Soviet Union," in *The Harlem Renaissance Revisited: Politics, Arts, and Letters*, ed. Jeffrey O. G. Ogbar (Baltimore: Johns Hopkins University Press, 2010), 211–44.

25. See, for example, Olabisi Ajala, *An African Abroad* (London: Jarolds, 1963); Andrew Richard Amar, *An African in Moscow* (London: Ampersand, 1963); Jan Carew, *Moscow Is Not My Mecca* (London: Secker and Warburg, 1964); Andrea Lee, *Russian Journal* (New York: Random House, 1981); Nicholas Nyangira, "Africans Don't Go to Russia to Be Brainwashed," *New York Times Magazine*, May 16, 1965, 64; S. Omor Okullo, "A Negro's Life in Russia—Beatings, Insults, Segregation," *U.S. News and World Report*, August 1, 1963, 59–60; and William Anti-Taylor, *Moscow Diary* (London: Robert Hale, 1967).

26. Everest Mulekezi, "I Was a Student at Moscow State," *Reader's Digest* 79, no. 471 (July 1961), 99–104.

27. TsKhSD, f. 5, op. 35, d. 149, l. 42, 44. For more on this and similar incidents, see Mazov, *Afriknaskie Studenty v Moskve*. See also "The Plight of Our Students in the USSR," *West African Pilot*, February 3, 1964.

28. "Africans Did Russians In by Rioting," *Chicago Defender*, December 28, 1963; see also Paul Wohl, "Africans Embarrass Reds," *Christian Science Monitor*, February 18, 1964.

29. An exhaustive study of this episode is found in Hessler, "Death of an African Student in Moscow."

30. "Students Demand 'Bill of Rights,'" *West African Pilot*, December 30, 1963.

31. Sunny Odulana, "Our Students in Moscow," *West African Pilot*, January 2, 1964.

32. See Roscoe Drummond, "Red Race Relations," *Washington Post*, January 5, 1964; "Africans Carry Knives for Protection in USSR," *Chicago Daily Defender*, May 11, 1964; Stephen Rosenfeld, "Soviet-African Student Fighting Reaches Kremlin," *Washington Post*, January 28, 1965; "African Students Trying Anew to Leave Russia," *Washington Post*, April 4, 1965; and "Kenya Students Tell Why They Left USSR," *Chicago Daily Defender*, April 8, 1965.

33. See "U.S. Diplomat Ordered to Leave Soviet Union," *Chicago Daily Defender*, May 12, 1965; and Henry Tanner, "Soviet Ousts U.S. Cultural Aide as Inciter of African Students," *New York Times*, May 12, 1965. See also William A. Payne, "Expelled Negro Diplomat Calls Soviet Charges Ridiculous," *Washington Post*, June 17, 1965.

34. "Africans Studying in Russia Allege Discrimination," *Christian Science Monitor*, November 11, 1975; see also "Kiev Strike Settled," *Africa Diary* 15, no. 49 (December 3–9, 1975): 7703–4.

35. "The Plight of Our Students."

36. Amar, *An African in Moscow*, 19.

37. Mulekezi, "I Was a Student," 102.

38. Lee, *Russian Journal*, 152.

39. "Savannah and Taiga," in Yevgenii Yevtushenko, *Vzmah ruki* [An outstretched hand] (Moscow: Molodaya Gvardia, 1962), 58–59. Translation by author.

40. Martin Luther King Jr., with his Christian gospel and Gandhi-inspired tactics of civil disobedience, had to be inconvenient for the Soviets. They far preferred such firebrand radicals as Dr. Angela Davis, whose famous 1971–1972 trial occasioned a massive propaganda campaign of support by the Soviet Union. See, for example, numerous commentaries and cartoons about the trial in issues of *Krokodil* for 1971–1972. A typical cartoon depicts a plucky Davis holding her head high in front of a racist judge. The sleeve of the judge's robe is in fact an executioner's ax ready to drop on the courageous black Communist (see *Krokodil* [5] [February 1972]: 10). But even Angela Davis inspired more than a sense of solidarity in the hearts of Soviet intelligentsia. In 1978, a leading Soviet nuclear physicist, Sergei Polikanov, was expelled from the Communist Party after having made a statement to Western reporters protesting restrictions on travel abroad. "It was easier to fight for the freedom of Angela Davis than for our own freedom," announced Polikanov, and predictably got into trouble with the authorities (see "Soviet Physicist Who Complained of Travel Curb Is Ousted by Party," *New York Times*, March 28, 1978).

41. Schomburg Center for Research in Black Culture, "Letter to Angela Davis from Valentina Nikolayeva-Tereshkova," Angela Davis Legal Defense Collection, Box 4, Folder 4 (1970).

42. James F. Clarity, "Angela Davis Warmly Welcomed in Moscow," *New York Times*, August 29, 1972. See also Open Society Archive, "Angela Davis in the GDR," Radio Free Europe, September 18, 1972, Box 99, Folder 1, Report 164 (1972).

43. Leonid Parfenov, *Namedni: Nasha Era, 1971–1980* [Recently: Our era, 1971–1980] (Moscow: KoLibri, 2009), 29.

44. Amar, *An African in Moscow*, 63.

45. Maxim Gorky, "O Muzyke Tolstykh" [On the music of the gross], *Pravda*, April 18, 1928.

46. *ASSA*, dir. Sergey Soloviev (Mosfilm, 1988).

47. See Louis Grachos, *Afrika* (Los Angeles: University of Southern California Fisher Gallery, 1991).

48. The lyrics of the song come from a popular children's poem. See Kornei Chukovskii, *Doktor Aibolit* [Doctor Dolittle] (Moscow: Detskaiia Literatura, 1961).

49. The lives and times of African Russians are the subject of two noteworthy memoirs—one by Lily Golden and another one by her daughter, the well-known journalist and TV personality Yelena Khanga. See Lily Golden, *My Long Journey Home* (Chicago: Third World Press, 2003); and Yelena Khanga, *Soul to Soul: A Black Russian American Family, 1865–1992* (New York: Norton, 1994).

50. See Mikhail Gorbachev, *Perestroika* (New York: Harper and Row, 1988).

51. L. Z. Zevin and E. L Simonov, "Pomosh' i Ekonomicheskoe Sotrudnichestvo

SSSR s Razvivayushimisia Stranami: Uroki, Problemy i Perspektivy" [Assistance and economic cooperation between the USSR and developing countries: Lessons, problems, and perspectives], *Narody Azii i Afriki* 2 (1990): 5–17.

52. See Mulekezi, "I Was a Student"; see also William Anti-Taylor, "Red Bias: African Lament," *Christian Science Monitor*, November 5, 1963.

53. RGASPI, "Stenogramma soveshaniya prepodavatelej vuzov g. Moskvy, Leningrada, i t.d." [The minutes of the meeting of university professors of Moscow, Leningrad, etc.], f. 1, op. 46, d. 339, April 23, 1963.

54. Composer V. Shainskii; translation by author.

55. *L'venok i Cherepakha Poyut Pesnyu* [The lion cub and the turtle sing a song], dir. Inessa Kovalevskaya, composer Gennady Gladkov (Soyuzmultfilm 1974); translation by author.

56. See Charles Quist-Adade, *In the Shadows of the Kremlin and the White House: Africa's Media Image from Communism to Post-Communism* (Lanham, MD: University Press of America, 2001).

57. Charles Quist-Adade, "Black Bashing," *West Africa*, October 8–14, 1990, 2606.

58. Quoted in Charles Quist-Adade, "Russian Roughshod," *West Africa*, July 9–15, 1990, 2056.

59. Ibid.

60. Quist-Adade, "Black Bashing," 2606.

61. Charles Quist-Adade, "Targets of AIDS-Phobia," *West Africa*, January 14–20, 1991, 8–9.

62. Quoted in ibid. See also the discussion in *The NIIA-RIAS Dialogue: A Report* (Lagos: Nigerian Institute of International Affairs, 1997), 105.

63. Vladimir Shubin, "Beyond the Fairy Tales: The Reality of Soviet Involvement in the Liberation of Southern Africa," in *Africa in Russia, Russia in Africa*, ed. Maxim Matusevich, 347.

64. See examples of such publications in Charles Quist-Adade, "After the Cold War: The Ex-Soviet Media and Africa," *Race and Class* 32, no. 2 (October–November 1993): 86–95.

65. New York African Film Festival, "A Screenplay Is Not a Guarantee," conversation between Abderrahmane Sissako and Kwame Anthony Appiah, *www.africanfilmny.org/network/news/Isissako.html* (accessed January 24, 2010).

References

ARCHIVES

Depository of Contemporary Documents (Tsentr Khranenia Sovremennoj Dokumentatsii), Moscow, Russia
Nigerian Institute of International Affairs Archive, Lagos, Nigeria
Open Society Archive, Budapest, Hungary
Russian State Archive of New History, Moscow, Russia
Russian State Archive of Social and Political History, Moscow, Russia
Schomburg Center for Research in Black Culture, New York, NY

PERIODICALS AND ONLINE SOURCES

Africa Diary
africanfilmny.org
bbc.co.uk
Chicago Daily Defender
Christian Science Monitor
The Crisis
fontanka.ru
inafran.ru
New York Times
New York Times Magazine
protivnenavisti.ru
Prozhektor
Reader's Digest
Reporter
U.S. News and World Report
Washington Post
West African Pilot

SELECTED PUBLISHED WORKS

Ajala, Olabisi. *An African Abroad*. London: Jarolds, 1963.

Amar, Andrew Richard. *An African in Moscow*. London: Ampersand, 1963.

Anti-Taylor, William. *Moscow Diary*. London: Robert Hale, 1967.

Brudny, Yitzhak M. *Reinventing Russia: Russian Nationalism and the Soviet State, 1953–1991*. Cambridge, MA: Harvard University Press, 2000.

Carew, Jan. *Moscow Is Not My Mecca*. London: Secker and Warburg, 1964.

Carew, Joy Gleason. *Blacks, Reds, and Russians: Sojourners in Search of the Soviet Promise*. New Brunswick, NJ: Rutgers University Press, 2008.

Davidson, A. B., and L. V. Ivanova. *Moskovskaya Afrika* [Africa in Moscow]. Moscow: Teatral'niy Institut, 2003.

Djagalov, Rossen, and Christine Evans. "Moscow, ca. 1960: Imagining a Soviet-Third-World Friendship." Unpublished paper, 2009.

Du Bois, W. E. B. *The Autobiography of W. E. B. Du Bois: A Soliloquy on Viewing My Life from the Last Decade of Its First Century*. London: Oxford University Press, 2007.

Golden, Lily. *My Long Journey Home*. Chicago: Third World Press, 2003.

Gorbachev, Mikhail. *Perestroika*. New York: Harper and Row, 1988.

Gorbatov, O. M., and L. Ia. Cherkasski. *Sotrudnichestvo SSSR so stranami Arabskogo Vostoka i Afriki* [Cooperation between the USSR and the countries of Arab East and Africa]. Moscow: Nauka, 1973.

Grachos, Louis. *Afrika*. Los Angeles: University of Southern California Fisher Gallery, 1991.

Hessler, Julie. "Death of an African Student in Moscow." *Cahiers du Monde Russe* 47, nos. 1–2 (January–June 2006): 33–63.

Ilyin, Yu. M. *Institut Afriki, 1960–2004* [Africa Institute, 1960–2004]. Moscow: RAN, 2005.

Khanga, Yelena. *Soul to Soul: A Black Russian American Family, 1865–1992.* New York: Norton, 1994.

Lee, Andrea. *Russian Journal.* New York: Random House, 1981.

Matusevich, Maxim, ed. *Africa in Russia, Russia in Africa: Three Centuries of Encounters.* Trenton, NJ: Africa World Press, 2007.

———. "An Exotic Subversive: Africa, Africans, and the Soviet Everyday." *Race and Class* 49, no. 4 (2008): 57–81.

———. "Journeys of Hope: African Diaspora and the Soviet Society." *African Diaspora* 1, nos. 1–2 (2008): 53–85.

Mazov, S. V. "Afrikanskie Studenty v Moskve v God Afriki" [African students in Moscow in the year of Africa]. *Vostok* 3 (May–June 1999): 89–103.

———. "Sozdanie Instituta Afriki" [The creation of Africa Institute]. *Vostok* 1 (January–March 1998): 80–88.

Ogbar, Jeffrey O. G., ed. *The Harlem Renaissance Revisited: Politics, Arts, and Letters.* Baltimore: Johns Hopkins University Press, 2010.

Parfenov, Leonid. *Namedni: Nasha Era, 1971–1980* [Recently: Our era, 1971–1980]. Moscow: KoLibri, 2009.

Quist-Adade, Charles. "After the Cold War: The Ex-Soviet Media and Africa." *Race and Class* 32, no. 2 (October/November 1993): 86–95.

———. *In the Shadows of the Kremlin and the White House: Africa's Media Image from Communism to Post-Communism.* Lanham, MD: University Press of America, 2001.

Robeson, Paul. *The Negro People and the Soviet Union.* New York: New Century Publishers, 1950.

Robinson, Robert. *Black on Red: My 44 Years inside the Soviet Union.* Washington, DC: Acropolis Books, 1988.

Smith, Homer. *Black Man in Red Russia: A Memoir.* Chicago: Johnson Publishing, 1964.

Starr, S. Frederick. *Red and Hot: The Fate of Jazz in the Soviet Union, 1917–1991.* New York: Limelight Editions, 1994.

Yevtushenko, Yevgenii. *Vzmah ruki* [An outstretched hand]. Moscow: Molodaya Gvardia, 1962.

Zevin, L. Z., and E. L Simonov. "Pomosh' i Ekonomicheskoe Sotrudnichestvo SSSR s Razvivayushimisia Stranami: Uroki, Problemy i Perspektivy" [Assistance and economic cooperation between the USSR and developing countries: Lessons, problems, and perspectives]. *Narody Azii i Afriki* 2 (1990): 5–17.

Zubok, Vladislav M. *A Failed Empire: The Soviet Union in the Cold War from Stalin to Gorbachev.* Chapel Hill: University of North Carolina Press, 2007.

CHAPTER 7

Crimes against Humanity in the Congo

Nazi Legacies and the German Cold War in Africa

Katrina M. Hagen

On November 30, 1964, Elfriede Lenz, a citizen of Ulm in the state of Baden-Württemberg, addressed a letter to West German chancellor Ludwig Erhard. In the letter, she raised concerns about recent press reports that German mercenaries were fighting in a civil war in the Congo. Under "Captain" Siegfried Müller, Germans were "taking part in murder, torture, plunder, and rapes (*Schänden*)," crimes that to Lenz evoked Nazi violence during the Second World War. "What has the German government done to stop this," Lenz wanted to know, "or what is it considering doing?" For Lenz, the situation had strong historical and personal dimensions. Voicing a common postwar apology for failing to speak out during the Nazi era, Lenz admitted that she had been "unable to protest against the crimes of the Third Reich because I first learned of them after the war." However, she implied that acting now would, in a sense, redress this failure. "I know about these crimes," Lenz wrote, "and protest against them with vehemence." The letter ended with an entreaty to Erhard, "not only as a politician, but rather also as a human being," to consider her plea.[1]

The civil war in the Congo in 1964–1965 pitted the Western-allied government under Moïse Tshombe against a vaguely Marxist rebel movement. The

166

rebels fought for a "second independence" in the name of the former prime minister, Patrice Lumumba, who had been murdered by Tshombe's men in 1961 in the course of the crisis following Congolese independence in June 1960. The Eastern and the Western blocs framed the civil war in 1964–1965 in Cold War terms, with Tshombe and his white mercenary army fighting against the Lumumbist rebels in what was characterized as a struggle between international Communism and Western capitalism. The connections between the civil war and the crisis surrounding decolonization, as well as the presence of white mercenaries in Tshombe's army, meant that the conflict was also racially coded. Although some hailed from Western Europe, the bulk of Tshombe's men came from South Africa and Rhodesia, two of the last bastions of white colonial power in Africa. For their supporters, Tshombe and his mercenaries fought to preserve Western civilization; for their critics they represented an attempt by the former colonial powers to turn back the clock on decolonization.

The two Germanys followed their Cold War allies in squaring off on the civil war in the Congo. The Federal Republic of Germany (West Germany) allied with the West in support of Tshombe, and the German Democratic Republic (East Germany) allied with the East in support of the Lumumbist rebels. The two states, however, were not directly involved in the conflict in the Congo in 1964–1965 and wielded little influence over the course of events during the civil war. Yet as the East German filmmaker Walter Heynowski put it in 1966, through the figure of Siegfried "Congo" Müller, the civil war in the Congo became a "German theme."[2] Müller was a former Wehrmacht soldier who fashioned himself as a "warrior of the free West." He claimed to be fighting against "bolshevism" in Tshombe's army as he had for the Nazi German Empire.[3] The presence of a handful of German mercenaries in Tshombe's army, including the notorious Müller, prompted Elfriede Lenz to write to Erhard and aroused the concern of many others in the two Germanies. From 1964 to 1966 a preoccupation with the mercenary army and reports of its brutality against Africans surfaced again and again in the press, in film, and in political debates within and between the two states.

Recent scholarship has shown that the German Cold War must be understood within an international framework that includes the decolonizing Third World.[4] This chapter contributes to this research by tracing the ways that the global Cold War shaped competing East and West German policies on the civil war in the Congo. Events in the Congo, however, were of interest not only to foreign policy makers. By combining political and cultural history, this chapter illustrates the broader significance of Cold War processes of decolonization in both German societies. Specifically, the chapter shows that the history of National Socialism and German overseas imperialism served as a backdrop that informed competing East and West German approaches to the civil war in the Congo.

Historians have linked the increasing critical engagement with the Nazi past in the early to mid-1960s, and especially with the actions of ordinary Germans and low-level functionaries, to Adolph Eichmann's trial in Jerusalem and the prosecution of Auschwitz personnel in the Frankfurt Auschwitz trials (1963–1965).[5] Concerns about violence, racism, and human rights in the Congo were entangled with East and West German responses to events such as the Eichmann and Auschwitz trials. What political and media commentary construed as a brutal "race war" in the Congo elicited comparisons to the Nazi genocide of European Jewry and to German imperial violence more generally. News from the Congo in 1964–1965 and German foreign policy with regard to the civil war raised concerns that the spirit of the Third Reich—and in particular a resurgent Nazi, colonialist masculinity—lived on in a new generation of "beasts in uniform" led by former Nazi soldiers such as Congo Müller.[6]

From the Congo Crisis to the War for a "Second Independence"

On June 30, 1960, the Congo proclaimed its independence from Belgium under the leadership of Lumumba. Inspired by pan-Africanism and the Bandung principle of nonalignment, Lumumba and his party, the Congolese Nationalist Movement, called for economic independence and Congolese unity.[7] Upon assumption of authority, however, Lumumba's government was put to the test by military revolt and political instability. Moïse Tshombe, who was among Lumumba's most powerful rivals and who advocated continued economic and political ties to Belgium and the West, launched a secessionist movement from the mineral-rich province of Katanga. Belgium exacerbated the situation, first by sending troops to protect whites in the Congo and then by providing financial and military support to the Katanga secession.

The United States viewed Lumumba as a Communist threat, and the Eisenhower administration actively sought to eliminate him. Lumumba, who had finally called on the Soviet Union for backing after being turned away by the United States, was ousted from office on September 14, 1960, by US asset General Joseph Désiré Mobutu. On January 17, 1961, Mobutu's forces handed Lumumba over to Tshombe's soldiers and Belgian police, who murdered him in Katanga with the support of high-ranking Belgian officials.[8] News of Lumumba's assassination unleashed a storm of angry protest. The Soviet Union and the Eastern bloc joined African heads of state and protestors across the world in condemning Tshombe for Lumumba's murder and denouncing Western intervention in the Congo. In death, Lumumba became a martyr to the cause of African nationalism and a symbol of the consequences of imperialist aggression.[9]

The secessionist civil war continued until UN forces defeated Tshombe, and he fled to Spain in self-imposed exile in January 1963. It was thus a remarkable turn of events when Tshombe returned to the Congo in June 1964 and soon after became prime minister of Joseph Kasa-Vubu's Western-oriented central government, which was currently under siege by Lumumbist rebels who had regrouped to fight for a "second independence." Gaston Soumialot and Christoph Gbenye (Lumumba's minister of the interior) founded the National Liberation Committee (CNL) in eastern Congo, while Pierre Mulélé (Lumumba's minister of education) launched a separate rebellion in Kivu province called the Youth Movement. The two groups shared a Marxist-Leninist language and a core anti-imperialist ideology. They proclaimed themselves Lumumba's heirs and called for the overthrow of Kasa-Vubu's government, which they identified as a puppet regime representing European and US neocolonial interests.[10] There was heavy fighting in summer 1964 between the Lumumbists and Tshombe's troops, which included the combined forces of the Congolese National Army (ANC) under Mobutu's command and white mercenaries recruited from South Africa, Rhodesia, and Western Europe, including West Germany. By August, the CNL took Kisangani (Stanleyville) and announced a new independent state, which included conquered territories in the east and the north making up almost half the Congo. By fall 1964, the rebellion represented a true challenge not only to the central government, but also to European and US interests in the Congo.

West German Responses

While some European members of the North Atlantic Treaty Organization (NATO), including Great Britain, France, and Portugal, had overtly or covertly lent support to Tshombe, West Germany had joined the United States in opposition to the secession.[11] Although Eisenhower had viewed Lumumba as a Communist threat, he had still supported a unified state, and the Kennedy administration, which came to power just after Lumumba's murder in January 1961, came out in full support of the UN mission that ended the secession and Tshombe's bid for power.[12] Kennedy worried that the balkanization of the country, which would splinter its resources, combined with the secession's neocolonial racial politics could leave the Congo vulnerable to Communist influence.[13]

Although not a member of the United Nations, West Germany had followed its US ally in siding with the UN effort to quash the secession for similar reasons. The Foreign Office believed that a unified Congo was the best defense against Communist inroads into the region, and moreover feared that support of Tshombe could provide fodder for the East German propaganda machine.[14] The East Germans, who joined their Soviet counterparts in condemnation of the secession and Lumumba's murder, were keen to exploit to would-be African allies any semblance of neo-imperialist aggression on the other side of the Cold War divide. Although Tshombe made overtures during the secession, West Germany ultimately refused to deal with him or to recognize Katanga.[15]

While the West German Foreign Office had some reservations about Tshombe's resumption of power in June 1964, he nonetheless seemed the best hope for political stability and a peace in line with Western interests.[16] This assessment conformed to US policy. Lyndon Johnson followed his predecessors Eisenhower and Kennedy by promoting a unified Congo even if that now meant backing Tshombe, who was still seen as an "old foe" to some Kennedy-era members of the State Department.[17] Prominent German Cold Warriors urged the West German government to offer Tshombe support as well. In early October the economist Wilhelm Röpke wrote a personal letter urging Chancellor Ludwig Erhard to take action.[18] Röpke was a longtime adviser and friend to Erhard and staunch defender of the free market, who still wielded influence in West Germany even though he remained in Switzerland following his wartime exile by the Nazi regime.[19]

Röpke described Tshombe as "an undeserved stroke of good luck for the free world."[20] In addition to espousing a politics of "reconciliation" aimed at unifying the Congo and increasing the power of the central government, Tshombe called for friendly relations and economic and political cooperation between Europe and the Congo. He surrounded himself with Belgian advisers and sought to forge ties with European business and political figures.[21] While some saw Tshombe's ties to European business as evidence of neo-imperialism, liberal Cold Warriors such as Röpke saw them as necessary for the defeat of the Communist opposition and for ensuring the opening of the Congo to Western markets, which would be a step toward bringing "order" and "freedom" to the country, while also contributing to international stability. In his reply to Röpke, Erhard assured him that through its development aid program, "the German government has proven its will to help the Tschombé government economically."[22]

By construing development aid to Tshombe as evidence that West Germany was indeed doing its part to support Western interests in the Congo, Erhard reflected current thinking about international relations and the Cold War. Participation in development aid signaled successful postwar rehabilitation and Western integration through a willingness to act as a responsible member of the "developed" world. Like its allies, West Germany subscribed to the theory that "modernization" along Western lines would stop the advance of Communism.[23] Although the West German aid program was ostensibly apolitical, it promoted specific German Cold War interests through development spending. Since the late 1950s, West Germany had attempted to block East German efforts to achieve international legitimacy under the Hallstein doctrine, the end goal of which was to force reunification. The doctrine held that West Germany was the sole legitimate representative of the German people. Accordingly, Bonn made diplomatic relations with other states contingent on their nonrecognition of East Germany. The decolonizing world was a locus of intra-German rivalries during this period. Especially during the mid-1960s, both Cold War states used aid packages and threats of sanctions in competition in the Third World.[24]

West German development theory and practice reflected not only the Cold War political constellation, but also shifts in thinking about the relationship between the North American and European powers and the formerly colonized world. Following the end of the Second World War, German notions of race underwent profound shifts. With the defeat of the Nazi regime, the international community and the allied forces charged the two Germanys with the moral imperative to eliminate all vestiges of the Nazi past. Retaking its place among the "civilized" nations after Nazi imperialism and genocide meant the thorough discrediting of eugenic definitions of racial difference; the very idea of "race" became taboo in East and West Germany. The eradication of eugenics and the language of race from the two German societies did not mean that race lost its salience as an organizing principle. Racial difference—in the two Germanys and in the context of racial liberalism in Western Europe and North America more generally—was instead increasingly articulated in psychological rather than biological terms.[25]

After 1945 imperialist visions of a world divided between the colonizers and colonized populations of various degrees of civilization gave way to conceptions of a global order founded on universalistic notions of progress, in which differences between peoples and nations were reconfigured in terms of stages of development. Not only did colonized populations pose increasing challenges to the colonial system, but also Nazi racism and genocide called into question European claims of cultural and racial superiority. Developmentalism, which carried over into postindependence governance and became the basis for international lending and aid programs, claimed and maintained power through the offer of improved political and living conditions through "modernization" and "development" under European tutelage.[26] While using the language of "partnership" and ostensibly eschewing racial categories, developmentalism—like other psychological or cultural understandings of difference—could also appeal to concepts of primitiveness and savagery compatible with biological racism. Behavior out of step with the proscribed path to "modernity" was an atavistic return of the uncivilized and a rejection of social and political "development."[27]

Unruly Masculinity and Threats to "Civilization" in the Congo

Cold War strategies in dealing with the Third World, as well as new understandings of the difference between the developed and developing worlds, are evident in West German reactions to Tshombe and the rebel movement in the Congo. As violence escalated in the autumn of 1964 and the rebel movement conquered more and more territory, West German diplomatic correspondence increasingly construed the civil war as a battle for Western civilization in which anti-Communist sentiment merged with anxieties about racialized danger and disorder.[28] One dispatch from the West German embassy in Léopoldville on August 12 described the rebels as a "feral gang" (*verwilderte Mannschaft*) barely under control of their leaders. The dispatch suggested that concern over the rebel's connections to the "Red Chinese" was less worrisome than the possibility that the rebellion could undo "civilizing" work done by Europeans in the Congo. Without Western intervention, the movement could draw the country into atavistic decline.[29] A report on August 17 expressed similar fears and described the rebel forces as "Halbstarke gone wild," who ushered in "pre-colonial" conditions as they took over new territories.[30] The term "Halbstarke," which can be translated as "hooligans," was used by the popular press, social scientists, and Cold Warriors in the 1950s to describe young, white German youth—primarily but not only adolescent boys—thought to transgress class and gender boundaries.[31]

Diplomatic reports framed the movement as a cultural and physical danger in particular to Europeans in the Congo. In light of the perceived weakness of the Congolese army, West German diplomatic correspondence in August called for European reinforcements, specifically, white mercenaries.[32] Such a move was in fact already in the works. After failing to convince European powers, including Belgium, France, and West Germany, to send troops to aid the ANC, the United States increased its military support, and in cooperation with Belgium covertly began to organize and finance a mercenary army consisting largely of white Rhodesians and South Africans, as well as some white Europeans, including a small number of Germans.[33] Some West German officials were involved in mercenary recruitment, even though military service under a foreign flag violated the West German legal code. Nonetheless, the minister of the interior for Nordrhein Westphalia, Willi Weyer, suggested to local police officers that they serve a one-year commitment of voluntary service in the Congo.[34]

Concern that the Congolese civil war was a race war in which whites were particularly vulnerable peaked in late October. Gbenye issued a radio appeal from Kisangani, the seat of his rebel government, in which he called on sympathetic African heads of state for assistance and threatened to resort to a "scorched earth policy" in response to attacks by the ANC and mercenary army.[35] This statement generated alarm in Europe and the United States about the safety of white Europeans and Americans in occupied territory, in particular in Kisangani, where Belgian and US citizens were reportedly held hostage by Gbenye's troops. In response, the West German embassy in Léopoldville worried that in the course of an attempt to retake Kisangani, rebel "excesses," which had until then been directed largely at the Congolese, would soon be "extended to the white population in occupied territories."[36]

In order to secure the safety of the European and American hostages at Kisangani, the United States and Belgium, with British cooperation, launched a military parachute operation code-named Dragon Rouge. On November 24, roughly 450 Belgian paratroopers dropped from US aircraft over Kisangani, where they engaged in combat with rebel forces and in cooperation with Tshombe's mercenaries retook the city and rescued 1,500 foreign nationals. In the days that followed, Belgium and the United States repeated similar missions in neighboring areas where the rebels were thought also to hold large numbers of white hostages. After paratrooper operations ceased, the mercenary army continued to drive back the rebellion and liberate hostages.

While dubbed a "humanitarian" operation, Dragon Rouge was nonetheless bloody. Rebels killed thirty-seven hostages during the parachute drop, and in the days that followed two thousand to twenty thousand Congolese were killed by the ANC in reprisal.[37] Clearly hoping to head off international criticism, Paul-Willem Segers, the Belgian minister of defense, issued a statement on the day of the parachute drop in which he insisted that it was not a military action but rather a humanitarian rescue mission to save foreign nationals, "among them women and children," from rebel violence. While only a portion of these foreign nationals were white Europeans and Americans, Segers made clear the racial politics behind the rescue when he attributed the sudden timing of the operation to news reports of an increasingly "menacing picture of the situation of the whites in Stanleyville [Kisangani]."[38]

Twenty-three of the fifty-one Germans known to be in the Congo were evacuated during Dragon Rouge and subsequent mercenary operations. Three had been killed by rebel soldiers, and by mid-December, twenty-five remained in territories still affected by the war.[39] In spite of the fact that there were Germans among the foreign nationals in the Congo, West Germany did not participate alongside its NATO allies in Operation Dragon

Rouge. By order of the constitution, or Basic Law, the West German military was a defensive force; military action outside the country's borders was thus illegal. Although it supported US goals, the Foreign Office was aware of the political dangers of interference in the civil war in the Congo. The East German propaganda machine could construe any involvement in the Congo as evidence of West German neo-imperialism.[40] This was indeed an issue of concern, as economic strategies were not the only tool in the German Cold War arsenal. In the course of attempts at achieving international recognition and legitimacy, each state accused the other of failing to come to terms with the German past. While West German officials identified East Germany as a "totalitarian" state along the lines of the Nazi regime, East Germans routinely pilloried West Germany as the neo-imperialist successor state of imperial and Nazi Germany, and thus the sole inheritor of the history of German racism, imperialism, and genocide.[41] However, in spite of a reluctance to contribute to the operation publicly, the diplomatic correspondence in the months leading up to the invasion, as well as the political and economic support that the West German ministries and chancellor's office had shown Tshombe, suggests a trend toward general governmental approval of even drastic measures to protect Western interests—and white Europeans and North Americans—in the Congo.

The West German press largely applauded Operation Dragon Rouge. As in diplomatic dispatches, reportage tended to depoliticize the rebellion by focusing not on political or economic goals, but rather on extreme acts of "primitive" violence—especially against whites. News reports displayed images of badly shaken white refugees, and the accompanying stories recounted harrowing testimony of captivity and rescue. *Die Welt* described the rebels as "hordes of wild warriors wearing feather headdresses and armed with rusty knives," and as "sons of anarchy" "who know the laws of the jungle but not of civilization."[42] Numerous accounts detailed atrocities committed against the white hostages. *Frankfurter Allgemeine Zeitung* published at least two stories recounting the rape of white women, and eyewitness testimony that the rebels fed the bodies of their victims to crocodiles.[43] Further reports described ominous broadcasts over Radio Stanleyville in the hours before the invasion that threatened to "cut the foreigners to pieces," or even to "devour (*auffressen*) all the whites."[44]

By construing the dangers the rebel army posed to whites in terms of rape, dismemberment. and cannibalism, news reportage drew on racialized and often gendered tropes long associated with Africans in the European colonialist imagination, in particular the "Black Peril," the idea that African men presented a physical and sexual danger to white women.[45] In the West German case, news reports in November and December 1964 about the "savage" and "cannibalistic" young rebels in the Congo, and in particular their sexual threat to white women, resonated with responses to the occupation of the Rhineland by French colonial troops following the First World War.[46]

The case of the rebel army in the Congo in 1964–1965, however, differed from the hysterical and reactionary "Black Shame on the Rhine" campaign and other cases of reported "Black Peril" in the European colonies before 1945, which did not necessarily correlate to actual incidents of violence or rape.[47] Gbenye's forces indeed held hostages and perpetrated documented violence against whites and blacks in Kisangani. Like the "Black Peril" discourse, however, news reports that emphasized the predatory and sexual danger of the black rebels acted to racialize the civil war. Such reports highlighted the necessity of European military intervention, not only to save "civilization" in the Congo, but to save actual white European women and children.

The East German Response to Operation Dragon Rouge

While the West German press focused on the liberation of white hostages and followed US and Belgian claims that the Kisangani operation was a humanitarian and not a military mission, the East German press described it as an imperialist invasion. In contrast to their West German counterparts, East German commentators politicized the rebellion and the invasion in anticolonial terms. According to East Germany, it was a legitimate "people's movement" for "true independence" and ownership of the Congo's resources, not an "insurrection" carried out by a few "rebel" leaders and their crazed followers.[48] To the East German leadership, the Kisangani operation was part of a neo-imperialist effort to invalidate Congolese independence and steal the country's resources from its fourteen million inhabitants. The invasion was the "highpoint" of a four-year-long Western "interventionist policy" that dated to the struggles surrounding independence.[49]

While identifying Western "monopoly bosses" and corporate shareholders as among the true instigators of the invasion, East German journalists downplayed the rebels' violence against white Europeans. Instead, press commentary highlighted the general brutality of the invading forces and denounced what in East Germany was termed the "hostage legend" that justified the operation. On the contrary, one report argued, the white Europeans in Kisangani were neither held hostage nor under threat.[50] This was a clear manipulation of the facts, given that Gbenye's forces executed thirty-seven hostages during the parachute drop. Other stories described life in Kisangani following the invasion as "an empty hell" marked by the erratic violence of Belgian forces.[51] According to East German reporters, it was clear that the true victims of torture and brutality were not white Europeans but black Congolese, civilian and rebel alike.

East Germany was not alone in its condemnation of the operation. The Soviet Union, the Organization for African Unity, and African heads of state immediately denounced Dragon Rouge as an aggressive neo-imperialist military action that violated the UN Charter by interfering in the internal affairs of a sovereign state. Other Eastern bloc countries and African leaders agreed that the rescue of white hostages was only a pretext to disguise the true goal of the operation: to quash the Congolese liberation movement.[52] In the days that followed, angry protestors demonstrated outside US and Belgian embassies in Africa, Asia, and Europe. In some cases, protest escalated to vandalism and violence. On November 26, students in Cairo burned the John F. Kennedy Library to the ground, and three days later over a thousand African students from Lumumba University in Moscow burned cars and broke windows at the US embassy.[53]

A group of UN member states, including Algeria, Tanzania, Ghana, Guinea, Sudan, the United Arab Republic, and Yugoslavia, called for a special session of the Security Council on December 9 to review and censure the invasion. The racial politics of the invasion and the international response to it were at the center of the proceedings. The complaining states, joined by the Soviet Union, condemned Tshombe as a stooge of the European powers and the invasion as a neo-imperialist intervention aimed at crushing national liberation.[54] The primarily African member states criticized the focus on the white hostages, both in the rationale behind the invasion and in reporting in the international press. Blatant racism, they argued, afforded white lives more value than black lives and diverted attention from the Congolese victims of the civil war and the invasion. The UN minister from Guinea provocatively compared the attack against the liberation movement to violent white suppression of the US civil rights movement, while the minister from Ghana suggested that according to the logic behind the invasion, it would be justified for an African coalition to launch a humanitarian intervention in the southern United States to save African Americans in danger from white violence.[55]

International attention to Operation Dragon Rouge brought increased aid—at least for the short term—to the Congolese rebels. In spite of rumors of Soviet backing of the Congolese rebel forces, the East German embassy in Moscow had reported in September 1964 that the Soviets had thus far abstained from lending significant military or financial assistance, primarily because of political incoherence and lack of unity among the various factions of the movement.[56] Despite attempts by rebel leaders to enlist East German help in spring and summer of 1964, Walter Ulbricht's government had also refrained from sending aid to the Congo.[57] Following the parachute drop, Algeria and Cuba both began to assist in the movement's military operations. Cuba sent troops under the leadership of Che Guevara to join in the fighting and train the rebel soldiers in guerilla tactics.[58] The Soviets also informed East Germany of plans to deliver military aid to the rebels. Although East Germany did not supply military equipment or personnel, by December it too began sending medical supplies and some economic aid to the Congolese rebels.[59]

For East Germany and the Soviet Union, Operation Dragon Rouge also provided the occasion for self-interested Cold War posturing. The Soviet Union, now under the leadership of Leonid Brezhnev, responded by castigating Western, neo-imperialist intervention and expressing solidarity with the "Congolese patriots."[60]

East Germany joined its Soviet ally in an attempt to capitalize on the moral and political significance of its new ties to the Congolese liberation movement in order to gain leverage in the German Cold War. Although West Germany was not involved Operation Dragon Rouge, when news of the parachute drop broke, East German politicians and propagandists immediately attempted to link West Germany to the invasion. The Afro-Asian Solidarity Committee denounced the invasion as evidence of the "aggressive character of the NATO forces," and implicated the West German military high command.[61] The press identified Bonn's development aid package to the Tshombe regime and West German private industrial investment in the Congo as perhaps the most damning evidence of neo-imperialist/monopoly capitalist intentions in the Congo.[62] Bonn, Tshombe, and the mercenary army connived to crush the liberation movement as a means of protecting this monopoly capitalist conspiracy. News reports in *Neues Deutschland* attested to the brutal human consequences of such neo-imperialist machinations. Meanwhile, East Germany offered material aid to the Congolese "freedom fighters" in "the spirit of camaraderie and human brotherhood," thus claiming the political and moral high ground for the East German people. As evidence of this, *Neues Deutschland* reprinted a letter reportedly received by the Solidarity Committee in which a Congolese representative offered thanks for recent shipments of medical supplies and expressed "how much solace and support" East German aid had "meant to [their] wounded and sick comrades."[63]

News and diplomatic commentary contrasted East German proletarian internationalism to West German neo-imperialism by placing the Kisangani operation within the history of European racism and imperialism and by highlighting what East German authorities identified as the historical continuities between West German policy and the German colonial and Nazi pasts. On November 26, the Ministry of Foreign Affairs declared the operation "a crude violation of the norms of human rights and a shameless encroachment upon the right to self-determination of the Congolese people" comparable to colonial conquest. The Kisangani operation was akin to the murderous "punitive expeditions" of the colonial era carried out to protect white settlers.[64] While not specifically naming Imperial Germany, the ministry's formulation resonated with knowledge in East Germany about the particularly brutal history of German colonial rule and the swift and vicious response of the colonial military to challenges to German imperial power. The ministry evoked, for example, the brutal suppression of the Maji Maji rebellion in German East Africa (Tanzania) in 1905–1907, and the assault on the Herero and Nama revolt in German South West Africa (Namibia) in 1904–1908 that ended in genocide.[65] Since the late 1950s, the East German academy had joined with the ministry in an effort to research and publicize the history of German overseas colonial violence.[66] One practical goal of this exposure campaign, like similar efforts to document Nazi legacies through publications detailing the "Brown" pasts of politicians and diplomats, was to reveal continuity with Nazi and imperial policies, in this case in order to counter West Germany's Cold War gains in Africa.[67] The colonial exposure campaign resulted in the publication and distribution—in East Germany and in Africa—of popular and academic histories and source material on German colonial violence.[68]

News coverage on the civil war in the Congo took part in the language of the exposure campaign by pointing to the presence of German mercenary forces, to make explicit connections to a specifically German history of colonial violence. An article in *Neues Deutschland* titled "Germans to the Front!" cited a German—or more accurately, *West* German—propensity for imperial military violence. The command "Germans to the front!" was the oft-quoted order delivered by the British admiral who led the international military force sent to defeat the Chinese Boxer rebellion in June 1900. Germany's participation not only marked its first experience in an international military operation, but also earned German forces the reputation for being particularly brutal.[69] According to *Neues Deutschland*, German mercenaries in the Congo thus joined a long tradition of Germans who had rallied to protect European colonial interests with the use of military force. Given this German reputation, it was only fitting that the forces of neo-imperialism in the Congo would once again "send 'Germans to the front!' As against the Chinese in 1900! As against the Herero in 1904! As against the Hottentots [Nama] in 1905!"[70] According to this interpretation, West Germany's participation in the Kisangani operation revealed an unbroken continuity between Bonn's Congo policy, the suppression of the Boxer Rebellion, and the Namibian genocide.

Nazi Atrocities in the Congo?

East German journalists were not alone in linking the mercenaries to a German history of imperialist violence. While much of the West German press lauded the mercenaries as heroes, some accounts figured Tshombe's men as savage perpetrators themselves rather than bulwarks against African primitivism.[71] A series of mercenary exposés told tales of brutality and violence that evoked comparisons to Nazism and inspired anxieties about the resurgence of particularly German forms of racism and uncivilized fascist masculinity. Just as news of Kisangani broke, Gerd Heidemann and Ernst Petry published a three-part series in the Hamburg illustrated weekly *Stern* that was the most widely cited of the stories.[72] The series detailed Heidemann and Petry's search for Siegfried Müller, the former Wehrmacht soldier who now led the 52nd Command in the Congo.

Heidemann and Petry described the Germans as especially "adventure hungry" and well suited to the violent, racially charged nature of the conflict. Even though most were young, "simple minded" men born too late to have fought for Hitler, they were nonetheless renowned among their mercenary companions and white European civilians "to be specialists in the solution of racial questions (*Rassenfrage*)." Whites in the Congo were especially "happy to know that a German captain, Siegfried Müller, is in command of the mercenaries." Unlike the others, the forty-four-year-old Müller *had* fought in Hitler's army. Müller still proudly wore a swastika-stamped iron cross that he explained he had earned in Russia in 1943. Like his men, Müller claimed to share "the same goal as West Germany: to fight against Bolshevism."[73] While Heidemann and Petry never explicitly connected Müller's campaigns for Tshombe to those he had fought for Germany during the Second World War, Müller's use of the term "Bolshevism," his Nazi iron cross, and references to Russia suggested terminological and possibly ideological continuity with the Nazi anti-Communism that, in combination with anti-Slavic and anti-Semitic racism, fueled the murderous invasion of Eastern Europe and the Soviet Union.

Heidemann and Petry's silence on the racial violence perpetrated by the German regular army during the Second World War conformed to general approaches to the topic in the years after 1945. Scholars typically credit a traveling exhibit of documents, photos, and letters from the Wehrmacht compiled by the Hamburg Institute for Social Research in 1995 with opening West German public discussion of the role of the Wehrmacht in Nazi imperialism and genocide. This included mass executions, deportations of Jews, and the killing of unarmed civilians.[74] While Heidemann and Petry did not highlight this aspect of the Wehrmacht in their discussion of Müller, the Nazi legacies of the regular army were certainly known to some of their readers.[75] In the end,

Heidemann and Petry defended Müller as an honorable "soldier," driven to brutality by the savage conditions of African warfare; he and his men had essentially "gone native."[76] However, scenes of racially motivated torture, images of black corpses, and descriptions of the sickening smell of decomposing bodies that surrounded Müller's encampment were reminders that he and his army of adventurers were nonetheless agents of mass death and destruction reminiscent of the Eastern Front.

The series ultimately conformed to the official West German position by concluding that Tshombe and his forces, combined with an inflow of Western development aid, were a "necessary evil" if "civilization" was to be preserved in the Congo. Heidemann and Petry's ambivalent portrayal, however, inspired public debate in which concerns about West German policy on the civil war merged with those about the Nazi past. Links to Nazism were all the more powerful because the Nazi concentration camp system and its perpetrators were at the moment under intense public scrutiny as a result of the West German trials of Auschwitz personnel. The Frankfurt Auschwitz trials (December 1963–August 1965) were part of a series of events in the early to mid-1960s, initiated by the trial of Eichmann in Jerusalem (1961) and the publication of a German edition of Hannah Arendt's *Eichmann in Jerusalem* (1964), that sparked widespread public discussion of the genocidal crimes that "ordinary" Germans and low-level functionaries committed under the Nazi regime.[77] The Auschwitz trials contributed to public engagement with the Nazi past by instigating historical exploration of the concentration camp system and the machinery of the entire Nazi racial state through a highly publicized and minutely detailed accounting of the extreme violence of Auschwitz and its Nazi personnel. The trial was attended by constant coverage in the major West German press and included testimony of camp survivors and perpetrators in harrowing and often gruesome detail. Sensationalistic reportage focused on camp personnel's sadism and on excessive violence and torture, and contributed to a conception of Auschwitz as "incomprehensible," a "hell on earth."[78]

Images of white mercenary violence against blacks in the racialized war in the Congo resonated with stories of the brutal and murderous actions of the German SS. The depiction of the Congo as a place of savage death and destruction littered with corpses and reeking of decomposing bodies, a place in which the laws of civilization did not apply, evoked allusions to Auschwitz. Indeed, it was the *Stern* series that prompted Elfriede Lenz from Ulm to write to Erhard on November 30, demanding to know what the government planned to do about mercenaries such as Müller. Lenz, who framed her call to action in terms of her own process of coming to terms with the Nazi past, and specifically her own failure to protest against National Socialism, was clearly influenced by recent efforts to seek justice for Nazi crimes. Lamenting the failure of German vigilance, and alluding to the Eichmann and the Auschwitz trials, Lenz concluded: "We search through the entire world . . . for criminals of the past in order to bring them to justice, but these same crimes against humanity should be allowed to go unpunished in the present? That would be a shame without comparison."[79]

The West German radical student movement expressed similar concern. Support of Tshombe and men like Congo Müller seemed to be further examples of the failure to learn from German history. One article in *Konkret* criticized the West German government for supporting military action equivalent to "genocide" in the Congo.[80] Alarm over West German relations to Tshombe and mercenary violence in the Congo dovetailed with other concerns of the nascent anti-authoritarian Left. The anti-authoritarian movement's political and social critique combined Third World internationalism with accusations of fascist tendencies in foreign and domestic policy. To anti-authoritarian critics, support of Tshombe was evidence not only of complicity in capitalist violence in the decolonizing world but also of the failure of the older generation to root out Nazi racism and imperialism.

While the anti-authoritarian wing of the Socialist German Students' League (Sozialistischer Deutscher Studentenbund, SDS) would not become the dominant political voice within the student movement until 1966, historical scholarship and participant memoirs identify the anti-Tshombe protest in December 1964 as the beginning of this phase of the movement.[81] Protest escalated in December when Tshombe traveled to West Germany during a multiweek trip to Europe for negotiations over development aid and investment in the Congo. Because of the anti-Tshombe backlash generated by the Communist bloc and nonaligned African states, the West German government was uneasy about the visit. The Foreign Office issued a press release clarifying that Tshombe's visit was of a private rather than a public nature.[82] In fact Tshombe came to West Germany at the invitation of the Rhein-Ruhr Club in Düsseldorf—an association of conservative businessmen and industrialists—where he delivered a lecture on December 17 aimed at encouraging private investment in the Congo. Tshombe also hoped to secure an increase in West German development aid to the Congo during his talks with Federal President Heinrich Lübke. While guaranteeing a commitment made in November of an additional DM 10 million in credits, Lübke refused further aid, citing budget shortfalls and concern over the continued instability in the Congo.[83]

Governmental attempts to create a degree of political distance from Tshombe did not lessen the controversy that his visit unleashed. The West German student Left protested Tshombe's appearance at the Rhein-Ruhr

Club and came out in force on December 18 when Tshombe met with Willy Brandt, the mayor of West Berlin.[84] The massive demonstration that began at Tegel Airfield and proceeded to the Berlin Senate was organized primarily by the SDS and African and Latin American student organizations.[85] Organizers distributed more than eight thousand leaflets to university students in Berlin that issued a call to action in terms that would resonate with the public, given the context of recent debate. They not only described Tshombe's war against the rebel movement as a neo-imperialist attempt to secure the interests of European capital but also criticized the West German reception of the civil war and the Kisangani operation by pointing to the violence and brutality of the mercenary army: "Tshombe's mercenary army includes South African and South Rhodesian racists, former French OAS officers, and former SS people. The deeds of these mercenaries have been made known through the West German press—Why is it believed today that these mercenaries carry out 'humanitarian actions'?"[86] More than eight hundred students participated in the demonstration, carrying placards reading, "No Money for White Mercenaries," "No Bloodbath in the name of Humanity," and "Kongo oui—Tschombé non!"[87] That some of the protest signs were in French highlighted the international nature of the demonstration. The student protest in Berlin against Tshombe's visit was indeed so successful that Brandt not only met with the protestors in person, but also cut short his visit with Tshombe.[88]

While accounts of mercenary violence inspired outrage among leftist students and concerned citizens, some West German commentators took exception to negative media portrayals of the mercenaries. The philanthropist Elsie Kühn-Leitz, who had traveled in the Congo in the years since independence, was one prominent Tshombe defender.[89] She sent an open letter to Foreign Minister Schröder to be distributed "at his discretion, for the good of the Western world."[90] Kühn-Leitz wrote that she was "shaken to the core" by the *Stern* series. Echoing Tshombe supporters such as the liberal Cold Warrior Röpke, Kühn-Leitz maintained that the mercenaries were neither Nazis nor savages, but rather a "plucky band of white volunteers" enlisted by "the clever and far sighted" Tshombe in an effort to save the Congo from Communism and a reversion to primitivism. Accounts such as Heidemann's and Petry's simply fueled anti-Western propaganda in the "Soviet Zone."[91]

Congo Müller and the German Cold War

Kühn-Leitz was likely aware of the sensation that stories of mercenary violence elicited in East Germany. Since it had no correspondents in the Congo, the East German press drew on reports from the West German media such as the *Stern* series to attack West German support of Tshombe and to link mercenary violence to Nazism. The East German press made this connection explicit by referring to the mercenaries as "German SS mercenaries," "Tshombe's SS executioners," or "German Gestapo thugs."[92] Such characterizations attempted to undermine West German claims to have overcome the past by implying an unbroken continuity between Nazi imperialism in Europe and West German neo-imperialism in Africa. One *Neues Deutschland* story asked how West Germans could "read the reports from the Auschwitz trials with indignation" yet "calmly observe" the violence against the Congolese perpetrated "by the same workers, brains and executioners."[93]

The controversy over Congo Müller lived on in the two Germanys even after Tshombe faded into the background following Mobutu's rise to power in November 1965. In May 1965, Gerd Heidemann had sold the materials he had used to write the *Stern* series to the East German filmmaker Walter Heynowski.[94] Heynowski used these sources in two highly publicized documentary films produced with Gerhard Scheumann, *Kommando 52* (1965) and *Der lachende Mann* [The laughing man] (1965–1966). The films sought to expose the genocidal tendencies of former Nazis such as Müller now fighting alongside a new generation of West German "fascists" in neo-imperialist wars in the Third World.[95] *Der lachende Mann*, the more famous of the two, featured a candid interview with Müller obtained under the false pretense of a documentary on modern warfare. Müller appeared in the film in battle fatigues and Nazi iron cross, recounting his military career from the German Wehrmacht to recent battles in the Congo. Grinning, shameless, and increasingly drunk on the Pernod supplied by Heynowski and Scheumann, Müller boasted before the camera of his "adventures" fighting against "Bolshevism" in the Congo as he had during the Third Reich.[96] Müller claimed to have been fighting a just and "civilized" war in the Congo, but the film juxtaposed Müller's words and visage with images of African bodies and gratuitous white violence against blacks. Fifty-five percent of viewers watched the film when it premiered on East German television on February 9, 1966.[97] Writing later about its reception, Heynowski and Scheumann reported having received thousands of letters from audience members who saw in Congo Müller the "Herrenmenschen" (so-called members of the master race) of the Nazi concentration camps. One East Berliner wrote that the film convinced him even more of his loyalty to the "German state that had cleaned out such beasts."[98]

The mercenary films were useful for Cold War purposes in Africa as well as for domestic propaganda. The Ministry of Foreign Affairs distributed both documentaries in Africa, where they contributed to efforts to expose purported Nazi continuities in West German foreign policy.[99] The films challenged West German claims of an anti-imperialist and noninterventionist foreign policy and implied that the failure to root out Nazism had led to its dangerous spread abroad. To make this point more forcefully, the ministry showed *Der lachende Mann* in early February 1966 to Pauline Lumumba, Patrice Lumumba's widow, convincing her to support a criminal complaint against Müller for murder.[100] It was no coincidence that it was Friedrich Karl Kaul, an East German prosecutor involved in the Auschwitz trials, who submitted the charge to the Frankfurt state's attorney on February 12, 1966.[101] In the press conference that followed, Kaul described Müller as a perpetrator of "crimes against humanity," akin to the Buchenwald and Auschwitz personnel who made lampshades out of human skin. Challenging West Germany to live up to its post-Nazi duty, Kaul concluded: "It is this mentality that we must all take a stand against in the interests of the Nation."[102]

The complaint was to have coincided with the West German premiere of *Kommando 52* at the Short Film Festival in Oberhausen. *Kommando 52*, however, was rejected from the festival, ostensibly on aesthetic grounds. West German authorities also hindered its importation through a law regulating the transport of propaganda material from the Eastern bloc. Similar measures were taken to prevent the importation of *Der lachende Mann* and its screening at the Mannheim Festival later that year.[103] By this time, Congo Müller had become a public relations liability for West Germany. The distribution of the films in Africa indeed produced the desired result. Beginning in December 1965, the Foreign Office and the Ministry of the Interior debated revoking Müller's passport in light of rumors that he was now fighting in a mercenary army in Rhodesia and because the constant bad publicity surrounding him endangered West German interests.[104] In the end the West German government neither revoked Müller's passport nor pursued charges against him. By the beginning of 1967, the consensus in the Foreign Office was that interest in Müller and its negative impact had begun to fade.[105] Müller had immigrated to South Africa, and by 1966–1967 events in Vietnam overshadowed those in the Congo.[106] Both the student Left and the East German state increasingly focused their anti-imperialist critique on the Vietnam War and West Germany's support of its US ally.[107]

Conclusion

Although East and West Germany were not party to the conflict, Congo Müller, Moïse Tshombe, and the civil war in the Congo had powerful resonance in the two Germanys. Debates about the Congo brought into relief concerns about racism, violence, and national self-determination in the Cold War context of decolonization and in relation to the Nazi and imperial pasts. West German participation in European and US projects for economic development in the Congo, as well as (at least tacit) support for military efforts to save civilization in the Congo from the barbarism of Communism and African primitivism, were undertaken against the backdrop of Germany's own recent history of barbarism. This fact was recognized both in West Germany, where it led to soul-searching and criticism of government policy, as well as in East Germany, where it became fodder for the Communist critique of German and US imperialism. The policy of the West German government highlighted its postwar Western integration and commitment to liberal capitalism and was, as such, an element of the project of legitimating the West German state. Ironically, West German support for Western intervention in the Congolese civil war played a similar role in East Germany, bolstering its claims to legitimacy as the self-identified *only* anti-imperialist and antiracist German state. East German journalists and filmmakers followed suit, drawing on West German media representations to challenge Western constructions of the civil war as a battle for civilization and to critique state support of Tshombe and his mercenary army.

The controversy over the civil war in the Congo was not only a battle between East and West. It prompted West German citizens and radical students to join their East German counterparts in pointing to the brutality of this seeming new generation of male perpetrators in order to criticize the West German–Tshombe alliance and, in some cases, to question West German claims to have overcome the Nazi and imperial pasts more generally. White mercenary violence resonated with the terrible accounts from the Auschwitz trials and raised concerns about the reemergence of Nazi racism and genocidal violence in decolonizing Africa. Mobilizing figures such as Congo Müller thus became a powerful way to combine a critique of the postwar German domestic and the international orders.

Notes

1. Elfriede Lenz to Chancellor Ludwig Erhard, November 30, 1964: Politisches Archiv des Auswärtigen Amts (hereafter PA/AA), Ref. IB3, B 34, Bd. 497. I use pseudonyms for private individuals.
2. Walter Heynowski and Gerhard Scheumann, *Der lachende Mann. Bekenntnis eines Mörders* [The laughing man: The avowal of a murderer] (Berlin: Verlag der Nation, 1966), 8.
3. Ibid., 38.

4. See especially William Glenn Gray, *Germany's Cold War: The Global Campaign to Isolate East Germany, 1949–1969* (Chapel Hill: University of North Carolina Press, 2003); and Young-Sun Hong, "'The Benefits of Health Must Be Spread among All': International Solidarity, Health, and Race in the East German Encounter with the Third World," in *Socialist Modern: East German Everyday Culture and Politics*, ed. Katherine Pence and Paul Betts, 183–210 (Ann Arbor: University of Michigan Press, 2008).

5. In 1960 Adolph Eichmann (1906–1962), a Nazi bureaucrat involved in the deportation of European Jews, was captured in Argentina by the Israeli security service and put on trial in Jerusalem for crimes against the Jewish people. Eichmann was found guilty and hanged in 1962. On the German response to the Eichmann and Auschwitz trials, see especially Harold Marcuse, *Legacies of Dachau: The Uses and Abuses of a Concentration Camp, 1933–2001* (Cambridge: Cambridge University Press, 2001); Rebecca Wittmann, *Beyond Justice: The Auschwitz Trial* (Cambridge, MA: Harvard University Press, 2005); and Devin O. Pendas, *The Frankfurt Auschwitz Trial, 1963–1965: Genocide, History, and the Limits of the Law* (Cambridge: Cambridge University Press, 2006).

6. "Invasion! Stanleyville von Imperialisten überfallen; die Aggressoren: Belgien, Bonn und die USA" [Invasion! Stanleyville attacked by imperialists; the aggressors: Belgium, Bonn, and the USA], *Neues Deutschland* (*ND*), November 25, 1964.

7. Georges Nzongola-Ntalaja, *The Congo from Leopold to Kabila: A People's History* (London: Zed Books, 2002), 96.

8. On the role of Belgian soldiers and governmental officials in Lumumba's murder, see Ludo de Witte, *The Assassination of Lumumba*, trans. Anne Wright and Reneé Fenby (London: Verso, 2001), 110–12. On the role of the CIA in the conspiracy to oust Lumumba from power and eventually assassinate him, see Madeline G. Kalb, *The Congo Cables: The Cold War in Africa, from Eisenhower to Kennedy* (New York: Macmillan, 1982); and US Congress, Senate, Interim Report, *Alleged Assassination Plots Involving Foreign Leaders*, by the Select Committee to Study Government Operations with Respect to Intelligence Activities, 1st Session, 94th Congress, November 20, 1975.

9. De Witte, *The Assassination of Lumumba*, 148–51. On the Soviet response, see Lisa Namikas, "Battleground Africa: The Cold War and the Congo Crisis, 1960–1965" (PhD diss., University of Southern California, 2002), 271.

10. David Gibbs, *The Political Economy of Third World Intervention* (Chicago: University of Chicago Press, 1991), 148. After an important military victory, Gaston Soumialot is reported to have announced over the radio: "Lumumba said that someone stronger than himself would come to complete his work. That man is me." Quoted in Kwame Nkrumah, *Challenge of the Congo* (New York: International Publishers, 1967), 252.

11. The position of each of these states on the secession was linked to their own stakes in African decolonization as well as business interests in Katanga. See Alan James, *Britain and the Congo Crisis, 1960–63* (Basingstoke, UK: Macmillan, 1996); and Gibbs, *Third World Intervention*, 114–17.

12. Kennedy was much clearer about his opposition to Tshombe and the secession than was Eisenhower, who only reluctantly opposed the secession. Under both

administrations there was support of the Katanga secession—what David Gibbs calls the procolonial bloc—particularly among members of the European Bureau of the State Department and among those with ties to business interests in Katanga. There was also a strong pro-Katanga lobby in Congress, most associated with Thomas Dodd; see Gibbs, *Third World Intervention*, 117–24.

13. Thomas Borstelmann, *The Cold War and the Color Line: American Race Relations in the Global Arena* (Cambridge, MA: Harvard University Press, 2001), 149.

14. "Kongo-Krise" [Congo crisis], Hasso von Etzdorf, Bonn, July 21, 1960 (forwarded to Chancellor Konrad Adenauer), PA/AA, Ref. IB3, B 34, Bd. 47.

15. Tshombe sent a telegram to the Foreign Office on July 14, 1966, asking for recognition of Katanga's independence. The Foreign Office never responded. See Telegram from Tshombe, Elizabethville, Katanga, to the Ministre des Affaires Étrangères de la République Fédérale allemande, Bonn, July 14, 1960, PA/AA, Ref. IB3, B 34, Bd. 46; and Telegram from Foreign Minister Heinrich von Brentano to Hellmut Kalbitzer, July 20, 1960, PA/AA Ref. IB3, B 34, Bd. 47.

16. "Regierungswechsel im Kongo" [Change in government in Congo], West German Embassy, Léopoldville, to the Foreign Office, Bonn, July 14, 1964, pg. 4, PA/AA, Ref. IB3, B 34, Bd. 496.

17. Namikas, "Battleground Africa," 417.

18. Röpke wrote to Erhard at the behest of Otto von Habsburg, the last heir to the Habsburg throne, now living in Bavaria, who hoped that Röpke would use his influence to provide development aid to Tshombe. Otto von Habsburg to Wilhelm Röpke, Pöcking u. Starnberg, February 10, 1964, Bundesarchiv-Koblenz (Federal Archive Coblenz) (hereafter BArch-K), Bundeskanzleramt, B 136, Bd. 6263.

19. A. J. Nicholls, *Freedom with Responsibility: The Social Market Economy in Germany, 1918–1963* (Oxford: Clarendon Press, 1994), 273–75.

20. Handwritten letter, Wilhelm Röpke to Chancellor Ludwig Erhard, Geneva, October 12, 1964, BArch-K.

21. In fact, CIA documents suggest that Belgian corporations such as the Sociéte Générale de Belgique and its subsidiary Union Miniére Haut Katanga played a role in Tshombe's appointment as prime minister. Gibbs, *Third World Intervention*, 154–56.

22. Since 1962 the government had granted the Congo DM 20 million in credits to be used for "vital capital and consumer goods." West Germany had also financed reconstruction projects to aid in the recovery effort following the end of the wars for secession in the amount of DM 3.7 million, and expected to contribute another DM 8 million in technical aid in 1965 (letter from Ludwig Erhard to Wilhelm Röpke, Bonn, November 30, 1964, BArch-K, Bundeskanzleramt, B 136, Bd. 6263). These numbers are comparable to other West German aid packages to sub-Saharan African countries during this period. For example, in 1961 the Adenauer government offered similar amounts to the following countries: Ivory Coast, DM 30 million; Senegal, DM 25 million; Upper Volta, Niger, and Dahomey, DM 15 million each (Gray, *Germany's Cold War*, 121).

23. This theory is most associated with US intellectual Walt Rostow in his *Stages of Economic Growth: A Non-Communist Manifesto* (Cambridge: Cambridge University Press, 1960). On the role of development aid in German Cold War politics, see

especially Klaus Bodemer, *Entwicklungshilfe—Politik für wen?* [Development aid—policy for whom?] (Munich: Weltforum Verlag, 1973); and Brigitte Schulz, *Development Policy in the Cold War Era: The Two Germanies in Sub-Saharan Africa, 1960–1985* (Munich: Lit Verlag, 1995).

24. West Germany used aid packages as an enticement and in some cases withdrew aid from countries that recognized East Germany, as in the case of Tanzania, Sri Lanka, Egypt, and Cuba. Rüdiger Marco Booz, *"Hallsteinzeit": Deutsche Außenpolitik, 1955–1972* ["Hallstein times": German foreign policy, 1955–1972] (Bonn: Bouvier, 1995); and Gray, *Germany's Cold War.*

25. On the rise of psychological understandings of racial difference in the two Germanys, see Heide Fehrenbach, *Race after Hitler: Black Occupation Children in Postwar Germany and America* (Princeton, NJ: Princeton University Press, 2005); and Uta G. Poiger, *Jazz, Rock, and Rebels: Cold War Politics and American Culture in a Divided Germany* (Berkeley: University of California Press, 2000). For the United States, see Ruth Feldstein, *Motherhood in Black and White: Race and Sex in American Liberalism, 1930–1965* (Ithaca, NY: Cornell University Press, 2000). For a general account, see Graham Richards, *"Race," Racism and Psychology: Towards a Reflexive History* (London: Routledge, 1997).

26. Frederick Cooper, *Decolonization and African Society* (Cambridge: Cambridge University Press, 1996), 173.

27. Frederick Cooper, *Africa since 1940: The Past of the Present* (Cambridge: Cambridge University Press, 2002), 83.

28. Borstelmann notes similar racial coding in US political and media perceptions of the civil war in Congo in 1964. Borstelmann, *The Cold War and the Color Line*, 185.

29. "Innenpolitische Lage Kongo" [Domestic political situation in Congo], West German Embassy, Léopoldville, August 12, 1964, PA/AA, Ref. IB3, B 34, Bd. 497.

30. "Aufentahalt in Léopoldville am 17. August 1964" [Stop in Léopoldville on 17 August 1964], Bonn, August 19, 1964, von Mirbach, PA/AA, Ref. IB3, B 34, Bd. 497.

31. Poiger, *Jazz, Rock, and Rebels*, 95–98.

32. "Lage im Kongo" [Situation in Congo], Bonn, August 21, 1964, PA/AA, Ref. IB3, B 34, Bd. 497; and "Innenpolitische Lage Kongo."

33. Piero Gleijeses, *Conflicting Missions: Havana, Washington, and Africa, 1959–1976* (Chapel Hill: University of North Carolina Press, 2005), 156.

34. Kum'a Ndumbe, *Was will Bonn in Afrika? Zur Afrikapolitik der Bundesrepublik Deutschland* [What does Bonn want in Africa? On the Africa policy of the Federal Republic of Germany] (Pfaffenweiler: Centaurus, 1992), 135. It is unlikely that Weyer's suggestion resulted in any significant increase in West German enlistments in Tshombe's mercenary army. While the exact number of German mercenaries in Congo is unknown, their numbers remained low. Christian Bunnenberg has established that at least nine individuals identified as "German" served under Siegfried "Congo" Müller in autumn 1964. However, Austrians and South Africans of German ancestry were also considered "German." In addition, to these men, two other West German citizens are known to have served and been killed in battle under Müller. Christian Bunnenberg, *Der "Kongo-Müller." Eine deutsche Söldnerkarriere* ["Congo-Müller": A German mercenary career] (Berlin: Lit Verlag, 2007), 50–52.

35. Gbenye's radio address called on Kwame Nkrumah (Ghana), Ahmed Ben Bella (Algeria), Gamal Abdel Nasser (Egypt), and Ahmed Sékou Touré (Guinea). "Appell des 'Präsidenten der Volksrepublik Kongo,' Gbenye, an N'Krumah, Ben Bella, Nasser und Sékou Touré" [Appeal of the "President of the People's Republic of the Congo" to N'Krumah, Ben Bella, Nasser, and Sékou Touré], West German Embassy, Léopoldville, November 4, 1964, PA/AA, Ref IB3, B 34, Bd. 497.

36. Ibid.

37. Namikas, "Battleground Africa," 437–38.

38. "Erklärung des beligischen Verteidigungsministers vom 24.11 (telefonisch durchgegeben von Botschaftsrat Dr. Röhring)" [Declaration of the Belgian minister of defense from 11/24 (transmitted by telephone by counselor of embassy Dr. Röhring)], Bonn, November 24, 1964, PA/AA, Ref IB3, B 34, Bd. 497.

39. Martin Bormann, the son of the high-ranking Nazi party official of the same name, was among the three casualties. While Bormann's death received considerable press, the Germans in Congo generally seem to have drawn little attention prior to Operation Dragon Rouge. It was not until after the parachute drop in mid-December that the Foreign Office was asked to report on Germans in Congo to the Bundestag. Deutscher Bundestag, Fragestunde, 154 Sitzung, Bonn, December 16, 1964, 7611–12, PA/AA, Ref IB3, B 34/497. For press accounts of Germans in Congo and Bormann in particular, see, for example, the series in the popular illustrated weekly *Quick*: "Gottes Wort am Kongo" [God's word in Congo], December 6, 1964; and "Kongo: Die Schreckenstage der Weißen Geiseln" [Congo: The white hostages' days of terror], December 13, 1964.

40. See, for example, the expression of such concerns in discussion of West German involvement in a Red Cross mission to Congo. "Appell an die Weltöffentlichkeit mit dem Ziel, die Einreise einer Delegation des Internationalen Komitees vom Roten Kreuz (IKRK) in das kongolesischen Aufstandsgebiet zu erwirken" [Appeal to the world public with the goal of obtaining the entry of a Red Cross delegation in the region of the Congolese insurrection], Abteilung I, AA VLR I Graf v. Posadowsky-Wehner, November 19, 1964, PA/AA, Ref IB3, B 34/497.

41. On this position and the ways that it contributed to East German policy, see especially Alfred Babing, introduction to *Against Racism, Apartheid, and Colonialism: Documents Published by the GDR, 1949–1977*, ed. Alfred Babing (Berlin: Staatsverlag der DDR, 1977), 45–63, 50–53.

42. "Die Rettung hätte Vorgang" [The rescue was necessary], *Die Welt*, November 25, 1964.

43. *Frankfurter Allgemeine Zeitung (FAZ)*, November 27, 1964; and "Berichte von kannibalismus im Kongo" [Reports of cannibalism in the Congo], *FAZ*, December 14, 1964.

44. "Die Rettung hätte Vorgang."

45. On the "Black Peril," see: Jock McCulloch, *Black Peril, White Virtue: Sexual Crime in Southern Rhodesia, 1902–1935* (Bloomington: Indiana University Press, 2000); Krista O'Donnell, "Poisonous Women: Sexual Danger, Illicit Violence, and Domestic Work in German Southern Africa, 1904–1915," *Journal of Women's History* 11, no. 3 (Autumn 1999): 32–54; and Pamela Scully, "Rape, Race, and Colonial Culture: The

Sexual Politics of Identity in the Nineteenth-Century Cape Colony, South Africa," *American Historical Review* 100, no. 2 (1995): 335–59.

46. On the German campaign against the "Black Shame on the Rhine" and its broad resonance across Europe, see especially Sally Marks, "Black Watch on the Rhine: A Study in Propaganda, Prejudice, and Prurience, 1914–1930," *European Studies Review* 13 (1983): 297–334; and Reiner Pommerin, *Sterilisierung der Rheinlandbastarde: Das Schicksal einer farbiger deutschen Minderheit, 1918–1937* [The sterilization of the Rhineland Bastards: The fate of a colored German minority, 1919–1937] (Dusseldorf: Droste, 1979).

47. Ann Laura Stoler, *Carnal Knowledge and Imperial Power: Race and the Intimate in Colonial Rule* (Berkeley: University of California Press, 2002), 58.

48. Lothar Killmer, "Hintergründe einer Aggression" [Background of the aggression], *ND*, November 25, 1964.

49. Manfred Shulman, "Stanleyville—Höhepunkt permanenter Intervention" [Stanleyville—high point of a permanent intervention], *ND*, November 27, 1964.

50. Killmer, "Hintergründe einer Aggression."

51. See especially "Ich sah die Hölle" [I saw the hell], *ND*, November 27, 1964, and "So wüten die Paras: Augenzeugen widerlegen den Schwindel von der 'humanitären Aktion'" [So rage the paratroopers: Eyewitnesses refute the swindle of the "humanitarian action"], *ND*, November 28, 1964.

52. "Scharfer Protest der UDSSR" [Fierce protest of the USSR], *ND*, November 26, 1964.

53. "Amerikanische Botschaft in Kairo gestürmt" [American embassy in Cairo stormed], *Die Welt*, November 27, 1964; and "Ausschreitung gegen US-Botschaft in Moskau" [Riot against the US embassy in Moscow], *Die Welt*, November 30, 1964.

54. "Sicherheitsrat zur Lage in Kongo" [Security Council on the situation in Congo], telegram from West German observer to United Nations, New York, to AA, no. 750, December 10, 1964, 1, PAAA B 34, Bd. 497.

55. Ibid., 3.

56. Gleijeses, *Conflicting Missions*, 75.

57. See, for example, "National Rat der Befreiung 'C.N.L.' an Das Zentralkomitee der Sozialistische Einheits Partei Deutschlands" (German translation) [National Liberation Council "C.N.L." to the Central Committee of the German Socialist Unity Party], Brazzaville, April 30, 1964; and "Aktenvermerk über ein Gespräch mit dem Vertreter der CNL Kongos/Leopoldville, Herrn Mumengy" [Note for the file on a conversation with the representative of the CNL of Congo/Léopoldville, Mr. Mumengy], General Consulate of the German Democratic Republic in the United Arab Republic, Cairo, August 22, 1964, *Stiftung Archiv der Parteien und Massenorganisationen der DDR* im *Bundesarchiv* (hereafter BArch-SAPMO), DY 30 IV/A 2/20/983.

58. On the Cuban detachment in the Congo, see Gleijeses, *Conflicting Missions*, chs. 4–5. On Guevara's experience fighting with the rebel movement, see his diaries from the period, Che Guevara, *Pasajes de la guerra revolucionaria: Congo* [Reminiscences of the revolutionary war: Congo] (Barcelona: Grijalbo, 1999).

59. Gleijeses, *Conflicting Missions*, 75. This funding was, however, short-lived. By spring 1965 East Germany, like the Soviet Union, had radically decreased its support because

of infighting and lack of unity among the various rebel factions, which showed no hope of resolution: "Nationale Befreiungsbewegung in Kongo/Leopoldville" [National liberation movement in Congo/Léopoldville], MfAA, March 4, 1965, PA/AA, MfAA C-807, Bd. 74.

60. Namikas suggests that after Khrushchev's fall from power in August 1964, interest in African liberation movements had actually waned in the Kremlin in favor of a renewed focus on domestic developments in the Soviet Union. While conforming to Khrushchev's ideological position on Congo, Brezhnev's regime was reluctant to commit significant funds to the cause despite its Cold War rhetorical posturing. Namikas, "Battleground Africa," 433.

61. "Invasion! Stanleyville von Imperialisten überfallen," *ND*, November 25, 1964.

62. "Kongolesene Patrioten Danken der DDR. Bonn paktiert immer enger mit den Putschisten" [Congolese patriots thank the DDR; Bonn is in ever closer cahoots with the putschists], *ND*, December 8, 1964.

63. Ibid.

64. "DDR verurteilt Bonner Schützhilfe in Kongo" [DDR condemns Bonn's aid to Congo], *ND*, November 26, 1964.

65. Germans perpetrated what has been since identified as the first genocide of the twentieth century in the colony of German South West Africa, in the course of which German military forces under the command of Lothar von Trotha annihilated the majority of the populations of Herero and Nama peoples. During these same years, German forces executed punitive expeditions against the Maji Maji rebellion in German East Africa (Tanzania). Military attack and famine resulting from a German scorched-earth policy resulted in African deaths estimated as high as 250,000–300,000. On the Herero genocide, see especially Helmut Bley, *South-West Africa under German Rule, 1894–1914*, English ed. (Evanston, IL: Northwestern University Press, 1971); Jürgen Zimmerer, *Deutsche Herrschaft über Afrikaner: staatlicher Machtanspruch und Wirklichkeit im kolonialen Namibia* [German rule over Africans: The state claim to power and reality in colonial Namibia] (Muenster: Lit, 2002); and Horst Drechsler, *Let Us Die Fighting: The Struggle of the Herero and Nama against German Imperialism (1884–1915)* (London: Zed Press, 1980). On the Maji Maji rebellion, see John Iliffe, *A Modern History of Tanganyika* (Cambridge: Cambridge University Press, 1979).

66. In 1960, a Politburo directive called for a more intensive documentation of the German colonial past as part of an official foreign policy offensive against West Germany in Africa. Politbüro Protokol: Sitzung des Politbüros des Zentralkomitees [Politburo protocol: Meeting of the Politbüro of the Central Committee], January 4, 1960, BArch-SAPMO, DY 30/ J IV 2/2/682.

67. See especially National Council for the National Front, ed., *Brown Book: War and Nazi Criminals in West Germany* (Dresden: Verlag Zeit im Bild, 1966); and Ministerium für aussenländische Angelegenheiten, ed., *From Ribbentrop to Adenauer: A Documentation of the West German Foreign Office* (Berlin: Ministry of Foreign Affairs, 1961). On the Nazi "exposure campaign" more generally, see Jeffrey Herf, *Divided Memory: The Nazi Past in the Two Germanys* (Cambridge, MA: Harvard University Press, 1997), 181–85.

68. See, for example, Kurt Büttner, *Die Anfange der deutschen imperialismus in Ostafrika. Eine Kritische Untersuchung an Hand Unveroffentlichter Quellen* [The origins of German imperialism in East Africa: A critical investigation based on unpublished sources] (Berlin: Akademie Verlag, 1959); Horst Drechsler, *Südwestafrika unter deutscher Kolonialherrschaft. Der Kampf der Herero und Nama gegen deutschen Imperialismus, 1884–1915* [South-West Africa under German colonial rule: The struggle of the Herero and Nama against German imperialism, 1884–1915] (Berlin: Akademie Verlag, 1966); and Manfred Nussbaum, *Togo, eine Musterkolonie?* [Togo, a model colony?] (Berlin: Akademie Verlag, 1961).

69. Isabel V. Hull, *Absolute Destruction: Military Culture and the Practices of War in Imperial Germany* (Ithaca, NY: Cornell University Press, 2005), 148.

70. "The Germans to the Front!," *ND*, December 2, 1964.

71. Such accounts also appeared in the international press. See Gleijeses, *Conflicting Missions*, 72–73.

72. Ernst Petry and Gerd Heidemann, "Auf der Straße der Landsknechte" [On the streets of the Landsknechte] (1), Stern 46 (November 22, 1964); Petry, "Auf der Straße der Landsknechte" [On the streets of the Landsknechte] (2), *Stern* 47 (November 29, 1964); and Petry, "Auf der Straße der Landsknechte" [On the streets of the Landsknechte] (3), *Stern* 48 (December 6, 1964). Similar stories appeared in *Quick* 38, 39 (1964) and *Revue* 41, 42, 43 (1964).

73. Petry, "Auf der Straße" (2), 97.

74. Marcuse, *Legacies of Dachau*, 380.

75. In his work on returning German POWs, Frank Biess has shown the tension in the postwar period between remembering and forgetting, and voicing and silencing the participation of the Wehrmacht in wartime atrocities and genocide on the Eastern Front. See *Homecomings: Returning POWs and the Legacies of Defeat in Postwar Germany* (Princeton, NJ: Princeton University Press, 2006). For scholarly treatments of the participation of the German Wehrmacht and reserve troops in genocide and atrocities against civilians and prisoners of war, see especially Christopher R. Browning, *Ordinary Men: Reserve Police Battalion 101 and the Final Solution in Poland* (New York: Harper Perennial, 1998); and Omer Bartov, *The Eastern Front, 1941–45: German Troops and the Barbarisation of Warfare* (London: Macmillan, 1985).

76. Petry, "Auf der Straße" (2), 98.

77. Hannah Arendt, *Eichmann in Jerusalem: A Report on the Banality of Evil* (New York: Penguin Books, 1987). On the West German response to Eichmann's capture and Arendt's book detailing the trial, see Marcuse, *Legacies of Dachau*, 212, and Wittmann, *Beyond Justice*, 14.

78. Wittmann, *Beyond Justice*, 176–77. On the Auschwitz trial, see also Pendas, *The Frankfurt Auschwitz Trial*.

79. Lenz to Erhard, November 30, 1964.

80. Michael Luft, "Kongo-Greuel" [Congo horror], *Konkret* 12 (December 1964).

81. Memoirs, biographies, and contemporary accounts that highlight the anti-Tshombe protest as a movement catalyst include: Gretchen Dutschke-Klotz, *Wir hatten ein barbarisches, schönes Leben: Rudi Dutschke: Eine Biographie* [We had a barbaric,

beautiful life: Rudi Dutschke—a biography] (Cologne: Kiepenheuer and Witsch, 1996), 60–61; Ulrich Enzensberger, *Die Jahre der Kommune I: Berlin, 1967–1969* [The Years of Commune I: Berlin, 1967–1969] (Cologne: Kiepenheuer and Witsch, 2004), 30–32; and Uwe Bergmann et al., *Rebellion der Studenten oder die neue Opposition* [The student rebellion or the new opposition] (Reinbek b. Hamburg: Rowohlt, 1968), 160–62. The anti-Tshombe demonstration receives mention in most general studies of the anti-authoritarian student movement, but the most comprehensive scholarly accounts are Quinn Slobodian, "Radical Empathy: The Third World and the New Left in 1960s Germany" (PhD diss., New York University, 2008), 98–121; and Niels Seibert, *Vergessene Proteste. Internationalismus und Antirassismus, 1964–1983* [Forgotten protest: Internationalism and antiracism, 1964–1983] (Muenster: UNRAST-Verlag, 2008), 27–34.

82. "Mitteilung an die Presse" [Communication to the press], Ref. IB4, December 11, 1964, PA/AA, Ref. IB3, B 34, Bd. 498. During his visit, Tshombe met with, among others, Federal President Heinrich Lübke, State Secretary Karl Carstens of the Foreign Office, Parliamentary President Eugen Gerstenmaier, and the mayor of West Berlin, Willy Brandt.

83. Notes on the Lübke-Tshombe meeting, December 16, 1964, PA/AA, Ref. IB3, B 34, Bd. 498.

84. See Peter Grubbe, "Der Held der westlichen Welt: Moishe Tschombe" [The hero of the Western world: Moïse Tschombe], *Konkret* 1 (January 1965): 17–18.

85. Hubertus Knabe has shown that East German secret police, or Stasi, had infiltrated parts of the German student movement and had influence over publications such as *Konkret*. Indeed, Quinn Slobodian points out that the East German youth organization, the Free German Youth, participated in the initial planning of the Tshombe demonstration but pulled out because some protestors wanted to carry signs critical of the Berlin Wall. In spite of such evidence of East German involvement in the protest, Slobodian's research suggests, the most significant external influence on the anti-Tshombe demonstration came not from East Germany but from African students, some of whom may have come from East Germany. Slobodian, "Radical Empathy," 98–121; and Hubertus Knabe, *Die unterwanderte Republik: Stasi im Westen* [The infiltrated republic: The Stasi in the West] (Berlin: Propyläen, 1999), 182–234.

86. "Schweigedemonsration! Am Freitag soll Tschombé vom Berlin Senat empfangen werden" [Silent vigil! On Friday Tshombe will be received by the Berlin Senate], in Siegward Lönnendonker and Tilman Fichter, eds., *Freie Universität Berlin. Hochschule im Umbruch, 1948–73, Teil IV: Die Krise* [Free University Berlin: Academia in upheaval, 1948–73, Part IV: The crisis] (Berlin: FU Berlin, 1974), 175.

87. "Zum Verlauf der Demonstration gegen den Empfang Tschombés" [On the course of the demonstration against Tshombe's reception], in ibid., 179.

88. Seibert, *Vergessene Proteste*, 31.

89. Kühn-Leitz was a prominent figure in West German foreign relations and in humanitarian circles. She corresponded with Adenauer in the 1950s and 1960s, and at his urging became the founding chairperson of the German-French Friendship Association. Kühn-Leitz was also known for her humanitarian work in Africa. She

was associated with the famous philanthropist Albert Schweitzer and carried out numerous private fund-raising efforts to aid various African countries and causes. *Who's Who in Germany* (Munich: Intercontinental Book and Publishing Company, R. Oldenbourg Verlag, 1964), 968–69.

90. Handwritten note from Kühn-Leitz to Foreign Minister Gerhard Schröder, November 30, 1964, PA/AA, Ref. IB3, B 34, Bd. 497. The letter was published later as a newspaper article. Dr. Elsie Kühn-Leitz, "Die Retter zu Marodeuren gestempelt: Wie den Kongo-Rebellen und ihren Hintermännern Hilfestellung geleistet wird" [The saviors branded as marauders: How the Congolese rebels and their backers are assisted], *Rheinischer Merkur*, December 11, 1964.

91. Elsie Kühn-Leitz, "Offener Brief über die gegenwärtigen Ereignisse im Kongo" [Open letter on the current events in Congo], PA/AA, Ref. IB3, B 34, Bd. 497.

92. See, for example, "Invasion! Stanleyville von Imperialisten überfallen," *ND*, November 25, 1964; and "Paras schlachte wahlos Kongolesen ab" [Paratroopers indiscriminately slaughter Congolese], *ND*, November 28 and December 1, 1964. For descriptions of the mercenaries as "beasts in uniform," see *ND*, November 25, 1964.

93. "Sehen Sie den Abgrund nicht?" [Don't they see the abyss?], *ND*, November 29, 1964.

94. Petry had also given film to Heynowski and was in the process of working out a similar deal. See confidential report on negotiations with Gerd Heidemann, Walter Heynowski, Berlin, May 28, 1965, BArch-SAPMO, DR 118/1550. See also Rüdiger Steinmetz and Tilo Prase, *Dokumentarfilm zwischen Beweis und Pamphlet. Heynowski & Scheumann und Gruppe Katins* [Documentary film between evidence and lampoon: Heynowski and Scheumann and the Katin group] (Leipzig: Leipziger Universitätsverlag, 2002), 73.

95. Heynowski and Scheumann also made a third film, *Der Fall Bernd K.* [The case of Bernd K.], which was particularly interested in the postwar generation and served as an indictment of West German culture. It followed the former East German Bernd Michael Kohlert. Kohlert had fled to West Germany and eventually joined Müller's commando in Congo, where he was among the first mercenary casualties. Unlike *Kommando 52* [Commando 52] and *Der lachende Mann* [The laughing man], however, this thirty-minute documentary received little critical attention. See Bunnenberg, Der "Kongo-Müller," 111–14; and Walter Heynowski and Gerhard Scheumann, *Der Fall Bernd K.* (Halle: Mitteldeutscher Verlag, 1968).

96. Heynowski and Scheumann, *Der lachende Mann*, 38.

97. Steinmetz and Prase, *Dokumentarfilm zwischen Beweis und Pamphlet*, 83.

98. Heynowski and Scheumann, *Der lachende Mann*, 92–93. The state recognized the films as such successful consciousness-raising tools that it funded the formation of H&S Studios, through which Heynowski and Scheumann would continue to produce anti-imperialist documentaries. Beschlußvorlage zur Gründung der DEFA-Gruppe Heynowski and Scheumann [Proposed resolution on the founding of the DEFA group Heynowski and Scheumann], circa 1967, BArch-SAPMO, IV A 2/2.02 A/35.

99. Arbeitsgruppe Auslandsinformation, KAG III—Heynowski an Stoff [Foreign information working group, KAG III—Heynowski to Stoff], January 26, 1966, BArch-SAPMO, DR 118/1551; and Heynowski and Scheumann, *Der lachende Mann*, 100.

100. Letter from Inge Kleinert, Director, DEFA Studios für Wochenschau und Dokumentarfilme [DEFA Studios for Newsreels and Documentary Film], to Gürke, MfAA, IV AEA, January 12, 1966, BArch-SAPMO, DR 118/1551. Kleinert in fact spun this differently to the press, claiming that Pauline Lumumba first saw the film and then contacted Kaul because he was known to have participated in the Auschwitz trials. Heynowski and Scheumann, *Der lachende Mann*, 143.

101. Heynowski and Scheumann, *Der lachende Mann*, 138. Heynowski and Scheumann made a third film, *P.S. zum lachenden Mann* [P.S. to the laughing man], that followed up on the public reception of the first film and also detailed the complaint against Müller. For an analysis, see Bunnenberg, *Der "Kongo-Müller,"* 101–11.

102. Heynowski and Scheumann, *Der lachende Mann*, 145.

103. On the exclusion of *Der lachende Mann* from the Internationale Kurzfilmwoche [International Short Film Week], Mannheim, in October 1966, see "Argumentation zur Vorlage über die Teilnahme von Filmschaffenden der DDR an der XV. Internationalen Filmwoche Mannheim 1966" [Rationale for the guidelines on the participation of DDR film technicians in the 15th Mannheim International Film Week 1966], Abteilung Kultur der ZK-SED [Culture Bureau of the Central Committee of the SED]; and "Kurzinformation über den Verlauf der XV. Internationalen Filmwoche Mannheim vom 10–15 Oktober 1966" [Brief information on the course of the 15th Mannheim International Film Week from 10 to 15 October 1966], Ministerium für Kultur, Abt. Filmproduktion [Ministry of Culture, Bureau of Film Production], BArch, IV A 2/9.06/121. For a discussion of West German policies on importation of the films, see Bunnenberg, *Der "Kongo-Müller,"* 100–103; and Heynowski and Scheumann, *Der lachende Mann*, 142–45.

104. Bunnenberg, *Der "Kongo-Müller,"* 81–84. See the following exchange: "Betr.: Fernschreiben Nr. 236 vom 23.12.1965 aus Accra" [Re: Telegram Nr. 236 from 12.23.1965 from Accra], Ref. V3 to Ref. IB3 AA, Bonn, December 29, 1965; "Betr.: Werbung von deutschen Söldnern; hier: Siegfried Müller" [Re: Promotion of German mercenaries; here: Siegfried Müller], Ref. V3 to the Minister of the Interior, Bonn, December 31, 1965; "Betr.: Anwerbung von deutschen Söldnern für fremden Wehrdienst durch Siegfried Müller" [Re: Enlistment of German mercenaries for foreign military service through Siegfried Müller], Minister of the Interior to the AA, Bonn, February 10, 1966; "Betr.: Siegfried Müller" [Re: Siegfried Müller], Ref. V3 to the Minister of the Interior, September 14, 1966, PA/AA, Ref. V3, B 82, Bd. 1116.

105. "Betr: Deutscher Staatsangehöriger Siegfried Müller genannt 'Kongo-Müller'" [Re: German national Siegfried Müller called "Congo-Müller"], Minister of the Interior to Ref. V3, AA, November 10, 1966; and "Betr.: 'Kongo-Müller'—hier: Paßentzug" [Re: 'Congo-Müller'—here: Passport revocation], Ref. V3 to Ref. IB3, Bonn, February 10, 1967, PA/AA, Ref. V3, B 82, Bd. 1116.

106. Demonstrations against the West German premiere of the Gualtiero Jacopetti and Franco Prosperi's film, *Africa Addio* (Italy, 1966), which included footage of the white mercenaries, had incited a new round of student protests invoking Müller's name in September 1966, and had earned the ire of some African diplomats and politicians. See Seibert, *Vergessene Proteste*, 35–50.

107. On anti-Vietnam protest, see especially Ingo Juchler, *Rebellische Subjektivität und Internationalismus. Der Einfluss Herbert Marcuses und der Nationalen Befreiungsbewegungen in der Sog. Dritten Welt auf die Studentenbewegung in der BRD* [Rebellious subjectivity and internationalism: The influence of Herbert Marcuse and the national liberation movements of the so-called Third World on the student movement in the FRG] (Marburg: Verlag Arbeiterbewegung und Gesellschaftswissenschaft, 1989); Wilfried Mausbach, "Auschwitz und Vietnam: West German Protest against America's War during the 1960s," in *America, the Vietnam War, and the World: Comparative and International Perspectives*, ed. Andreas W. Daum, Lloyd C. Gardner, and Wilfried Mausbach, 279–98 (Washington, DC: German Historical Institute; Cambridge: Cambridge University Press, 2003); and Günter Wernicke, *'Solidarität hilft siegen!' Zur Solidaritätsbewegung mit Vietnam in beiden deutschen Staaten. Mitte der 60er bis Anfang der 70er Jahre* ['Solidarity Aids Victory!' On the solidarity movement with Vietnam in the two German states; middle of the 1960s to the beginning of the 1970s] (Berlin: Gesellschaftswissenschaftliches Forum, 2001).

References

ARCHIVES
Bundesarchiv (Federal Archive), Berlin, Germany
Bundesarchiv (Federal Archive), Coblenz, Germany
Politisches Archiv des Auswärtigen Amts (Political Archive of the Foreign Office), Berlin
Stiftung Archiv der Parteien und Massenorganisationen der DDR im Bundesarchiv (Foundation Archive of Parties and Mass Organizations of the DDR at the Federal Archive), Berlin, Germany

PERIODICALS
Frankfurter Allgemeine Zeitung
Neues Deutschland
Quick
Revue
Stern
Die Welt

PUBLISHED GOVERNMENT DOCUMENTS
Babing, Alfred, ed. *Against Racism, Apartheid, and Colonialism: Documents Published by the GDR, 1949–1977*. Berlin: Staatsverlag der DDR, 1977.
US Congress, Senate, Interim Report. "Alleged Assassination Plots Involving Foreign Leaders, by the Select Committee to Study Government Operations with Respect to Intelligence Activities." 1st Session, 94th Congress, November 20, 1975.

SELECTED PUBLISHED WORKS

Arendt, Hannah. *Eichmann in Jerusalem: A Report on the Banality of Evil*. New York: Penguin Books, 1987.

Bartov, Omer. *The Eastern Front, 1941–45: German Troops and the Barbarisation of Warfare*. London: Macmillan, 1985.

Bergmann, Uwe, Rudi Dutschke, Wolfgang Lefevre, and Bernd Rabehl. *Rebellion der Studenten oder die neue Opposition* [The student rebellion or the new opposition]. Reinbek b. Hamburg: Rowohlt, 1968.

Biess, Frank. *Homecomings: Returning POWs and the Legacies of Defeat in Postwar Germany*. Princeton, NJ: Princeton University Press, 2006.

Bley, Helmut. *South-West Africa under German Rule, 1894–1914*. English ed. Evanston, IL: Northwestern University Press, 1971.

Bodemer, Klaus. *Entwicklungshilfe—Politik für wen?* [Development aid—policy for whom?]. Munich: Weltforum Verlag, 1973.

Booz, Rüdiger Marco. *"Hallsteinzeit" Deutsche Außenpolitik, 1955–1972* ["Hallstein Times": German foreign policy, 1955–1972]. Bonn: Bouvier Verlag, 1995.

Borstelmann, Thomas. *The Cold War and the Color Line: American Race Relations in the Global Arena*. Cambridge, MA: Harvard University Press, 2001.

Browning, Christopher R. *Ordinary Men: Reserve Police Battalion 101 and the Final Solution in Poland*. New York: Harper Perennial, 1998.

Bunnenberg, Christian. *Der "Kongo-Müller." Eine deutsche Söldnerkarriere* ["Congo-Müller": A German mercenary career]. Berlin: Lit Verlag, 2007.

Büttner, Kurt. *Die Anfange der deutschen imperialismus in Ostafrika. Eine Kritische Untersuchung an Hand Unveroffentlicher Quellen* [The origins of German imperialism in East Africa: A critical investigation based on unpublished sources]. Berlin: Akademie Verlag, 1959.

Cooper, Frederick. *Africa since 1940: The Past of the Present*. Cambridge: Cambridge University Press, 2002

———. *Decolonization and African Society*. Cambridge: Cambridge University Press, 1996.

de Witte, Ludo. *The Assassination of Lumumba*. Translated by Anne Wright and Reneé Fenby. London: Verso, 2001.

Drechsler, Horst. *Let Us Die Fighting: The Struggle of the Herero and Nama against German Imperialism (1884–1915)*. London: Zed Press, 1980.

———. *Südwestafrika unter deutscher Kolonialherrschaft. Der Kampf der Herero und Nama gegen deutschen Imperialismus, 1884–1915* [Southwest Africa under German colonial rule: The struggle of the Herero and Nama against German imperialism, 1884–1915]. Berlin: Akademie Verlag, 1966.

Dutschke-Klotz, Gretchen. *Wir hatten ein barbarisches, schönes Leben: Rudi Dutschke: Eine Biographie* [We had a barbaric, beautiful life: Rudi Dutschke—a biography]. Cologne: Kiepenheuer and Witsch, 1996.

Enzensberger, Ulrich. *Die Jahre der Kommune I: Berlin, 1967–1969* [The years of commune I: Berlin, 1967–1969]. Cologne: Kiepenheuer and Witsch, 2004.

Fehrenbach, Heide. *Race after Hitler: Black Occupation Children in Postwar Germany and America*. Princeton, NJ: Princeton University Press, 2005.

Gibbs, David. *The Political Economy of Third World Intervention*. Chicago: University of Chicago Press, 1991.

Gleijeses, Piero. *Conflicting Missions: Havana, Washington, and Africa, 1959–1976*. Chapel Hill: University of North Carolina Press, 2002.

Gray, William Glenn. *Germany's Cold War: The Global Campaign to Isolate East Germany, 1949–1969*. Chapel Hill: University of North Carolina Press, 2003.

Guevara, Che. *Pasajes de la guerra revolucionaria: Congo* [Reminiscences of the revolutionary war: Congo]. Barcelona: Grijalbo, 1999.

Herf, Jeffrey. *Divided Memory: The Nazi Past in the Two Germanys*. Cambridge, MA: Harvard University Press, 1997.

Heynowski, Walter, and Gerhard Scheumann. *Der Fall Bernd K.* [The case of Bernd K.]. Halle: Mitteldeutscher Verlag, 1968.

———. *Der lachende Mann. Bekenntnis eines Mörders* [The laughing man: The avowal of a murderer]. Berlin: Verlag der Nation, 1966.

Hong, Young-Sun. "'The Benefits of Health Must Be Spread among All': International Solidarity, Health, and Race in the East German Encounter with the Third World." In *Socialist Modern: East German Everyday Culture and Politics*, edited by Katherine Pence and Paul Betts, 183–210. Ann Arbor: University of Michigan Press, 2008.

Hull, Isabel V. *Absolute Destruction: Military Culture and the Practices of War in Imperial Germany*. Ithaca, NY: Cornell University Press, 2005.

Iliffe, John. *A Modern History of Tanganyika*. Cambridge: Cambridge University Press, 1979.

James, Alan. *Britain and the Congo Crisis, 1960–63*. Basingstoke, UK: Macmillan, 1996.

Kalb, Madeline G. *The Congo Cables: The Cold War in Africa, from Eisenhower to Kennedy*. New York: Macmillan, 1982.

Knabe, Hubertus. *Die unterwanderte Republik: Stasi im Westen* [The infiltrated republic: The Stasi in the West]. Berlin: Propyläen, 1999.

Lönnendonker, Siegward, and Tilman Fichter, eds. *Freie Universität Berlin. Hochschule im Umbruch, 1948–73*. Teil IV: Die Krise [Free University Berlin: Academia in upheaval, 1948–73; Part IV: The crisis]. Berlin: FU Berlin, 1974.

Marcuse, Harold. *Legacies of Dachau: The Uses and Abuses of a Concentration Camp, 1933–2001*. Cambridge: Cambridge University Press, 2001.

Marks, Sally. "Black Watch on the Rhine: A Study in Propaganda, Prejudice, and Prurience, 1914–1930." *European Studies Review* 13 (1983): 297–334.

Ministerium für aussenländische Angelegenheiten [Ministry of Foreign Affairs], ed. *From Ribbentrop to Adenauer: A Documentation of the West German Foreign Office*. Berlin: Ministry of Foreign Affairs, 1961.

Namikas, Lisa. "Battleground Africa: The Cold War and the Congo Crisis, 1960–1965." PhD diss., University of Southern California, 2002.

Ndumbe, Kum'a. *Was will Bonn in Afrika? Zur Afrikapolitik der Bundesrepublik Deutschland* [What does Bonn want in Africa? On the Africa policy of the Federal Republic of Germany]. Pfaffenweiler: Centaurus, 1992.

Nkrumah, Kwame. *Challenge of the Congo*. New York: International Publishers, 1967.

Nzongola-Ntalaja, George. *The Congo from Leopold to Kabila: A People's History*. London: Zed Books, 2002.

Pendas, Devin O. *The Frankfurt Auschwitz Trial, 1963–1965: Genocide, History, and the Limits of the Law.* Cambridge: Cambridge University Press, 2006.

Poiger, Uta G. *Jazz, Rock, and Rebels: Cold War Politics and American Culture in a Divided Germany.* Berkeley: University of California Press, 2000.

Pommerin, Reiner. *Sterilisierung der Rheinlandbastarde: Das Schicksal einer farbiger deutschen Minderheit, 1918–1937* [The sterilization of the Rhineland Bastards: The fate of a colored German minority, 1919–1937]. Dusseldorf: Droste, 1979.

Richards, Graham. *"Race," Racism and Psychology: Towards a Reflexive History.* London: Routledge, 1997.

Schulz, Brigitte. *Development Policy in the Cold War Era: The Two Germanies and Sub-Saharan Africa, 1960–1985.* Muenster: Lit, 1995.

Seibert, Niels. "Proteste gegen den Film *Africa Addio.* Ein Beispiel für Antirassismus in den 60er-Jarhen" [Protest against the film *Africa Addio*: An example of antiracism in the 1960s]. In *Widerstandsbewegung. Antirassismus zwischen Alltag und Aktion* [Resistance movement: Antiracism ranging from everyday to political campaign], edited by Jetti Hahn Titus Engelschaft, Tobias Pieper, and Tim Zülch, 280–89. Berlin: Verlag Assoziation A, 2005.

———. *Vergessene Proteste. Internationalismus und Antirassismus, 1964–1983* [Forgotten protest: Internationalism and antiracism, 1964–1983]. Muenster: UNRAST-Verlag, 2008.

Slobodian, Quinn. "Radical Empathy: The Third World and the New Left in 1960s Germany." PhD diss., New York University, 2008.

Steinmetz, Rüdiger, and Tilo Prase. *Dokumentarfilm zwischen Beweis und Pamphlet. Heynowski & Scheumann und Gruppe Katins* [Documentary film between evidence and lampoon: Heynowski and Scheumann and the Katin group]. Leipzig: Leipziger Universitätsverlag, 2002.

Stoler, Ann Laura. *Carnal Knowledge and Imperial Power: Race and the Intimate in Colonial Rule.* Berkeley: University of California Press, 2002.

Wittmann, Rebecca. *Beyond Justice: The Auschwitz Trial.* Cambridge, MA: Harvard University Press, 2005.

Zimmerer, Jürgen. *Deutsche Herrschaft über Afrikaner: Staatlicher Machtanspruch und Wirklichkeit im kolonialen Namibia* [German rule over Africans: The state claim to power and reality in colonial Namibia]. Muenster: Lit Verlag, 2002.

CHAPTER 8

Race and the Cuban Revolution

The Impact of Cuba's Intervention in Angola

Henley Adams

The transformation of the Angolan Civil War from a localized power struggle among three rival national liberation movements—the Popular Movement for the Liberation of Angola (MPLA), the National Front for the Liberation of Angola (FNLA), and the Union for the Total Independence of Angola (UNITA)—into a major source of geopolitical tensions between the United States and the Soviet Union constituted one of the most surprising developments of the Cold War. Equally surprising would be the conflict's impact on the domestic and international policies of the Caribbean island of Cuba. Until its emergence as an improbable flashpoint in the ideological confrontation between East and West, Angola had been an obscure Portuguese colony in southwest Africa, a continent neither superpower regarded as strategically important. Yet the battle for Angola became more than ideological.

The issue of race would shape the overwhelmingly negative reaction to South Africa's intervention in Angola on behalf of the FNLA, and later UNITA, helping consolidate diplomatic support for the MPLA among African and other countries, even those previously hostile to the liberation movement's Marxist leanings. Cuban troops, mostly of African descent, served as a bulwark against South African ambitions. Inside South Africa itself, events in Angola would inspire the black majority's resistance to apartheid. In June 1976, high school students in Soweto, the country's largest segregated black township, staged a massive protest against a government-imposed plan to teach Afrikaans, derided as the language of the oppressors by most blacks. The security force's violent response led to the deaths of hundreds, among them numerous schoolchildren shot by the police, and signaled the beginning of a heightened internal resistance to apartheid. Some anti-apartheid activists cite the reversals experienced by the South African Defence Force (SADF) in Angola as having emboldened them in their challenge to the South African state. Another beneficiary of Cuba's presence would be the people of South-West Africa (present-day Namibia), who had been struggling against the illegal administration of the country by South Africa. Racial affinity helped inoculate Cuba, a geographical outsider, from accusations of imperialist behavior, a sensitive issue for African countries, most of which were barely a decade removed from painful histories of colonial domination. Finally, as a result of its involvement in Angola, Cuba itself would begin to examine issues associated with its own internal racial dynamics.

This analysis of Cuban foreign policy focuses on the racial aspect of Cuba's actions in Africa, especially the mission in Angola, a departure from the majority of studies, which have focused on the ideological, geostrategic, or economic implications of the island's activism. The internationalist commitment in Angola not only served as a decisive stage in Cuban foreign policy but also constituted a critical juncture in the official attitude toward race. Consequently, the story of Cuba's policy in Africa cannot be understood fully unless the myriad racial dimensions of the Cuban government's decisions and actions are explored.

End of Colonial Rule and Arrival of Independence

On April 25, 1974, the Armed Forces Movement (MFA), a cabal of reform-minded junior military officers, staged a virtually bloodless coup in Portugal, ending five decades of authoritarian rule under the Estado Novo, or New State. Initially, the revolutionary junta expressed reservations about ending colonial rule before announcing its intention to begin a process of immediate decolonization.[1] In Angola, a transition to independence proved problematic, the process complicated by the existence of the three bitter rivals for power. Not only did each movement believe itself best suited to govern an independent Angola, but also relations among the respective group's leaders were characterized by suspicion and mutual enmity.

Despite reconciliation efforts supervised by the Organization of African Unity (OAU) during the early days of January 1975, and a subsequent agreement among the adversaries and Portugal establishing a framework for mutual cooperation, the sharing of political power, and a formal independence date of November 11, 1975, accommodation proved elusive.[2] In addition to the personal enmity among Agostinho Neto (MPLA), Holden Roberto (FNLA), and Jonas Savimbi (UNITA), ethnic and to a lesser degree ideological differences separated the movements. The MPLA, dominated by black Angolan intellectuals, but also including members of the country's tiny *assimilado* and *mesticio* social classes among its leadership, professed allegiance to Marxism, and derived the majority of its support from the Mbundu ethnic group. More controversially, the MPLA allowed whites to join, a decision that not only engendered the derision of the rival movements, but also created dissension among rank-and-file MPLA members. UNITA, supported by the Ovimbundu, Angola's largest ethnic group, initially embraced no specific ideology, at one time endorsing democratic socialism before later adopting a staunch anti-Communist, pro-Western outlook once it began receiving South African and US military aid. The FNLA, similar to UNITA, espoused no clearly articulated political philosophy except for a virulent hatred of the Portuguese, its uncompromising militancy succeeding in attracting vocal support from some of the foremost African nationalists, such as Patrice Lumumba, Kwame Nkrumah, Ahmed Sékou Touré, and Frantz Fanon.[3] Serious armed clashes erupted between the MPLA and FNLA in March 1975 and a series of short-lived truces failed to end the fighting. Ultimately, in July 1975 the MPLA succeeded in expelling FNLA troops from the capital, Luanda, signaling the start of a sustained battle for military hegemony and effectively dashing any hopes for a proposed national government of unity.

Notwithstanding the corrosive relations among the three liberation movements, the blame for escalating hostilities in the buildup to independence must be attributed to the actions of foreign actors—specifically the transfers of large quantities of armaments to the FNLA and MPLA—although the covert nature of such transactions obviates against any consensus about the chronology. UNITA entered into an uneasy alliance with the FNLA, but the immediate military impact of this coalition proved negligible as the MPLA seized control of twelve out of a total sixteen provincial capitals and extended its authority throughout much of the country, positioning itself to be recognized as Angola's legitimate government with the arrival of independence.[4]

The Soviet Union had increased its provision of weapons to the MPLA during the March–April 1975 intensification of fighting, funneling its support through neighboring Congo-Brazzaville, and also directly into Angolan ports with the connivance of sympathetic Portuguese authorities.[5] According to the former head of the CIA Angolan task force, the United States began its own insertion of substantial lethal aid into Angola in August 1975, using Zaire as the base for what would become a massive and controversial covert operation to assist the FNLA and UNITA.[6] South Africa's decision to invade in October

1975 dramatically reversed the military situation on the ground, the well-trained and equipped South Africans easily overwhelming the resistance of the MPLA in the southern region of the country and rapidly advancing across wide swaths of territory.

The introduction of South African soldiers transformed the conflict from a confrontation primarily featuring Angolans fighting each other and ushered in a new phase—one in which foreign armies would occupy center stage. South Africa's entry led to an alarming reversal of the MPLA's military fortunes, threatening both its control of the country and its formerly secure position in Luanda.[7] Cuban military personnel had been trickling into Angola beginning in June 1975, an initial contingent of 230 advisers dispatched to train MPLA cadres in the use of increasingly sophisticated weapons supplied by the Soviet Union. Now, the addition of South African soldiers served as the catalyst for Cuba's buildup of its troop strength, significantly altering the nature of its involvement. By this time, approximately 1,500 Cubans already were participating in Angola's conflict, although the Cuban government regarded them as "instructors" rather than actual "troops," a distinction viewed as factually correct since these personnel did not participate "as separate, integral units."[8] These forces proved instrumental in organizing the defense of Luanda against a combined FNLA/Zairian assault, decisively routing the attackers and ensuring MPLA control of the capital upon the formal arrival of independence.[9] However, negative outcomes in early clashes with the superior SADF forces convinced Cuba of the need for additional forces, setting in motion the formal introduction of combat troops.

Under the code name Operation Carlota, in honor of "Black Carlota," a female slave and leader of a November 1843 slave rebellion in Matanzas province, Cuba initiated the buildup of troops that would inaugurate its sixteen-year mission in Angola. In a semi-official account of the operation written by Gabriel García Márquez, the celebrated Colombian author and a close friend of Fidel Castro, in its initial phase Carlota consisted of an airlift on November 7, 1975, of an elite 650-man contingent of special forces troops from the Ministry of Interior and additional troops, including men trained in the use of heavy artillery, departing Cuba on five ships. Subsequent military defeats during December 1975 and clashes with the SADF hastened a further introduction of troops, the rate of arrival climbing from an estimated four hundred in December to about a thousand a week in January 1976.[10] An estimated 2,800 Cubans at independence increased to 15,000 by the end of major fighting and the MPLA consolidation of authority in mid-February 1976.[11] Only during the latter stages of the operation did the Soviet Union provide needed transportation for soldiers bound for Angola.[12] On March 27, 1976, South Africa withdrew its forces from Angola after receiving assurances from the MPLA that the hydroelectric project at Cunene on the Angolan-Namibian border would not be destroyed and thus deprive northern Namibia of water and electricity.[13] With the FNLA virtually extinct in the north and UNITA on the run in the south, the CIA initiated a last-ditch effort to stave off defeat by recruiting white mercenaries, primarily from Europe, but also from the United States.[14] In an action denounced as "anti-African" by the OAU, anti-Communist sympathizers in the United States toyed with the idea of creating a contingent of black Americans to fight alongside FNLA-UNITA.[15] However, this proposed gambit ultimately failed because Congress passed the Clark Amendment on December 19, 1975, prohibiting further American aid to the anti-MPLA alliance. Moreover, this coalition already had dissolved into internecine bloodshed. As the MPLA consolidated its advantage on the battlefield, Angola was formally recognized and admitted into both the OAU and United Nations. Unquestionably, Cuba's willingness to send its military personnel into Angola had allowed the MPLA to assert its authority over its rivals and their foreign supporters.

The first official acknowledgment that Cuban troops were involved in Angola's civil war occurred on December 22, 1975, during Fidel Castro's closing speech at the revamped Cuban Communist Party's First Congress. As Castro stated in his address to the party faithful, Cuba's foreign relations would be guided first and foremost by the principle of proletarian internationalism: "The starting point of Cuba's foreign policy . . . is the subordination of Cuba's positions to the international needs of the struggle for socialism and for the national liberation of the peoples. Cuba, which has already proved its international solidarity by all possible means—with blood, with work, and with technical cooperation—will continue to make this condition the basis of its international attitudes." However, justification for the Angolan mission did not rest solely on the fulfillment of an internationalist duty; simultaneously, race and racial solidarity with black Africans against the virus of South Africa racism was equally important. During the same speech, in an emotional and lengthy proclamation of Cuba's racial brotherhood with Africa, the Cuban leader asserted:

> The blood of Africa runs abundantly through our veins. And from
> Africa, came many of our ancestors as slaves to this land. And
> many [of them] struggled as slaves, and many [of them] fought in
> the Liberation Army for our fatherland! We are brothers of the
> Africans, and for the Africans we are ready to struggle. In our
> country discrimination existed. Who does not know it? Who does not
> remember? In many parks, here the whites and here the blacks. Who
> does not remember that in many places, recreation centers, schools,

the descendants of Africans were not permitted to enter? Who does not remember that in study, work, and all aspects discrimination existed? And who are today the representatives, the symbols of the most hated, and the most inhuman discrimination? The fascists and racists of South Africa.[16]

The implications of these comments were obvious: Cubans had a duty to prevent the imposition of racial discrimination in Angola such as existed in Cuba under slavery and the prerevolutionary social order, especially since people of African descent had contributed so much to the struggle for independence. In this characterization, Castro had underscored the connection between Cuba and Africa as one based on mutual experiences of shared suffering experienced by large numbers of Africans and Cubans because of their racial origins. Thus began the Caribbean island's reinvention of its national identity as a hybrid "Latin-African" nation.

While Cuba's action has been characterized as "unprecedented" in the sense of a small, poor undeveloped country sending military forces to a far-away land, in other respects Angola represented continuity with previous Cuban behavior on the African continent. During the 1960s, the Cubans had engaged in a brief flirtation with the MPLA, before deciding the movement lacked the capability of becoming a viable revolutionary force in Angola. However, the overriding motive for Cuba's interest was ideology, not race. Stymied in his efforts to foment revolutions in Latin America, Fidel Castro regarded Africa, then in the midst of anticolonial turmoil, as the most fertile region for revolutionary adventures. To be fair, the Cuban leader did acknowledge a historical link between Cuba and Africa as early as September 1960, during a speech to the United Nations Fifteenth General Assembly. Nevertheless, the focus of this speech centered on a common interest in the progress of Africa's decolonization struggles.[17] Similarly, in his initial visit to the continent in 1972, Castro toured radical African countries and primarily discussed the mutual fight against Western imperialism.

After long insisting on internationalism and ideological solidarity as the guiding principle for its foreign policy, the elevation of race as justification for its actions constituted a notable departure for Cuba. It had been the MPLA's multiracial composition and refusal to emphasize racial identity that solidified its relations with Cuba, rather than the existence of any historical or cultural linkage.[18] However, radical African countries made up a minority of the continent, and the Cuban government realized the success of its mission in Angola would depend on the political support, or at least acquiescence, of other African governments. Consequently, race became the factor that would permit the Caribbean island to argue that it was not an interloper, and notwithstanding geography, deserved membership in the community of African nations. Acknowledging potential concerns held by some African governments about the thousands of Cuban soldiers in Angola, Fidel Castro attempted to assuage their fears in a spring 1976 speech when he stated: "No country of black Africa has anything to fear from Cuban military personnel. We are a Latin-African people—enemies of colonialism, neocolonialism, racism, and apartheid, which Yankee imperialism aids and protects."[19]

Once the conflict had erupted into major confrontations between Cuban troops and the SADF, the Soviet Union was forced to act or face questions about its revolutionary credentials. Nonetheless, the Communist superpower, concerned about the negative effects of the Angolan crisis on détente, publicly appealed to the United States not to let the war hinder cooperation. Consequently, even as the fighting raged and the two superpowers were arming their respective allies, Soviet officials continued to insist that Angola should not be an obstacle to US-Soviet relations, since it "remained tangential to the course of foreign policy."[20] According to a high-ranking Soviet diplomat who defected to the United States, while Cuban and Soviet interests converged, it had been the former who had taken the lead role in becoming involved in Angola.[21]

Undoubtedly, Cuba's sizable population of African descent allowed the island to pursue activities on the continent that would have been unthinkable for a country with a white-led government. Yet, racial solidarity constituted a necessary but by no means sufficient factor as an explanatory variable for the acceptance by most African and other predominantly black countries of Cuba's presence in Africa.

Race and Cuban Foreign Policy:
The Encounter with Black America

The role of race in Cuba's socialist revolution historically has been complex and arguably the most elusive topic. Its emergence as a linchpin of Cuban foreign policy must be viewed as one of the more surprising developments given the ambivalence toward racial issues on the island. Afro-Cubans had failed to participate in significant numbers during the revolutionary struggle, a fact acknowledged by the revolutionary government.[22] The catalyst for Fidel Castro to openly address race in Cuba appears to have been the shabby treatment of black veterans of the guerrilla army at some Havana hotels and clubs. Following a pair of speeches by the Cuban leader criticizing prejudice among some whites, and a structural assault on socioeconomic equality through redistributive policies and egalitarian legislation, he confidently declared an end to racial discrimination, describing it as a vestige of the old social order. In an interview with an American journalist, Castro summarized his revolution's position on the issue: "We believe that the problem of discrimination has an economic basis appropriate to a class in which man is exploited by man. . . . Discrimination disappeared when class privileges disappeared, and it has not cost the Revolution much effort to resolve the problem."[23] Thus, with the implementation of socialist economic programs, race as an issue faded from the national agenda. At the same time, it became an integral factor in the island's foreign relations, strategically deployed in pursuit of ambitious high-profile international policies.

If Africa represented the gestation of Cuba's use of race as a foreign policy weapon, the United States should be considered its embryonic phase. Race made its debut in Cuban-US relations during a 1960 visit to the United Nations in New York City, when Fidel Castro abandoned upscale hotel accommodations for more modest living arrangements in Harlem, creating a stir among black Americans and making a powerful international statement.[24] Cuba became a champion of the rights of African Americans, earning the admiration of many in the black community, including political militants.

Overall, the Cuban–black American relationship followed a rocky trajectory, a mixture of misunderstanding, suspicion, and outright hostility by some black radicals toward the government's racial policies, and a corresponding reaction by the Cuban authorities to certain currents within the radical black movement. Thus, although Cuba maintained consistent support for the black struggle in the United States, strains soon became evident in the relationship. The thorniest disagreement centered on black power ideology, an explicitly race-centered program to acquire political power, which had gained popularity among some African Americans during the mid-1960s. Consequently, one Cuban commentary pointedly highlighted the differences between black Americans and Afro-Cubans, criticizing the former for their "emotional" and unsophisticated perspectives on racial discrimination.[25] This served as a prelude to both a direct critique of black power and the idea of an ostensible brotherhood among blacks throughout the world. In effect, by focusing on the political superstructure rather than on capitalism's economic structure, black power theorists were flawed in their analytical approach to understanding the causes of American racism.[26]

The fact that this rebuke of black power ideology occurred around the same time as a highly visible tour of Cuba by Stokely Carmichael—one of the intellectual authors of the ideology—during which he received an enthusiastic welcome by Afro-Cubans, suggests official reservations had more than theoretical or ideological motivations. Cuba considered the black Americans to be involved in a liberation struggle that, although waged under special circumstances and in a unique context, was ultimately no different from other anticapitalist Third World struggles across Africa, Asia, and Latin America, the only solution being the destruction of capitalism and its replacement with socialism.[27] In terms of this analysis, black Americans were perceived as one segment, albeit a highly visible one, among myriad social groups oppressed by capitalism, their socioeconomic inequality a function primarily of their class status rather than their racial group membership. Thus, at its core, the black struggle was a confrontation with the capitalist system in which racial discrimination existed as an expression of this system's distortions. The solution lay in the creation of class alliances with other exploited groups, including poor and progressive whites.

The Cuban perspective clashed directly with the beliefs embraced by most radical black Americans, and more specifically those embracing a black nationalist philosophy, concerning the reasons for their disadvantaged status in American society. As viewed by these militants, African Americans were a distinct group whose experiences and history in the United States separated them from all other social classes. African Americans, conditioned by a history of experiences with whites of all classes in which race shaped the interaction process, tended not to distinguish among whites based on their class origins. Within the racial hierarchy of the United States, poor whites were often more racist and willing to violently express these sentiments than were whites of other classes, bolstered by the knowledge that despite their poverty, white skin possessed a certain social currency.

According to the political scientist Mark Sawyer: "Cuba played a central role in defining revolutionary and cultural nationalism in opposition to each other in the 1960s and 1970s."[28] In effect, their encounter with the island and its racial dynamics profoundly affected many of the leading figures of black nationalism, ultimately dividing the movement against itself. Black cultural nationalists decried the lack of racial self-determination on the island, their distinctly single-minded focus on race allowing them to criticize and reject the Cuban government's racial policies as well as the possibility of any white-led state, regardless of ideology, leading the fight for black liberation. With respect to Cuba's policy toward black American radicalism, Cuban policy makers wrestled with a desire to capitalize politically by exploiting US racial problems while simultaneously ensuring none of the more "regressive" ideas emanating from segments of this radical movement would infect the Afro-Cuban population and allow race to escape official control. Consequently, throughout the 1960s and into the early 1970s, the most intense period of engagement with radical black Americans, Cuba struggled to balance official support for the struggle by the oppressed black community in the United States and official disapproval of black Cubans who embraced any sense of racial consciousness.

Internationalism and the Politics of Race in Angola and Cuba

Notwithstanding the mutual recriminations and suspicions that accompanied this collapse of the relationship between socialist Cuba and prominent figures within the radical black movement, it did not appear as though the island's authorities harbored similar reservations about becoming involved in Africa. Nonetheless, Angola presented special circumstances that forced Cuba to maneuver around that African country's racial legacy that had been shaped by colonialism. This racial cleavage violently exploded in an abortive coup by disaffected ex-members of the MPLA leadership against their erstwhile colleagues. The origins of the attempted seizure of power stemmed from the MPLA's reluctance to address or even acknowledge racial tensions among its members devolving from the liberation movement's status as a *mesticio*-dominated party in a predominantly African country. This tension burst into the open just two months after a visit by Fidel Castro when marginalized members from within the leadership mounted an armed challenge to the authority of President Neto. On May 27, 1977, the country's recently dismissed interior minister and member of the Politburo, Nito Alves, staged a coup against the government, espousing a combination of militant African nationalism, anti-*mesticio*, and antiwhite sentiments.[29]

At one level, the coup was an ideological power struggle between proponents of a highly exclusive vanguard party and those of mass participatory people's organs.[30] Intraparty disagreements related to the institutional power of the Popular Committees were a source of contention. An irony of these political cleavages was the forging of a curious anti-Neto coalition of radical black nationalists, led by Alves, and white Portuguese Communists, many of whom later were expelled from Angola after being accused of involvement in the conspiracy.[31] Notwithstanding these political disputes, the fact remains that an appeal to race served as the driving force in galvanizing support for the seizure of power among functionaries in key party organs and mobilizing ordinary supporters. The coup's racial dynamic and government concern about its popular appeal among segments of the party was evident in a pre-coup speech by Neto in which he insisted Angola's true divisions were those of class and declared war against racial division.[32] In remarks following the failure of the coup, the Angolan president pointedly highlighted the contributions of four mixed-race Politburo members to the country.[33] The MPLA also conducted a purge in which thousands of sympathizers of Alves's viewpoint were killed.

The presence of members from these social classes in high-level government and party positions and Neto's overt attempt to rally public opinion in their defense underscored the MPLA's difficulty in attracting support from some segments of the populace. Although the government engaged in further damage control, denouncing the conspirators as "factionalists" allied with Zaire and stressing their nonproletarian character, the specter of race cast a lingering shadow over insistent claims of party unity. Cuban troops acted decisively to help crush the coup.[34] Raúl Castro paid a brief visit to Angola to demonstrate Cuba's solidarity with the Angolan government, and the official Cuban statement of support delivered to Neto castigated the conspirators for succumbing to personal ambition and furthering imperialism's interests.[35] This rebuke served as the only direct public commentary on the Alves affair, the Cuban government never formally acknowledging its role in crushing the coup. However, Cuba's ambassador to Angola was replaced almost immediately, suggesting displeasure with his performance during the crisis by either Fidel Castro or perhaps the MPLA. The rescue of Neto's government constituted a departure from previous Cuban actions in comparable circumstances, as the island had until then avoided taking sides in the intraparty, ethnoracial disputes of its African allies.[36]

It is certainly worthwhile to speculate whether such racial resentment would influence black Cubans sent to Angola. In fact, the claim has been made that some Afro-Cubans returned with a renewed sense of racial consciousness.[37] If true, this could have been behind the resentments of a black Cuban veteran who complained about his experiences in Angola: "The foot soldiers are always black and the commanders are always white. If you try to talk about that, it is counterrevolutionary subordination."[38] Conversely, it appears likely that exposure to African poverty and severe underdevelopment left black Cubans with ambivalent if not negative perceptions of the continent, its people, and the very notion of blackness. The experience of African students in Cuba provides an illustrative example. It was not difficult for a visitor to meet ordinary Cubans, many of them Afro-Cubans, willing to express their dislike for the African visitors.[39] The mutual antagonism sometimes erupted into confrontations, such as an episode involving a group of students from Zimbabwe deported from Cuba after their scholarships were revoked for fighting. This brief insight into interpersonal Cuban-African relations indicated that in certain aspects the situation was less than harmonious.[40]

The extent to which racial considerations influenced selections for internationalist duty constitutes one of the more intriguing aspects of Cuba's overseas missions. The tactical use of race in the deployment of Cuban troops in the beginning stages of the Angolan intervention, given the need for secrecy, is certainly understandable—almost the entire initial contingent of fighters had been Afro-Cubans. However, as the operation intensified and significant numbers of combat troops arrived, the inclusion of higher percentages of blacks

Table 8.1. Racial composition of Cuba, 1953 and 1981 (in percentage)

Year	Total Pop.	Whites	Blacks	Mulattoes	Asians
1953	5,829,029	72.8	12.4	14.5	0.3
1981	9,723,605	66.0	12.0	21.9	0.1

Source: Cuba, Comite Estatal de Estadisticas, *Censo de poblacion y viviendas, 1981* [State Committee of Statistics, Census of Population and Housing, 1981], *Republica de Cuba*, 16 vols. (Havana, 1983); "Report about the Definitive Results of the 1981 Population and Housing Census," *Granma*, September 19, 1983.

and mulattoes seemed to reflect strategic determinations. One estimate of the nonwhite proportion of these soldiers placed their presence at 40–50 percent.[41] The 1981 census calculated the proportion of Afro-Cubans at 32.9 percent of the island's population, underscoring their overrepresentation among those dispatched to Angola (see Table 8.1).

Fragmentary data also support this assertion of strategic racial engineering. Fidel Castro, in a July 1988 speech celebrating the thirty-fifth anniversary of the storming of the Moncada garrison, applauded Santiago de Cuba, a province with a 70 percent Afro-Cuban majority, for providing six thousand citizens for internationalist service.[42] The Cuban president also hailed the twenty-four thousand internationalists from Oriente on missions overseas.[43] While he failed to provide specifics, except to note that the "overwhelming majority" of these individuals were located at the front lines in Angola, it is nevertheless possible to obtain a rough calculus of the racial composition of Cuban troops (see Table 8.2).

At the time of this speech, Cuba had fifty thousand combat troops fighting in Angola and an indeterminate number of civilians (est. five thousand to eight thousand). This represented an increase from the combined forty thousand military and civilian personnel in autumn 1986.[44] Since an estimated 80–85 percent of all Cubans overseas were stationed in Angola, the province of Santiago de Cuba alone provided at least 10 percent of these forces. The other provinces in Oriente contributed approximately 30 percent or more of these soldiers, and the entire region collectively was responsible for 40 percent or more of Cuban military personnel fighting against UNITA and South Africa. These five provinces, containing 35.6 percent of the island's population, therefore provided a slightly disproportionate share of the total troop contingent. With the black and mulatto proportion of Oriente representing 51.9 percent of the total nonwhite population, the most conservative estimate of their presence among Oriente internationalists was 49.3 percent.[45] Admittedly, this does not constitute unassailable evidence of Afro-Cuban overrepresentation,

Table 8.2. Racial composition of Cuba, by province, 1981 (in percentage)

Province	Population	Whites	Blacks	Mulattoes	Asians
Camaguey	667,539	77.0	11.0	11.9	0.1
Ciego de Avila	321,015	80.8	9.5	9.6	0.1
Cienfuegos	326,383	76.6	9.6	13.7	0.1
Granma	739,234	42.7	4.4	52.7	0.2
Guantánamo	466,039	26.3	18.8	54.5	0.4
Havana	585,912	82.2	9.5	8.2	0.1
Ciudad de Havana	1,929,432	63.0	16.4	20.4	0.2
Holguín	912,853	78.8	6.1	14.9	0.2
Isla de la Juventud	58,058	66.8	10.9	22.1	0.2
Las Tunas	437,198	74.4	7.2	18.3	0.1
Villa Clara	765,823	82.5	6.9	10.5	0.1
Matanzas	559,260	76.0	12.7	11.2	0.1
Pinar del Rio	640,726	78.3	14.3	7.4	0.0
Sancti Spíritus	400,026	84.1	7.4	8.5	0.0
Santiago de Cuba	914,107	30.2	22.2	47.3	0.3

Source: Comite Estatal de Estadisticas, *Censo de poblacion y viviendas*, 1981 [State Committee of Statistics, Census of Population and Housing, 1981] (Havana, 1983).

but it does establish the active role of the majority nonwhite eastern provinces in furnishing personnel for internationalist duty. Other information provides a more definitive picture about the use of racial criteria in the selection of Cubans for overseas service. Using data released about Cubans following two incidents—the US invasion of Grenada, and UNITA's bombing of an apartment building housing construction workers and other personnel in Huambo, Angola—certain conclusions about race and internationalist service can be drawn.[46]

The 784 Cubans in Grenada primarily originated from the capital, Havana (37.9 percent), and the provinces of Matanzas (31.5 percent) and Holguín (7.7 percent), all of which according to the 1981 census data were at least 60 percent white. Surprisingly, the representation of internationalists from predominantly Afro-Cuban provinces was virtually nonexistent, with Granma (1.3 percent), Guantánamo (1.5 percent), and Santiago de Cuba (2.0 percent) providing few personnel. Therefore, the three provinces containing approximately 43 percent of Afro-Cubans collectively contributed only 4.8 percent of Cubans in Grenada, suggesting race was a nonfactor. A different conclusion emerges when the twenty-four men killed during fighting at the Point Salinas airstrip become the focus of analysis. Using this sample, race becomes more salient than suggested by the aggregate data. Nonwhites constituted 37.5 percent of those killed, a 26.3 percent overrepresentation of their population share in the three main provinces from which the majority of internationalists originated.[47] This approximates the 25 percent Afro-Cuban overrepresentation, if the specific provinces for all the dead are measured.[48] Thus, blacks and mulattoes made up a disproportionate share of Cubans in Grenada, even though a majority of internationalists belonged to predominantly white provinces.

The Angolan bombing incident demonstrated similar dynamics. The attack claimed fourteen Cuban lives, four of the dead being Afro-Cubans. Twelve of the fourteen men hailed from the provinces of Ciego de Avila (15.9 percent) and Sancti Spíritus (19.1 percent), both of which contained relatively small proportions of blacks and mulattoes. In this instance, the sample of those killed revealed nonwhites to have been overrepresented by 70 percent in the construction brigades from these majority white provinces.[49] These indications of disproportionate shares of Afro-Cubans among internationalists in predominantly black countries could simply reflect the greater willingness among the ideologically committed to volunteer for service in these countries; it is more than likely the product of a conscious policy decision by an ostensibly color-blind government.

As Cuban involvement deepened in Angola and relations expanded with other African countries, the role of the most prominent nonwhite in the Cuban leadership hierarchy, Juan Almeida Bosque, appeared to reflect a certain racial gamesmanship. Almeida's role as Cuba's official "black" face in Africa expanded, and he became much more visible in Cuban policy dealing with Africa and the international struggle against racism. The event that appeared to set in process a period of increased visibility was Fidel Castro's March 1977 visit to Africa and Eastern Europe, in the midst of which Almeida was summoned to join the delegation during the Angolan phase of the journey.[50] Subsequently, Almeida led Cuba's delegation to the funeral of Marien Ngouabi, the assassinated president of Congo, and at that time arguably one of Cuba's most important allies on the continent.[51] This started a series of African or race-related missions in which Almeida participated during the subsequent three years: he led the Cuban delegation to a UN General Assembly meeting on Namibian independence; accompanied Fidel Castro to Ethiopia's celebrations of its revolution's fourth anniversary; headed Cuba's delegations to the funerals of the presidents of Algeria and Angola; and represented the island at Zimbabwe's independence in 1980. In 1980, Almeida also served as Castro's envoy to seven African countries; attended independence celebrations in Madagascar, a close African ally; visited Jamaica; and acted as Cuba's representative to an international conference on racial discrimination. Almeida was omnipresent in the conduct of Cuban foreign policy in Africa and matters of race.

Inside Cuba itself, Almeida's prominent role continued. Whereas in the first half of the 1970s Almeida's function during state visits by foreign leaders had been as their host in Santiago de Cuba, where he served as the Politburo's representative to Oriente Province, during the latter part of the decade this changed. Prominently featured in the welcoming parties at Jose Martí airport in Havana during visits to Cuba by African dignitaries, Almeida frequently occupied the first position in the receiving line after Fidel and Raúl Castro. Invariably, in the Cuban press during this period, Almeida's name was listed immediately after those of the Castro brothers rather than included in the amorphous "rest of the Politburo members," as had occurred previously. Frequently, he tended to be strategically placed beside one of the brothers, ensuring that his photograph would appear regularly in press coverage of state functions, again suggesting an effort to highlight Almeida's position within Cuba's leadership.

In the revolution's twentieth-anniversary editorial that praised living revolutionaries for initiating and consolidating Cuba's revolutionary process, Almeida was the only member of the leadership hierarchy singled out for special recognition besides Fidel and Raúl Castro.[52] Admittedly, as a veteran of the attack on the Moncada barracks, head of a guerrilla front during the anti-Batista struggle, and a decorated Hero of the Revolution, Almeida possessed an impeccable revolutionary pedigree. In addition, as a Politburo member and one of the vice presidents on the Council of State, he belonged to two of the premier decision-making organs in the country. Yet his ubiquity appeared at odds with his actual responsibilities in the island's hierarchy, since the veteran revolutionary held no major party or government portfolios. Further evidence of Cuba's willingness to politicize Almeida's race occurred in a published interview with the black American entertainer Harry Belafonte, during which Belafonte expressed his pride at witnessing Almeida's prominence in Cuba's governing hierarchy and the influence exercised by this Afro-Cuban when some black leaders in other countries served as mere political figureheads.[53] After years of neutralizing his racial background, Almeida in essence became a symbol of Cuban racial progress, a transnational figure with whom other blacks could identify, regardless of nationality.

Assessment of the impact of Cuba's Africa policy on the sociopolitical fortunes of Afro-Cubans on the island has elicited contrasting perspectives. Africa, according to one argument, brought about the incorporation of blacks and mulattoes as full participants in revolutionary society. Citing developments such as: (1) an increase in the number of black announcers appearing on television; (2) the selection of Arnaldo Tamayo, a mixed-race Cuban astronaut, as the first Latin

American to travel to space; (3) greater official tolerance toward black Cubans displaying symbols of racial pride; and (4) the calculated use of Afro-Cubans as ambassadors in the Caribbean, one analyst concluded: "By 1980, blacks in Cuba seemed to have become more integrated into the Revolution. This was not because of any active domestic policy on the part of the government but, instead, because of the spillover effects of its foreign policy on the African continent. The point is that the praxis of the Revolution abroad generated a dynamism that perforce produced greater racial integration within the island."[54] Moreover, Cuba's activities on the continent, especially the rescue of the MPLA and the successful facing down of South Africa, garnered the island significant goodwill among neighboring black-led Caribbean countries, strengthening diplomatic relations with these governments. In the aftermath of Angola, Cuba developed especially strong relations with Guyana and Jamaica, the leaders of these countries being vocal proponents of Cuban policy in Africa.

A contrasting examination regards the entire African policy with deep cynicism. The island's virtually all-white revolutionary elites have been accused of paternalism at best, and unreconstructed racism at worst. Knowing little about Africa, and caring even less, Fidel Castro has been criticized for adopting an "Afrocentric" foreign policy as a cynical ploy to ensure political survival. In this view, Africa represented an arena for Castro to pursue his dream of revolutionary change and to attract diplomatic and political support. In this endeavor he exploited Cuba's sizable population of African descent to establish a foothold on the continent, Afro-Cubans themselves receiving little of benefit in return for their sacrifices. Moreover, this activist African policy occurred in tandem with "Afrophobic" domestic policies designed to suppress autonomous forms of self-expression or the development of racial consciousness among black Cubans.[55] With respect to an enhanced Cuban presence in the international arena, the policy could be judged a success, since as Fidel Castro himself boasted, Cuba's diplomatic contacts had increased to 121 by the time of the PCC Third Congress, up from 81 in 1975.[56] In addition to a growth in relations with Africa and the English-speaking Caribbean, this almost 50 percent increase in Cuba's diplomatic presence included ties with Asia and a reestablishment of relationships with most Latin American countries. The bold Angolan mission had made Cuba relevant beyond the group of like-minded radical states, broken its regional isolation, and underscored its status as one of the foremost Third World actors in international politics.

Nevertheless, the latter half of the 1970s and the 1980s constituted a period during which the Cuban government devoted its most sustained attention to issues of race on the island, and Afro-Cubans began to demonstrate measurable gains in securing positions in the bureaucracy and party and state institutions. A sizable number of black Cubans served as ambassadors in Africa and the Caribbean in the 1970s and 1980s, calculated to be between fifteen of twenty-one accredited diplomats in Africa and five out of six in the English-speaking Caribbean.[57] Black functionaries were assigned ministerial portfolios and began receiving appointments as provincial party first secretaries. The ruling Council of State and the legislature, the National Assembly of Popular Power, showed similar diversity, as the number of black members increased with each successive five-year incarnation of these bodies. Racial politics and the inclusiveness of nonwhites reached its highest phase in February 1986, when during his closing address at the PCC Third Congress, Fidel Castro acknowledged the underrepresentation of nonwhites among the leadership of the party. In subsequent selections, black representation on the central committee elected at the congress increased by 90.3 percent compared to the previous congress in 1980, which itself had registered a 69.9 percent positive advance when measured against the 1975 First Congress.[58] Even so, the country's top decision-making institution—the Politburo—remained closed to Afro-Cubans, with only one person of color elevated to its ranks alongside the long-tenured Almeida.

The only published study of race in the Revolutionary Armed Forces (FAR), a mid-1970s treatise, had concluded nonwhites were disproportionately concentrated at the troop level and underrepresented in the upper levels of the officer corps, although their numbers appeared to be on the rise in the lower-to midlevel ranks.[59] While Afro-Cubans such as the brigadier generals Rolando Kindelan Bles, Victor Scheug Colas, and Rafael Moracen Limonta, all of whom had served with distinction in Cuba's various African missions, were rewarded with membership in the Communist Party's Central Committee in the 1980s, service in Africa does not appear to have boosted significantly the proportion of blacks in the army's hierarchy.[60] A sample of military officers elected to the central committees of the three congresses during which those who served in Angola could be expected to receive such promotions revealed that of ninety-eight FAR members, only sixteen, or 16.3 percent, were black. Of these officers, the majority held the rank of brigadier general or higher, but among those of lower rank, 40 percent were black. In effect, a black FAR officer on the central committee was more than three times as likely to be elected as a lower-ranked officer.[61] Further insight into the racial composition of the military could be gleaned from information released in the aftermath of an airplane accident in Angola. Of eighteen active-duty FAR officers who perished in the crash, blacks constituted 22 percent, although none held a rank above major. Of the twenty-six military officials who lost their lives, including eight noncommissioned officers, Afro-Cubans accounted for the majority. While conclusions from such a tiny sample must be viewed with caution, the collective evidence suggests that within the FAR, internationalist service did not translate immediately into an appreciable number of black Cubans advancing into its upper ranks.

In the mid-1980s, Cuba found itself receiving diminishing returns with respect to its presence in Angola. The immediate political benefits secured by defeating South Africa already had dissipated. Cuba had been elected to a three-year term as head of the Non-Aligned Movement in 1979, but the Soviet Union's invasion of Afghanistan and Fidel Castro's silence effectively neutered his presidency of the organization. In Angola, a revived UNITA had developed into a relentless foe and the country's borders remained vulnerable to SADF incursions. The Angolan government, without consulting Cuba, accepted an offer by the United States to mediate with South Africa, culminating in the signing of the Lusaka Accords in 1984—a tactical defeat for the liberation struggle in southern Africa, since the agreement curtailed support for the African National Congress (South Africa) and South-West African Peoples Organization (SWAPO) in Namibia. As a result, Cuba found itself in an untenable situation in Angola: diminishing political influence as an assertive MPLA demonstrated its independence by pursuing an alternate agenda; a decrease in military prestige as the SADF and UNITA continued to threaten Angola's security; an unhappy FAR subordinated to a Soviet military strategy it regarded as misguided; and difficulty engineering a dignified exit that would justify to the Cuban people more than a decade of sacrifice.[62]

The end of Cuba's military role in Angola occurred following a failed offensive by the Angolan army against UNITA during which the South Africans, who once again crossed the border and intervened in the fighting, pursued the retreating government forces to Cuito Cunavale, a small, nondescript town in southern Angola. Responding to the MPLA request for assistance to save its trapped army, Fidel Castro authorized the dispatch of additional advisers in December 1987, augmenting this group with reinforcements in January 1988. These additional fifteen thousand combat troops allowed Cuba to recapture the military initiative in southern Angola and establish defensive positions close to the Namibian border. The SADF abandoned efforts to capture Cuito Cunavale, and on March 17, 1988, the Angolans and Cubans declared victory. Rather than a major defeat of the SADF, the significance of this final confrontation between the foreign armies was in its alteration of the military status quo.[63] Cuba had upped the ante of any future South African military operations, and the apartheid state was loath to pay the price. The shift in military advantage was dramatized on June 27, 1988, when in retaliation for an artillery attack, Cuban planes bombed South African installations on the Namibian-Angolan border.[64] Following negotiations, an agreement ending external involvement in Angola was brokered, and on December 22, 1988, Cuba, South Africa, and Angola signed a tripartite accord at UN headquarters in New York City, providing simultaneously for a Cuban withdrawal from Angola and Namibian independence.[65]

The end of the military phase of internationalist activity in Africa came with both the Angolans and the Cubans searching for a way to bring this type of collaboration to a close. Although Fidel Castro created a stir during his speech to the eighth Non-Aligned Movement's conference when he promised to maintain Cuban soldiers in Angola until the demise of apartheid, in essence redefining the purpose of the military mission from preserving Angolan sovereignty to overthrowing the South African government, changed global circumstances rendered his statement unsustainable. The Soviet Union, under Mikhail Gorbachev, had begun to reassess the prudence of foreign entanglements. Foreign interference was blamed for the prolongation of the fighting in Angola.[66] The economic cost to the Soviet Union of imbroglios such as that in Angola was cited as a reason to abandon such foreign adventures.[67] Inside Angola, the MPLA had begun a process of political and economic reform that would culminate in its abandonment of Marxism-Leninism and a claim to monopoly on power and lead to the start of reconciliation talks with UNITA and a privatization of the economy, this last measure probably the least momentous of the changes. Even as a putative socialist country, Angola's economic relations had been oriented to the capitalist world; the country had never even bothered to disrupt the colonial pattern of economic integration with the West.[68]

Not surprisingly, Cuba appeared to be more interested in trumpeting Namibian independence as the signature foreign policy achievement of its sixteen-year military presence in southern Africa than the successful preservation of the MPLA government in Angola. While the Cuban government never publicly chastised its erstwhile ideological ally for the ease with which it had abandoned its allegiance to Marxism, the turnabout no doubt elicited some consternation. In searching for meaning to account for its sacrifices, Cuba plausibly could focus on race, even if ideology had provided the impetus for its actions. Consequently, in contrast to a studious silence about events in Angola, the independence process in Namibia received much more emphasis. The former colony's independence celebrations were accorded splashy coverage in the Cuban press and a high-powered delegation headed by Almeida attended the ceremony transferring power to a SWAPO-led government. Shortly after his election as president, Sam Nujoma, SWAPO's leader, paid an official visit to Cuba during which he formally inaugurated Namibia's embassy in Havana and expressed his people's gratitude for the island's support. A team of medical internationalists soon departed Cuba for Namibia. Cuba's ties with the ANC in South Africa also became progressively closer as the non-Marxist liberation movement and the Communist island bonded over a shared commitment to fighting for racial justice. Cuba justified the pursuit of its mission in Angola in terms of the principles of ideology and race, of which it regarded the former as more important. However, in the final analysis, it was the latter that allowed the Caribbean island to solidify its presence on the African continent.

Conclusion

Cuba's bold gambit in Angola elevated the small, undeveloped Caribbean island to the front ranks of the Third World countries. Yet, while the scope and intensity of the intervention in Angola captured international attention and enhanced Cuba's prestige, the action represented continuity with the island's long history of activism on the continent. Characterized as a small country with a big country's foreign policy, involvement in Africa allowed Cuba to escape isolation in Latin America and the Caribbean, ensuring the survival of the region's only socialist country even while thrusting the island into the center of the Cold War. By any measure, Cuba's intervention transformed southern Africa, the hundreds of thousands of internationalists garnering an impressive set of accomplishments. Besides the initial accomplishment of bringing to power a socialist government in Angola, a byproduct of the Cuban military presence was independence for Namibia, a shattering of the perceived omnipotence of South Africa's military, and the galvanization of the black majority's struggle against apartheid inside South Africa.

Race provided Cuba with moral authority to justify its foreign policy, and the large Afro-Cuban population helped the country pursue its agenda in Africa. Simply put, Cuba's activism in Africa would have been impossible if not for the black Cubans who executed the policy in significant numbers. Ironically, by political philosophy and cultural inclination, Cuba should have been among the most unlikely candidates to adopt a race-based policy, as the topic historically was avoided on the island, notwithstanding its multiracial population. Moreover, an initial attempt to use race as a foreign policy weapon against the United States ultimately provided few lasting benefits to Cuba, its relationship with radical black Americans cooling perceptibly after an initial period of rapprochement. The experience in Africa proved to be more successful, racial affinity serving as the bridge that helped Cuba leave large international footprints.

Notes

1. Henry Giniger, "Portuguese Junta Opposes Freeing of African Lands," *New York Times*, April 28, 1974. General António de Spínola, head of the first MFA-

led administration, cautioned during a meeting with newspaper editors that in spite of Portugal's willingness to extend significant autonomy to its colonies, "self determination should not be confused with independence." Instead, Spínola proposed that the colonies would be offered an opportunity to enter into a federation with Portugal on an equal footing.

2. The so-called Alvor Accords, signed on January 15, 1975, stipulated that the three liberation movements participate in a transitional government with Portugal until elections in October 1975.

3. Basil Davidson, *In the Eye of the Storm: Angola's People* (Garden City, NY: Doubleday, 1972).

4. Colin Legum, "The Soviet Union, China, and the West in Southern Africa," *Foreign Affairs* 54, no. 4 (July 1976): 745–62.

5. Raymond Garthoff, *Détente and Confrontation: American-Soviet Relations from Nixon to Reagan.* (Washington, DC: Brookings Institution, 1985).

6. John Stockwell, *In Search of Enemies: A CIA Story* (New York: Norton, 1978).

7. On the eve of Portugal's scheduled departure from Angola on November 10, 1975, MPLA authority had been reduced to control of only three of Angola's fifteen provinces, down from the twelve that had been held just two months previously.

8. William J. Durch, "The Cuban Military in Africa and the Middle East," *Studies in Comparative Communism* 11, nos. 1/2 (Spring/Summer 1978): 67.

9. The then head of the CIA Angola Task Force, John Stockwell, provides a vivid description of the November 11, 1975, encounter in which FNLA soldiers, their Zairian allies, and about a hundred Portuguese Angolan commandos were defeated about twelve miles from Luanda. Following this defeat, the FNLA ceased to be a serious contender for power, as its forces fled in panic as the MPLA/Cubans mounted a counteroffensive in the north of the country.

10. Gabriel García Márquez, "Operation Carlota," *New Left Review* 101–2 (February–April 1977): 123–37.

11. Edward González, "Complexities of Cuban Foreign Policy," *Problems of Communism* 26, no. 6 (November–December 1977): 1–15.

12. Although the initial contingent of soldiers was transported by Cuban planes and ships, these flights soon began experiencing difficulty in refueling because of intense US pressure on Caribbean countries. Later in January 1976, the Soviet Union supplied aircraft with greater flight range for troop transport. The initial efforts by Cuba to transport its troops to Angola represented an adventure in geographical maneuverability with a constant search for alternate routes to replace those that were lost.

13. Most South African troops had actually ceased fighting by January 22, 1976.

14. Daniel Anable, "U.S. Halts Secret Training for Angola," *Christian Science Monitor*, January 5, 1976.

15. Mary Russell, "200 on Hill Oppose Angola Aid," *Washington Post*, January 27, 1976.

16. Fidel Castro, "Closing Speech on December 22, 1975 at the First Congress of the Cuban Communist Party," *Granma*, December 24, 1975.

17. Edward Glick, "Cuba and the Fifteenth UN General Assembly: A Case Study in

Regional Disassociation," *Journal of InterAmerican Studies and World Affairs* 6, no. 2 (April 1964): 235–48.

18. Jorge I. Domínguez, "Cuban Foreign Policy in Africa," *Foreign Affairs* 57, no. 1 (Fall 1978): 83–108.

19. Fidel Castro, "Speech on April 19, 1975 at the Main Ceremony for the 15th Anniversary of the Victory at Giron Beach," *Granma*, December 24, 1975.

20. Leslie H. Gelb, "Ford Said to Bar a Combat Role in Angolan War," *New York Times*, December 17, 1975.

21. Arkady Shevchenko, *Breaking with Moscow* (New York: Knopf, 1985).

22. José Felipe Carneado, "La Discriminacion Racial en Cuba No Volvera Jamas" [Racial discrimination in Cuba will never return], *Cuba Socialista* 2 (January 1962): 168–82. This lack of participation was explained in terms of a propaganda campaign by the dictatorship of Fulgencio Batista, himself of mixed race, that portrayed the revolutionaries as whites who would offer little of benefit to Afro-Cubans.

23. Lee Lockwood, *Castro's Cuba, Cuba's Fidel* (New York: Macmillan, 1967), 128.

24. The symbolism of Fidel Castro's actions was obvious and generated significant negative publicity for the United States at a time when international attention was focused on events at the United Nations. Neither can the domestic implications of Castro's actions be ignored, since this event certainly had some resonance among Cuba's nonwhite population. However, the primary audience was most likely the black community in the United States. It may have been these considerations that were responsible for the belated appearance of Juan Almeida, Cuba's highest-ranking nonwhite figure, in the Cuban UN delegation. Almeida appeared only after Castro's move to Harlem and from then on was featured prominently at the Cuban leader's side in public appearances and publicity photographs.

25. *Granma Resumen Semanal*, December 31, 1967.

26. Alberto Pedro, "Poder Negro" [Black power], *Casa de las Américas* 53 (March–April 1969): 134–44.

27. Tony Fernandez, "The United States: Nation of Ghettos," *Granma*, March 20, 1974, 2.

28. Mark Sawyer, *Racial Politics in Post-Revolutionary Cuba* (New York: Cambridge University Press, 2006), 100.

29. Paul Fauvet, "Angola: The Rise and Fall of Nito Alves," *Review of African Political Economy* 9 (May–August 1977): 88–104. The sophisticated conspiracy involved almost every key institution within the MPLA's organizational framework; Alves, in his capacity as Interior Minister, had infiltrated and gained control of them, installing his loyalists. An important aspect of the coup involved creating artificial shortages by diverting food supplies and spreading general discontent through nonpayment of salaries. The objective was to create an image of an incompetent government and capitalize on public disaffection. The coup instigators succeeded in imprisoning and murdering seven high-level MPLA leaders belonging to the Politburo and Central Committee.

30. Davis Ottaway and Mariana Ottaway, *Afrocommunism* (New York: Africana Publishing, 1986).

31. Daniel Kempton, *Soviet Strategy toward Southern Africa: The National Liberation Movement Connection* (New York: Praeger, 1989).

32. "Rally Held in Luanda in Support of the Political Position of the MPLA Central Committee and the Angolan Government," *Granma*, May 24, 1977.

33. "Seditious Intent in Luanda by Factionist Elements," *Granma*, May 28, 1977.

34. Insight into the crucial role of Cuban personnel was provided in recollections of the exploits in Angola of Rafael Moracen Limonta, an Afro-Cuban brigadier general selected as one of five recipients awarded the title Hero of the Cuban Republic in 1989. Moracen Limonta, an adviser to the head of Neto's Presidential Guard at the time of the coup, organized and led the government assault that recaptured Luanda's radio station from supporters of Nito Alves. "Heroes of the Republic of Cuba: Assault on the National Radio," *Granma*, January 3, 1989. Although Cuba's role in crushing the coup had long been an open secret, at the time of the event the Cuban government never acknowledged or divulged any information about actions by its forces, its only response being the suspension of troop withdrawals. This account represents the only discussion from an official source about Cuban actions during the event.

35. "Raul Carries Out an Official Visit to the People's Republic of Angola," *Granma*, June 13, 1977.

36. Aaron Seagal, "Cubans in Africa," *Caribbean Review* 7, no. 3 (July–September 1978): 38–43.

37. Edward González and David Ronfeldt, *Castro, Cuba, and the World* (Santa Monica, CA: Rand, 1986).

38. Howard W. French, "Blacks Say Castro Fails to Deliver Equality," *New York Times*, December 4, 1990.

39. Many Cubans appear to have resented the presence of the African students and the money allocated to financing their education. The Africans also had to confront the stigma of coming from a poor continent and overcoming the myths associated with their origins, and the very real social effects of their disadvantaged economic situations. In a color-conscious society such as Cuba's, dark skin often tended to be correlated with perceptions of inferiority, and the presumed deprivation of their backgrounds conferred a certain negative status that the Africans could not escape.

40. According to the official Cuban explanation, the returning students had fallen ill and requested to return home. The Zimbabwean newspaper publishing the story registered its skepticism of Cuba's version of events. Curiously, in the Cuban article there was no denial of the facts of the incident, just an implication that the Zimbabwean newspaper's exposé, published during an official visit by Cuba's foreign minister, had been a deliberate but ultimately unsuccessfully effort to embarrass Cuba and tarnish its image in the African country ("The Editor of the *Daily Mail* in Zimbabwe Dismissed," *Granma*, April 24, 1987). Nonetheless, the indirect admission of problems with this group of students confirmed long-standing rumors of periodic clashes between the African students and their hosts.

41. Jiri Valenta, "The Soviet-Cuban Intervention in Angola, 1975," *Studies in Comparative Communism* 11, nos. 1/2 (Spring/Summer 1978): 3–33.

42. Fidel Castro, "Speech on 26th of July in Santiago de Cuba at the Main Ceremony for the 35th Anniversary of the Attack on the Moncada Barracks," *Granma*, August 1, 1988.

43. The five regions that Oriente had comprised prior to its administrative restructuring were Holguín, Granma, Guantánamo, Las Tunas, and Santiago de Cuba.

44. Francisco Forteza, " Cuba and Angola Reiterate Willingness [to] Negotiate," *Granma*, September 11, 1988.

45. The actual figure is probably higher, but this conservative estimate is based on the Afro-Cuban share in the internationalist contingents from the various provinces corresponding exactly to their proportions in that province. Obviously, it is impossible to argue this in fact occurred, but the methodology does achieve a balance among provinces such as Guantánamo (73.7 percent) and Santiago de Cuba (69.8 percent) with substantial Afro-Cuban populations and Holguín (21.2 percent) and Las Tunas (25.2 percent) with more modest totals.

46. While Grenada geographically belongs to the Caribbean, it is a predominantly black island and can serve as a useful example in the effort to understand whether Cuba deployed personnel according to racial considerations.

47. Figures computed from the list of all Cubans in Grenada at the time of the invasion and published photographs/biographies of the dead. "Report to the People," *Granma*, November 4, 1983; and "Our Fallen Brothers in Grenada," *Granma*, November 14, 1983.

48. Jorge I. Domínguez, *To Make a World Safe for Revolution: Cuba's Foreign Policy* (Cambridge, MA: Harvard University Press, 1989), 276–77.

49. Ibid.

50. "Almeida's Arrival," *Granma*, March 31, 1977. Although Almeida's appearance seemed reminiscent of earlier incidents, such as that in Harlem and Fidel Castro's first African tour in 1972, the dynamics of this occasion were different. The arrival of Cuba's highest-ranking nonwhite was announced in a splashy front-page photograph and article of him and Fidel Castro holding an interview with the African National Congress's (ANC) Oliver Tambo, and Joshua Nkomo, leader of the Zimbabwe African People's Union (ZAPU). It is difficult not to conclude this was an orchestrated event intended to convey the impression of Almeida as a serious and important policy maker in Cuba's leadership.

51. "Almeida Departs the Republic of the Congo, after Having Attended the Burial of Marien Ngouabi," *Granma*, April 4, 1977.

52. "In the 20th Year of the Triumph of the Revolution [We Are] Continuing to Advance on the Victorious Road to Socialism," editorial, *Granma*, December 31, 1978.

53. Gabriel Molina, "Paul Robeson Always Told Me: Keep the People United and the Enemy Will Not Be Able to Destroy You; If You [Don't] the People Belong to the Enemy," *Granma*, August 23, 1978.

54. Frank Taylor, "Revolution, Race, and Foreign Relations Since 1959," in *Cuban Studies*, ed. Carmelo Meso-Lago (Pittsburgh: University of Pittsburgh Press, 1988), 18:35.

55. Carlos Moore, *Castro, the Blacks, and Africa* (Los Angeles: Center for Latin American Studies, University of California Press, 1988); and Moore, "Race Relations in Socialist Cuba," in *Socialist Cuba: Past Interpretations and Future Challenges*, ed. Sergio Roca, 175–206 (Boulder, CO: Westview Press, 1988).

56. Fidel Castro, "Resolution about International Policy," *Granma*, February 8, 1986; and *Bohemia* 67, no. 23, June 6, 1975.

57. This could be explained by an official policy of recycling ambassadors with regional expertise, and thus top diplomats often have multiple missions in the same region. However, it also suggests Cuba might have had a deliberate policy of concentrating its nonwhite foreign policy personnel in its sub-Saharan African and Caribbean departments of the Foreign Ministry and Communist Party. Regardless of the reason, an expansion in relations with Africa and the Caribbean clearly benefited Afro-Cuban diplomats, creating opportunities for career advancement in the state and party bureaucracies focusing on foreign relations. Moore, *Castro, the Blacks, and Africa* and "Race Relations in Socialist Cuba."

58. Henley Adams, "Fighting an Uphill Battle: Race, Politics, Power, and Institutionalization in Cuba," *Latin American Research Review* 39, no. 1 (2004): 175.

59. Domínguez, *To Make a World Safe*.

60. Kindelan Bles participated as the commander of Cuban forces in the Congo operation; Scheug Colas commanded troops that routed the FNLA in Angola; Moracen Limonta participated in the Cuban column in Zaire headed by Che Guevara, served as one of early instructors of MPLA guerrillas, and later helped foil the Alves coup to preserve Neto's government.

61. Henley Adams, "Race and the Cuban Revolution: The Impact of Cuba's Intervention in Angola" (PhD diss., University of North Carolina at Chapel Hill, 1999).

62. Olga Nazario, "Cuba's Angola Operation," in *Cuban Internationalism in Sub-Saharan Africa*, ed. Sergio Diaz-Briquets, 102–23 (Pittsburgh: Duquesne University Press, 1989).

63. Jeffrey Herbst, "The Tripartite Accords," in *Cuban Internationalism in Sub-Saharan Africa*, ed. Sergio Diaz-Briquets (Pittsburgh: Duquesne University Press, 1989), 144–53.

64. "Report from the Ministry of the Revolutionary Armed Forces," *Granma*, June 30, 1988, 1.

65. The United States and Soviet Union were active participants in the accord's negotiations, the United States as an arbiter among the three sides and the Soviet Union as a strong behind-the-scenes actor pressuring its allies to reach an agreement with South Africa. Despite the unresolved issues of Angola's conflict, each superpower achieved its primary objective through the signing of the accord. The United States secured the departure of approximately fifty thousand Cuban troops from Angola, a long-standing foreign policy obsession, and the USSR removed an irritant to improved East-West relations. While the peace accords made no specific reference to the future of the guerrilla movements, SWAPO and UNITA, the former clearly emerged as a winner, since its objective of Namibian independence had been achieved.

66. Yevgeni Primakov, "USSR Policy on Regional Conflicts," *International Affairs* 6 (June 1988): 3–9.

67. Alexi Izyumov and Andrei Kortunov, "The USSR in the Changing World," *International Affairs* 8 (August 1988): 45–56.

68. Gillian Gunn, "The Angolan Economy: A History of Contradictions," in *Afro-Marxist Regimes: Ideology and Policy*, ed. Edmond J. Keller and Donald Rothchild (Boulder, CO: Lynne Rienner, 1987), 78–101.

References

PERIODICALS
Bohemia
Christian Science Monitor
Granma
New York Times
Washington Post

SELECTED PUBLISHED WORKS
Adams, Henley C. "Fighting an Uphill Battle: Race, Politics, Power, and Institutionalization in Cuba." *Latin American Research Review* 39, no. 1 (2004): 168–82.
———. *Race and the Cuban Revolution: The Impact of Cuba's Intervention in Angola.* PhD diss., University of North Carolina at Chapel Hill, 1999.
Carneado, José Felipe. "La Discriminacion Racial en Cuba No Volvera Jamas" [Racial discrimination in Cuba will never return]. *Cuba Socialista* 2 (January 1962): 54–67.
Davidson, Basil. *In the Eye of the Storm: Angola's People.* Garden City, NY: Doubleday, 1972.
del Aguilar, Juan. *Cuba: Dilemmas of a Revolution.* Boulder, CO: Westview Press, 1984.
Diaz-Briquets, Sergio, ed. *Cuban Internationalism in Sub-Saharan Africa.* Pittsburgh: Duquesne University Press, 1989.
Domínguez, Jorge I. "Cuban Foreign Policy in Africa." *Foreign Affairs* 57, no. 1 (Fall 1978): 83–108.
———. "Racial and Ethnic Relations in the Cuban Armed Forces: A Non-Topic." *Armed Forces and Society* 2, no. 2 (February 1976): 273–90.
———. *To Make a World Safe for Revolution: Cuba's Foreign Policy.* Cambridge, MA: Harvard University Press, 1989.
Durch, William J. "The Cuban Military in Africa and the Middle East." *Studies in Comparative Communism* 11, no. 1/2 (Spring/Summer 1978): 34–74.
Fauvet, Paul. "Angola: The Rise and Fall of Nito Alves." *Review of African Political Economy* 9 (May–August 1977): 88–104.
García Márquez, Gabriel. "Operation Carlota." *New Left Review* 101–2 (February–April 1977): 123–37.
Garthoff, Raymond. *Détente and Confrontation: American-Soviet Relations from Nixon to Reagan.* Washington, DC: Brookings Institution, 1985.
Gleijeses, Piero. *Conflicting Missions: Havana, Washington, and Africa, 1959–1976.* Chapel Hill: University of North Carolina Press, 2002.
———. "The First Ambassadors: Cuba's Contribution to Guinea-Bissau's War of Independence." *Journal of Latin American Studies* 29, no. 1 (February 1997): 45–88.
Glick, Edward. "Cuba and the Fifteenth UN General Assembly: A Case Study in Regional Disassociation." *Journal of InterAmerican Studies and World Affairs* 6 (April 1964): 235–48.
González, Edward, and David Ronfeldt. *Castro, Cuba, and the World.* Santa Monica, CA: Rand, 1986.
Kahn, Owen Ellison. "Cuba's Impact on Southern Africa." *Journal of InterAmerican Studies and World Affairs* 29, no. 3 (Fall 1987): 33–54.

Kempton, Daniel. *Soviet Strategy toward Southern Africa: The National Liberation Movement Connection*. New York: Praeger, 1989.

Klinghoffer, Arthur Jay. *The Angolan War: A Study in Soviet Policy in the Third World*. Boulder, CO: Westview Press, 1980.

Legum, Colin. "The Soviet Union, China, and the West in Southern Africa." *Foreign Affairs* 54, no. 4 (July 1976): 745–62.

LeoGrande, William M. *Cuba's Policy in Africa, 1959–1980*. Berkeley: University of California Press, 1980.

Lockwood, Lee. *Castro's Cuba, Cuba's Fidel*. New York: Macmillan, 1967.

Loney, Martín. "Social Control in Cuba." In *Politics and Deviance*, edited by Ian Taylor and Laurie Taylor, 42–60. New York: Penguin Books, 1973.

Moore, Carlos. *Castro, the Blacks, and Africa*. Los Angeles: Center for Latin American Studies, University of California Press, 1988.

———. "Race Relations in Socialist Cuba." In *Socialist Cuba: Past Interpretations and Future Challenges*, edited by Sergio Roca, 175–206. Boulder, CO: Westview Press, 1988.

Nazario, Olga. "Cuba's Angola Operation." In *Cuban Internationalism in Sub-Saharan Africa*, edited by Sergio Diaz-Briquets, 102–23. Pittsburgh: Duquesne University Press, 1989.

Pedro, Alberto. "Poder Negro" [Black power]. *Casa de las Américas* 53 (March/April 1969): 134–44.

Primakov, Yevgeni. "USSR Policy on Regional Conflicts." *International Affairs* 6 (June 1988): 3–9.

Ratliff, William. "Cuban Military Policy in Sub-Saharan Africa." In *Cuban Internationalism in Sub-Saharan Africa*, edited by Sergio Diaz-Briquets, 29–47. Pittsburgh: Duquesne University Press, 1989.

Sawyer, Mark. *Racial Politics in Post-Revolutionary Cuba*. New York: Cambridge University Press, 2006.

Seagal, Aaron. "Cubans in Africa." *Caribbean Review* 7, no. 3 (July–September 1978): 38–43.

Stockwell, John. *In Search of Enemies: A CIA Story*. New York: Norton, 1978.

Taylor, Frank. "Revolution, Race, and Foreign Relations since 1959." *Cuban Studies*, vol. 18, edited by Carmelo Mesa-Lago, 19–45. Pittsburgh: University of Pittsburgh Press, 1988.

Thomas, Hugh. "Cuba in Africa." *Survey: A Journal of East and West Studies* 23 (Autumn 1977–1978): 181–88.

———. *Cuba: The Pursuit of Freedom*. New York: Harper and Row, 1971.

Valenta, Jiri. "The Soviet-Cuban Intervention in Angola, 1975." *Studies in Comparative Communism* 11, no. 1/2 (Spring/Summer 1978): 3–33.

PART IV

Ethnicity and the Interplay of Domestic and International Politics

CHAPTER 9

Ethnic Nationalism in the Cold War Context

The Cyprus Issue in the Greek and Greek American Public Debate, 1954–1989

Zinovia Lialiouti and Philip E. Muehlenbeck

On August 18, 1974, an estimated seventy thousand Americans—the majority of Greek descent—marched in protest in front of the White House. The crowd was protesting Turkey's recent invasion of the Mediterranean island of Cyprus—and the United States' perceived assent to the invasion—and calling for President Gerald Ford, who had been in office a mere ten days, to cut off military aid to Washington's NATO ally in Ankara.[1]

The next day halfway around the world similar protests took place outside of the US embassy in Athens, Greece. A wave of anti-Americanism had taken over the country as a result of Turkey's invasion of Cyprus, for which many Greeks held the United States culpable. US Secretary of State Henry Kissinger took the brunt of the criticism for his apparent pro-Turkish leanings, "wanted" signs were posted for his arrest across the city, and protestors outside the embassy chanted "Kissinger Murderer."[2] Explosives were placed underneath US government cars and a statue of Harry Truman was defaced, as "the doctrine that bore his name had never been in lower repute within Greece."[3]

Meanwhile, that same day on Cyprus itself an angry mob of approximately two thousand Greek Cypriots attacked the US embassy in Nicosia. Soon automatic gunfire was directed at the compound, causing the embassy staff to run for cover. In the chaos Antoinette Darnaya, a Cypriot who worked at the embassy, was shot in the head. Ambassador Davies attempted to catch her falling body and in the process was shot himself. The bullet went through both his lungs and severed the top of his heart—he died immediately.[4] In the face of such animosity toward his guidance of US policy on the Mediterranean, Kissinger was not moved. Rather than seeking to understand the reasons for these outbursts of spontaneous violence against US interests, the American secretary of state instead dismissed Greek Americans as disloyal and threatened the governments of Greece and Cyprus with the possibility that Washington would wash its hands of the Cyprus issue if Athens and Nicosia did not take action to curb such anti-Americanism.[5]

The Cyprus crisis, which precipitated all these protests, illustrates the interaction between ethnic nationalism and the cohesiveness of the NATO alliance, as well as the interaction between elite and mass perceptions.[6] Greek nationalism, ignited by ethnic conflict between Greeks and Turks on Cyprus, undermined Greece's devotion to the Atlantic alliance, became a basic source of anti-Americanism, and ultimately weakened the American position in the Eastern Mediterranean.

Early US-Greek Relations

The first half of the twentieth century was a stormy period in Greek history marked by intense political struggles, military coups, and a series of war adventures. As a consequence of the two Balkan wars (1912–1913, 1913–1914) and the First World War, Greek territory was significantly increased.[7] As a result, nationalism and irredentism became prevailing features in the country's political culture.[8] However, the Greco-Turkish War (1919–1922)—known as the Turkish War of Independence in Turkey and the Asia Minor Catastrophe in Greece—led to the uprooting of the Greek population in Asia Minor and the defeat of the Megali Idea (an ethnic nationalist irredentist goal of uniting all ethnic Greeks in the former Ottoman Empire into a single Greek state). The failure of the Megali Idea was experienced as a deep national trauma in Greece. Nationalist ideology was reinterpreted after this defeat but remained active and influential. During the Second World War, Greece endured significant losses in human lives and infrastructure.[9] Moreover, the end of the war was not the end of turbulence, as a brutal civil war raged on until 1949.[10]

The Greek Civil War cannot be fully understood unless it is examined in the context of the emerging Cold War between the United States and the Soviet Union. After the American intervention in the Greek Civil War following the enactment of the Truman Doctrine in 1947, Greece would become part of the American sphere of influence, and an anti-Communist regime with serious democratic shortcomings was established. With the implementation of the Marshall Plan, Greece became a recipient of American financial aid and American officials gained considerable control over the country's economic, political, and social life.[11] As a result, the Greek political Left and gradually certain components of the Center began to denounce American interventionism and to lament the loss of Greek national sovereignty.

Greeks in the United States

On the eve of the Second World War there were only an estimated five hundred thousand Greeks living in the United States—a figure that was minuscule in relation to other European nationalities—accounting for only 1.3 percent of total European immigration to the United States.[12] Greek Americans demonstrated their loyalty to the United States and were at the forefront of opposition to both Nazism and Fascism (especially after Germany and Italy invaded Greece in 1941).

Despite this demonstration of loyalty to their new homeland, Greek Americans tended to retain their ethnic distinctiveness to a greater degree than did other European immigrants to the United States. According to Peter Marudas, the homogeneity of the Greek American community was largely a result of the "ethnic-religious life centering around the Greek Orthodox parish and extensive use of the Greek language [which] discouraged interaction with other groups."[13] This was in contrast to other immigrants—Poles, Italians, Mexicans, Portuguese, Irish, and others—who as Catholics attended church with other ethnicities and sent their children to be educated in heterogeneous schools. This did not, however, mean that Greek Americans isolated themselves from mainstream American society. Most tended to be politically active and a great many become successful small businessmen.[14] This combination of retained homogeneity and political activism would allow Greek Americans to have their collective voice be heard in Washington during the Cyprus crisis.

The Emergence of the Cyprus Issue: Cold War Ideology and Ethnic Nationalism

The Greek post–civil war official ideology, the so-called *ethnikofrosyn* (national mindedness), consisted of anti-Communism, pro-Americanism, pro-Atlanticism, and nationalism.[15] However, these elements often contradicted one another, revealing the inconsistencies of the ideology of national mindedness.[16] In particular, the emergence of the Cyprus issue brought to the surface the contradiction between pro-Americanism or pro-Atlanticism and nationalism.[17] Cyprus's quest for independence from the British Empire and the prospect of a union with Greece (*enosis*) became a sort of national passion for Greek public opinion.

Cyprus, which had been a British colony since 1878, had a Greek-speaking, Greek Orthodox population estimated to make up 80 percent of the Cypriot population of approximately 570,000, while the Turkish-speaking Muslim minority represented 18 percent of the island's population.[18] The United Kingdom and the United States were initially opposed to the claim of independence, let alone the prospect of Cyprus's union with Greece. Turkey had its own claims over the island—both Ankara and the Turkish Cypriots advanced the alternative goal of *taksim*, the partition of the island into separate Greek and Turkish sectors.[19]

Athens had to find a compromise between cooperation with its NATO allies and the pressure for *enosis* stemming from Greek public opinion.[20] The political elite were initially very reluctant to support Cyprus's claim because of NATO constraints.[21] The argument made in 1950 by George Papandreou, at the time vice president of a centrist government, is indicative of this reluctance. When a Cypriot delegation visited Athens and urged the Greek government to support its bid for independence, Papandreou responded: "Greece breathes at the moment with two lungs, one British and the other American. And that's why she cannot risk suffocation for the sake of Cyprus."[22] However, the equilibrium between NATO conformity and national desires proved to be difficult to maintain.

The Greek government attempted to raise the Cyprus issue at the United Nations for the first time in 1954. Several Latin American nations indicated to Greek officials that they would support the motion, but American and British lobbying caused them to change course.[23] The motion was thus denied; the US action was very disappointing for the Greek government.[24]

In the United States, Greek Americans lobbied Washington to support either Cypriot independence or the island's *enosis* with Greece through the creation of the Justice for Cyprus Committee and other similar organizations. However, it was clear that at the time Cyprus was not the most important issue in the lives of most Greek Americans, because most voted to reelect President Dwight D. Eisenhower, despite his administration's noted lack of support for Cypriot independence. Finally, after a series of complicated and tense diplomatic negotiations, an agreement between the United Kingdom, Greece, and Turkey was reached in 1959 (the Zurich and London Agreement). Cyprus became independent in 1960, but its sovereignty was limited by the oversight of three guarantor powers, the United Kingdom, Greece, and Turkey. The agreements had outlined a presidential regime that represented a delicate balance between the Greek Cypriot majority and the Turkish Cypriot minority: executive power was to be shared by a president of Greek Cypriot origin and a vice president of Turkish Cypriot origin.[25] The prospect of union with Greece was specifically excluded. Greek public opinion viewed the agreement as a painful compromise.

Throughout this period, nationalist and anti-Western attitudes prevailed in Greek political culture despite the government's effort to appease public opinion and the limited freedom of expression allowed in the authoritative postwar republic.[26] These tendencies were also manifested in the student and youth movements from the mid-1950s to the 1960s and in the emerging Center-Left. The role of America as the leader of the free world was questioned even by the pro-American Greek Right. Conservative columnists often urged the Atlantic allies to alter their policy toward Greece and Cyprus, fearing that otherwise Greek public opinion would ultimately oblige Athens to withdraw from NATO.[27]

The Cyprus issue also gave the Communist Left the opportunity to acquire new legitimization and to appear as the genuine defender of Greek nationalist claims for the first time since the end of the civil war.[28] The Greek Communist Party had been stigmatized as traitorous for its attitude toward the so-called Macedonian issue and its support for the creation of a socialist Macedonian state consisting of parts of Greek, Yugoslavian, and Bulgarian territory. But in the case of Cyprus, the Communist Party actually supported the integration of an island outside Greek borders into the Greek state.[29] The issue was also organically integrated into the party's political and electoral campaigns, based on the argument that the liberation of Cyprus was both a national and a social goal.[30]

The Greek Orthodox Church also played an important role in the public support for union with Cyprus. But the focus was on the ethnic and not the religious dimension of the Cyprus conflict. Greek clergy were present in public protests and demonstrations concerning Cyprus, made repeated references to the "liberation" of "our Cypriot brothers" in their sermons, and expressed their frustration for the delay of that liberation in the official journal of the Greek Orthodox Church, *Ekklesia*. However, the Greek Church was fiercely anti-Communist and therefore very restrained in its anti-American and anti-Western critique.

Furthermore, the preeminent Greek Cypriot political leader and emblematic figure of the Cypriot struggle for independence was a priest, Archbishop Makarios. But even in his discourse, the religious element in the struggle against the British and the confrontation with the Turks was downgraded.

Under Makarios, the Orthodox Church of Cyprus operated as a political player with a clear anti-Communist orientation and nationalist aspirations.[31] Yet, after the declaration of Cyprus's independence and his election as president of the republic, Makarios approached the Non-Aligned Movement and followed an ambiguous policy of flirtation with the Soviet Union that provoked the displeasure of the United States.

Another important consequence of the Cyprus struggle was the re-emergence of intense anti-Turkish feelings among the Greek public, along with the deterioration of relations between Athens and Ankara. Turkey had been for more than a century the enemy par excellence for Greek public opinion. Greece became an independent state in 1830 after a decade of struggle against the Ottoman Empire.[32] Greece and Turkey had also fought on opposite sides during the Balkan wars and the First World War. Yet the two countries had both become NATO members in 1951, so in the context of the Atlantic alliance, the traditional hostility toward Turkey was downgraded in Greek public discourse. Even prior to the creation of NATO, however, the political leadership in both countries had opted for a policy of détente through the Lausanne Treaty of 1923, but by the mid-1950s this truce was seriously challenged by the emergence of the Cyprus issue.[33]

The dispute over Cyprus, which began as a dispute with the British Empire, was rapidly transformed into a Greek-Turkish conflict. In the anti-Turkish rhetoric, historical memory was selectively applied in order to sustain the Greek belief that Turks were impeding Greece's historical right to Cyprus. Greece's contribution during the Second World War compared to Turkey's neutrality and the demand for compensation by the Western allies was the most common argument.[34] A crucial issue in this debate was the amount of American Marshall Plan aid to Greece compared to that received by Turkey. Furthermore, all American announcements of cutbacks in the level of aid given to Greece were perceived as a form of blackmail tied to the Cyprus issue.[35] The American attitude toward Turkey was measured by American friendship toward Greece, and Washington's perceived pro-Turkish policies were treated as an immediate threat, revealing a zero-sum game perception.[36]

The hostility became even more intense after the Istanbul pogrom against the city's Greek minority in September 1955.[37] The violence, a response to the bombing of the Turkish consulate in Thessaloniki, resulted in attacks against churches, schools, shops, and houses in the Greek community—over sixty Greek Orthodox churches were badly damaged and a Greek monk was burned to death.[38] The Turkish press helped fan the fire of ethnic nationalism and anti-Greek sentiment by running headlines of alleged Greek atrocities against Turks in Cyprus.[39] Greeks were outraged by the Turkish brutality and by their Atlantic allies', and particularly Washington's, reluctance to intervene. The accusations against the United States centered on Washington's unwillingness to protect Greeks from Turkish aggression, to arbitrate justice as the leader of the Western alliance, and to recognize the Greeks' perceived historical, moral, and cultural superiority over the Turks.[40] The Greek newspaper *Kathimerini* editorialized on September 15, 1955: "We knew who the Turks were. And we knew who the British were as well. . . . But we hadn't realized who the Americans were and we are just beginning to find out with profound bitterness. Our friends are after all cold and indifferent and inconsistent." Similar sentiments prevailed in the pro-Communist press: "The patriotism of the Greek people has finally rebelled. They have the right, they have the power, they have the obligation to stigmatize the grave diggers and the sextons. . . . It's the British imperialists, the Turkish 'allies,' the whole pantheon of colonial powers. . . . All of them and with them and above them, the 'great allies of little Greece,' the 'leaders of the free world,' the Americans!"[41]

The Greek press presented the events of 1955 as a national tragedy and a shameful humiliation, since there was no retaliation. From the Greek perspective, Greece appeared to be an innocent, helpless victim betrayed by her allies and those obliged to protect her.[42] The press, even traditional publications of the Right, urged the government to withdraw from NATO and to revise Greek foreign policy toward Cold War neutrality.[43] Additionally, the execution by the British in 1956 of young Cypriot freedom fighters Michalis Karaolis and Andreas Dimitriou, and the deportation of Archbishop Makarios to Seychelles, intensified the feeling that the Greek nation was facing the aggression of both the West and the Turks.[44]

Despite the agreement of 1959 and the declaration of Cypriot independence in 1960, the tension between the two ethnic communities on the island did not abate. The newly founded republic was tormented by the fact that the two communities remained physically and politically separated, with political parties divided strictly along ethnic lines.[45] The two communities remained distinguished by their Greek or Turkish ethnicity, language, culture, and religion. The newly designed Cypriot flag, a yellow map of the island on a white background, purposely excluded blue, red, and green colors as well as crosses, stripes, stars, and crescents—colors and symbols of Greece, Turkey, or Islam. Since the days of Ottoman rule, schools on the island were established along ethnic lines using separate languages and curriculum, which served to further stunt the development of a unified Cypriot nationalism.[46]

As president of the Cypriot Republic, Makarios's intention to revise the constitution in order to reduce the political power of the Turkish minority as part of the Akritas Plan (which aimed to weaken the Turkish Cypriot wing of the government with the ultimate goal of *enosis* with Greece) met with opposition from the Turkish Cypriot leadership and led to the intensification of intercommunal violence.[47] After a series of Greek Cypriot attacks on Turkish and mixed villages, the Turkish military eventually intervened by bombing Greek Cypriot positions. The escalation of tension between Greece and Turkey over Cyprus is apparent in the following statement of Greek prime minister George Papandreou: "A war clash between Greece and Turkey would be madness, but if Turkey decides to enter the insane asylum, we shall not hesitate to follow her."[48]

But in Greece the overall responsibility for the violence endured by the Greek Cypriots was attributed to Washington's support of Ankara and the Turkish Cypriots.[49] The Left also exploited the fact that the Turks used American and NATO weaponry in their operations, their object being to establish that the "Atlantic Allies" of Athens were in reality lethal enemies of Greece: "NATO isn't anymore just the 'alliance' that undermines our national independence. . . . Today, blood stands between us and NATO: the blood and the burned flesh of our murdered innocent Cypriot brothers."[50]

Washington, fearing that animosity between two of its NATO allies would weaken the alliance's southern flank, sought to mediate an end to the ethnic strife on Cyprus and pull Greece and Turkey back from the brink of war. The United States believed that it was serving as a neutral intermediary between Athens and Ankara, and if anything slightly favoring Athens, as it was only through US pressure and a personal letter from President Lyndon Johnson to Turkish prime minister Ismet Inonu that Turkey refrained from invading the island in support of the Turkish Cypriot cause. Yet the American diplomatic intervention went unappreciated, viewed with skepticism in both Athens and Ankara, both of whose media characterized the United States as biased toward the other side.[51]

The Greek American press felt much the same way. Greek Americans viewed the Acheson Plan, Washington's attempt to find a middle road between the interests of Cyprus, Greece, and Turkey, as synonymous with *taksim*—the solution favored by both Ankara and the Turkish Cypriots.[52] When Turkey began bombing Greek Cypriot positions, the front page of the *National Herald* proclaimed: "This is Cyprus: The Greek Hiroshima of 1964."[53] Greek Americans criticized the Johnson administration for its handling of the Cyprus crisis through full-page ads in the *New York Times* and by distributing a special issue of the *Ahepan* magazine devoted to Cyprus to nearly every newspaper, library, and city, state, and federal government office in the United States.[54] Greek Americans adamantly believed that their new homeland had the diplomatic and economic means to pressure Turkey into acceding to the Greek position over Cyprus and expected Washington to compel Ankara to do so.

The United States instead pressured its NATO allies to accept a mediated solution to the Cyprus problem, a move that was viewed in Athens as a form of blackmail.[55] In the summer of 1964 Papandreou became prime minister and visited Washington in order to discuss the Cyprus issue with President Lyndon Johnson, but the Acheson Plan was rejected as unacceptable to Greece, and the Greek media emphasized the harshness of American diplomatic pressure and anti-American demonstrations frequently occurred outside the US embassy in Athens.[56] In the Greek public debate, the rejection of the American proposals was presented as a means to safeguard national interests, while pro-Soviet references appeared even in the conservative press.[57] Mass demonstrations were held outside the United States embassy in Athens that included the burning of pictures of President Johnson.[58] Finally, the subversion against the Papandreou government in the summer of 1965, which resulted in the pro-American King Constantine II dismissing the government, was attributed by a large part of Greek public opinion to American manipulations as revenge for Athens's earlier noncompliance in US plots against Cyprus.[59]

The Cyprus Issue as a Greek National Tragedy and Its Impact on the Cold War

In April 1967 a military coup led by a group of junior officers took place in Athens, and an anti-Communist junta was established (1967–1974). For the overwhelming majority of the Greek people, the junta was believed to have American guidance and support and to serve American interests in the region.[60] This increased anti-Americanism in Greece, which manifested itself in numerous forms of protest—including several attempts to bomb the statue of President Truman in Athens. The coup also served to further fragment the already weak Greek American lobby in the United States as Greek Americans split over whether to support the new military government or protest against it for having killed democracy in its birthplace.

However, the Greek Colonels (as the group became known) had a problematic relationship with Archbishop Makarios, the elected leader of Cyprus, who resisted the new government's demands for Cyprus's absorption into greater Greece. In 1974, after Makarios sent Athens an ultimatum to withdraw the 650 Greek officers serving in the Cyprus National Guard (as he rightly believed, they owed allegiance to Greece rather than to Cyprus and were working to undermine his government), the Colonels sponsored a coup against him. After Makarios narrowly escaped death and fled the island, the Greek junta inserted Greek Cypriot Nicos Sampson as Cyprus's provisional president. He was known as the "butcher of Omorphita" or "the Turk killer" by Turkish Cypriots for his role in intercommunal violence in the early 1960s and labeled the "Al Capone of Cyprus" by the *New York Times*, and Cypriots of Turkish descent were understandably concerned about his ascension to the Cypriot presidency.[61] Acting on its right to intervene as a guarantor power under the terms of the 1959 Zurich and London Agreement, Turkey invaded the island in order to protect the interests and well-being of Turkish Cypriots.[62] Even though Makarios was eventually restored to the presidency, the Turks did not withdraw from the island, occupying 38 percent of its northern part. The invasion had a direct impact on the country's demographics, orchestrating Turkish ethnic cleansing against Cypriots of Greek descent and a massive influx of Turkish mainland settlers.[63]

The Greek American Reaction

Four days after Turkish troops landed on Cyprus, the national presidents of fourteen Greek American organizations met in Washington, DC, to decide how to respond. The delegates issued a statement in the name of nearly three million Americans of Greek descent in support of UN Resolution 353, which called for a cease-fire and respect for Cypriot sovereignty, and implored the US government to take whatever action necessary for the preservation of Cypriot independence. This message was sent to President Richard Nixon, Secretary of State Kissinger, every member of Congress, and the media.[64] The Turkish invasion of Cyprus spontaneously united the Greek American community, which previously had been divided over whether to support or oppose the Greek military junta. Within weeks about twenty new Greek American organizations were created to mobilize support for the Greek Cypriot cause. Working alongside the nearly fifty Greek American fraternal organizations that had existed prior to the Turkish invasion, new organizations such as the American Hellenic Institute combined with long-established groups like the American Hellenic Educational Progressive Association (AHEPA) to form a well-organized and powerful lobbying effort whose main goal was the withdrawal of Turkish troops from Cyprus, and in lieu of that withdrawal a US arms embargo against Turkey.[65]

AHEPA received over $165,000 in contributions to its publicity campaign.[66] Its first advertisement was a full-page ad in the *New York Times* on August 24, 1975, which ran under the headline: "We Demand Withdrawal of Turkish Invaders From Cyprus."[67] A grassroots campaign designed to influence public opinion and executive and congressional policy making was also launched, which resulted in over forty thousand letters to the White House and tens of thousands of Greek Americans boycotting the *Washington Star* for its opposition to a Turkish arms embargo.[68]

Greek Americans were also mobilized through the Greek Orthodox Church. The day after the Turkish invasion of Cyprus, Archbishop Iakovos, primate of the Greek Orthodox Archdiocese of North and South America, held a special prayer service at Holy Trinity Cathedral in New York attended by Archbishop Makarios of Cyprus, Archbishop Athenagoras of London, and Zenon Rossides, the Cypriot ambassador to the United Nations. Iakovos also directed every Greek Orthodox parish in the United States to hold vigils for Cyprus that day. The following week Iakovos organized a meeting between church leaders and the presidents of the Greek fraternal organizations to coordinate the combined efforts of Greek Americans. Iakovos continued to play an important role as a spokesman of the Greek American position in subsequent meetings with Kissinger and President Gerald R. Ford (who ascended to the presidency following Nixon's resignation only three weeks after the coup against Makarios). The church also set up committees in all fifty states to collect donations for Greek Cypriot refugees and to distribute procedural information on how to press local legislators to support an arms embargo against Turkey.[69] Eventually, Greek Orthodox priests would damn by name from the pulpit congressmen who voted against the Turkish arms embargo.

A key cog in the Greek American lobbying effort was Eugene T. Rossides, a former all-American quarterback at Columbia University, law partner of William Rogers, and assistant secretary of the treasury from 1969 to 1972. Through his newly formed American Hellenic Institute, Rossides provided the Greek American lobby a permanent presence in Washington, legal counsel, and contacts within the State Department and Nixon/Ford administration that resulted in AHEPA leaders meeting three times with Secretary of State Kissinger; once with Jack Kubisch, the newly appointed US ambassador to Greece; and once with President Ford himself. Rossides was also instrumental in developing the legal approach that Greek Americans used to seek an arms embargo against Turkey. It is important to note that the Greek American lobby never claimed to represent the interests of Greeks, Greek Cypriots, or even Greek Americans, but instead argued that as US citizens they were seeking a US foreign policy toward Greece, Turkey, and Cyprus consistent with US law and traditional American values and beliefs (in fact most abhorred being identified as the Greek American lobby, preferring to be referred to as "an American lobby for law and decency").[70] As an AHEPA press release put it: "Upholding the rule of law, opposition to aggression, and support of freedom and representative government—are basic to American foreign policy and concern all Americans. They are not the concern of only Americans of Greek descent."[71]

This emphasis on US and international law was the brainchild of Rossides, who argued that in its invasion of Cyprus, Turkey had violated US law, the UN

Charter, the NATO treaty, the Geneva Convention of 1949, and the European Convention on Human Rights. Spearheading the congressional campaign to enforce an arms embargo against Turkey were the five Greek Americans who served in the House of Representatives—Paul Sarbanes (D-MD), Peter Kyros (D-MD), Gus Yatron (D-PA), Louis Bafalias (D-FL), and John Brademas (D-IN), who in 1959 had become the first Greek American to serve in the US Congress. With no Greek Americans in the Senate, the issue was carried forward by Thomas Eagleton (D-MO), Ted Kennedy (D-MA), Claiborne Pell (D-RI), and Adlai Stevenson (D-IL).

Initially, the Ford administration was not concerned about the possibility of Greek American backlash against its Cyprus policies. President Ford, who had been an honorary member of AHEPA for over a quarter of a century and had attended fourteen of their previous twenty-two annual meetings prior to 1975, assured Secretary of State Kissinger that Greek Americans had never concerned themselves with foreign affairs.[72] Ford likely realized the folly of this assertion when he was speaking to the 1975 AHEPA Supreme Convention and two protestors held up a sign reading "Ford is a Turkey."[73] Once it became evident that Greek Americans would in fact attempt to influence US policy toward Cyprus, Ford and Vice President Nelson Rockefeller both publicly questioned the group's loyalty to the United States. Kissinger repeatedly criticized the actions of the "Greek lobby" and the "Greek congressmen" for playing "ethnic politics" and implied that they were funded by, if not taking orders from, the Greek foreign ministry. He further demeaned Greek Americans by saying that they were "so passionate that their leaders were deprived of any flexibility" and lamenting that "ethnic passions can overwhelm serious thought."[74] The implication was clear: while Kissinger portrayed the White House and State Department as acting in the best interest of the United States as a whole, Greek Americans were characterized as acting on parochial interests which were in opposition to US national interests.

Partly because of this attitude, many Greek Americans vilified Kissinger as the "killer of Cypriots" or the "greatest menace in America's history" and blamed his alleged pro-Turkish sympathies as being the chief reason for Cyprus's troubles—some going as far as to suggest that the US secretary of state should be prosecuted for his "crimes." which were characterized as "the proximate cause of more than one thousand deaths."[75] This mindset was frequently demonstrated in political cartoons in the Greek American press. One such cartoon from the *National Herald* subtitled "Behold Our Ally—The Noble Turk" pictured a figure resembling Kissinger with a bloody sword labeled "Cyprus" in one hand and a heroin needle in the other labeled "Heroin Production," the bodies of Greek Cypriots and American youths at his feet.[76]

One thing that Kissinger and the Greek American lobby agreed on was that the only way to negotiate Turkey's withdrawal from Cyprus was if Washington used its leverage on its NATO ally. They differed, however, in how that leverage should be applied. Kissinger believed that an arms embargo against Turkey, which Greek Americans supported, eliminated any leverage that Washington might have over Ankara. He thought that Washington could better apply its leverage by offering positive incentives. The main reason for Kissinger's unwillingness to place an embargo on Turkey, however, was related to its strategic location along the Soviet Union's southern border and his fear that Ankara would close the more than two dozen US military installations in its country in response.

Congress members sympathetic to the Greek American position introduced House Resolution 1319 on August 14, 1974, calling for the suspension of economic and military aid to Turkey until all Turkish forces had been withdrawn from Cyprus. The resolution passed in late September by a vote of 64–27 in the Senate and 307–90 in the House of Representatives. Shortly after the voting, the Greek American lobby took out a full-page ad in the *New York Times* listing the name of every congressman who voted in favor of the legislation, referring to them as the "conscience of the nation."[77]

There was, however, more to this story than the mere effectiveness of the Greek American lobby. Given that there were only five Greek Americans in the House of Representatives and none in the Senate, and that Greek Americans numbered only between half a million and three million in 1974, it is not plausible to assume that Greek Americans could have succeeded in enacting this legislation alone.[78] Indeed, they were aided by other ethnic minorities with their own anti-Turkish sympathies—namely, Armenian Americans and Jewish Americans.[79] However, a more significant factor in the success of the Greek American lobbying effort was general congressional dissatisfaction with the direction of US foreign policy under Kissinger. The issue of the Turkish arms embargo happened to be the first opportunity for Congress to reassert its constitutional role in foreign policy making following Watergate and Vietnam. Therefore, for the majority of congressmen who voted in support of the arms embargo, the issue was not one of supporting Greece over Turkey, of succumbing to the political pressure of Greek Americans, or even of morality. They were voting against Kissinger and his policies and perceived the vote to be a constitutional issue: the executive branch's usurpation of Congress's constitutional role in the formulation of foreign policy. This circumstance does not diminish the role of the Greek American lobby for having brought the issue to the fore, and all parties concerned recognized Greek Americans as the driving force behind the passage of the legislation.[80]

The embargo on aid to Turkey went into effect in February 1975, fueling anti-Americanism in Turkey and prompting the Turkish government to respond by closing all but one of the twenty-seven US military and intelligence bases on its territory. The embargo proved to have little impact on Turkish behavior toward Cyprus, however, and served only to open the door to Soviet influence. After the arms embargo went into effect, Moscow stepped in to fill the void and Turkey became the top Soviet aid recipient in the world, receiving $650 million in 1975, which increased to $800 million in 1978.[81] Conversely, once the embargo was repealed in 1978, Greece responded by improving its relations with Moscow. Thus American policy in the Mediterranean managed to alienate Greece, Turkey, and Cyprus simultaneously—a situation that the Kremlin was able to exploit to moderately improve its relations with its southern neighbors at the expense of the United States (although all three nations remained more closely aligned with Washington than Moscow).

The effective advocacy of the Greek American lobby hampered not only the Ford administration's foreign policy but also Ford's chances for reelection. Many prominent Greek American Republicans, such as Eugene Rossides and George Christopher, the former mayor of San Francisco, came out against the Ford administration. Christopher published an op-ed in the *Hellenic Chronicle* that asked God for "deliverance" from the "Ford-Rockefeller-Kissinger triumvirate" and called on Greek Americans to initiate a "crusade" to teach the Ford administration that "our ballots can be more effective than their bullets."[82] Such letters caused concern within the administration that the ethnic vote would spoil Ford's chances at retaining the presidency in 1976.

Partly in response to such letters and the fears for the president's political future that they elicited, the administration in January 1976 created a new White House staff position—special assistant for ethnic affairs—naming Ukrainian American Myron Kuropas to the position.[83] Other efforts to stem the tide of "hyphenated Americans" migrating to the Democratic Party included publishing a pamphlet titled *The Ford Presidency from an Ethnic Perspective*, which detailed the president's fondness for ethnic Americans and claimed that Ford had "done more than merely *talk* about this desire to have ethnic Americans participate in his Administration. . . . [He had] met with more ethnic American leaders than any other American President."[84] The administration also asked a prominent Greek American lawyer, Dennis Livadas, to send a letter to Greek Americans imploring them to vote for President Ford's reelection. In fact, Ford's vulnerability among ethnic voters was so well known that even Greeks wrote administration members, such as White House Chief of Staff Dick Cheney and Secretary of Defense Donald Rumsfeld, offering schemes to win over the ethnic vote.[85]

The Greek Reaction

The Turkish invasion of Cyprus destabilized the Greek military regime and led to its collapse, since it was held responsible for a national tragedy. The Turkish occupation of Cyprus and the division of the island was a traumatic experience for Greeks and led to widespread anti-Americanism. President Nixon and Secretary of State Kissinger were depicted in the darkest colors and became symbols of US animosity toward Greece.

The Greek public held Washington responsible for having tolerated the Turkish invasion, and some Greeks even suspected that the United States was the mastermind behind Turkey's aggression.[86] A conservative populist newspaper described the anti-American feelings as "a huge wave of indignation that stems from the depths of the folkish soul," which transformed the Greek people "into a massive entity that moves with the power of an avalanche and seeks revenge."[87] American credibility within Greece had already been tarnished by the close relationship between Washington and the Greek military government, and, for many, Cyprus was the last straw, especially for younger Greeks who lacked the historical reservoir of goodwill that many older Greeks had. Greek public opinion made its disenchantment with its NATO ally clear by distancing itself from anything that represented the United States. Militant demonstrations took place in the capital and other major cities. Soldiers renounced their medals from the Korean War, academics returned their diplomas obtained in the United States, and artists and intellectuals refused to participate in events organized by the Hellenic-American Union.[88] A Greek columnist even went so far as to claim that the word "Greek American" itself was absurd, arguing the two adjectives were mutually exclusive.[89]

As a result of the public uproar against the United States, the formerly pro-American prime minister, Konstantinos Karamanlis, who replaced the Greek junta as the head of an interim government, announced Athens's withdrawal from the military sector of the NATO integrated command, saying that Greeks felt betrayed by the United States.[90] Karamanlis said that it saddened him to see Greeks, "once the most pro-American people in the world," now hostile toward the United States because of its Cyprus policy.[91] The entire spectrum of the Greek press saluted this decision in patriotic terms, calling it "the first decent political action of our postwar history."[92] Politicians and columnists began to call for Greece's integration into a unified Europe as a counterbalance against the United States and as a potential guarantee for Greek national interests and a "fair" solution to the Cyprus problem.[93]

These events also signified the bankrupt ideology of national-mindedness, since the military dictatorship that had preached the identification of anti-Communism with patriotism had seriously wounded Greek ethnic nationalism.

Furthermore, the period of détente between Washington and Moscow in the early 1970s had already facilitated the weakening of earlier Cold War definitions of "friends" and "enemies" in the Greek psyche.[94]

It is also worth noting that the idea of a wider plot that targeted the Greek nation, whether within Greece or outside its borders in areas that are historically believed to be parts of Hellenism such as Cyprus, became very common among the Greek populace. The plot was thought to have been designed by the United States and other major powers, with the Turks as simple marionettes serving the interests of Washington.[95] Like most conspiracy theories, this one combined facts and historical memories with unprovable assumptions and irrational elements.

Conspiracy scenarios continued to grow in popularity after a series of terrorist activities. In the autumn of 1975, Turkish ambassadors were murdered in Vienna and Paris. The Greek press argued that the murders were a part of a wider conspiracy against Greece and that the American secret services were behind the assassinations.[96] In December of that year Richard Welch, the CIA station chief in Athens, was murdered after his identity and address had been made public by the editors of the *Athens News*. Much later it became known that his murder had been carried out as the first act of a new anti-American Greek terrorist group, 17N (the Revolutionary Organization 17 November). However, at the time, Greek public opinion was convinced that the assassination was the work of foreigners and would be used to further exploit Greece.[97]

The concept of conspiracy against Hellenism was integrated into the discourse of both the Greek Communist Party and the growing Pan-Hellenic Socialist Movement (PASOK).[98] PASOK's leader, Andreas Papandreou (son of former prime minister George Papandreou), repeatedly argued that the United States and NATO had set out to enfeeble the Greek nation. As he put it, Hellenism faced a "tactical, guided, deadly threat."[99] In particular, the younger Papandreou, as leader of the opposition and later as prime minister, insisted that American and NATO policies aimed at altering the status quo in the Aegean Sea in favor of Turkey.[100] The Center-Left press was also filled with emotional references to the allegedly pro-Turkish attitude of the United States and to the consequent danger that posed for Greek territorial rights.[101] According to historian James E. Miller: "The Greek political establishment and Greek public opinion were united on one issue, blaming their errors on the United States. For the next two decades, the United States served as the national piñata, trooped out by Left and Right, on every possible occasion, to assuage national feelings of humiliation and to avoid a national debate over the real causes of both the rise of the Colonels and the Cyprus disaster."[102]

With the Greek public especially bitter toward the reestablishment of US military aid to Turkey, the country's Western orientation was seriously contested in public debate. This was particularly intense in the political strategy of the Pan-Hellenic Socialist Movement and of Andreas Papandreou personally. Campaigning on a platform filled with anti-American and anti-Western discourse, PASOK was elected to power with an overwhelming majority for the first time in 1981.[103] Some scholars argue that this was more rhetoric than actual policy. After all, after PASOK came to power the Greek government did not withdraw from NATO or the European Community as it had promised to do during its time as the opposition. Andreas Papandreou did pursue a foreign policy more independent of the United States, however, by seeking relations with leaders of the Non-Aligned Movement such as Olof Palme, Indira Gandhi, Yasser Arafat, and Muammar al-Gaddafi. He also made a series of visits to Warsaw Pact countries such as Bulgaria and Romania and became the first head of state of a Western country to visit Wojciech Jaruzelski's Poland after the imposition of martial law in that country.[104]

As far as the Cyprus issue is concerned, the matter took a dramatic turn in the early 1980s. In November 1983 the leaders of the Turkish Cypriot community unilaterally declared the independence of the northern Turkish-occupied part of the island. This action was a further step toward the de facto division of the island and was condemned by the international community and the United Nations. The Turkish Republic of Northern Cyprus was diplomatically recognized only by Turkey, on which it remains dependent economically, politically, and militarily to this day.

The creation of an independent Northern Cyprus provoked new tension in the relationship between Greece and Turkey as well as between Greece and the Western community, and especially the United States. The Greek media accused the United States of having sponsored the actions of Rauf Denktash, the leader of the Turkish Cypriot community and a militant proponent of the independence of northern Cyprus.[105] The Left and the Center-Left political parties also argued that the ultimate motive behind Washington's supposed support for Denktash was to punish Athens for its autonomy from the West and its neutral attitude toward the Cold War.[106] Athens and other Greek cities experienced passionate anti-American outbursts in the wake of Northern Cyprus's unilateral declaration of independence.

The creation of Northern Cyprus was viewed as an "attack against the national and the historic domain of Hellenism" by Greeks, Greek Americans, and Greek Cypriots alike.[107] This new national loss again stirred up anti-Western sentiment, since it was added to a long list of perceived injustices suffered by the Greek people for which the West was believed to be culpable. Greek history was reinterpreted as a series of continuous victimizations that the national body had managed to overcome. The sense of national victimization became an essential component of Greek ethnic identity and contributed to the belief that diplomatic isolation was a special quality of the Greek nation.

This widespread belief found emblematic phrasing in the statement of Greek president Christos Sartzetakis, who in 1985 referred to Greece as a "brotherless nation."[108] At the level of mass communication, this belief was a common feature in both the left-wing and right-wing media during the mid-1980s, and the extremes of the Greek political spectrum held this view in common. For example, the socialist newspaper *Elefterotypia* wrote: "We are reminded that in the past, in the present and in the future, we are alone; without any real allies, without any loyal friends. We have to face our enemies alone, we have to fight alone and we have to sacrifice ourselves alone." Further, "threats are the leitmotiv of our history. We are a lonely nation that struggles to find its fate between East and West, between Russians and Americans, between Israelis and Arabs."[109] In a similar vein, the conservative newspaper *Kathimerini* observed that the Greek nation "has been a victim during the war, a victim during truce, a victim during the reconstruction of Europe, a victim during the time of peace, a victim of Turkish bulimia, a victim of the deceitfulness of its friends, [and] a victim of its allies' policies."[110]

The public discourse was also dominated by rumors about impending political and territorial threats and political assassinations by 17N. Continued Greek frustration with the implacable Cyprus issue coincided with the murder of George Tsantes, a Greek American and the chief of the naval section of the Joint US Military Aid Group in Greece, at the hands of 17N. Greek press reports claimed that the victim was a CIA agent and made allusions to the agency's involvement in his murder.[111] They also tried to establish that the murder was directly linked to developments in Cyprus and was part of a Turkish American plan to destabilize the Greek government: "We sense, we understand, we smell, we see through the eyes of logic and experience that there is a tight link between the murder of the American officer and the collective crime against Cyprus."[112] 17N attempted to justify the assassination as an outgrowth of Greek anti-Americanism and the need to safeguard national independence.[113]

The anniversary of the November 17, 1973, student uprising at the Polytechnic School (Polytechneio) against the Colonels' junta, which ended in bloody suppression, was the inspiration for the name of 17N. This anniversary evolved through the years into an institutionalized expression of anti-Americanism that condemned the US role in Greece, and particularly the Nixon administration's ties with the Greek military regime and the Ford administration's acceptance of the Turkish invasion of Cyprus. The ritual of the November 17 anniversary involved a demonstration outside the American embassy in Athens featuring passionate anti-imperialist speeches and slogans.

The 1983 celebration was dominated by popular indignation for Denktash's unilateral declaration of independence for Northern Cyprus and the attitude of the United States toward this development. The demonstration, one of the most massive in Greek history, lasted five hours and an estimated one million people participated. This incident and the discursive strategies that evolved around it reflect the close ties between nationalism and anti-Americanism in Cold War Greece.

In the following years, during the diplomatic negotiations regarding Cyprus, the notion of Western hostility toward Greek national claims was established as a powerful stereotype. In contrast, positive references were made to the attitude of the Soviet Union and the Eastern bloc countries by the pro-government and left-wing media.[114] A constant source of Greek discontent was the amount of American aid and Western armament given to Turkey despite its continued occupation of Cypriot territory.[115] In September 1984, when the Greek government canceled a combined Greek American military exercise code-named Zeus, the pro-government press saluted the decision by arguing that Greece and the United States disagreed on their perception of the enemy—while the United States designed its military exercises based on the threat of a northern enemy (Bulgaria and the rest of the Soviet bloc), Greece did not fear a northern threat and wished to focus on her eastern enemy (Turkey), which the United States completely discounted as a danger to Greece.[116] This disconnect between Greek and American perceptions explains why a large part of Greek public opinion had distanced itself from NATO's definition of the enemy and instead defined their enemy based on nationalist, rather than Cold War, ideology.

This mood was demonstrated by an opinion poll that found that the majority of the Greek populace (91 percent) viewed Turkey as a threat to Greece, while 55 percent felt that the United States was an even greater threat. The percentage dropped to 22 percent when the pollsters replaced the United States with the Soviet Union, while only 3 percent regarded Albania as a threat.[117] This attitude was clear even when Greece returned to NATO. The opposition parties and press repeatedly argued that the alliance had lost its defensive significance for Greece, since the only real enemy for Greece was fellow NATO member Turkey, whom the Atlantic allies were unwilling to confront.[118]

Conclusion

On the one hand, Cold War commitments and ties to the United States served to restrain Athens and Ankara from direct clashes with each other and helped prevent large-scale civil war and genocide on Cyprus. On the other hand, however, the Atlantic alliance was unable to facilitate a diplomatic resolution to the island's ethnic strife, because Greece and Turkey both gave priority to their national aspirations over NATO solidarity and wider Cold War concerns.[119] The Cyprus issue was therefore a vivid example of the incompatibility between ethnic nationalist aspirations and Cold War security commitments.

Ethnic nationalism during the Cyprus crisis influenced US foreign policy on both the international and domestic fronts, leading Christopher Hitchens to label Cyprus "the site, and the occasion, of perhaps the greatest failure of American foreign policy in postwar Europe."[120] Internationally, ethnic nationalism hurt Washington's Cold War readiness because it undermined its eastern Mediterranean allies' commitment to the Atlantic alliance. Greece briefly left the military arm of NATO, while Turkey temporarily closed several US bases and listening posts on its territory. Moreover, each country began to see the other as their main enemy rather than focusing on the Soviet bloc. Domestically, Greek Americans effectively mobilized to take advantage of congressional irritation at its loss of oversight in foreign affairs and the executive branch's flaunting of American law to successfully lobby for an arms embargo against Turkey. The force of ethnic nationalism proved stronger than the will of the White House, both in the Mediterranean and on Capitol Hill.[121]

For Greece, ethnic nationalist sentiment toward Cyprus undermined Athens's devotion to the Atlantic alliance and poisoned her relationship with her allies (mainly the United States, Turkey, and the United Kingdom). It also made Athens aware of the asset that Greek Americans could be in pursuing Greek interests within the United States.[122] In terms of mass perception, the Cyprus crisis intensified anti-Turkish feelings and became the main source of anti-Americanism. The importance of the Cyprus issue for Greek public opinion led to its incorporation into the political and communicative agenda of nearly every Greek political party without much differentiation in platform and came to be seen as a measure of patriotism.

The legacy of the 1974 Cyprus crisis remains active in the post–Cold War era. Despite Cyprus's membership in the European Union, the northern part of the island remains occupied by Turkish forces and the divide between Cypriots of Greek and of Turkish ethnicity has not been resolved. Greek public opinion continues to remain sensitive to the issue and prone to anti-Turkish and anti-American sentiment in times of crisis.

Notes

1. *Hellenic Times*, August 19, 1974.
2. See Theodore A. Couloumbis, *The United States, Greece, and Turkey: The Troubled Triangle* (New York: Praeger, 1983), 98; and Jon V. Kofas, *Under the Eagle's Claw: Exceptionalism in Postwar U.S.-Greek Relations* (Westport, CT: Praeger, 2003), 132.
3. Laurence Stern, *The Wrong Horse: The Politics of Intervention and the Failure of American Diplomacy* (New York: Times Books, 1977), 133.
4. For a firsthand account of Ambassador Davies's death, see Thomas D. Boyatt, "1974 in Retrospect and Its Importance Today," in *The United States and Cyprus: Double Standards and the Rule of Law*, ed. Eugene T. Rossides and Van Coufoudakis (Washington, DC: American Hellenic Institution Foundation, 2002), 62. See also Jan Asmussen, *Cyprus at War: Diplomacy and Conflict during the 1974 Crisis* (London: I. B. Tauris, 2008), 246–47.
5. Kissinger quoted in Asmussen, *Cyprus at War*, 247.
6. For a comprehensive overview of the Cyprus problem, see Alexis Heraclides, *The Cyprus Problem, 1947–2004: From Union to Dichotomy* (Athens: Sideris, 2006).
7. Hellenic Army General Staff, *A Concise History of the Balkan Wars, 1912–1913* (Athens: Army History Directorate Publication, 1998).
8. Keith R. Legg and John M. Roberts, *Modern Greece: A Civilization on the Periphery* (Boulder, CO: Westview Press, 1997), 33–38; and Ioannis D. Stefanidis, *Isle of Discord: Nationalism, Imperialism, and the Making of the Cyprus Problem* (London: Hurst, 1999), 254–57.
9. Mark Mazower, *Inside Hitler's Greece: The Experience of Occupation* (New Haven, CT: Yale University Press, 1995); and Violetta Hionidou, *Famine and Death in Occupied Greece, 1941–1944* (Cambridge: Cambridge University Press, 2006).
10. David Close, *The Origins of the Greek Civil War* (Essex: Longman, 1995).
11. Argyris Fatouros, "Pos kataskevazete ena episimo plesio dyesdissis: He Inomenes Polities stin Ellada, 1947–1948" [The construction of an official structure for penetration: The United States in Greece, 1947–1948], in *He Ellada sti dekaetia 1940–1950: Ena ethnos se krisi* [Greece in the 1940s–1950s: A nation in crisis], ed. Nikos Alivizatos (Athens: Themelio, 1994), 419; Konstantinos Tsoukalas, "He ideologiki epidrasi tou Emfyliou polemou" [The ideological consequences of the civil war], in *He Ellada sti dekaetia, 1940–1950* [Greece in the 1940s–1950s: A nation in crisis], ed. Nikos Alivizatos (Athens: Themelio, 1994), 562; and Yiannis Yianoulopoulos, *O Metapolemikos kosmos: Elliniki kai evropaiki istoria (1945–1963)* [The postwar world: Greek and European history (1945–1963)] (Athens: Papazisis, 1992).
12. John Peter Paul, "A Study in Ethnic Group Political Behavior: The Greek-Americans and Cyprus" (PhD diss., University of Denver, 1979), 2–3.
13. Peter N. Marudas, "Greek American Involvement in Contemporary Politics," in *The Greek American Community in Transition*, ed. Harry J. Psomiades and Alice Scourby (New York: Pella Publishing, 1982), 95.
14. Clifford P. Hackett, "The Role of Congress and Greek-American Relations," in

Greek-American Relations: A Critical Review, ed. Theodore A. Couloumbis and John O. Iatrides (New York: Pella Publishing, 1980), 142.

15. Historically, the Greek Center-Right did not have a concrete ideological identity and was primarily defined negatively, by its opposition to Communism. Stathis Kalyvas, *The Greek Right: Between Transition and Reform*, in *The European Center-Right at the End of the Twentieth Century*, ed. F. L. Wilson (New York: St. Martin's Press, 1998), 102–4.

16. Despina Papadimitriou, *Apo ton lao ton nomimofronon sto ethnos ton ethnikofronon: He syntiritiki skepsi stin Ellada* [From the law-abiding people to the nation of the nationally minded: Conservative thought in Greece] (Athens: Savvalas, 2007), 178–207.

17. Despina Papadimitriou, *O ethnikismos ton "ethnikofronon" ke to Kypriako, 1950–1959* [The nationalism of the "nationally minded" and the Cyprus issue, 1950–1959], *Sygxrona Themata* 68, 69, 70 (July 1998–March 1999): 230.

18. Joseph S. Joseph, "Post–Colonial Period, 1960–1974: Expectations and Failures," in *Cyprus in the Modern World*, ed. Michalis S. Michael and Anastasios M. Tamis (Thessaloniki: Vanias Publishing, 2005), 26.

19. Joseph S. Joseph, *Cyprus: Ethnic Conflict and International Politics: From Independence to the Threshold the European Union* (London: Macmillan, 1999), 18; and Stefanidis, *Isle of Discord*, 206–17.

20. Nancy Crawshaw, *The Cyprus Revolt: An Account of the Struggle for Union with Greece* (London: George Allen and Unwin, 1978), 67–71.

21. Stefanidis, *Isle of Discord*, 257–65.

22. Spyros Linardatos, *From the Civil War to the Junta*, vol. 1 (Athens: Papazisis, 1986), 1:123–24.

23. William Mallinson, *Cyprus: A Modern History* (London: I. B. Tauris, 2005), 27–28.

24. Regarding the first Greek appeal to the United Nations, see Crawshaw, *The Cyprus Revolt*, 83–89. For the impact on Greek public opinion, see "US Adopts the Colonial Policy of the Foreign Office," *Ta Nea*, October 25, 1954; "Greece Caught in the Nest of a Mean Conspiracy," *Ta Nea*, December 15, 1954; and "With Indignation," *Ta Nea*, December 16, 1954.

25. Evanthis Hatzivassiliou, *The Cyprus Question, 1878–1960: The Constitutional Aspect* (Minneapolis: University of Minnesota Press, 2002), 73–92.

26. Ioannis Stefanidis, *Stirring the Greek Nation: Political Culture, Irredentism, and Anti-Americanism* (Burlington, VT: Ashgate, 2007), 55–77.

27. "Greece and NATO," *Kathimerini*, December 10, 1957; and "Greece and NATO," *Kathimerini*, November 29, 1957.

28. Kyrkos Doxiadis, "Ethnikofron dichasmos kai ethniki syspeirosi: I dipli ideologiki apotychia tis diktatorias" [Nationalist division and national rallying: The double ideological failure of the dictatorship], in *He Diktatoria, 1967–1974. Politikes Praktikes-Ideologikos Logos-Antistasi* [The dictatorship, 1967–1974: Political practices, ideological discourse, resistance], ed. Gianna Athanassatou, Alkis Rigos, and Serafeim Seferiades (Athens: Hellenic Association for Political Science, Kastaniotis, 1999), 173.

29. Yannoulopoulos, *The Post-War World*, 331.

30. "The Struggle for Cyprus Is a Struggle for Independence and for Bread," *Avgi*, June 3, 1956.

31. Stefanidis, *Isle of Discord*, 231–36.

32. Douglas Dakin, *The Greek Struggle for Independence, 1821–1833* (Berkeley: University of California Press, 1973); David Brewer, *The Greek War of Independence* (Woodstock, NY: Overlook Press, 2001); and Peter H. Paroulakis, *The Greek War of Independence* (Darwin, Australia: Hellenic International Press, 1984).

33. Joseph S. Joseph, *Cyprus: Ethnic Conflict and International Concern* (New York: Peter Lang, 1985), 80–81.

34. See "Some Memory," *Kathimerini*, January 6, 1956; "The American Attitude," *Kathimerini*, September 15, 1955; "Provocative Statements by Foreign Minister Dulles," *Ta Nea*, October 15, 1955; "Us and Others," *Ta Nea*, October 28, 1955; "Continuity," *Kathimerini*, July 10, 1957; "History," *Ta Nea*, October 26, 1954; "Our Contribution," *Ta Nea*, February 2, 1955; "Their Duty," *Ta Nea*, February 25, 1956; and "Miserable Oblivion," *Ta Nea*, May 9, 1955.

35. See "New Unexpected Decision of the American Government; the US Decided to Cut Back the Aid to Greece," *Kathimerini*, January 4, 1957; "The Aid," *Kathimerini*, January 5, 1957; and "Some Memory," *Kathimerini* January 6, 1957.

36. "Without Envy," *Kathimerini*, June 10, 1955; "Why Are They So Pro-Turkish?," *Kathimerini*, September 8, 1957; and "Let's Learn from It," *Ta Nea*, October 11, 1958.

37. Speros Vryonis, *The Mechanism of Catastrophe: The Turkish Pogrom of September 6–7, 1955, and the Destruction of the Greek Community of Istanbul* (New York: Greekworks, 2005).

38. Mallinson, *Cyprus*, 26.

39. Joseph, *Cyprus: Ethnic Conflict and International Politics*, 72.

40. See "The Chamomile Tea," *Ta Nea*, September 14, 1955; "A Terrible Indifference of the Western World," *Ta Nea*, September 12, 1955; "Moral Shuttering," *Ta Nea*, September 15, 1955; and "New Orientations," *Ta Nea*, September 21, 1955.

41. "National Rally," *Avgi*, December 16, 1954.

42. "It's Time to Explain Ourselves with the Allies," *Kathimerini*, May 24, 1955; "Mr. Allen," *Apogevmatini*, September 30, 1955; "No Confusion . . . ," *Kathimerini*, December 19, 1954; "We Urge the Government and the People of the US Not to Waste Their Last Chance," *Apogevmatini*, September 21, 1955; "The Second Step," *Kathimerini*, December 17, 1954; "The Riots," *Kathimerini*, December 18, 1954; "The British-American Conspiracy Has Been Revealed after the Speech of the US Representative in the UN," *Ta Nea*, February 21, 1957; "After Yesterday's Amputation of the Cyprus Issue . . . ," *Ta Nea*, September 19, 1957; and editorial, *Avgi*, March 31, 1957.

43. "While Public Indignation Becomes More Intense, the Cabinet Re-examines the Country's Place in the World," *Ta Nea*, September 21, 1955.

44. See "Pallikarides the Patriot Will Be Hanged Tomorrow in Cyprus," *Ta Nea*, March 13, 1957; and "Harting Had Pallikarides Hanged in the Midst of Generalized Apathy of the Allies," *Ta Nea*, March 14, 1957.

45. Joseph, *Cyprus*, 19, 25–30.

46. Ibid., 74–80.

47. M. A. Ramady, "The Role of Turkey in Greek-Turkish Cypriot Communal Relations," in *Essays on the Cyprus Conflict*, ed. Van Coufoudakis (New York: Pella Publishing, 1976), 1–11.

48. Joseph, *Post-Colonial Period*, 46.

49. "A Critical Moment," *Ta Nea*, August 11, 1964. In the student demonstrations in Athens, which had an intense anti-imperialist tone, the slogan "The Turkish invaders [are] US's and Britain's puppets" became popular. See editorial, *Ta Nea*, August 11, 1965; "Light from the Holocaust," editorial, *Avgi*, August 11 and August 15, 1964; and "The Triptych of Conspiracy against Makarios," *Apogevmatini*, August 18, 1964.

50. See "The 'National-Mindedness,'"*Avgi*, August 20, 1964, and January 23, 1965.

51. For the Greek side, see "A Council of Naïveté," *Apogevmatini*, August 14, 1964; "The Trip," editorial, *Kathimerini*, June 14, 1964; "Daily News," *Kathimerini*, June 21, 1964; "Daily News," *Kathimerini*, June 28, 1964; and "The 'Bluff,'" *Kathimerini*, July 31, 1964. For discussion of the Turkish reaction, see H. W. Brands Jr., *The Wages of Globalism: Lyndon Johnson and the Limits of American Power* (New York: Oxford University Press, 1995).

52. For a discussion of the Acheson Plan, see Douglas Brinkley, *Dean Acheson: The Cold War Years, 1953–1971* (New Haven, CT: Yale University Press, 1992), 210–19.

53. *National Herald*, August 16–23, 1964.

54. Paul, *A Study in Ethnic Group Political Behaviour*, 155.

55. See *Apogevmatini*, July 2 and July 4, 1964; "The Unthinkable 'Plan,'" *Kathimerini*, July 28, 1964; "A Council of Naïveté," *Apogevmatini*, August 14 and September 7, 1964; and "US Involvement in the Cyprus Issue Provoked Deep and Negative Reactions," *Kathimerini*, June 14 and July 31, 1964.

56. See "The Negotiations between Johnson and Papandreou Came to an End," *Ta Nea*, June 26, 1964; "Americans Acted Like Turkey's Servants," *Ta Nea*, June 27, 1964; "A New Air," *Ta Nea*, June 29, 1964; *Avgi*, June 25, 1964; "The New Blackmails Failed," *Ta Nea*, July 21, 1964; and editorial, *Apogevmatini*, May 7, 1964.

57. See "At Their Convenience," editorial, *Ta Nea*, August 11, 1964, and May 21, 1965.

58. George Ball, *The Past Has Another Pattern* (New York: Norton, 1983), 349.

59. See "Cyprus Alone Faces the Enemy; America and Britain on the Side of Turkey," *Ta Nea*, August 3, 1965; and "Ankara Demands an Immediate Solution for the Cyprus Issue; with Washington's Encouragement She Toughens Her Attitude," *Ta Nea*, September 28, 1965.

60. Recent scholarship has concluded that the US government was likely not involved in the 1967 coup in Greece. Nonetheless, the Nixon administration was the regime's most ardent international supporter, which served to alienate Greek public opinion. See Louis Klarevas, "Were the Eagle and the Phoenix Birds of a Feather? The United States and the Greek Coup of 1967," *Diplomatic History* 30, no. 3 (June 2006): 471–508; and James Edward Miller, *The United States and the*

Making of Modern Greece: History and Power, 1950–1974 (Chapel Hill: University of North Carolina Press, 2009).

61. H. Ibrahim Salih, *Cyprus: Ethnic Political Counterpoints* (Lanham, MD: University Press of America, 2004), 14.

62. Christopher Hitchens, *Cyprus* (London: Quartet Books, 1984), 61–100.

63. Van Coufoudakis, "The United States and Cyprus in the Post–Cold War Era," in *Cyprus in the Modern World*, ed. Michalis S. Michael and Anastasios M. Tamis (Thessaloniki: Vanias Publishing, 2005), 335.

64. Paul, *A Study in Ethnic Group Political Behaviour*, 182–83.

65. "The New Lobby in Town: The Greeks," *Time*, July 14, 1975, 12.

66. Paul, *A Study in Ethnic Group Political Behaviour*, 259.

67. *New York Times*, August 24, 1975.

68. Paul, *A Study in Ethnic Group Political Behaviour*, 236–37.

69. Ibid., 185, 257.

70. For an example of Greek Americans preferring to be referred to as "an American lobby for law and decency," see the comments of Representative Paul Sarbanes in Bernard Gwertzman, "House Refuses Arms to Turkey, Rebuffing Ford," *New York Times*, July 25, 1975.

71. AHEPA press release, April 25, 1975; and Theodore C. Marrs Files, 1974–76, Box 63, Folder "Meeting with AHEPA Group," Gerald R. Ford Presidential Library (hereafter GRFL), Ann Arbor, MI.

72. Henry Kissinger, *Years of Renewal* (New York: Simon and Schuster, 2000), 232.

73. Myron Kuropas, special assistant to President Ford for ethnic affairs, telephone interview with author, January 26, 2010.

74. Kissinger, *Years of Renewal*, 226, 194.

75. George Christopher, "Hellenes Must Join 'Crusade' in 1976," *Hellenic Chronicle*, May 29, 1975, Myron Kuropas Files, 1976–77, Special Assistant for Ethnic Affairs, Box 3, Folder "Greek-American Ethnic Groups (File 1)," GRFL; and Eugene T. Rossides, "American Foreign Policy Regarding Cyprus and the Rule of Law," in Eugene T. Rossides and Van Coufoudakis, eds., *The United States and Cyprus: Double Standards and the Rule of Law* (Washington, DC: American Hellenic Institution Foundation, 2002).

76. *National Herald*, August 25, 1974.

77. *New York Times*, September 23, 1974.

78. The number of Greek Americans in this time period is disputed. According to the 1976 census there were 640,000 Americans of Greek descent living in the United States. However, in their lobbying efforts many Greek Americans cited the figure of 3 million and others used the figure of 1.25 million. Part of the discrepancy stems from the fact that the census figures record as Greek Americans only those who emigrated directly from Greece (someone of Greek descent who emigrated from Bulgaria, for instance, would be listed as a "Bulgarian American" by the US census despite being ethnically Greek). The figure of 1.25 million seems the most accurate to this author. By way of comparison there were approximately 50,000 Turkish Americans at this time, most of whom were recent arrivals and had not yet

become politically acculturated to the United States. The Turkish American lobby was therefore practically nonexistent.

79. Armenian Americans held bitter feelings toward Turkey as a result of the 1915–1917 Armenian Genocide perpetrated by the Ottoman Empire (of which Turkey was the successor state). Jewish Americans identified with the Armenian cause because of their own history of being victims of genocide during the Holocaust.

80. Alexander DeConde, *Ethnicity, Race, and American Foreign Policy: A History* (Boston: Northeastern University Press, 1992), 173.

81. Kofas, *Under the Eagle's Claw*, 164. Turkey also had additional sources for military supplies, especially Italy and West Germany, and Ankara was even able to continue to procure some US military equipment through NATO's Maintenance and Supply Agency.

82. Christopher, "Hellenes Must Join 'Crusade.' "

83. The initial impetus to create the White House special assistant for ethnic affairs position came from US congressmen Frank Annunzio (D-IL) and Ed Derwinski (D-IL) in recognition of the fact that while the president had special advisers for Hispanic, black, and women's affairs, there was no adviser for white ethnic Americans. During the 1968 presidential campaign, Richard Nixon promised to create the position if elected but did not keep his word upon entering the White House. It was not until after the Greek American lobbying effort of 1974–1975 that Ford's advisers suggested that he revisit Nixon's campaign promise to create the position. Myron Kuropas was selected partly as a compromise candidate, as it was determined that the position should go to neither an Italian American or Polish American (which were the two largest white ethnic groups and the respective constituencies of Congressmen Annunzio and Derwinski) nor a Greek American (which would create the impression of pandering to the Greek American lobby). Kuropas, a Ukrainian American, seemed an ideal alternative. Myron Kuropas, special assistant to President Ford for ethnic affairs, telephone interview with author, January 26, 2010.

84. See Robert P. Visser Papers, 1972–1978, Legal Counsel for the President Ford Committee, Box 11, Folder "Ford Presidency from an Ethnic Perspective," GRFL. This claim is hard to believe given Ford's short term in office, but Kuropas is adamant about its validity. Kuropas interview.

85. See, for example, letter from Nicholas Casnakides to White House Chief of Staff Richard Cheney, December 29, 1975, President Ford Committee Records, 1975–1976, Box A13, Folder "Greek," GRFL.

86. See "The Imperialism of the Starveling," *Kathimerini*, January 10, 1975; "Holding Reservations," *Kathimerini*, February 7, 1975; "US Role in the Cyprus Issue," *Apogevmatini*, August 31, 1974; "Indignation," *Apogevmatini*, February 17, 1975; "The Privilege of Extraterritoriality Should Be Abolished," *Rizospastis*, September 28, 1974; "American Cynicism," *Rizospastis*, December 12, 1974; "The Provocative Turkish Actions Are Guided," *Rizospastis*, April 10, 1975; "A Plate of Lentils," *Ta Nea*, August 8, 1974; and "No," *Ta Nea*, August 17, 1974.

87. "Peoples and Governments," *Apogevmatini*, September 14, 1974.

88. See "When History Doesn't Repeat Itself," *Ta Nea*, August 19, 1974; *Apogevmatini*, August 19, 1974; and "Kissinger Is Up to Something," *Ta Nea*, March 11, 1975.
89. "No," *Ta Nea*, September 2, 1974.
90. Greece's withdrawal was temporary. Greece returned to NATO in 1980.
91. Karamanlis quoted in Asmussen, *Cyprus at War*, 235.
92. See "American and British Intervention for the Partition of Cyprus," *Ta Nea*, January 23, 1975; "We Are Leaving NATO; New Turkish Attack," *Ta Nea*, August 14, 1974; "When History Doesn't Repeat Itself," *Ta Nea*, August 20, 1974; "The Wishful Thinking of Mr. Luns," *Kathimerini*, December 13, 1974; and "Greece and NATO," *Kathimerini*, January 29, 1975.
93. See "Greece's Place in the European Superpower; Genuine Democracy as the Ultimate Ideal," *Ta Nea*, September 27, 1974; "What May Be Revealed," *Ta Nea*, June 2, 1975; "United Europe," *Ta Nea*, June 21, 1975; and "The New Karamanlis Seeks New Support," *Apogevmatini*, October 11, 1975.
94. See "Greece and the East," *Kathimerini*, December 24, 1974; "New Policy and Its Conditions," *Kathimerini*, May 25, 1975; "The Generators of the Dictatorship," *Rizospastis*, August 2, 1975; and "The Military Alliance That Changed Its Orientation," *Apogevmatini*, August 24, 1974.
95. See "These Are Their Goals," *Kathimerini*, January 23, 1975; "With Determination and Unity," *Kathimerini*, January 24, 1975; "We Won't Give In," *Kathimerini*, January 28, 1975; "The Unholy Alliance," *Kathimerini*, February 15, 1975; "An Additional Confirmation," *Kathimerini*, May 24, 1975; "Their Plans and Us," *Kathimerini*, September 3, 1975; and "Let's Not Get Carried Away," *Kathimerini*, September 7, 1975.
96. See "The Two Murders Are an International Scheme Which Aims to Incriminate Greece," *Eleftherotypia*, October 25, 1975; "An Evil Plan Aiming to Provoke Rupture between Greece and Turkey," *Eleftherotypia*, October 27, 1975; "Cyprus Is Their Ultimate Goal," *Ta Nea*, October 27, 1975; "Both Murders Were Designed by a Dark 'Brain,'" *Ta Nea*, October 29, 1975; "Criminal Challenges," *Rizospastis*, October 26, 1975; "The Role of the CIA in Creating Tension in Greek-Turkish Relations," *Rizospastis*, October 28, 1975; and "A Third Murder; a Rupture between Greece and Turkey Has Been Designed," *Ta Nea*, October 30, 1975.
97. See "Major Provocation," *Ta Nea*, December 24, 1975; "Who Murdered Him and Why," *Apogevmatini*, December 24, 1975; "In the Ruthless War of Foreign Spies," *Apogevmatini*, December 27, 1975; "The Motives of the Murder Remain in the Dark," *Ta Nea*, December 27, 1975; "A US Embassy Consultant Has Been Murdered in Athens," *Rizospastis*, December 24, 1975; and "CIA Sacrificed Welch," *Eleftherotypia*, December 27, 1975.
98. See "The New Conspiracy," *Rizospastis*, September 11, 1977; "The Conspiracy Continues," *Rizospastis*, September 13, 1977; "NATO's Conspiracy," *Rizospastis*, September 15, 1977; "NATO's Conspiracy," *Rizospastis*, December 10, 1977; "The New US Scheme," *Rizospastis*, October 11, 1977; and "US Promoted a New Plan for the Partition of Cyprus," *Rizospastis*, November 3, 1977.
99. Announcement of Andreas Papandreou on the occasion of the national holiday of October 28, cited in *Eleftherotypia*, October 27, 1977.

100. Speech by Andreas Papandreou during the first summit of PASOK's Central Committee, September 3, 1977 (transcript in *Ta Nea*, September 4, 1977); speech by Papandreou on the island of Rhodes, August 9, 1981 (transcript in *Ta Nea*, August 10, 1981); and programmatic statements by Papandreou in the Greek Parliament, November 23, 1981 (official transcripts of the Hellenic Parliament, Library of the Hellenic Parliament, Athens).

101. See "New Gratuitous US Offer towards Turkey," *Ta Nea*, July 14, 1981; "The Cannons of the Aegean; US Strengthens the Turkish Fleet," *Ta Nea*, July 17, 1981; and "US and NATO Offer Military Equipment to Turkey," *Ta Nea*, October 6, 1981.

102. Miller, *The United States and the Making of Modern Greece*, 207.

103. Michalis Spourdalakis, *The Rise of the Greek Socialist Party* (New York: Routledge, 1988); Christos Lyrintzis, "Between Socialism and Populism: The Rise of the Panhellenic Socialist Movement" (PhD diss., London School of Economics, 1983), and "The Rise of PASOK: The Greek Election of 1981," *West European Politics* 5, no. 3 (July 1982): 308–13; Theodore C. Kariotis, *The Greek Socialist Experiment: Papandreou's Greece, 1981–1989* (New York: Pella Publishing, 1992); and Angelos Elefantis, "PASOK and the Elections of 1977: The Rise of the Populist Movement," in *Greece at the Polls: The National Elections of 1974 and 1977*, ed. Howard R. Penniman (Washington, DC: American Enterprise Institute, 1981), 105–29.

104. Yannis Voulgaris, *He Ellada tis Metapolitefisis, 1974–1990* [Postauthoritarian Greece, 1974–1990] (Athens: Themelio, 2002), 223–27.

105. See "US and NATO Are Guilty," *Rizospastis*, November 16, 1983; "The Dark Plans of Imperialism Are Revealed," *Ethnos*, November 17, 1983; "Our Mistakes and Turkey's Patrons," *Eleftherotypia*, November 19, 1983; and "A Wider Plan against Cyprus and Greece," *Rizospastis*, November 17, 1983.

106. See "US and NATO Are Guilty" *Rizospastis*, November 16, 1983; "Imperialism Strikes Again in Greece," *Ethnos*, November 16, 1983; "The Dark Plans of Imperialism Are Revealed," *Ethnos*, November 17, 1983; "The Double Operation of Fraud and Crime," *Ethnos*, November 24, 1983; and "Conspiracy against Greece of Change and against Cyprus," *Ta Nea*, November 16, 1983.

107. See "The National Soul on the 'Green Line,'" *Ethnos*, November 17, 1983; "The Ultimate Frontier of Hellenism," *Ethnos*, November 18, 1983; and "A Warning for Turkey," *Eleftherotypia*, November 25, 1983.

108. Zinovia Lialiouti, *Christos Sartzetakis*, in *H Ellada sti dekaetia tou 1980: Koinonia, Politiki, Maziki Koultoura* [Greece during the 1980s: Society, politics, and mass culture], ed. Vassilis Vamvakas and Panayis Panayotopoulos (Athens: Perasma, 2010), 534–36.

109. See "An Old Love Threatens Hellenism," *Eleftherotypia*, October 27, 1984; and "Finally an Oscar!," *Eleftherotypia*, June 22, 1985.

110. "Carrington Day," editorial, *Kathimerini*, July 27, 1984.

111. "Imperialism Strikes Again in Greece," *Ethnos*, November 16, 1983; "The Double Operation of Fraud and Crime," *Ethnos*, November 24, 1983; "The Situation Looks Very Bad; Greece Is Numb," *Apogevmatini*, November 16, 1983; and "Conspiracy against Greece of Change and against Cyprus," *Ta Nea*, November 16, 1983.

112. "Double Operation of Fraud and Crime," *Ethnos*, November 24, 1983.

113. *17 Noemvri, 1975–2002: Ola ta keimena tis organosis* ["November 17," 1975–2002: All the Brochures of the Group] (Athens: Kaktos, 2002).

114. "What Do You Have to Say Now, Mr. Reagan?," *Eleftherotypia*, June 30, 1985.

115. See "New Intense Greek Démarche to the Americans," *Eleftherotypia*, February 4, 1984; "US Budget," *Ethnos*, February 3, 1984; and "Reagan Overturns the 7:10; He Suggests a Bigger Amount of Aid for Turkey," *Apogevmatini*, February 2, 1984.

116. "On the Cancellation of the 'Zeus' Exercise," *Ethnos*, August 24, 1984.

117. The opinion poll originally appeared in the American press and was republished by the Greek newspaper *Ta Nea*, August 12, 1984.

118. See "The Bitter Task of Re-accession; Alliance with the Enemy," *Eleftherotypia*, October 10, 1980; "Severe Criticism on the Re-accession in the Parliament," *Eleftherotypia*, October 22, 1980; "You Can Forget Your Banana Republic," *Eleftherotypia*, October 4, 1980; "Greek Contribution to Peace," *Ethnos*, October 15, 1981; speech by Andreas Papandreou on the island of Rhodes, August 9, 1981 (transcript in *Ta Nea*, August 10, 1981); and press conference by Papandreou in Volos with Greek and foreign journalists, September 20, 1981 (transcript in *Ta Nea*, September 21, 1981).

119. Joseph, *Cyprus: Ethnic Conflict and International Politics*, 87–92.

120. Christopher Hitchens, *Hostage to History: Cyprus from the Ottomans to Kissinger* (London: Verso, 1997).

121. Greek Americans and their supporters, however, failed to sustain this pressure on Washington, and in August 1978 President Jimmy Carter restored arms shipments to Turkey after the embargo had failed to move Ankara on the Cyprus issue.

122. DeConde, *Ethnicity, Race, and American Foreign Policy*, 174.

References

ARCHIVES
Gerald R. Ford Presidential Library, Ann Arbor, MI

PERIODICALS
Apogevmatini
Avgi
Baltimore Sun
Ekklesia
Eleftherotypia
Ethnos
Hellenic Chronicle
Hellenic Times
Kathimerini
National Herald
New York Times

Rizospastis
Ta Nea
Washington Star

SELECTED PUBLISHED WORKS

Asmussen, Jan. *Cyprus at War: Diplomacy and Conflict during the 1974 Crisis*. London: I. B. Tauris, 2008.

Couloumbis, Theodore A. *The United States, Greece, and Turkey: The Troubled Triangle*. New York: Praeger, 1983.

Crawshaw, Nancy. *The Cyprus Revolt: An Account of the Struggle for Union with Greece*. London: George Allen and Unwin, 1978.

DeConde, Alexander. *Ethnicity, Race, and American Foreign Policy: A History*. Boston: Northeastern University Press, 1992.

Doxiadis, Kyrkos. "Ethnikofron dichasmos kai ethniki syspeirosi: I dipli ideologiki apotychia tis diktatorias" [Nationalist division and national rallying: The double ideological failure of the dictatorship]. In *He diktatoria, 1967–1974: Politikes praktikes-ideologikos logos-antistasi* [The dictatorship, 1967–1974: Political practices, ideological discourse, resistance], edited by Gianna Athanassatou, Alkis Rigos, and Serafeim Seferiades, 166–73. Athens: Hellenic Association for Political Science, Kastaniotis, 1999.

Elefantis, Angelos. "PASOK and the Elections of 1977: The Rise of the Populist Movement." In *Greece at the Polls: The National Elections of 1974 and 1977*, edited by Howard R. Penniman, 106–29. Washington, DC: American Enterprise Institute, 1981.

Fatouros, Argyris. "Pos kataskevazete ena episimo plesio dyesdissis: He Inomenes Polities stin Ellada, 1947–1948" [The construction of an official structure for penetration: The United States in Greece, 1947–1948]. In *He Ellada sti dekaetia, 1940–1950. Ena ethnos se krisi* [Greece in the 1940s–1950s: A nation in crisis], edited by Nikos Alivizatos, 419–60. Athens: Themelio, 1994.

Hackett, Clifford. "The Role of Congress and Greek-American Relations." In *Greek-American Relations: A Critical Review*, edited by Theodore A. Couloumbis and John O. Iatrides, 131–48. New York: Pella Publishing, 1980.

Hitchens, Christopher. *Cyprus*. London: Quartet Books, 1984.

———. *Hostage to History: Cyprus from the Ottomans to Kissinger*. London: Verso, 1997.

Joseph, Joseph S. *Cyprus: Ethnic Conflict and International Concern*. New York: Peter Lang, 1985.

———. *Cyprus: Ethnic Conflict and International Politics: From Independence to the Threshold of the European Union*. London: Macmillan, 1999.

———. "Post-Colonial Period, 1960–1974: Expectations and Failures." In *Cyprus in the Modern World*, edited by Michalis S. Michael and Anastasios M. Tamis, 25–56. Thessaloniki: Vanias Publishing, 2005.

Kalyvas, Stathis. "The Greek Right: Between Transition and Reform." In *The European Center-Right at the End of the Twentieth Century*, edited by F. L. Wilson, 87–116. New York: St. Martin's Press, 1998.

Kissinger, Henry. *Years of Renewal*. New York: Simon and Schuster, 2000.

Klarevas, Louis. "Were the Eagle and the Phoenix Birds of a Feather? The United States and the Greek Coup of 1967." *Diplomatic History* 30, no. 3 (June 2006): 471–508.

Kofas, Jon V. *Under the Eagle's Claw: Exceptionalism in Postwar U.S.-Greek Relations.* Westport, CT: Praeger, 2003.

Lialiouti, Zinovia. "Christos Sartzetakis." In *He Ellada sti dekaetia tou 1980: Koinonia, politiki, maziki koultoura* [Greece during the 1980s: Society, politics, and mass culture], edited by Vassilis Vamvakas and Panayis Panayotopoulos, 534–36. Athens: Perasma, 2010.

Lyrintzis, Christos. "Between Socialism and Populism: The Rise of the Panhellenic Socialist Movement." PhD diss., London School of Economics, 1983.

———. "The Rise of PASOK: The Greek Election of 1981." *West European Politics* 5, no. 3 (July 1982): 308–13.

Mallinson, William. *Cyprus: A Modern History.* London: I. B. Tauris, 2005.

Marudas, Peter N. "Greek American Involvement in Contemporary Politics." In *The Greek American Community in Transition*, edited by Harry J. Psomiades and Alice Scourby, 93–110. New York: Pella Publishing, 1982.

Michael, Michalis S., and Anastasios M. Tamis, eds. *Cyprus in the Modern World.* Thessaloniki: Vanias Publishing, 2005.

Miller, James Edward. *The United States and the Making of Modern Greece: History and Power, 1950–1974.* Chapel Hill: University of North Carolina Press, 2009.

Papadimitriou, Despina. *Apo ton lao ton nomimofronon sto ethnos ton ethnikofronon: He syntiritiki skepsi stin Ellada* [From the law-abiding people to the nation of the nationally minded: Conservative thought in Greece]. Athens: Savvalas, 2007.

Paul, John Peter. "A Study in Ethnic Group Political Behaviour: The Greek-Americans and Cyprus." PhD diss., University of Denver, 1979.

Rossides, Eugene T., and Van Coufoudakis, eds. *The United States and Cyprus: Double Standards and the Rule of Law.* Washington, DC: American Hellenic Institution Foundation, 2002.

Salih, H. Ibrahim. *Cyprus: Ethnic Political Counterpoints.* Lanham, MD: University Press of America, 2004.

Spourdalakis, Michalis. *The Rise of the Greek Socialist Party.* New York: Routledge, 1988.

———. *Stirring the Greek Nation: Political Culture, Irredentism, and Anti-Americanism.* Burlington, VT: Ashgate Publishing, 2007.

Tsoukalas, Konstantinos. "He ideologiki epidrasi tou Emfyliou polemou" [The ideological consequences of the civil war]. In *He Ellada sti dekaetia, 1940–1950: Ena ethnos se krisi* [Greece in the 1940s–1950s: A nation in crisis], edited by Nikos Alivizatos, 561–94. Athens: Themelio, 1994.

Voulgaris, Yannis. *He Ellada tis metapolitefsis, 1974–1990* [Postauthoritarian Greece, 1974–1990]. Athens: Themelio, 2002.

Yianoulopoulos, Yiannis. *O Metapolemikos kosmos: Elliniki kai evropaiki istoria (1945–1963)* [The postwar world: Greek and European history (1945–1963)]. Athens: Papazisis, 1992.

CHAPTER 10

God Bless Reagan and God Help Canada

The Polish Canadian Action Group and Solidarność in Toronto

Eric L. Payseur

"Freedom will never die in Afghanistan," "Trudeau! Condemn Martial Law and Soviets," and "Mulroney Finances Red Army" were just a few of the slogans on placards and banners at demonstrations organized by the Polish Canadian Action Group (PCAG). The PCAG was a Toronto-based group created in 1980 by naturalized Canadian citizens to support Solidarność (Solidarity) in Poland. They conducted a direct action campaign to demand support for Solidarity and to influence the Canadian government and society at large to adopt a more critical stance against Communism in Poland and the Soviet Union. Though small in number, the PCAG served an important function for the Polish Canadian community in that they exuded a greater militancy than was possible or desirable for the majority of larger, established Polish Canadian organizations.

Events in Poland in the early 1980s reinvigorated ethnic political activism in Canada, effecting a unity of purpose among those of Polish descent. Individuals and groups who were not political in nature became so, and those who were already engaged in politics became even more so. As a result, leaders of the PCAG promoted direct action and an ideologically driven strategy that veered too far right for an acceptable Canadian conservative perspective, in that it differed from the more pragmatic approach of Solidarność in Poland and the mainstream Polish Canadian organizations in Canada.

The Polish Canadian Action Group was important for the greater participation of Polish and non-Polish Canadians in the support of Solidarność and for offering a new political means of expressing this solidarity. However, outside of a few events and activities such as hunger strikes, their rigid ideology and tactics often went beyond issues related directly to Poland and prohibited the group from attracting or maintaining widespread support against the Soviet Union from Canadians of Polish descent and others.

Background

Prior to 1914, most Polish immigrants were sojourning males, and those who settled did so in the prairies. Indeed, Winnipeg was the center of Polish Canadian activities up to World War II, but between 1919 and 1931 over forty thousand Poles came to Canada, and Toronto gradually became the center of Polish Canadian activities. World War II hastened this change, as approximately five thousand Polish engineers, technicians, skilled workers, and military personnel settled in Canada between 1941 and 1947. The majority of arrivals immediately following the war were displaced persons (DPs) who brought a militant anti-Communism with them. These professionals and other postwar immigrants refreshed and renewed institutions in Montreal and Toronto and created many new organizations and services to meet their needs as exiles and political refugees. In fact, the vast majority of this fourth phase of Polish immigration (1945–1956) settled in Canada's two largest cities. A total of sixty-four thousand Polish exiles and refugees settled in Canada during these eleven years. By 1971, Toronto had the largest concentration of the Polish ethnic group in Canada, 51,180 persons, or more than 16 percent of the 316,430 total.[1]

The Polish immigrants to Canada during and after World War II were the most highly educated and skilled of all the previous waves, and most importantly, as DPs who refused to return to a Communist Poland, they brought a militant anti-Communist ideology to bear on the organizational structure of Polonia.[2] Indeed, as Anna Jaroszyńska-Kirchmann found in the US context, "the Cold War defined their generational identity as political refugees and exiles," and political activity took precedence in these exiles' mission.[3] Many of these immigrants joined existing organizations and transformed them into even greater ideological instruments, although they did not succeed in reorienting the Canadian Polish Congress (CPC) from an equal or greater focus on Canada to a greater focus on Poland and

Europe.[4] Others, like the veterans groups (Polish Combatants), formed their own associations to meet their desired level of anti-Communism and political orientation.

Polish Canadian Organizations

Even before the end of the World War II, the political lines of Polish Canadian organizations were drawn. In 1944, the Canadian Polish Congress was founded as an umbrella association to bring together the various Polish Canadian organizations (115 charter group members), the majority of which were secular. The CPC supported total independence for Poland before most Polish Combatants arrived in November 1946.[5] In contrast, the Polish Alliance of Canada was a large organization with a tradition dating back to 1907. The founders and the majority of its members had agrarian roots and little formal education. They were left of center politically, although their main focus shunned politics in favor of the preservation of Polish traditions and culture in Canada.[6] According to former CPC president Edward Sołtys: "The approach adopted by the Polish Alliance of Canada was realistic whereas the political statements of the Congress veered toward the romantic idealism of its 'indominable' [sic] adherents."[7] The "*niezłomni*," or the indomitable, were proponents of the extreme pro-Polish independence platform advocated by exile organizations like the Polish Combatants.

Even after 1956, when relations and connections with Poland relaxed a little, some groups continued to refuse recognition to the Communist government, claiming the Polish government in exile (in London, England) was the only legitimate authority.[8] The attitude toward the Polish Communist government was such that leaders of the CPC in Montreal and Toronto who had tried to organize a Christmas visit to Poland in 1961 were stopped by the CPC Executive. However, more independent and certainly less ideological member organizations, like the Polish Alliance of Canada, regularly organized trips to Poland.[9] The differences between the Alliance and Congress lay dormant for the first two decades of the post–World War II period but started to erupt in the late 1960s and early 1970s.[10] In these years, young Polish Canadians of the second generation who had come of age challenged the relevancy of such ideological divisions for Polish Canadian identity and their existence in a multicultural Canada.[11] In 1973, the Alliance left the CPC because supporters of total independence for Poland controlled the Congress; the CPC had close ties to the government in exile; and there were accusations that the Alliance had pro-Communist leanings. As Sołtys and Kogler observe: "Once the Polish Alliance of Canada was no longer a member, the Congress was free to give full support to the political undertakings of Polish immigrants."[12]

The next year, 1974, the Canadian Committee for Captive European Nations was founded in Toronto to organize collectively to protest the thirtieth anniversary of the Yalta agreement. The six groups who joined the CPC were Estonians, Latvians, Lithuanians, Hungarians, Czechoslovaks, and Ukrainians. Their main activity was to direct accurate information on the Soviet regime and its satellites to the federal and provincial governments, but in 1981 and 1982, the bulk of their work concerned support for Solidarność.[13] Also in 1974, the CPC tried to persuade the Polish American Congress (PAC) to join together and support the unifying of Polonia in the Free World. They reached an agreement and jointly declared: "Polonia has a responsibility to inform public opinion in the Free World of the situation in Poland and to expose deceits of the official propaganda of the regimes [in Poland]. It has a responsibility to defend the Polish Nation's rights to full freedom, sovereignty, and self-determination. The Polish government [in Poland] realizes the significance of the truth delivered by Polonia and has increased infiltration into Polonia in order to cause divisions, to weaken it, to control it, and to make it into its own tool."[14] These events in the 1970s foreshadowed a most incredible reinvigoration of the "exile mission" that came with Solidarność and martial law. In Canada, Prime Minister Pierre Trudeau's reaction to martial law in Poland added fuel to the political activism of Polish Canadians. In fact, the events in Poland in the early 1980s created a more unified and politicized Polish Canadian ethnic identity than post–World War II Canada had ever seen.

Polish Canadians and Canada

Immediately after the end of World War II, Polish Canadians, like other anti-Communist immigrant and ethnic groups, supported the Cold War consensus at home.[15] Polish Canadians were a model ethnic group for the Canadian government—that is, until Solidarność captured the focus of Poles (and those of Polish descent) everywhere. In *Gatekeepers*, Franca Iacovetta has shown how immigrants, "especially political émigrés," and non-Communist ethnic Canadians played a vital role in shaping the early Cold War discourse in Canada.[16] They assimilated into Canadian life rather quickly. But things started to change when Quebec nationalism rose in the late 1950s and early 1960s, along with its demand to preserve French language and culture in Quebec and Eastern Canada, and the federal government of Lester Pearson responded with the 1963 Royal Commission on Bilingualism and Biculturalism. While its purpose had been to address the French-English divide, the public hearings and briefs brought unintended consequences related to other ethnic groups. Ukrainian Canadians led the charge against a bicultural narrative of Canada's history, along with Polish Canadians and other groups eager to stress their own importance in the history and development of the country.[17] Among other factors, this advocacy helped lead to the introduction of multiculturalism as state policy in 1971. As a result, hyphenated Polish Canadian identity had become largely accepted and even celebrated. By the 1980s, however, events in Poland would change again the relationship between Polish Canadians and their hyphenated identity. The renewed Cold War rhetoric emanating from the United States, and most importantly Solidarność and Canadian reactions to it, reawakened a more militant advocacy in Polish Canadians.

The evidence from PCAG and CPC documents shows Polish Canadians still fulfilling the role of a model Canadian ethnic group in the 1980s, but the social, political, and cultural context had changed in the late Cold War. Nonetheless, Polish Canadians were able to make Solidarność and Polish political refugees central to Canadian concerns and to affect the policies of the Canadian government. Although the PCAG promoted a rigid Cold War ideology that went beyond the acceptable Canadian discourse, they were an important part of the ethnic political activism that was crucial to getting the Canadian government to respond to events in Poland, to force the Polish government to meet the demands of hunger strikers, and to mobilize support for Solidarność in Canada. The Polish government caved to the pressure from Canadian politicians and clergy to allow hunger strikers' families to join them in Canada. In the House of Commons, Canadian politicians from all political parties voted unanimously for resolutions in support of Solidarność.

The PCAG

The PCAG led this new movement, which went further in its actions than any previous anti-Communist Polish organization or group of members in an ethnic organization. Although they were members of the Canadian Polish Congress, they differed greatly in their political rigidity and strategies to achieve the same goal.[18] Because it was founded in 1980 by Polish immigrants from the previous decade and because of momentous developments in Poland, the group was most active during the early to middle 1980s. Among its main activities were demonstrations outside the Polish consulate in Toronto, including two high-profile hunger strikes for Solidarity immigrants who desired family reunification, fund-raising to support Solidarity in Poland, and an organized campaign aimed at the media and government to promote a fierce anti-Communist sentiment to reinvigorate the Canadian Cold War mentality.

In the PCAG's "Statute" of 1981, the stated aim of actions in Canada was to: "Educate politicians, opinion-leaders and the public in general regarding the true situation in Poland, and to solicit their help for our cause. By our activities we shall aim to convince Canadian society that the emergence of a free Poland is in Canada's best interest and indeed in the interest of the entire free world."[19]

They promised to work with the Canadian Polish Congress and any other member organizations of the post–World War II umbrella group who were for a free and independent Poland. Indeed, the PCAG was sometimes praised for joining protests led by other ethnic groups, such as the Czechoslovaks, and some Polish Canadians thought it refreshing to see a Polish group not myopically focused on Poland.[20] In their bulletins from late 1982, the PCAG was still advertising that it needed members who could speak excellent English and who had impeccable personal communications skills. On the PCAG letterhead, the group promoted itself as a member of the Canadian Polish Congress, but left this off the heading on its regular bulletins.[21]

The PCAG offers an interesting case for several reasons. First of all, one can see the extent to which Solidarność motivated some Polish Canadians to move beyond the activities of existing organizations in Toronto. The direct action campaign the PCAG waged in Toronto was a clear departure from the history of Polish immigrants and their organizations in Canada, with the exception of individual Polish socialist and labor activists. Their militancy extended beyond their public demonstrations to the tone of their letters to Canadian politicians and the media. Finally, and most importantly, the PCAG allows one to see the extent to which anti-Communist Polish Canadians who had immigrated since World War II and had assimilated to Canadian political culture to varying degrees reacted to the tumultuous events in Poland.

The evidence from the PCAG shows that Polish Canadians in the 1980s were still helping to shape the Cold War discourse in Canada, as they had since the end of World War II.[22] However, the relationship and role of the federal government had changed. By the 1970s, the need for an intense, top-down anti-Communist effort from the government—like the one Iacovetta writes about—had diminished, precisely because the "gatekeepers" and their ethnic allies had been so successful in the early years.[23] In addition, Canadian and Polish Canadian opinion had shifted in the intervening years. The core anti-Communism of post–World War II Polish Canadians had not disappeared, but Solidarność and events in Poland quickly reinvigorated it. The social, cultural, and political context of the late Cold War had also changed. From the start, PCAG members seemed to wear ideological blinders, as many of them thought Communism could overtake Canada. "The realities of life under Soviet-style communism should serve as a warning to all democratic countries of what could happen within their own borders should they succumb to propaganda."[24] The idea that Canada was actually threatened by Communist subversion able to overthrow its government was too far-fetched for most citizens in the 1970s and 1980s. Despite the election of right-wing politicians in Britain, the United States, and Canada during the 1980s, fewer Canadians supported an extremely militant Cold War mentality than in the 1950s. Many Polish Canadians accepted the geopolitical realities but felt greater concern about the Soviet Union after the imposition of martial law in Poland in December 1981. In this way, they were most similar to the movement in Poland, which focused on simple and reasonable reform in that country.[25] Yet there is little evidence that the degree of support in Canada would have been as pronounced without a sizable number of both militant and moderate Polish Canadians mobilizing others.

Solidarność in Toronto

Solidarność and martial law in Poland spurred a worldwide mobilization of the Polish diaspora, and Polish Canadians were leaders of the support movement.[26] The CPC and the Polish Alliance of Canada sprang into action and the new Polish Canadian Action Group was formed. The Canadian Council of Poles in the Free World, as soon as martial law was declared, "appealed to all members of the Council to intervene with their country's governments in defence of the Polish nation and Solidarity."[27] Following the declaration of martial law in Poland, 2,500 Polish Canadians and other sympathetic Canadians held a major rally in Nathan Phillips Square in downtown Toronto.[28] The demonstration culminated in a resolution in support of Solidarność that was presented to the House of Commons the following day. The leader of the opposition, Conservative Joe Clark, introduced the motion by emphasizing that "thousands of concerned Canadians, including members of all political parties," approved the resolution. Its four points read:

> We, Canadians of Polish descent, are deeply concerned about the current events in Poland, and we call upon the Canadian government as cosignatory of the Helsinki Accords to undertake the following actions:
> 1. To press for the immediate lifting of martial law in Poland and the release of all Solidarity officials.
> 2. To press for the reinstatement of the rights of workers to form free trade unions.

3. To publicly state that no intervention by third parties into the internal affairs of Poland will be tolerated.

4. To send to Poland, for distribution by non-government organizations, significant economic aid in the form of food, medical supplies and agricultural machinery and feedstuffs in order that the people of Poland survive the coming winter.

We trust that the voice of the Canadian government as international mediator will be heard and that the conflicts in Poland will be resolved in a just and lasting manner.[29]

The motion was seconded by New Democratic Party leader Ed Broadbent.[30] With Canadian politicians from all parties supporting the motion, the Liberal government minister responded that Canada had contributed "$100,000 to the Canadian Polish Congress to enable food and medicines and any other useful materials to be sent to the Polish people."[31] After martial law was declared in Poland, all political parties and the government agreed again that Canada had to react against such human rights abuse. The language and position of Prime Minister Pierre Trudeau and of his ministers were more tempered than Polish Canadians and the Progressive Conservatives desired. However, Polish Canadians did not react to this more diplomatic approach in exactly the same way. Even the usually more diplomatic CPC conveyed the urgency of the situation with a more forceful tone. As Sołtys and Kogler note: "In its normal dealings with the Canadian government, the Congress would usually send polite petitions. Now it made demands. The situation in Poland was most unusual."[32]

Indeed, the unusual situation in Poland created an unusual situation in Canada. Begun in 1981 and completed in early 1982, the Polish Alliance of Canada rejoined the CPC because they both wanted to be united to help the Polish people during this extraordinary time.[33] The president of the CPC, in reporting the acceptance of the Alliance back into the CPC, noted the urgency of working together "due to the current situation demanding unity and strength among Canadian Poles in their actions and initiatives."[34] On March 2, 1981, the minister of employment and immigration signed an Immigration Accord with the CPC; up to December 1981, the CPC sponsored 168 Polish immigrants and up to September 1982, another 521. The Polish Refugee Committee of the Polish Alliance of Canada campaigned with unions and churches of all denominations and during 1981 and 1982 sponsored six hundred individuals under a separate agreement with the federal government. An additional 550 refugees were sponsored by Catholic, Presbyterian, and United Churches in Canada.[35] "The Congress strategy was intended to elicit the greatest support for the Polish affair through [separate] meetings with trade union leaders, the Minister of Multiculturalism, and the Leader of the Opposition, Joe Clark."[36] Trade unions in Canada helped the CPC organize International Solidarity Day on January 30, 1982, and cooperation with other ethnic groups helped gather forty thousand signatures in support of Solidarność.

The PCAG frequently led protests at the Polish Consulate in Toronto; major demonstrations, excluding hunger strikes, numbered around ten and occurred largely in the early and middle 1980s.

Unsurprisingly, the declaration of martial law in Poland was a major impetus for ratcheting up the direct action campaign. Apart from the declaration of martial law in Poland, the hunger strikes in late 1983 galvanized the most support within the Polish Canadian community and Canadian society at large, because they were based not on a Cold War mentality as much as on the notion of a human right to be together with one's family. Canadians could understand and sympathize with this situation regardless of their political views or knowledge of Poland and Soviet Communism. For most Polish Canadians and especially the PCAG, the event proved the evilness of the Polish state and the need to continue to fight the Cold War; for most non-Polish Canadians, the Cold War realities were less important than reuniting these hunger strikers with their families.

Martial Law and Trudeau

The difference in strategy between mainstream Polish Canadian leaders and the PCAG came to a head over Trudeau's reaction to the declaration of martial law in Poland. During the House of Commons question period of January 25, 1981, one month after the enactment of the law, the prime minister declared: "I do not believe that in advance we can or should condemn the use of troops by any of our friends if it is to avoid a worse result."[37] After Trudeau disapprovingly sided with the Polish government, separate meetings were held with the minister of multiculturalism and then the opposition leader, Joe Clark. On January 25, 1981, Polish Canadian leaders (the CPC, Polish Alliance, Polish Canadian MP Jesse Flis, and others) met with Trudeau himself and the minister of multiculturalism. After an hour-long meeting, Trudeau made a statement in Parliament the next day that supported the main points the leaders had emphasized and corrected somewhat his ill-perceived comments on events in Poland.[38] The Canadian Labour Congress joined Polish Canadians in the massive protests, and the Communists used Trudeau's comments as proof that what they did (martial law) was right. In response to "domestic dissatisfaction as well as the increasing pressure from the U.S.," the Canadian government gradually shifted its stance.[39] Canada's initial stance on the Polish crisis was similar to West Germany's; both were dovish and seemed driven by fear of a new, reinvigorated Cold War.[40] Trudeau wrongly compared Solidarność to Canadian labor unions and used the Canadian context to interpret Polish events. His views of martial law also echoed his own response to the October 1970 crisis with the FLQ.[41]

A *Toronto Star* article mentioned that Trudeau had met with leaders of the Polish Canadian community, and "surprisingly, they were apparently satisfied with the Canadian government's attitude and actions."[42] On December 28, 1981, CPC wrote Trudeau that they were "deeply distressed" by Trudeau's comments and they "certainly do not agree with his opinion that Solidarity is responsible for this crisis by voicing 'excessive demands on the Polish communist regime.'"[43] Even the president of the Canadian Polish Congress had expressed his regret that the prime minister was not using "stronger language because this is the only thing that they [the Polish government] understand," but his tone was different from previous CPC letters to government officials prior to Solidarność and from the tone of PCAG letters.[44] The CPC leaders showed deference to Trudeau while presenting the Polish Canadian view, while the PCAG decided to ratchet up the demonstrations and campaign.[45] Both groups had the same goal and the help of two Liberal Polish Canadians on Parliament Hill (Jesse Flis in the House of Commons and Stanley Haidasz in the Senate), but the PCAG believed a direct action campaign and a more militant anti-Soviet position was the best means to achieving the defeat of Communism in Poland.

One prominent example of this strategy and the PCAG's more demanding tone was a letter requesting further action from their most fervent ally, US president Ronald Reagan. On July 30, 1981, *Słowo* reprinted an open letter from the Friday, July 10, 1981, *New York Times* to Reagan which thanked the president for his public pronouncements on "Poland's God-given right to determine her own destiny, without foreign interference," and urged stronger statements on the Polish people's behalf.[46] The signatures were mainly from US organizations and prominent individuals but included the PCAG and the Polish Combatants Association from Ontario; neither the Polish Canadian Congress nor the Polish American Congress signed the letter.

PCAG's Campaign

Officially, the PCAG wrote to politicians of all the major parties (Progressive Conservatives, Liberals, and New Democrats), not only to those of ridings (electoral districts) with substantial Polish constituencies. Behind the scenes, however, they disdained Trudeau and most Liberals, as well as the NDP. They found their most sympathetic ear with the Conservatives. The PCAG showed their greatest admiration for politicians who were further to the right than Canada's Conservatives, namely Ronald Reagan and Margaret Thatcher. The group penned a letter to the American president in early 1982 that heaped on paragraph after paragraph of praise for his hard-line foreign policy and attitude toward the Soviet Union. The letter closed: "Thank you, Mr. President, thank you America."[47]

The PCAG believed that the NDP, as Canada's democratic socialist party, was necessarily too close to the wrong side in the Cold War, and that they did not view Solidarność with the appropriate hard-line, anti-Communist lens. The most prominent example of the PCAG view came in October 1982 from PCAG president Lech Prusinski, who wrote to one of the several Tory MPs he knew on a first-name basis: "That party's performance on the Polish issue is little short of scandalous. We have been unable to find in Hansard any substantive statements made by Pauline Jewett [foreign affairs critic for the New Democratic Party during the 1980s]. It behooves the P.C.'s to point out the N.D.P.'s hypocracy [*sic*] as well as the Liberal Government's timidity."[48] The NDP, like the Liberal government, disagreed with the strategy and ideology of the PCAG, and preferred to frame the Polish crisis in rhetoric that they thought would not reignite the Cold War.

Earlier, in June 1982, the PCAG and CPC had collected forty thousand signatures for a petition to the House of Commons: to condemn martial law and call for its end, to release Lech Wałęsa from prison, and to recognize Solidarność. Polish Canadians' trusted Liberal MP, Jesse Flis, submitted the petition to the House of Commons and thanked the PCAG "for keeping Canadians informed of the wishes of the people in Poland."[49] Flis was a second-generation Polish Canadian and a member of the Polish Alliance of Canada, an organization that differed with the Canadian Polish Congress in that it focused more on the integration and assimilation of Polish immigrants to Canada but worked to preserve Polish language and culture.[50] Yet during the months of martial law and the Solidarity era in general, events in Poland took precedence. As a result, political tensions between the Polish ethnic groups in Canada diminished.

The PCAG supported Flis because of his concern for events in Poland and his position in and ability to influence the Liberal government. Yet Flis was not completely immune to criticism. The PCAG leaders asked him to present the petition, with careful instructions on how to speak to the House of Commons with maximum effect. Later, PCAG president Prusinski and secretary Andrew Piekarski would question, and even chide him, over the manner in which he presented the document. Piekarski remarked: "In fact, according to *Hansard*, you presented it on your own initiative, with no reference to the Committee and no publicity. The impact seems to be minimal. It may be that there has been some misunderstanding in all this. We would appreciate your opinion on what happened, how such misunderstanding (if there was one) can be avoided in the future, and how we can still use that petition to better effect."[51] The measure was passed unanimously. However, Flis reminded the PCAG that "we have no control over the media as to what they report and do not report."[52] Despite these tensions, in the end, Flis had played an important role by speaking on behalf of Polish Canadians in the House of Commons. Indeed, years later, in a documentary on the hunger strike, Flis would take partial credit for convincing Trudeau and his minister of immigration, Lloyd Axworthy, to allow Polish refugees from martial law to stay in Canada.[53]

The PCAG tried to pressure right-wing politicians and both the left- and right-leaning media in Canada beyond their usual positions to adopt what was essentially a right-wing Polish Canadian perspective. The Conservatives, as the official opposition, were most sympathetic to this perspective. For example, Conservative MP John Crosbie agreed completely with the PCAG's views on Poland and the Cold War sent to him and confessed his disagreement "with the attitudes expressed by Mr. Trudeau which can do nothing but give aid and comfort to the present Polish government."[54] While the PCAG found ideological sympathy with right-wing Canadian politicians, the MPs' general concern for Canada's best interest took precedence over their sympathies for a small group of right-wing Polish Canadians.

The PCAG's views on the Cold War did not fit the dominant view in Canadian society, and especially those held by fellow Torontonians. In a 1982 civic election, for instance, 78.8 percent of Toronto voters endorsed a call for efforts toward multilateral nuclear disarmament.[55] Yet the PCAG joined and supported smaller groups that opposed the Canadian peace movement. Many of them worked for, marched with, and promoted organizations like the Canadian Coalition for Peace through Strength. Both the Canadian Coalition for Peace through Strength and the Polish Canadian Action Group supported the testing of cruise missiles in Canada at the same time that nuclear disarmament became a central issue on the Canadian Left.

On February 20, 1983, more than a year after the resolution on martial law in the House of Commons, the PCAG invited Toronto MPs of the three federal parties to debate their parties' position on the current situation in Poland. The event confirmed the PCAG's views of the parties and the way the group used rhetoric in support of Solidarność or anti-Sovietism. In fact, the PCAG did not live up to some of their own public statements, except as they applied to Poland or the Soviet Union. In a subsequent letter to the NDP participant, Prusinski supposedly summarized the reaction he solicited from those in attendance, and after praising the MP's professionalism, took issue with his stance. "Your comment on supporting freedom everywhere, not just Poland, caused some problems. When support is spread that widely, it is spread thinly. Should it not be concentrated in area's [*sic*] where it is most needed? Right-wing dictatorships are often unspeakably brutal, but they have no 'staying power' as they lack ideology and infrastructure, and they tend not to spread. Communist regimes on the other hand, once in, stay in."[56] A PCAG circular printed in English a few months later seemed to contradict this hard-line stance. In a preamble to nine resolutions they thought the Canadian government should adopt, the PCAG noted that "the Free World should not stand idly by. So long as it ignores the plight of peoples enslaved by any political system anywhere in the world, and so long as it aids the very regimes responsible for their enslavement, its own freedom is bereft of moral value, and ultimately cannot be secure."[57] Most likely, the PCAG was carefully framing their concerns in terms more appealing to Canadians.

One event that captured the attention of Canadians, and the one most associated with the Polish Canadian Action Group, was the hunger strike of ten Polish Solidarity immigrants that began on November 7, 1983. Ten hungry men, the subject of the 2005 Omni TV film of the same name, camped out in front of the Polish consulate in Toronto.[58] The hunger strike lasted for nineteen days, and during these weeks, thousands of Canadians of all ethnicities marched in support of the strikers.[59] The drama of this hunger strike and a subsequent one were covered in the *Toronto Star* and other newspapers, often on the front page. There one could read about MP Jesse Flis crediting Canadians of all backgrounds for the victory against the Polish Communist government's emigration rules: "Thanks to the help of Canadians, not only of Polish descent, but Canadians of all heritages."[60] The PCAG organizational efforts around the hunger strike, along with the support of Flis and thousands of other Canadians, assured that the Canadian government would pressure the Polish government to permit the hunger strikers' families to come to Canada.

As the 1980s continued, the PCAG continued their media and political campaigns, but the international events in the middle of the decade were not as salient for other Polish Canadians (or non-Polish Canadians) as those in the early part of the decade. Yet the lack of widespread support did not deter the PCAG. One event that attracted a fair amount of their attention was a Peace Conference at the University of Toronto in 1984. A small group of PCAG members and supporters went to pass out leaflets and protest a panel discussion sponsored by the Toronto Association for Peace at which ex-premier Jozef Cyrankiewicz; Professor Yevgeny Primakov, president of the Soviet Peace Congress; and Lt. Col. Wiesław Gornicki, adviser to General Wojciech Jaruzelski were scheduled to speak. The PCAG activists were asked to leave, along with a Polish journalist sent to open Solidarity offices in North America. He worked for the *Toronto Sun* and was apparently accosted before being forced out of the meeting by security. The PCAG had taken issue with the speakers, who they felt should not be allowed to promote their lies. Dismissed from the event before it began, the PCAG members and supporters, including a University of Toronto professor, wrote to the university president to complain. The most revealing letter they wrote after this event was one directed to the Canadian Security Intelligence Service (CSIS). After describing the altercations, the PCAG noted that "it was shocking to witness those KGB type tactics and realize that Soviet infiltration and subversive activities were operating on a Canadian campus." They then asked why these individuals were admitted to Canada, when apparently they were denied visas to the United States, and ended with an offer of assistance to CSIS in this matter or any other.[61]

Other PCAG letters provide even greater evidence of their members' ideology in the mid-1980s and showed the demarcation line between a right-wing Canadian conservative position and a right-wing American conservative one. When the Canadian government declined the invitation to join Reagan's Star Wars initiative, the PCAG wrote to their usual list of conservative MPs, now in power, about their displeasure.[62] The responses the PCAG received criticized the pro-SDI (Strategic Defense Initiative) position as against Canadian public opinion. In their answers, politicians highlighted the differences between their country and the United States. One of them wrote: "After careful and detailed consideration, the Government of Canada concluded that our nation's own policies and priorities do not warrant a government-to-government effort in support of SDI research. . . . I wish to reassure you that Canada's foreign policy will always be conducted in the best interest of this nation and with the firm commitment to our national integrity."[63] Other MPs insisted that the government was involved with Canadian priorities, and they delineated a position clearly distinct from right-wing Polish Canadians and the US government.[64]

The following year, in 1986, the PCAG asked the Canadian media to cover the story of Adam Winkler, a Polish citizen who had spent two years fighting in Afghanistan against the Soviets. They organized a press interview with Winkler, and when the mainstream Canadian media did not show, the PCAG wrote letters criticizing them. In a letter to the *Globe and Mail*, the PCAG couched their criticism in terms of morality and responsibility.[65] In their answers, the Canadian media—even the more right-wing *Toronto Sun*—took Prusinski and the PCAG to task over its claim that the Afghanistan war was the largest conflict in the world at the time. Downing of the *Toronto Sun* wrote:

> I would suspect that no other newspaper in Ontario, indeed in
> Canada, has written more about what is happening in Afghanistan
> even though it is not as you say "the biggest armed conflict taking
> place in the world today." How you can overlook the Iran-Iraq war is
> beyond me. It is obvious from your letter that you are not aware of the
> coverage that the Toronto Sun has given Afghanistan over the years. If
> you had you would not have presumed to lecture us on the subject.[66]

The *Toronto Star* city editor similarly chastised Prusinski: "It is not [the
editor's] job to make moral judgments to influence public opinion."[67] Prusinski
and the PCAG did not let these responses end the exchange. Prusinski continued to hammer away at the media for their lack of coverage of Afghanistan,
even in one instance reprimanding an editor for the tone of his reply.[68] One
might be tempted to dismiss this conflict with the media as Prusinski's alone.
However, evidence in the PCAG's documents point to a tight organizational
structure with subcommittees for various tasks such as media campaigns, and
there is no evidence of disagreement from other executive members.

Conclusion

The PCAG's documents reveal that their attempts to raise awareness of
Solidarność were part of the promotion of a much more stringent Cold War
mentality, very rarely diluted. Their strategy was driven by a more militant
right-wing ideology than that of the other leaders of the Polish Canadian
community. Immediately after martial law was declared in Poland, in 1981,
and throughout the early 1980s, the PCAG's direct action campaign fit well
with other Polish Canadian efforts to make the plight of Polish people important to Canadians. The PCAG efforts in these years were directly related to
events happening in Poland, and the activities for Solidarność and martial
law immigrants were such that all Polish and most Canadians could support. Later, however, petitions against the Soviet war in Afghanistan and
other non-Polish activities did not draw the wide support seen in the early-
1980s demonstrations and hunger strikes. Although the group maintained
its media campaign and contacts with Canadian politicians for several years
after the fall of Communism, the PCAG's activities seemed to wane beginning in 1985.

The most successful events, which garnered the most attention from the
Canadian public, were the initial martial law demonstration and the hunger
strikes to reunite Solidarity immigrants with their families. Canadians of

all political stripes unanimously supported multiple House resolutions condemning martial law, calling on the Polish government to allow Solidarność, and showing Canadian displeasure at the events in Poland. The PCAG did help to bring this about. They organized events and engaged in activities that attracted the support of politicians, Polish Canadians, and many other Canadians. Of course, the hunger strikers, who merely wanted the Polish government to allow their families to come to Canada, generated a wealth of sympathy from all across the country. Yet in the complete history of the organization, these events were the exceptions, in that they attracted widespread support among both Polish Canadians and non-Polish Canadians. Outside of raising money for Solidarność in Poland, the PCAG activities from the middle of the 1980s did not elicit the same support, even among Polish Canadians.

Unlike the leadership of larger, older organizations, the leadership of the PCAG comprised Polish Canadians who had come to Canada in the 1960s or 1970s, at least for those individuals who are easily traceable. The evidence here suggests that whether one immigrated prior to World War II, immediately after as a displaced person, or from Communist Poland had a noticeable effect on how one reacted to Polish developments in the 1980s. Most of the leaders of the PCAG had been Canadian citizens for at least a decade before Solidarity. They appeared well integrated and they knew how to try to influence Canadian media and politicians.

As a small, more independent group, the PCAG could take a more militant stance and tone than could the CPC, because the latter had to balance competing interests among its member organizations and to maintain its crucial links to Canadian government officials. The CPC could ill afford to alienate its friends in government and other sectors of Canadian society that were vital to achieving its objectives. When the Polish Canadian Action Group focused on issues directly relating to Poland or Polish Canadians, they received widespread support and their efforts, despite differences in strategy, complemented those of the Canadian Polish Congress. However, by the middle of the 1980s, PCAG's activities became more about a rigid anti-Sovietism and events taking place elsewhere in the European Cold War world than solely about Poland, and as a result, support for the group waned.

Thus, the PCAG does not fit neatly into the two main cohorts that Mary Erdmans found among Polish residents of Chicago: "ethnics" and "newcomers."[69] The PCAG was located in the difficult to define space between immigrants and ethnics, and the generalities about immigrants and ethnics and politics and culture Erdmans observed in Chicago were not quite as sharply drawn in Toronto.[70] There was a bit of a complementary relationship between ethnics and immigrants, but the PCAG were ethnics and not newcomers, so they had more in common with the older cohorts.[71] The CPC had more established and better connections in Canada and were more adept at using them effectively, at least initially during the Polish crisis. The PCAG were closer to being new immigrants than were the leaders of the CPC, but they were still ethnics who had been in Canada about a decade. The lines between an immigrant defining Polishness in political terms and an ethnic maintaining Polishness as a cultural identity were further blurred when the monumental events of Solidarność happened in the homeland.

Of the first hunger strikers, the majority were post–martial law immigrants who, by the time of the strike, were landed Canadian residents. However, the PCAG documents do not reveal that any of them became highly involved in the PCAG. In fact, the PCAG and the *Toronto Sun* highlighted the fact that nine of the first hunger strikers visited the three currently demonstrating in a special show of solidarity.[72] If, indeed, there were not many Solidarity immigrants in the rank and file, then the political identity the PCAG carved out for itself was a unique aspect of Polish Canadian ethnic identity formation. In other words, this is an instance of newer and older immigrants showing major similarities in identifying with, and being politically active for, Poland but differing in the means they used to achieve their common goals. As Erdmans suggests: "Struggles in the homeland triggered collective action in Polonia, and this action energized and reinforced ethnic identity."[73] Indeed, events in Poland effected a new approach to promoting Polish issues in Canada with the creation and success of the PCAG. Polish Canadians were mobilized by events in Poland in the early 1980s, and they made certain that Canadian politicians and the Polish government were affected by events in Canada.

In this way, Polish Canadians were similar to other ethnic groups, such as the Ukrainians, who since the 1960s and the rise of multiculturalism have increasingly "brought new political questions to the fore."[74] For example, in the 1980s, Jewish Canadians lobbied on both sides of the issue in the summer of 1982 when Israel invaded Lebanon, Pakistani Canadian groups protested and welcomed President Zia ul-Haq in the same year, and some Japanese Canadian groups were successful in attaining an apology and reparations from the Canadian government for the unjust internment of Japanese Canadians during World War II.[75] Such cases have been quite divisive issues for the ethnic group or groups involved.[76] However, Polish Canadians during the early 1980s, despite differing on strategy, were comparatively more unified in their goals. Such was the powerful effect of Solidarność on Canadian Polonia.

In the end, for many people of Polish descent in Toronto, Solidarność effected a new attitude toward Poland and how their country should help it. To borrow Pawel Boski's term, the movement became a salient "symbol of cultural relevance" for Polish Canadians.[77] However, because of the momentous events in Poland, an increase in cultural sentiment quickly gave way to political activism. This activism proved its relevancy in the early 1980s, as Canadian rhetoric and policy around martial law and political refugees changed. Yet, despite these successes, the most fervent advocate for Solidarność in Canada had an agenda closer to a right-wing US position, as well as a strategy and Cold War rigidity, that went beyond what was acceptable for the majority of Polish Canadians, and certainly the majority of other Canadians.

Notes

1. Henry Radecki, *Ethnic Organizational Dynamics* (Waterloo, ON: Wilfred Laurier University Press, 1979), 37.
2. Victor Turek, *Poles in Manitoba* (Toronto: Polish Alliance Press, 1967), 44–48. "Polonia" is the term used to refer to those of Polish descent living outside Poland.
3. Anna D. Jaroszyńska-Kirchmann, *The Exile Mission: The Polish Political Diaspora and Polish Americans, 1939–1956* (Athens: Ohio University Press, 2004), 222.
4. Radecki, *Ethnic*, 82. See also *www.multiculturalcanada.ca/Encyclopedia/A-Z/p6/5*. To be clear, there was a significant lag time before members of the exile cohort could rise to positions of power. As an umbrella organization, the CPC had to at least give the appearance of balancing the demands and agendas of all its member organizations if it wanted to be the lobby for all of Polonia, as it claimed to be.
5. Edward Sołtys and Rudolf Kogler, eds., *Half a Century of Canadian Polish Congress* (Toronto: Canadian Polish Research Institute, 1996), 44.
6. Ibid., 59–60, and Polish Alliance of Canada, "Pionierska Droga: Związku Polaków w Kanadzie, Przyczynek do Dziejów Organizacji Polonijnej" [The pioneer path: The organizational activities of the Polish Alliance of Canada] (Toronto: Polish Alliance Press, 1973), 23.
7. Sołtys and Kogler, eds., *Half a Century of Canadian Polish Congress*, 4–14.
8. Alexander J. Matejko, "The Double Identity of Polish Canadians," in *Two Nations, Many Cultures: Ethnic Groups in Canada*, 2nd ed., ed. Jean Leonard Elliott (Scarborough, ON: Prentice-Hall Canada, 1983), 368.
9. Sołtys and Kogler, *Half a Century*, 59.
10. Ibid., 64–65.
11. Eric L. Payseur, "*Echo*-ing the Spirit of the Times: A Polish-Canadian Youth Experiment in the 1970s," *Canadian Ethnic Studies* 39, no. 3 (2007): 153–56, 159.
12. Sołtys and Kogler, *Half a Century*, 65.
13. *Kongres Polonii Kanadyjskiej* [Canadian Polish Congress]: *Report of the Twenty-Seventh Convention of the Canadian Polish Congress*, Winnipeg, Manitoba, November 12–14, 1982, 24, Clara Thomas Archives and Special Collections, York University Library, CPC 1982 0010.
14. Jaroszyńska-Kirchmann, *The Exile Mission*, 233.
15. The Cold War consensus in Canada put Canada clearly on the side of capitalism, led

by the United States. In addition, "any perceived political and other threats to the body politic at home" were contained or removed. By the 1950s, the consensus was firmly entrenched in Canadian society, with the result that "all forms of criticism and nonconformist behaviour" were viewed as "attacks on democratic decency." Franca Iacovetta, *Gatekeepers: Reshaping Immigrant Lives in Cold War Canada* (Toronto: Between the Lines, 2006), 15, 18.

16. Ibid., 100, 134.

17. Kenneth McRoberts, *Misconceiving Canada: The Struggle for National Unity* (Toronto: Oxford University Press, 1997), 122–24.

18. Sołtys and Kogler, *Half a Century*, 71–72.

19. "Statut Grupy Solidarność i Niepodległość" [Statutes of PCAG], Toronto, March 1981, *PCAG Polish Canadian Action Group Grupa Solidarność i Niepodległość, 1980– 1994: Raport z projektu dokumentacji dzialalnosci grupy* (hereafter *PCAG*), Toronto, October 26, 1994.

20. *Biuletyn Informacijny Grupa Solidarność i Niepodległość* [Information bulletin of the Polish Canadian Action Group], nr. 11, September 1981, 3, Thomas Fisher Rare Books Library, University of Toronto (hereafter TFRBL).

21. *Biuletyn Informacijny Grupa Solidarność i Niepodległość*, nr. 1, August 1982, 1. TFRBL.

22. Iacovetta, *Gatekeepers*, 100, 134.

23. Iacovetta defines the "gatekeepers" as all the organizations and institutions (and the individuals working for them) that encountered, received, and regulated immigrants, attempting to socialize the newcomers to Canada. See Iacovetta, *Gatekeepers*, xii.

24. Marek Celinski and Adam Kossowski to Editor of the *Globe and Mail*, April 16, 1981, *PCAG*, October 26, 1994. The similarity of this comment to the earlier joint statement from the CPC and the Polish American Congress in 1974 shows the ideological similarities between cohorts active in different decades. See Iacovetta, *Gatekeepers*, xii, and Jaroszyńska-Kirchmann, *The Exile Mission*, 233.

25. Harald von Riekhoff, "The Desirability of a Graduated Increase of International Pressure," in *Canada's Response to the Polish Crisis*, ed. Adam Bromke, Harald von Riekhoff, Jacques Levesque, and J. R. Federowicz (Toronto: Canadian Institute of International Affairs, 1982), 20–21. The New Democratic Party, the party left of the centrist Liberal Party, and the Canadian Labour Congress framed support for Solidarność as support for free trade unions.

26. During the early 1980s, *Słowo*, a Polish Canadian weekly, reprinted the entire Solidarność newspaper from Poland. This was most often printed as a stand-alone issue but occasionally was inserted into the two or four pages of *Słowo*'s print run. Even in these instances, the news from Canada or Polonia was almost always about Solidarność. In surveying thousands of pages from Polish Canadian serials from the 1950s to the 1980s, the mostly mundane content gave way to an almost singular focus on events in Poland at key moments, the most prominent (before the collapse of Communism) of which were Solidarność and martial law.

27. *Kongres Polonii Kanadyjskiej*, 66.

28. Susan Pigg, "Silent Prayer Marks Vigil in Toronto," *Toronto Star*, December 17, 1981.

29. Debates, House of Commons Canada, 1st Session, 32nd Parliament, Vol. 13, 14151.

30. The New Democratic Party was Left of the governing Liberal (centrist) party and to the Far Left of the Conservatives.

31. Debates, House of Commons Canada, 1st Session, 32nd Parliament, Vol. 13, 14152.

32. Sołtys and Kogler, *Half a Century*, 70.

33. Ibid., 73.

34. *Kongres Polonii Kanadyjskiej*, 59.

35. Ibid., 11–13.

36. Ibid., 18.

37. Andrew Szende, "Crisis in Poland Just Like Ulster, Trudeau Declares," *Toronto Star*, January 26, 1982. Trudeau's comments must be seen in the context of his own political reference points: in this case, the October Crisis of 1970 when a Quebec nationalist fringe group, the Front de liberation du Québec (FLQ), kidnapped two high-profile individuals and Trudeau responded by invoking the War Measures Act for the first time during peacetime. Trudeau had declared martial law himself and arrested more than five hundred people merely on suspicion. See *www.cbc.ca/news/indepth/october/*.

38. Sołtys and Kogler, *Half a Century*, 70.

39. Adam Bromke, "Distant Friends: The Evolution of the Canada-Poland Relationship," in Bromke et al., *Canada's Response to the Polish Crisis* (Toronto: Canadian Institute of International Affairs, 1982), 11.

40. Riekhoff, "Desirability," 18.

41. Ibid., 19. For a discussion on why Trudeau's statements did not make sense to those knowledgeable about Poland and Solidarność, see pages 20–21. Also, the early 1970s in Canada saw many major public-service strikes, unions who were highly critical of the Liberal government, and three major union leaders were arrested and imprisoned in 1973. R. Douglas Francis, Richard Jones, and Donald Smith, eds., *Journeys: A History of Canada* (Toronto: Thomas Nelson, 2006), 513.

42. "Polish-Canadian Leaders content with PM's Stand," *Toronto Star*, January 26, 1982, A16.

43. Riekhoff, "Desirability," 18–19.

44. Ibid.

45. Of course, not all Liberal MPs agreed with Trudeau's reaction to martial law in Poland, and the PCAG took note of instances when this was apparent. "Burghardt Counters Trudeau's Position," newspaper clipping, *London Free Press* [London, ON], February 1, 1982, *PCAG*.

46. *Biuletyn Informacyjny Grupa Solidarność i Niepodległość*, nr. 8, lipca 1982, 3, TFRBL.

47. Letter from PCAG to President Reagan, January 16, 1982, "Kontakty z Politykami Kanadyjskim" [Contacts with Canadian politicians], *PCAG*, 26 Wrzesnia 1994, Robarts Library, University of Toronto (hereafter cited as Kontakty). The PCAG were not the only Polish Canadians writing admiring letters to Reagan. Following the assassination attempt on the US president, the CPC president and the president of Polonia in the Free World expressed the "deepest indignation and shock felt by all of us" and prayed "to God Almighty for your speedy recovery, personally and as

leader of the free world during these difficult times." *Kongres Polonii Kanadyjskiej* [Canadian Polish Congress], 67.

48. Letter to Michael Wilson, M.P., October 12, 1982, Kontakty. *Hansard* is the official record of the House of Commons.

49. Jesse Flis to Les Prusinski, June 16, 1982, Kontakty.

50. Frank Glogowski, "The Importance of the Polish Alliance of Canada to the Canadian Polonia," in *A Community in Transition: The Polish Group in Canada*, ed. Benedykt Heydenkorn (Toronto: Canadian Polish Research Institute, 1985), 111–18.

51. Andrew Piekarski to Jesse Flis, September 14, 1982, Kontakty.

52. Jesse Flis to Andrew Piekarski, November 16, 1982, Kontakty.

53. *Ten Hungry Men*, dir. Richard Pawlowski, Omni TV, 2005, *www2.omnitv.ca/ programming/*.

54. John Crosbie to Les Prusinski, January 22, 1982, Kontakty.

55. *The Peace Calendar* 2 (11), December 1984, *www.peacemagazine.org/*.

56. Les Prusinski to Ian Deans, April 7, 1983, Kontakty.

57. "Poland: What Should Canada Do?," June 1983, in *"Sprawy Organizacyjne"* [Organizational issues], Kontakty.

58. *Ten Hungry Men*.

59. Ibid.

60. Laurie Monsebraaten and Paul Todd, "Polish Hunger Strikers Triumph," *Toronto Star*, June 30, 1984.

61. Les Prusinski to Director General, CSIS, December 17, 1984, "Demonstracja w University of Toronto" [Demonstration at the University of Toronto], Kontakty.

62. Andrew Piekarski to Michael Wilson, Dan Blenkarn, Patrick Boyer, and Andrew Witter, November 8, 1985, Kontakty.

63. Patrick Boyer to Andrew Piekarski, March 12, 1986, Kontakty.

64. Michael Wilson to Andrew Piekarski, December 13, 1985; and Patrick Boyer to Andrew Peikarski, March 12, 1986, Kontakty.

65. Les Prusinski to Editor, *Globe and Mail*, June 8, 1986, "Media Kanadyjskie," PCAG.

66. John Downing, Editor, to Les Prusinski, June 19, 1986, ibid.

67. Rod Goodman to Les Prusinski, June 30, 1986, ibid.

68. Les Prusinski to Jesperson, July 13, 1986, and Les Prusinski to Rod Goodman, July 13, 1986, ibid.

69. Mary Patrice Erdmans, *Opposite Poles: Immigrants and Ethnics in Polish Chicago, 1976–1990* (University Park: Pennsylvania State University Press, 1998), 7–8, 11. According to Erdmans: "A cohort is a group of people who experience similar events in similar social settings at similar points in their life cycles" (7). I find it more useful in the Canadian case to speak of five major immigrant cohorts who arrived in Canada: pre–World War II, during and immediately after as DPs, between 1956 and 1981, during martial law in Poland, and after martial law was lifted.

70. Ibid., 222.

71. Ibid., 157.

72. *Toronto Sun*, May 23, 1984, "Glodowka Druga" [Hunger strikes], Kontakty.

73. Erdmans, *Opposite Poles*, 215.

74. Francis, Jones, and Smith, *Journeys*, 566.

75. Elizabeth Riddell-Dixon, *The Domestic Mosaic: Domestic Groups and Canadian Foreign Policy* (Toronto: Canadian Institute of International Affairs, 1985), 3.
76. *www.multiculturalcanada.ca/Encyclopedia/A-Z/j3/10* and *-/A-Z/j2/10*. See also Harold Troper and Morton Weinfeld, *Old Wounds: Jews, Ukrainians, and the Hunt for Nazi War Criminals in Canada* (Chapel Hill: University of North Carolina Press, 1989).
77. Pawel Boski, "Remaining a Pole or Becoming a Canadian: National Self-Identity among Polish Immigrants to Canada," *Journal of Applied Social Psychology* 21, no. 1 (1991): 41–77.

References

ARCHIVES

Clara Thomas Archives and Special Collections, York University Library, Toronto, Ontario, Canada

Polish Canadian Action Group Archives, Robarts Library, University of Toronto, Ontario, Canada

Thomas Fisher Rare Book Library, University of Toronto, Ontario, Canada

PERIODICALS

Toronto Star
Peace Calendar

PUBLISHED GOVERNMENT DOCUMENTS, REPORTS, AND SERIALS

Debates, House of Commons of Canada, 1st Session, 32nd Parliament, Vol. 13.

SELECTED PUBLISHED WORKS

Biuletyn Informacijny Grupa Solidarność i Niepodległość [Information bulletin of the Polish Canadian Action Group], September 1981–August 1982. Thomas Fisher Rare Book Library, University of Toronto.

Boski, Pawel. "Remaining a Pole or Becoming a Canadian: National Self-Identity among Polish Immigrants to Canada." *Journal of Applied Social Psychology* 21, no. 1 (1991): 41–77.

Bromke, Adam. "Distant Friends: The Evolution of the Canada-Poland Relationship." In *Canada's Response to the Polish Crisis*, edited by Adam Bromke, Harald von Riekhoff, Jacques Levesque, and J. R. Federowicz, 3–14. Toronto: Canadian Institute of International Affairs, 1982.

Erdmans, Mary Patrice. *Opposite Poles: Immigrants and Ethnics in Polish Chicago, 1976–1990.* Harrisburg: Pennsylvania State University Press, 1998.

Francis, R. Douglas, Richard Jones, and Donald Smith, eds. *Journeys: A History of Canada.* Toronto: Thomas Nelson, 2006.

Glogowski, Frank. "The Importance of the Polish Alliance of Canada to the Canadian

Polonia." In *A Community in Transition: The Polish Group in Canada*, edited by Benedykt Heydenkorn, 97–100. Toronto: Canadian Polish Research Institute, 1985.

Iacovetta, Franca. *Gatekeepers: Reshaping Immigrant Lives in Cold War Canada.* Toronto: Between the Lines, 2006.

Jaroszyńska-Kirchmann, Anna D. *The Exile Mission: The Polish Political Diaspora and Polish Americans, 1939–1956.* Athens: Ohio University Press, 2004.

Kongres Polonii Kanadyjskiej: Report for the Twenty-Seventh Convention of the Canadian Polish Congress, Winnipeg, Manitoba, November 12–14, 1982. Clara Thomas Archives and Special Collections, York University Library, CPC 1982 0010.

Matejko, Alexander J. "The Double Identity of Polish Canadians." In *Two Nations, Many Cultures: Ethnic Groups in Canada*, 2nd ed., edited by Jean Leonard Elliott, 363–82. Scarborough, ON: Prentice-Hall Canada, 1983.

McRoberts, Kenneth. *Misconceiving Canada: The Struggle for National Unity.* Toronto: Oxford University Press, 1997.

Pawlowski, Richard. *Ten Hungry Men.* Omni TV, Toronto, 2005.

Payseur, Eric L. "*Echo*-ing the Spirit of the Times: A Polish-Canadian Youth Experiment in the 1970s." *Canadian Ethnic Studies* 39, no. 3 (2007): 151–72.

PCAG Polish Canadian Action Group Grupa Solidarność i Niepodległość, 1980–1994: Raport z projektu dokumentacji dzialalnosci grupy [Documentary report of the group's activities], Toronto, 1994. Polish Canadian Action Group Archives, Robarts Library, University of Toronto, FC 106.P7 P67 1981.

Polish Alliance of Canada. "*Pionierska Droga: Związku Polaków w Kanadzie, Przyczynek do Dziejów Organizacji Polonijnej*" [The pioneer path: The organizational activities of the Polish Alliance of Canada]. Toronto: Polish Alliance Press, 1973.

Radecki, Henry. *Ethnic Organizational Dynamics.* Waterloo, ON: Wilfred Laurier University Press, 1979.

———. "Poles." In *Encyclopedia of Canada's Peoples*, ed. Paul R. Magosci. Toronto: Multicultural History Society of Ontario, University of Toronto Press, 1999. *www.multiculturalcanada.ca/Encyclopedia/A-Z/p6/1.*

Riddell-Dixon, Elizabeth. *The Domestic Mosaic: Domestic Groups and Canadian Foreign Policy.* Toronto: Canadian Institute of International Affairs, 1985.

Riekhoff, Harald von. "The Desirability of a Graduated Increase of International Pressure." In *Canada's Response to the Polish Crisis*, edited by Adam Bromke, Harald von Riekhoff, Jacques Levesque, and J. R. Federowicz, 15–24. Toronto: Canadian Institute of International Affairs, 1982.

Sołtys, Edward, and Rudolf Kogler, eds. *Half a Century of Canadian Polish Congress.* Canadian Polish Research Institute, Toronto, 1996.

Troper, Harold, and Morton Weinfield. *Old Wounds: Jews, Ukrainians, and the Hunt for Nazi War Criminals in Canada.* Chapel Hill: University of North Carolina Press, 1989.

Turek, Victor. *Poles in Manitoba.* Toronto: Polish Alliance Press, 1967.

CHAPTER 11

Ethnic Nationalism and the Collapse of Soviet Communism

Mark R. Beissinger

That nationalism should be considered among the causes of the collapse of Communism is not a view shared by everyone.[1] A number of works on the end of Communism in the Soviet Union, for instance, have argued that nationalism played only a minor role in the process—that the main events took place within official institutions in Moscow and had relatively little to do with society, or that nationalism was a marginal motivation or influence on the actions of those involved in key decision making. Failed institutions and ideologies, an economy in decline, the burden of military competition with the United States, and instrumental goals of self-enrichment among the nomenklatura instead loom large in these accounts.[2] In many narratives of the end of Communism, nationalism is portrayed merely as a consequence of Communism's demise, as a phase after Communism disintegrated—not as an autonomous or contributing force within the process of collapse itself.

Such a story, however, leaves a number of critical issues unaddressed. For one thing, it completely ignores the critical mobilizational dimension of politics during the 1987–1992 period. Within the Soviet Union enormous mobilizations involving millions of people occurred during these years, with nationalist demands being the most prominent among the banners under which people mobilized. Indeed, in the Soviet case regime change and the breakup of the Soviet state were not entirely separable phases in the unfolding events that brought about the end of Communism, but were rather more overlapping and interrelated than many analyses portray them to be. In 1988 and 1989, institutional opening politicized nationalism across multiple contexts in the Soviet Union. These conflicts in turn magnified divisions within the Communist Party over how to deal with them, encouraged the spread of contention to other groups, created enormous disorder within institutions, and eventually led to the splintering of the Soviet state into national pieces. This was an outcome that seemed utterly unimaginable to the vast majority of Soviet citizens (and even most Soviet dissidents) when glasnost began in late 1986. It was the unintended result of Gorbachev's policies—one that was made possible not just by the widening political space that glasnost afforded, but also by the social forces that moved into that space and used it to reconfigure regime and state. Agency and contingency, not just structural determination, were important elements of Communism's demise. Moreover, where nationalist mobilization was weak (as in Central Asia), Communist elites survived the end of the Soviet Union, even while the Soviet state collapsed around them. Indeed, to say that Communism ended in these cases begs the question, "In what respects?" None of the post-Soviet states were entirely new. They were all fragments of preindependence state authority, and the extent to which governing elites and bureaucracies were reconfigured in the post-Communist period ultimately depended on the degree to which they were challenged from below by society during the glasnost period, principally through nationalist mobilization.[3]

But the argument that nationalism was marginal to Communism's demise also provides an inadequate answer to the question of why some Communist regimes (China, North Korea, Vietnam, Laos, Cambodia, and Cuba) survived the 1987–1992 period. Many of these Communist regimes also experienced ideological crises and failed economies, were moving decisively toward market reform, or were facing the threat of increased military competition with the United States in the late 1980s and early 1990s. Their economies were just as irrational, their governments just as repressive, and their bureaucracies just as corrupted as those European and Eurasian Communist regimes that failed. Yet Asian and Latin American Communist regimes survived, while European and Eurasian Communist regimes did not. Of course, the chief reason that Asian and Latin American Communist regimes survived is that they never initiated the kind of political liberalization undertaken inside the Soviet Union, unleashing political forces that eventually overwhelmed the state. But another important difference has been the ability of Asian and Latin American Communist regimes to harness the nationalism of dominant national groups as a core legitimating force, enabling these Communist regimes to stigmatize foreign influences, to marginalize more easily the oppositional challenges they have confronted, and to maintain their legitimacy within key sectors of society.[4]

By contrast, within European and Eurasian Communist regimes in the late 1980s nationalism largely failed as a legitimating force for Communist regimes and served instead as a major source for delegitimation and opposition.[5] Whereas Russian nationalism was long considered the linchpin of Soviet power, sustaining the Soviet regime since the 1930s and mobilizing critical support within Soviet society for Soviet political domination throughout Eastern Europe and Eurasia, for the most part Russian nationalism failed to come to the defense of either Communism or the Soviet empire in the late 1980s.[6] Instead, many Russians joined in the attacks, ironically coming to identify themselves as victims of Soviet "imperial" domination and declaring Russian sovereignty vis-à-vis the Soviet government. In this sense, Soviet Communism was brought down in part by what Roman Szporluk perceptively termed the "de-Sovietization of Russia"—that is, the growing disassociation of Russians and of Russian national identity from a state with which they had been routinely identified in the past.[7]

But it was not only the weakening Russian identification with the Soviet state and its imperial project that facilitated Communism's collapse. The struggle against what were widely viewed as repressive alien regimes imposed from without by Soviet power was also a central animus underlying the events of 1989–1991, both within the Soviet Union and among its Eastern European satellites. Communism in Europe and Eurasia was more than just tyrannical rule, an idiotic economic system, and a ritualized ideology. It was also an international and multinational hierarchy of such polities established and managed by Moscow—an interrelated structure of control that replicated patterns of politics, economics, and social organization across geopolitical space. Within Soviet-dominated Eastern Europe, calls for popular sovereignty could not be easily disentangled from independence from Muscovite tutelage, since these regimes had largely been imposed and maintained through intervention and externally imposed controls. Thus, behind the desire for freedom in 1989 also stood the desire for national sovereignty. In this sense, 1989 in Eastern Europe was not merely a series of revolts against Communism as a repressive political and social system; it was also a series of national revolts against Soviet domination, and as such closely related to the same revolt that, by fall 1989, had already become widespread within Soviet society itself.

Precisely because nationalism was an underlying factor in the demise of Communism, the process of collapse largely spread along the two institutional forms that were used to structure multinational and international control: ethnofederalism and the Warsaw Pact. Both these institutions used faux forms of sovereignty to mask centralized control, so that the collapse of Communism revolved in significant part around making genuine the bogus sovereignties of Communist-style ethnofederalism and the Warsaw

Pact. With the exception of Albania (explicable as a simple case of regional spillover effects, and in fact the last of the Eastern European Communist regimes to collapse), all the other nine Communist regimes that collapsed in the late 1980s and early 1990s were either members of the Warsaw Pact, were under strong political domination by the Soviet Union (Mongolia), or were ethnofederal states like the Soviet Union (Yugoslavia). By contrast, the six Asian and Latin American Communist regimes that survived stood outside the system of Soviet institutional control, had established themselves independently from Soviet power, and did not employ ethnofederalism as an institutional form for mediating relations with their own internal minorities.

In what follows, I develop three arguments related to the role of nationalism in the collapse of Communism.[8] First, nationalism (both in its presence, in its absence, and in the various conflicts and disorders it unleashed) played an important role in structuring the way in which the collapse of Communism unfolded. Of course, to argue that nationalism was an important factor in structuring the collapse of Communism should not be interpreted as saying that nationalism "caused" the collapse of Communism. History involves complex causation, and we would be fools to constrain a series of events as complex as the collapse of Communism within the confines of any single causal factor. But as we will see, we would also be foolish to ignore the national dimension to Communism's demise, not only because it was central to the dynamic by which the demise of Communism materialized, but also because we would seriously misunderstand post-Communist politics and societies without elucidating the national dimension of Communism's demise. Second, nationalist mobilization during this period was not a series of individual nationalist stories. Rather, it was a set of interrelated streams of activity in which action in one context exercised a profound effect on action in other contexts—what I have called the "tidal" context of nationalism. Indeed, neither the Soviet state nor Eastern European Communism would likely have collapsed had these nationalist revolts occurred in isolation from one another, so that these interconnections were critical to the production of the collapse itself. Third, while clearly structured, acts of nationalist mobilization did not simply reflect a preexisting logic of institutions, structures, and identities. Rather, acts of mobilization also played independent roles in *transforming* institutions, structures, and identities, so that while the collapse of Communism is often portrayed as a structurally overdetermined drama (some would even say that Communism's collapse was predetermined from its very establishment), its manifestation depended on myriad acts of defiance and contention whose outcomes themselves were hardly predetermined.[9]

Nationalism's Extraordinary Appeal under Glasnost

Gorbachev's policy of glasnost and the political liberalization that it produced were obviously the critical institutional conditions that allowed the collapse of Communism to occur. Without glasnost, the forces that most directly brought about the collapse could never have materialized or have been able to act. But despite the absolute importance of the Gorbachev factor and the broader factors that led Gorbachev to choose this path, we should also remember that the collapse of Communism was in fact the unintended result of Gorbachev's policies, not its conscious goal, and that the collapse occurred precisely because other social forces moved into the widening political space that glasnost afforded. Gorbachev sought to reform Communism both domestically and internationally, not to dismantle it. As Gorbachev recalled about the early years of perestroika: "We talked not about revolution, but *about improving the system*. Then we believed in such a possibility."[10] Gorbachev's disavowal of the Brezhnev doctrine in late 1988 similarly was not aimed at dismantling socialism in Eastern Europe or undoing the division of Germany, but rather at remaking Soviet relations with its allies while undoing the Cold War division of Europe. Of course, there was a great deal about Gorbachev that was naive. But Communism collapsed not only because of Gorbachev's policies, but also because social forces (in some places but not others) used the opportunities that Gorbachev's policies produced in order to mobilize oppositions, transform institutions and identities, and appropriate power.

There is an unfortunate tendency in the literature on the collapse of Communism to draw a sharp line between events within the Soviet Union and those in Eastern Europe. Scholars of the Soviet collapse tend not to speak about a single annus mirabilis, but of a five-year intense and protracted period in which new revelations filled the newspapers every day, a dizzying array of institutional changes were enacted, and dozens (at times hundreds) of protests were mounted daily—many of them spectacular events.[11] From this perspective, the Eastern European revolutions were but one set of episodes (though a very critical set) in the events that constituted Communism's collapse. An accurate understanding of the collapse of Communism needs to view its Soviet and Eastern European dimensions as interrelated rather than separate processes. What stood beneath this interrelationship was the ability of oppositions to draw analogies across a wide expanse of political and cultural space because of subjection to common modes of domination and a shared sense of alien rule. It is here that nationalism played a critical role in providing a frame through which analogies across cultural and political boundaries were drawn.

The issues that effectively mobilized populations within the Soviet Union during these years revolved precisely around nationalism. To be sure, issues of democratization, labor unrest and consumer shortages, and environmental justice constituted autonomous vectors of mobilization, at times intersecting with nationalism and at times diverging from it. But as my own study of thousands of protest demonstrations throughout the Soviet Union during the glasnost period has shown, nationalism gained a particular force and appeal not enjoyed by these other streams of contention. For example, not only were demonstrations that voiced nationalist demands but did not voice democratizing demands almost three times more frequent than those that voiced democratizing demands but did not voice nationalist demands, but also demonstrations that voiced nationalist demands and did not raise democratizing demands mobilized ten times more participants than those voicing democratizing demands but not raising nationalist demands. The patterns are quite striking. Moreover, demonstrations that combined both democratizing and nationalist demands mobilized five times more participants than those voicing democratizing demands but not raising nationalist demands. In other words, the strongest pressures from society for democratization came precisely from those movements that also pulled on nationalist tropes, and without nationalism to underpin them demands for liberalization on their own had relatively weak resonance within Soviet society. A similar but even more pronounced difference occurred between mobilization over nationalist demands and mobilization over economic demands—in spite of the enormous decline in living standards that occurred during this period.[12] In short, nationalism exercised an unusual force of attraction within the Soviet society during these years that was unparalleled by any other set of issues.

The deeper causes for this attraction were rooted in Soviet history and in the institutional crisis of the Soviet state. Significant grievances revolving around the brutality of the Stalinist past and the struggle for historical truth played prominent roles in motivating nationalist mobilization during glasnost. The Brezhnev era bred a sclerotic political system, a declining economy, widespread corruption, and a deepening malaise and cynicism within society—all of which contributed to a growing identification of the Soviet ruling elite as an alien other, even among many ordinary Russians. The Soviet state and Communist regime were closely fused, since the multinational state had been founded by the Communist regime, and the regime sought to legitimate itself primarily as an internationalist revolution. Yet beneath the veneer of formal equality the reality of Russian dominance persisted, reinforced in particular during Stalin's rule, when a once multiethnic political elite tipped toward disproportionate Russian representation, and a discourse of cultural and political stratification came to be embraced. As a result of the fusion of state and regime, any political opening that led to challenges against the regime was also bound to politicize issues of membership in the state, particularly for groups like the Balts, who had been incorporated forcefully into the Soviet Union as a result of the Molotov-Ribbentrop Pact of 1939.[13] And because the state had been the creation of the regime, widespread separatist challenges also necessarily assumed the form of anti-regime activity and were unambiguous challenges to Communist rule. Thus, regime change and the breakup of the Soviet state were not easily separable phases in the demise of Communism, but were interrelated and partly concurrent phenomena.

As a number of scholars have pointed out, many of the everyday institutional practices of the Soviet state in the nationalities sphere—the ethnofederal system, the primordialized passport system of ethnic identification and its use as a source of discrimination in everyday life, the promotion of minority cultures within the framework of the socialist state, and official personnel policies that promoted cadres in part on the basis of nationality—also reinforced ethnicity over other (specifically, class) modes of identity.[14] Class identities had of course provided the initial underpinning for Communist ideology. But as modernization and upward mobility proceeded, the class basis of Communism receded and the ethnic dimension of everyday life grew more prominent.

Still, until glasnost, secessionist sentiments remained very much on the margins of Soviet society—even in regions like the Baltic, where Soviet rule had come to be seen as an unalterable fact of life and "a permanent state of affairs." When glasnost first began in late 1986 and early 1987, it contained no strong nationalist component, and as an Estonian sociologist later observed, "neither its chief architects nor the broad public were prepared for the possible rise of national movements."[15] Glasnost initially manifested itself almost entirely in the operation of official institutions—in the press, movie theaters, and government offices. But already by spring 1987 glasnost had begun to escape official control, as small groups of hippies, Crimean Tatars, ecologists, Jewish refuseniks, Russian nationalists, and Baltic dissidents tested the boundaries of the permissible by taking politics to the street, engaging in small-scale demonstrations. The new atmosphere of press freedom, growing factionalism within the Politburo, and toleration of small-scale protest encouraged deeper politicization. In the early years of glasnost nationalist mobilization followed closely on the heels of institutional reform, with key periods of institutional reform precipitating thickenings of nationalist activity: the October 1987 Central Committee Plenum; the Nineteenth Party Conference in June 1988; the March 1989 elections; and meetings of the First Congress of People's Deputies in July 1989. But by the spring and summer of 1989, large-scale nationalist demonstrations involving hundreds of thousands of participants had spread across multiple republics and had become a relatively frequent affair. By this time the effect of institutional constraints on nationalist action had largely faded, and nationalist mobilization had increasingly became its own autonomous progenitor of events, influencing the character of political institutions instead of being contained by them.

Just how rapidly this transformation occurred is one of the astounding features of the collapse of Communism. It was not until over a year after the initiation of glasnost—in February 1988—that the first major eruptions of nationalism occurred in the Soviet Union: the massive Armenian protests over Karabakh, involving up to a million people in Yerevan alone. But over the following nineteen months—from February 1988 through August 1989—the USSR experienced a veritable explosion of nationalist mobilization in the Baltic, the Transcaucasus, Ukraine, and Moldova. Already by the end of 1988 and the beginning of 1989, the coherence of Soviet control over its own territory had been compromised by the rise of nationalist movements to dominance within the Baltic republics and the veritable loss of control by the Soviet state over events in Armenia and Azerbaijan. The massive mobilizations in Tbilisi in April 1989 that incited violent suppression by the Soviet army and the political backlash that this evoked had not only undermined completely Communist control in that republic, but also convinced many throughout the Soviet Union and in the Soviet government itself to question the utility of the deployment of the army as a means for containing nationalist revolt. By the summer of 1989, the tide of nationalist contention spread to the point that the Soviet regime appeared highly unstable. Enormous demonstrations (involving hundreds of thousands of people, and sometimes up to a million people) racked all the republics of the Baltic and Transcaucasus at the time, spreading as well to western Ukraine and Moldova. During the summer of 1989 multiple violent interethnic conflicts also broke out across the southern tier of the USSR: between Uzbeks and Meskhetian Turks, Kazakhs and Lezgins, Abkhaz and Georgians, Armenians and Azerbaijanis, and Kyrgyz and Tajiks. Massive miner strikes in eastern Ukraine, western Siberia, and northern Kazakhstan—though non-national in character—reflected the spread of large-scale protest to the Russian community as well, and the growing disaffection of Russians from the Soviet state.

This mounting domestic incoherence and instability of the Soviet state was an important part of the political opportunity structure that presented itself to Eastern Europeans in fall 1989. If Balts could get away with declaring sovereignty vis-à-vis the Soviet state at the end of 1988 and early 1989, and up to a million of them could hold hands across the Baltic in August 1989 in favor of independence from the Soviet Union, why should Poles and Czechs not be expected to press their own claims for popular sovereignty against their repressive, Kremlin-controlled regimes? Why should Russians be afforded a greater degree of press freedom than Bulgarians or East Germans (particularly when Soviet newspapers were readily available for purchase throughout Eastern Europe)? And if the Soviet state could not contain mass revolts within its own borders, why should its client states in Eastern Europe be expected to contain them, even if they had been able to rely on Soviet help (which Gorbachev had privately indicated would not be forthcoming)? Up through early 1989 the pace of political change inside the Soviet Union outstripped the pace of change within the Soviet Union's Eastern bloc allies, so that the example of political change within the Soviet Union emboldened political reformers throughout the Communist world (and not only in Eastern Europe, as the Chinese example illustrates). By early 1989 reform efforts were already under way in Poland and Hungary, leading to free elections in Poland in June 1989 and to the opening of borders and the transition to political pluralism in Hungary. This in turn led to a dizzying three-month cascade of events in late 1989: massive demonstrations in East Germany, the fall of the Berlin Wall, the Velvet Revolution in Czechoslovakia, unrest and the removal of Zhivkov in Bulgaria, and the violent overthrow of the Ceaușescu regime in Romania.

In turn, the collapse of Communism in Eastern Europe enormously accelerated and radicalized processes of nationalist revolt within the Soviet Union itself, leading to a sense that a momentum had built up against the Soviet state that could no longer be contained. The Ukrainian nationalist movement Rukh, for instance, actively used the Eastern European example to mobilize support to its cause. "The peoples of Poland, Hungary, East Germany, and Czechoslovakia have said no to Communist dictatorship," its banners at a demonstration read. "The next word is ours, citizens!"[16] The first half of 1990 saw a sharp rise in the number of groups pressing separatist demands inside the Soviet Union, spurred on in particular by republican elections, which brought to power nationalist movements in many republics and led to a bifurcation of authority (*dvoevlastie*) and increasingly bitter disputes over sovereignty. It was at this time as well that Gorbachev's popularity plummeted among Russians, and nomenklatura elites began to defect from the center in significant numbers, reinventing themselves as nationalists in anticipation that Soviet power would not last long. The classic example was Leonid Kravchuk. A party propagandist who once had been an implacable enemy of Rukh, Kravchuk came, in the course of 1990, to embrace the cause of Ukrainian sovereignty and independence. That once loyal nomenklatura like Kravchuk could reconfigure themselves as "fathers" of their respective nations was not a plausible outcome outside of these cross-case influences, for there would be no reason why, in isolation from what had occurred elsewhere, these elites would have ever considered defection.

The Transnationalism of Nationalism

Thus, nationalist mobilization during the collapse of Communism was not a collection of separate stories, but a series of interrelated streams of activity in which action in one context exercised a profound effect on action in other contexts—what I have called elsewhere a "tide" of nationalism. This tidal dimension is often lost in the literature on the collapse that focuses on single country or national cases. The interconnectedness produced by common targets of mobilization, common institutional characteristics, common ideologies, and common modes of domination meant that oppositions also perceived a linkage of political opportunities, feeding the spread of contention across cultural and political boundaries. The upsurge of mobilization across multiple contexts was not produced by a single shock, but rather by the way in which agents forged connections with the challenging actions of others through analogy and emulation. Institutional arrangements like ethnofederalism or the Warsaw Pact became lightning rods for the spread of contention laterally because they connected populations in analogous ways. When such analogies cohered, the example of successful contention in one context weakened political order in other contexts by raising expectations among challengers that authority could be successfully challenged. Challengers looked toward each other for inspiration and ideas, widely borrowing tactics, frames, and even programs from those who had demonstrated prior successes. Nationalism is often portrayed as parochial and inward looking, lacking empathy and incapable of identifying with others. But the collapse of Communism illustrates the limits of such stereotypes. Most nationalist movements are actually transnational in orientation, forced by strategic circumstances to conceive of their fates as intertwined with others.

But the transnational spread of nationalist mobilization was more than just a matter of analogy and emulation. Those movements that gained early successes also consciously sought to spread their contention laterally so as to increase the overall chances of consolidating their victories by gaining allies and by further disrupting the coherence of the state they wished to undermine. After the Nineteenth Party Conference in June 1988, attempts to challenge the Soviet regime proliferated with great rapidity, defusing across multiple groups. At this very time, challenging groups engaged in a widespread sharing of information, pamphlets, expertise, modes of challenge, and mobilizational frames. By June 1988 representatives of Ukrainian, Armenian, Georgian, Latvian, Lithuanian, and Estonian dissident nationalist movements had initiated contact with one another and established a coordinating committee among themselves. Indeed, in the summer and fall of 1988 popular fronts created along the lines of the Baltic model sprang up throughout most of the Soviet

Union. Representatives of these groups met frequently, shared documents and ideas, and occasionally aided each other by providing material support or organizing demonstrations in solidarity with each other's demands. The tide of nationalism thus assumed concrete form during the collapse of Communism in the ways in which nationalist paradigms were consciously exported and borrowed, organizational resources were shared, and challenging groups sought inspiration from one another.

Arguably the most important mobilizational frame to emerge within the Soviet Union during the glasnost era was the anti-imperial sovereignty frame that played such an important role in the ultimate demise of the Soviet state. In its final years of existence, the imperial persona implicit within the Soviet state came to be openly affirmed, as nations claimed sovereignty, up to and including their place on the political map of the world. This anti-imperial sovereignty frame first gained mass resonance in the Baltic in summer 1988 and subsequently spread massively to Georgia, Armenia, Azerbaijan, Moldova, Ukraine, and eventually to Russia itself. When Boris Yeltsin embraced Russia sovereignty vis-à-vis the Soviet Union in June 1990, he was borrowing from the tide of nationalism that had already swept across much of the USSR (or as one Politburo member put it: "To make Russia sovereign is the golden daydream of the Balts").[17] So successful was the spread of this sovereignty frame that over the course of 1990 every Soviet republic (as well as autonomous republics and even one island in the Far East) issued its own declarations of sovereignty vis-à-vis the Soviet government in what came to be known as the "parade of sovereignties." The diffusion of this anti-imperial sovereignty frame beyond the Baltic was partly an attempt to capitalize on the prior success of others— a process of emulation typical of modular phenomena like nationalism. But it was more than this. Baltic popular fronts consciously attempted to reproduce themselves throughout the Soviet Union out of both philosophical and strategic considerations. They vigorously organized to extend their influence throughout the Soviet Union to aid the spread of the master frame they themselves had pioneered. A conscious strategy of spreading secessionist revolt laterally was pursued, both as an effort to consolidate secessionist movements through the power of numbers and to weaken the regime by undermining its ability to defuse nationalist challenges.[18]

It is unlikely that the Soviet state or Eastern European Communism would have ever collapsed had these revolts occurred in isolation from one another. Certainly, had the Balts engaged in their struggle alone, there is little doubt that they would have been easily repressed. By contrast, the fact that claims of sovereignty against the center had spread broadly throughout the fabric of Soviet society made rebellion difficult to contain. Part of the dilemma that had confronted opponents of Soviet Communism throughout its history was that past Eastern European revolts against Soviet control had exerted only limited influence inside the Soviet Union and had been repeatedly cut short by Soviet intervention and pressure.[19] In 1989, however, extensive revolt inside the Soviet Union was occurring at the same time as Eastern Europeans pressed their own freedom, so that the Kremlin for the first time faced multiple, simultaneous revolts both within and outside the country. The modular spread of revolt across the Soviet Union and Eastern Europe represented an unusual period of heightened contention that transcended cultural and international borders and in which challenges to the state multiplied and fed off one another, overwhelming the capacity of the state to contain them and evoking large-scale tectonic change in the character of the state system.

The Weakness of Russian Defense of the Soviet State

Nationalism was conspicuous in the collapse of Communism not only by its presence, but also by its absence. By all measures of conventional wisdom, Russians should have been expected to come to the defense of Soviet Communism and the Soviet empire. Soviet Communism was widely viewed as Russian Communism, and Leninist ideology was said to have resonated powerfully with embedded elements of Russian political culture.[20] Indeed, one of the reasons why earlier waves of revolt against Soviet control had failed was precisely the way in which Russians had come to the defense of the realm. Yet, in the late 1980s, at a time when the Soviet state liberalized and Russian dominance was under attack, this did not happen. Instead, large numbers of Russians protested against the Soviet state and acquiesced in its forfeiture of empire.

How does one explain the weakness of Russian imperial nationalism in the context of glasnost? To be sure, glasnost itself is to a large extent responsible, for its constant revelations of Soviet abuses and atrocities drove a wedge between many ordinary Russians and the Soviet state. But part of the explanation is also to be found in the multiple political roles that Russians could and did assume during these years. Russians were the dominant nationality of the Soviet Union and had the most to lose from attempts to undermine the Soviet empire. But Russians also constituted a disproportionate share of the Soviet intelligentsia and working class relative to most other nationalities.[21] The former were strongly attracted to ideas of liberalization, while the latter (because of their vulnerable position at a time of growing economic shortage and insecurity) were most likely to protest the regime's economic policies. This split structural position in relationship to the changes introduced by perestroika in fact led to a trifurcation of Russian mobilization into nationalist-conservative, liberal, and labor-economic streams, each of which comprehended its relationship to the Soviet state in different terms.

In this respect Russian mobilization differed substantially from that of other groups in the Soviet Union, for it was unusually divided. Not only was there a plethora of Russian movements by 1988 and 1989, but these movements stood for quite distinct and in some instances opposing frames. Rather than generating a nationalist backlash among Russians, as many observers had expected, the tide of nationalism instead drove a wedge more deeply among Russians, politicizing and polarizing cleavages among them. Russian liberals eventually forged an alliance with non-Russian separatists against the Soviet regime, borrowing their sovereignty and anticolonial frames. They did not define themselves as nationalists. They saw themselves as struggling primarily against the Communist regime, not for the nation. Yet in the first half of 1990 they adopted many of the tropes of national liberation then extant elsewhere in the Soviet Union, coming to advocate a brand of liberal nationalism in which Russian sovereignty and self-determination were seen as necessary parts of the democratization process. In 1990 and 1991 this defense of Russian sovereignty against an overbearing and imperial all-union government became the dominant theme of Russian mobilization. Similarly, as the economy deteriorated and the Soviet state disintegrated, labor activism radicalized, coming in many cases to embrace dismantlement of central planning and the sovereignty paradigm.

Conservative-nationalists, by contrast, remained highly divided. Some distanced themselves from the Communist regime; indeed, demands for Russian sovereignty initially emerged not from liberals but from Russian nationalists, who, seeking to counter the "Russophobia" prevalent at the time, noted that Russians also had been discriminated against and victimized by Communism. Others embraced a conservative Communism that emphasized defense of the party and the state. But nationalist-conservatives failed to find a mass base for themselves within Russia. Their attempts to court the coal miners of Ukraine, Siberia, and Northern Kazakhstan also came to naught. Their support proved to be greatest within the Russian-speaking communities of the Baltic and Moldova, but even here much of their capacity to mobilize opposition to nationalist movements weakened in 1990 and 1991, as the breakup of the Soviet state grew immanent. In short, Russian nationalism fizzled as a force for defending the Soviet empire because glasnost significantly undermined Russian support for the Communist regime, Russians were deeply divided politically, and Russians increasingly embraced the sovereignty paradigm championed by nationalist oppositions under the influence of the tide of nationalism.

Structure and Agency within "Thickened History"

While the events in Eastern Europe in 1989 are widely referred to as revolutions, with the exception of the Baltic states it is not fashionable today to talk about the collapse of the Soviet Union in these same terms. After all, in some Soviet republics political power ultimately remained in the hands of Communist officials, while in other republics nationalist revolts descended into intraethnic violence and even civil war. But the disintegration of the Soviet Union unambiguously deserves to be understood as revolutionary. It easily falls within Tilly's minimalist, processual understanding of revolution (a situation of dual sovereignty in which nonruling contenders mobilize large numbers of citizens for the purpose of gaining control over the state).[22] Even if we assume a more robust, outcome-oriented definition such as that used by Skocpol (the rapid transformation of a country's state and class structures and its dominant ideology), there is little doubt that the collapse of Communism was revolutionary.[23] In most (though not all) Soviet republics, property relations were totally reconfigured in the wake of Communism's collapse, long-standing social institutions were dismantled, new ideologies and new classes came to the fore, and new forms of social behavior sprang into existence.

The disintegration of the Soviet Union was accompanied by immense transformations in political discourse and in public perceptions of politics. A population that could barely imagine the breakup of their country came, within a compressed period of time, to view its disintegration as inevitable. The record of public opinion polling during these years demonstrates massive transformations in attitudes toward the Soviet state—even for groups like the Balts, among whom the notion of independence, once considered the pipe dream of dissidents, came to be almost unanimously embraced under the shifting boundaries of the possible. In the case of the Ukrainians the transformation in attitudes under the influence of external events was stark—to the point that 90 percent of the Ukrainian population voted in December 1991 for independent statehood in a national referendum. As Bohdan Nahaylo described it: "What appears to have happened is that swiftly and almost imperceptibly . . . a revolution occurred in the minds of Ukraine's inhabitants. Somehow, during a remarkably short period, the idea of Ukrainian independence, for so long depicted in the Soviet press as the hopeless cause of diehard nationalists in Western Ukraine, took hold throughout the republic."[24] Even large numbers of Russians, under the influence of events elsewhere, eventually came to support the dissolution of the Soviet Union by December 1991, as public opinion polls at the time showed (although nostalgia for the USSR quickly developed thereafter).[25]

This enormous transformation in outlooks was of course facilitated by specific structural conditions: the institutional and ideological crisis of the Soviet

state, the fusion between state and regime, the submerged sense of ethnic grievance across multiple groups, and the Soviet state's overreach abroad. Moreover,
patterns of nationalist mobilization broadly reflected such factors as the degree
of urbanization of a nationality, the size of an ethnic group, its ethnofederal
status, and the degree to which it had been assimilated to the dominant Russian
culture. But the specific events that transformed institutions and brought movements to power also contained a heavy dose of contingency, and their outcomes
were hardly predetermined. Repression could have easily shut down challengers
in 1988 and early 1989. At other moments the backlash effects of repression, the
outrage that erupted from intergroup violence, and the anger that materialized
out of callous government responses to popular demands played important roles
in transforming the opinion climate of politics and affecting the prisms through
which individuals related to the state and to others. Indeed, those who organized challenges often sought to provoke responses from states or other groups
that heightened a sense of conflict and identity, so as to drive the engine of history more quickly, while other movements sought to ride the momentum generated from the successful prior actions of others. In short, the agency of ordinary
people needs to be placed squarely in the center of any accurate understanding
of Communism's collapse.

As E. H. Carr noted, in real life there is no contradiction between the influence of structure and the role of agency, because structure exercises its effects
not by rendering outcomes inevitable, but rather by making action possible,
more probable, and more likely to meet with success.[26] But it is also true that
as actions accumulate, they also can exercise a structurelike effect, having the
capacity to render subsequent action possible, more probable, and more likely
to meet with success. Rather than simply being a manifestation of structurally
predetermined conditions, the collapse of Soviet Communism materialized over
a five-year period of what I have called "thickened history"—in which events
acquired a sense of momentum, transformed identities and political institutions,
and increasingly assumed the characteristics of their own causal structure. As
one Soviet journalist put it in fall 1989: "We are living in an extremely condensed
historical period. Social processes which earlier required decades now develop
in a matter of months."[27] This heightened pace of contention affected both governing and governed—the former primarily in the state's growing incoherence
and inability to fashion relevant policies, the latter by introducing an intensified
sense of contingency, possibility, and influence from the example of others.

One of the characteristic features of "thickened" history is that the pace
of events outstrips the movement of institutions and the understanding of
leaders. In the collapse of Communism the pace of events was itself a causal
factor in the outcome, as events simply moved far faster than institutions
were capable of reacting. This was most glaringly evident with regard to the

nationalities issues, in which formulas embraced by Gorbachev in 1988, 1989, and 1990 soon grew outdated as a result of shifting events on the ground. The tide of nationalism also produced enormous confusion and division within Soviet institutions, making it even more difficult to find institutional solutions to the challenge of holding the Soviet state together. The pull of alternative movements within the Communist rank and file was particularly strong in many parts of the country. In the course of 1989, nationalist movements came to dominate republican politics in the Baltic republics, Georgia, and Armenia, so that party organizations largely went "underground," as one Communist official put it. In the 1990 republican elections, nationalist movements or those sympathetic with them came to power in practically every republic with the exception of Azerbaijan and Central Asia, institutionalizing the waves of nationalism that had swept across the country. This was soon followed by what came to be known as the "war of the laws"— a struggle between the center and the republics over whose laws actually were sovereign. Gorbachev insisted that the central government's laws had precedence over republics and localities and declared invalid a whole series of laws that contradicted all-union laws. In turn many republics refused to recognize the authority of the center over them. The conservative reaction to this disorder pushed the Soviet state toward its final, tumultuous demise in the failed August 1991 coup.

Nationalist mobilization not only undermined the authority of state institutions; it also helped dissipate the state's capacity to repress. In the wake of the April 1989 Tbilisi events, the use of the Soviet Army as a tool to contain ethnic revolt grew heavily politicized, and as authority shifted to the republics, actions by the central government's institutions of order to quell the nationalist unrest became embroiled in controversy. The constant deployment of the military and special police units to nationalist "hot spots" around the country bred a sense of exhaustion among them. The declining morale of those charged with keeping order was a constant theme during these years, and over the course of 1990–1991 discipline within the armed forces began to unravel in a serious way. Most of the officers who commanded key units during the August 1991 coup had been intimately involved in putting down nationalist unrest in various parts of the country. Given the effect that many of these earlier actions had on morale within the police and the military, it hardly seems accidental that these same officers, when called on to use force against a civilian population of their own nationality on an even larger scale for the sake of preserving the Soviet Union, refused to carry out their superiors' orders.

Nationalism within and beyond the Collapse

It would be impossible to understand post-Communist politics today without reference to the national dimension of the Communist collapse—one of the reasons why any serious discussion of Communism's demise needs to explicate nationalism's role in this process rather than treat it merely as a consequence of the collapse. A glance at the front page of a randomly chosen Russian newspaper almost two decades after the collapse included stories about continuing conflicts between Estonia and Russia over demarcation of their borders, claims by Moscow mayor Yuri Luzhkov that Ukrainian authorities were discriminating against the Russian-speaking population of Ukraine, and the opening of regular passenger ship routes between Russia and Abkhazia despite Georgian objections that this was a gross violation of Georgian sovereignty.[28] The collapse of Soviet Communism remains a fundamental reference point, both positive and negative, for populations throughout the region. It is either mourned, in Putin's words, as "the greatest geopolitical catastrophe of the century" or celebrated as the foundation of a national political community and marked as a national holiday by fireworks and military parades (as in Ukraine).[29] These identity narratives are woven into the fabric of new national histories and continue to manifest themselves politically in issues like NATO and EU expansion, the geopolitics of energy, policies toward Russians and Russophones living in the post-Soviet republics, and desires for and fear of a resuscitation of Russian power in the region. Thus, not only did nationalism occupy a central role in the way in which the collapse of Communism unfolded, but the fundamental identity conflicts that gave structure to the collapse remain with us, manifested now more in the realm of interstate relations but nevertheless still central to the ways in which individuals understand themselves and their relationship to political authority.

Notes

1. This chapter first appeared in a special issue of *Contemporary European History* that revisited the causes, course, and consequences of 1989. For original, see Mark Beissinger, *Contemporary European History* 18, no. 3 (August 2009): 331–47. Reprinted with the permission of Cambridge University Press.
2. See, for instance, Jerry F. Hough, *Democratization and Revolution in the USSR, 1985–1991* (Washington, DC: Brookings Institution, 1997); Steven Solnick, *Stealing the State: Control and Collapse in Soviet Institutions* (Cambridge, MA: Harvard University Press, 1998); and Stephen Kotkin, *Armageddon Averted: The Soviet Collapse, 1970–2000* (Oxford: Oxford University Press, 2001).

3. Keith Darden and Anna Grzymala-Busse, "The Great Divide: Literacy, Nationalism, and the Communist Collapse," *World Politics* 59, no. 1 (October 2006): 83–115.

4. See Martin K. Dimitrov, "Why Communism Didn't Collapse: Exploring Regime Resilience in China, Vietnam, Laos, North Korea, and Cuba," paper presented at the conference "Why Communism Didn't Collapse: Understanding Regime Resilience in China, Vietnam, Laos, North Korea, and Cuba," Dartmouth College, Hanover, NH, May 25–26, 2007.

5. The major exception was Yugoslavia. Minority nationalisms obviously played a major delegitimating role in the collapse of Yugoslav Communism and in the unmaking of the Yugoslav state. But Serbian commitment to maintaining Yugoslavia's territorial integrity and to Serbian Communists who peddled such an undertaking remained considerably stronger than the commitment of Russians to maintaining the territorial integrity of the Soviet Union, accounting for the outbreak of ethnic civil war in Yugoslavia and the persistence of the Communist control in Serbia (in the guise of the Socialist Party) over the decade of the 1990s. See Veljko Vujačić, "Historical Legacies, Nationalist Mobilization, and Political Outcomes in Russia and Serbia: A Weberian View," *Theory and Society* 25, no. 6 (December 1996): 763–801.

6. David Brandenberger, *National Bolshevism: Stalinist Mass Culture and the Formation of Modern Russian National Identity, 1931–1956* (Cambridge, MA: Harvard University Press, 2002).

7. See, in particular, Roman Szporluk, *Russia, Ukraine, and the Break-up of the Soviet Union* (Stanford, CA: Hoover Institution Press, 2000).

8. These arguments are drawn from or are elaborations on my own work on the Soviet collapse. See Mark R. Beissinger, *Nationalist Mobilization and the Collapse of the Soviet State* (Cambridge: Cambridge University Press, 2002).

9. For a critique of the heavy determinism in the literature on the breakdown of Communism, see Stathis N. Kalyvas, "The Decay and Breakdown of Communist One-Party Systems," *Annual Review of Political Science* 2 (1999): 323–43.

10. Mikhail Gorbachev, *Zhizn' i reformy* [Life and reforms], vol. 1 (Moscow: Novosti, 1995), 203.

11. Michael Howard, "The Springtime of Nations," *Foreign Affairs* 69, no. 1 (1990): 17–32.

12. Beissinger, *Nationalist Mobilization*, 75–79.

13. Valerie Bunce, *Subversive Institutions: The Design and the Destruction of Socialism and the State* (Cambridge: Cambridge University Press, 1999).

14. Philip G. Roeder, *Red Sunset: The Failure of Soviet Politics* (Princeton, NJ: Princeton University Press, 1993); Ronald Grigor Suny, *The Revenge of the Past: Nationalism, Revolution, and the Collapse of the Soviet Union* (Stanford, CA: Stanford University Press, 1993); and Rogers Brubaker, "Nationhood and the National Question in the Soviet Union and Post-Soviet Eurasia: An Institutionalist Account," *Theory and Society* 23 (1994): 47–78.

15. K. S. Hallik, quoted in "S'ezd Narodnykh Deputatov SSSR, 6-ogo Iunia, utrennaia sessia" [USSR Congress of People's Deputies, June 6, morning session], *Pravda*, June 7, 1989.

16. "41 godovshchina priniatiia vseobshchei deklaratsii prav cheloveka" [The 41st anniversary of the Universal Declaration of Human Rights], *Ekspress khronika*, December 17, 1989.

17. Vadim Medvedev, quoted in *Soiuz mozhno bylo sokhranit'* [The union could have been preserved] (Moscow: Izdatel'stvo "Aprel'-85," 1995), 64.

18. Nils R. Muiznieks, "The Influence of the Baltic Popular Movements on the Process of Soviet Disintegration," *Europe-Asia Studies* 47, no. 1 (1995): 3–25.

19. See Roman Szporluk, ed., *The Influence of Eastern Europe and the Soviet West on the USSR* (New York: Praeger, 1975).

20. Nikolai Berdyaev, *The Origins of Russian Communism* (Ann Arbor: University of Michigan Press, 1960).

21. Darrell Slider, "A Note on the Class Structure of Soviet Nationalities," *Soviet Studies* 37, no. 4 (October 1985): 535–40.

22. Charles Tilly, *European Revolutions, 1492–1992* (Oxford: Blackwell, 1993).

23. Theda Skocpol, *States and Social Revolutions: A Comparative Analysis of France, Russia, and China* (Cambridge: Cambridge University Press, 1979).

24. Bohdan Nahaylo, "The Birth of an Independent Ukraine," *Report on the USSR* 3, no. 50 (December 13, 1991): 1–2.

25. See Matthew Wyman, *Public Opinion in Postcommunist Russia* (New York: St. Martin's Press, 1997), 166.

26. Edward Hallett Carr, *What Is History?* (New York: Knopf, 1962), 124.

27. Ibid.

28. *Vremia*, July 2, 2008, 1.

29. Poslanie Prezidenta Rossiiskoi Federatsii V. V. Putina Federal'nomu Sobraniiu Rossiiskoi Federatsii [Address of the president of the Russian Federation V. V. Putin to the Federal Assembly of the Russian Federation], April 25, 2005 (*www.kremlin.ru/appears/2005/04/25/1223_type63372type63374type82634_87049.shtml*).

References

PERIODICALS

Ekspress khronika
Literaturnaia gazeta
Pravda
Soiuz mozhno bylo sokhranit'
Vremia

SELECTED PUBLISHED WORKS

Beissinger, Mark R. *Nationalist Mobilization and the Collapse of the Soviet State.* Cambridge: Cambridge University Press, 2002.

Berdyaev, Nikolai. *The Origins of Russian Communism.* Ann Arbor: University of Michigan Press, 1960.

Brandenberger, David. *National Bolshevism: Stalinist Mass Culture and the Formation of Modern Russian National Identity, 1931–1956.* Cambridge, MA: Harvard University Press, 2002.

Brubaker, Rogers. "Nationhood and the National Question in the Soviet Union and Post-Soviet Eurasia: An Institutionalist Account." *Theory and Society* 23 (1994): 47–78.

Bunce, Valerie. *Subversive Institutions: The Design and the Destruction of Socialism and the State.* Cambridge: Cambridge University Press, 1999.

Carr, Edward Hallett. *What Is History?* New York: Knopf, 1962.

Darden, Keith, and Anna Grzymala-Busse. "The Great Divide: Literacy, Nationalism, and the Communist Collapse." *World Politics* 59, no. 1 (October 2006): 83–115.

Dimitrov, Martin K. "Why Communism Didn't Collapse: Exploring Regime Resilience in China, Vietnam, Laos, North Korea, and Cuba." Paper presented at the conference "Why Communism Didn't Collapse: Understanding Regime Resilience in China, Vietnam, Laos, North Korea, and Cuba," Dartmouth College, Hanover, NH, May 25–26, 2007.

Gorbachev, Mikhail. *Zhizn' i reformy* [Life and reforms]. Vol. 1. Moscow: Novosti, 1995.

Hough, Jerry F. *Democratization and Revolution in the USSR, 1985–1991.* Washington, DC: Brookings Institution, 1997.

Howard, Michael. "The Springtime of Nations." *Foreign Affairs* 69, no. 1 (1990): 17–32.

Kalyvas, Stathis N. "The Decay and Breakdown of Communist One-Party Systems." *Annual Review of Political Science* 2 (1999): 323–43.

Kotkin, Stephen. *Armageddon Averted: The Soviet Collapse, 1970–2000.* Oxford: Oxford University Press, 2001.

Muiznieks, Nils R. "The Influence of the Baltic Popular Movements on the Process of Soviet Disintegration." *Europe-Asia Studies* 47, no. 1 (1995): 3–25.

Nahaylo, Bohdan. "The Birth of an Independent Ukraine." *Report on the USSR* 3, no. 50 (December 13, 1991): 1–2.

Plakans, Andrejs. *The Latvians: A Short History.* Stanford, CA: Stanford University Press, 1995.

Roeder, Philip G. *Red Sunset: The Failure of Soviet Politics.* Princeton, NJ: Princeton University Press, 1993.

Skocpol, Theda. *States and Social Revolutions: A Comparative Analysis of France, Russia, and China.* Cambridge: Cambridge University Press, 1979.

Slider, Darrell. "A Note on the Class Structure of Soviet Nationalities." *Soviet Studies* 37, no. 4 (October 1985): 535–40.

Solnick, Steven. *Stealing the State: Control and Collapse in Soviet Institutions.* Cambridge, MA: Harvard University Press, 1998.

Suny, Ronald Grigor. *The Revenge of the Past: Nationalism, Revolution, and the Collapse of the Soviet Union.* Stanford, CA: Stanford University Press, 1993.

Szporluk, Roman, ed. *The Influence of Eastern Europe and the Soviet West on the USSR.* New York: Praeger, 1975.

———. *Russia, Ukraine, and the Break-up of the Soviet Union.* Stanford, CA: Hoover Institution Press, 2000.

Tilly, Charles. *European Revolutions, 1492–1992.* Oxford: Blackwell, 1993.

Vujačić, Veljko. "Historical Legacies, Nationalist Mobilization, and Political Outcomes in Russia and Serbia: A Weberian View." *Theory and Society* 25, no. 6 (December 1996): 763–801.

Wyman, Matthew. *Public Opinion in Postcommunist Russia.* New York: St. Martin's Press, 1997.

Contributors

Henley Adams is adjunct assistant professor at Queensborough Community College (CUNY) and the author of "Fighting an Uphill Battle: Race, Political Power, and Institutionalization in Cuba," *Latin American Research Review* 39, no. 1 (February 2004).

Mark R. Beissinger is professor of politics at Princeton University. His main fields of interest are nationalism, state building, imperialism, revolutions, and social movements, with special reference to the Soviet Union and the post-Soviet states. In addition to numerous articles and book chapters, he is the author or editor of four books, including *Nationalist Mobilization and the Collapse of the Soviet State* (Cambridge University Press, 2002) and *Scientific Management, Socialist Discipline, and Soviet Power* (Harvard University Press, 1988).

Michael Donoghue is assistant professor of history at Marquette University. His publications include "Murder and Rape in the Canal Zone: Cultural Conflict and the U.S. Military Presence in Panama, 1955–1956," in *Decentering America: Culture and International History II*, ed. Jessica C. E. Gienow-Hecht (Berghahn Books, 2007), and *Borderland on the Isthmus: Zonians, Panamanians, West Indians, and the Struggle for the Canal Zone, 1939–1979* (Duke University Press, forthcoming).

Katrina M. Hagen is a lecturer in history and literature at Harvard University.

Ryan M. Irwin is an international historian who writes about the changing mechanics and shifting perceptions of American global power in the twentieth century. His first book, *The Gordian Knot: Apartheid and the Unmaking of the Liberal World Order, 1960–1970* (Oxford University Press, forthcoming), is an international history of the 1960s that looks closely at the symbolic and political importance of apartheid during the years after decolonization. His current book project is an international history of the early Cold War, which explores how the United Nations—with Washington at its helm—confronted the dilemma of settler colonialism in the 1940s and 1950s. He teaches classes on decolonization and world affairs at Yale, and coordinates activities connected to Yale's international history program. He is the deputy director of International Security Studies.

Michael L. Krenn is professor of history at Appalachian State University. His most recent books include *The Color of Empire: Race and American Foreign Relations* (Potomac Books, 2006), *Fall-Out Shelters for the Human Spirit: American Art and the Cold War* (University of North Carolina Press, 2005), and *Black Diplomacy: African Americans and the State Department, 1945–1969* (M. E. Sharpe, 1999).

Zinovia Lialiouti is a scholar of political science and history. Her doctoral dissertation was entitled "Greek Anti-Americanism, 1947–1989." She currently works as a research fellow at the Andreas Papandreou Institute for Strategic and Development Studies (ISTAME). Her publications include "Challenging Americanism: The Public Debate about the 'American Way of Life,'" in *The United States and the World: From Imitation to Challenge*, ed. Andrzej Mania and Lukasz Wordliczek (Jagiellonian University Press, 2010); "The Concept of Anti-Americanism and Obama's Presidential Campaign," *Ad Americam: Journal of American Studies* 11 (2011); and "Greek Anti-Americanism and the War in Kosovo," *National Identities* (forthcoming).

Maxim Matusevich is associate professor of world history at Seton Hall University, where he also directs the program in Russian and Eastern European Studies. He is the author of *No Easy Row for a Russian Hoe: Ideology and Pragmatism in Nigerian-Soviet Relations, 1960–1991* (Africa World Press, 2003), and editor of *Russia in Africa, Africa in Russia: Three Centuries of Encounters* (Africa World Press, 2007).

Philip E. Muehlenbeck is professorial lecturer at George Washington University. His publications include *Betting on the Africans: John F. Kennedy's Courting of African Nationalist Leaders* (Oxford University Press, 2012) and, as editor, *Religion and the Cold War: A Global Perspective* (Vanderbilt University Press, 2012).

Eric L. Payseur is a PhD candidate in the Department of History at York University in Toronto. His dissertation explores Polish Canadian identity since the Second World War.

Luís Nuno Rodrigues is associate professor in the Department of History of ISCTE, Lisbon University Institute, where he coordinates the graduate program in history, defense, and international relations and conducts research at the Center for the Study of Portuguese Contemporary History. His books include *Spínola* (Esfera dos Livros, 2010) and *Kennedy-Salazar: A crise de uma aliança. As relações luso-americanas entre 1961 e 1963* [Kennedy-Salazar: The crisis of an alliance; Portuguese-American relations between 1961 and 1963] (Notícias Editorial, 2002).

Nico Slate is assistant professor of history at Carnegie Mellon University. His research and teaching focus on the transnational history of social movements in the United States, with a particular emphasis on South Asia and on the history of struggles against racism and imperialism worldwide. He is the author of *Colored Cosmopolitanism: The Shared Struggle for Freedom in the United States and India* (Harvard University Press, 2011).

David Webster is assistant professor of international studies at the University of Regina. He is the author of *Fire and the Full Moon: Canada and Indonesia in a Decolonizing World* (University of British Columbia Press, 2009) and the editor of *East Timor Testimony* (Between the Lines, 2004).

Index